Women, children and the family in Palmyra

Abstract

The present volume includes articles stemming from a two-part workshop on the representations of women and children and their roles in the families in Roman period Palmyra. The workshops were held at Aarhus University, Denmark, under the auspices of the Palmyra Portrait Project in October 2016 and February 2017. During the workshops concerning women, children and family constellations, various aspects of representations of women and children as well as the wider family groups within which they were shown in Palmyra were explored, as well as the implications these might have carried in relation to the Palmyrene family structure and wider Palmyrene society. Since the evidence from the public sphere does not give much insight into how women and children were perceived in Palmyra, the material from the funerary sphere remains central to these issues. We wish to thank the contributors for sharing their expert insights on the topics covered during the workshops as well as for their large endorsement and enthusiasm. This induced many interesting discussions that are reflected in the contributions in this volume.

Signe Krag and Rubina Raja,
Aarhus University, September 2018

Acknowledgements

Without the support of the Carlsberg Foundation, the Palmyra Portrait Project would not have been possible. The foundation has made it possible for the group of researchers working within and around the framework of the project to undertake important research, which otherwise could not have been done. I thank the foundation most gratefully. Furthermore, I thank the Royal Academy of Sciences and Letters and in particular its editor Marita Akhøj for taking so good care of the manuscript for the series Palmyrenske Studier, which I founded shortly after the project began. I would also like to thank the Ny Carlsberg Glyptotek and its staff, in particular its director Christine Buhl Andersen and curator Anne Marie Nielsen, for all the support and help they have given the project over the years. Last but not least, a large thank you goes to the members of the Palmyra Portrait Project and here in particular research assistants, Olympia Bobou, Jesper Vestergaard Jensen, Nathalia Breintoft Kristensen and Rikke Randeris Thomsen for helping with the editing of the manuscript. Without them, this book would not have come to completion this fast.

Rubina Raja, Aarhus, September 2018

Women, children and the family in Palmyra

Edited by Signe Krag and Rubina Raja

Scientia Danica. Series H, Humanistica, 4 · vol. 10

DET KONGELIGE DANSKE VIDENSKABERNES SELSKAB

Palmyrenske Studier bind 3 · Palmyrene Studies Vol. 3

Printed in Denmark by Specialtrykkeriet Arco A/S
ISSN 1904-5506 · ISBN 978-87-7304-419-3

Submitted to the Academy July 2018
Published May 2019

Contents

INTRODUCTION
Krag, S. and R. Raja. Families in Palmyra – the evidence from the first three centuries CE 7

Part I: Women, children and the family in the funerary sphere

CHAPTER 1
Henning, A. The representation of matrimony in the tower tombs of Palmyra 19

CHAPTER 2
Krag, S. Palmyrene funerary buildings and family burial patterns 38

CHAPTER 3
Cussini, E. Daughters and wives: Defining women in Palmyrene inscriptions 67

Part II: Women, children and the family in civic and religious spheres

CHAPTER 4
Kaizer, T. Family connections and religious life at Palmyra 82

CHAPTER 5
Raja, R. It stays in the family: Palmyrene priestly representations and their constellations 95

CHAPTER 6
Klaver, S. The participation of Palmyrene women in the religious life of the city 157

CHAPTER 7
Andrade, N. J. Burying Odainath: Zenobia and women in the funerary life of Palmyra 168

Part III: Comparative aspects

CHAPTER 8
Boatwright, M. T. Model families in Imperial Rome and Palmyra 184

CHAPTER 9
Vuolanto, V. Children and religious participation in Roman Palmyra 201

List of contributors 214

Abbreviations 215

Subject index 217

Index of geographical places 221

Index of personal names 222

Index of divine and mythological names 227

Antique authors 228

BANQUETING RELIEF DEPICTING A SEATED WOMAN AND RECLINING MAN WITH TWO MEN STANDING BEHIND THE RECLINING MAN, 200–273 CE. *FITZWILLIAM MUSEUM, CAMBRIDGE, GR6.1888 (© THE FITZWILLIAM MUSEUM, CAMBRIDGE).*

INTRODUCTION

Families in Palmyra – the evidence from the first three centuries CE

Signe Krag and Rubina Raja

SCI.DAN.H.4.10 · WOMEN, CHILDREN AND THE FAMILY IN PALMYRA
THE ROYAL DANISH ACADEMY OF SCIENCES AND LETTERS · 2019

Palmyra, located in Syria, flourished during the Roman imperial period, and most of the archaeological remains found in the city can be ascribed to the first to third centuries CE.[1] Queen Zenobia rose to power in the city in 267/68 CE and started expanding the Palmyrene territory. However, this was not looked upon mildly by the Romans who entered the city in 272 CE defeating Zenobia, and one year later, after a second Palmyrene uprise, they returned to the city and overthrew it.[2] Since the rediscovery of Palmyra, portraits and inscriptions from the city have often been removed from the site and distributed amongst museums and private collections across the entire world.[3] This has particularly taken place during the nineteenth and twentieth centuries. In this way, the Palmyrene material have become world-known as many collections, large and small, often hold one or more of the Palmyrene portraits or relief slabs with Palmyrene inscriptions.

Monographs providing more in-depth research on the ancient city of Palmyra have been circulating since the early twentieth century.[4] One of the earliest more extensive publications on Palmyrene portraits by Harald Ingholt examined the funerary portraits and their chronology.[5] His focus was on both male and female portraits and less on portraits of children. In the book by Malcolm A. R. Colledge from 1976, portraits of both women and men were addressed but once again, children did not receive much attention.[6] It was not until 1984 that portraits of children were examined in more detail in an article by Françis Pierson.[7] He especially addressed the clothing worn by children, searching for differences between the costume worn by boys and girls. In the book by Anna Sadurska and Adnan Bounni on in situ contexts in Palmyra, family groupings in the funerary reliefs and sculptures were, among other things, addressed.[8] The authors underlined the importance of men in these scenes and that women and children played a secondary role.[9] In recent years, Sara Ringsborg has been studying the portraits of children resulting in an article from 2017.[10] However, overall fairly little is known about children and childhood in Palmyra, as these themes have received little attention in scholarly research publications on the city.

Women on the other hand, has been the focus of several publications. Sadurska published several articles on the roles of women in Palmyra. She examined

1. For example, see Gawlikowski 1970; Stoneman 1992; Will 1992; Kaizer 2002; Yon 2002; Smith 2013.
2. See Hartmann 2001.
3. For example, see Dentzer-Feydy and Teixidor 1993; Hvidberg-Hansen and Ploug 1993; Albertson 2000.
4. For example, see Ingholt 1928; Colledge 1976; Gawlikowski 1970; 1974; Schmidt-Colinet 1992; Stoneman 1992; Will 1992; Millar 1993; Higuchi and Izumi 1994; Sadurska and Bounni 1994; Dirven 1999; Hartmann 2001; Higuchi and Saito 2001; Sartre 2001; Kaizer 2002; Yon 2002; Satre et al. 2005; Andrade 2013; Henning 2013; Smith 2013; Seland 2016.
5. Ingholt 1928.
6. Colledge 1976.
7. Pierson 1984.
8. Sadurska and Bounni 1994.
9. Sadurska and Bounni 1994, 190-191.
10. Ringsborg 2017.

the roles held by women through their funerary portraits, tying these roles to the domestic sphere.[11] More recent studies by Maura K. Heyn as well as by Signe Krag and Rubina Raja have explored the relations between women and their relatives.[12] Here, for example, a strong bond between women and children is pointed out and how motherhood was an important social role for women. Cynthia S. Finlayson has focused especially on the headgear worn by Palmyrene women and their embroidered textiles (in her opinion, the headbands signal tribe affiliations).[13] The jewellery worn by women in their portraits has also received much attention in research.[14] The jewellery has been used to establish chronologies for the funerary portraits and to examine aspects of wealth and female beautification in the funerary portraits. Moreover, the uncovered hairstyles found in some of the female funerary portraits, have been examined in previous research, especially focusing on the circulation of ideas between the Roman Empire and Palmyra, and here especially the work by Klaus Parlasca should be underlined.[15] In the 2002 monograph by Jean-Baptiste Yon, the roles of men and women in the Palmyrene society were investigated.[16] Based on especially civic and religious epigraphy, Yon underlined that women's main access to influence and status was dependant on their roles in families in connection to men.[17] Moreover, Eleonora Cussini has since the 1990s undertaken important research on the roles of women in the construction and transfer of funerary buildings, or sections of these.[18] She has also addressed women in the civic and religious epigraphy from the city, pointing out that women are not well represented in these spheres of the city.[19] As such, several aspects of Palmyrene women are addressed in previous research providing an understanding of the female positions and roles in society. Nevertheless, many aspects of both female and child representations still need to be explored in order for us to gain a deeper and better understanding of the roles of women and children in the Palmyrene society. This can further provide a better understanding of the social structure of the Palmyrene families. This volume offers several insights into women and children as well as the families in Palmyra. The volume is divided into three sections. The first section addresses women, children and the family in the funerary sphere. The second section focuses on women, children and the family in civic and religious spheres and, finally, the third section includes comparative aspects.

Part I: Women, children and the family in the funerary sphere

Archaeological material from Palmyra testifies to the central role the family held in society. From epigraphy, it can be inferred that this emphasis on family continued throughout the centuries in which the city prospered.[20] Portraits of families are especially found in the funerary spheres, whereas epigraphy found across the entire city demonstrates a strong focus on family relations in all sorts of aspects whether on a religious, funerary or civic level.[21] That Palmyrenes were members of certain groups in society, whether tribes or families, was therefore important to display in order to establish and underline social connections and status. In this respect, both women and children held important roles as being part of Palmyrene families.[22]

11. Sadurska 1983; 1994; 1995; 1996. For research on Palmyrene women, see also contribution by Klaver in this volume.
12. Heyn 2010; Krag and Raja 2016; 2017; Krag 2018.
13. See Finlayson 1998; 2002–2003; 2008.
14. On jewellery in Palmyra, see Mackay 1949; Gawlikowski 1966; El-Chehadé 1972; Colledge 1976; Deppert-Lippitz 1987; Schenke 2003; 2004; Palmieri 2010; Zenoni 2010; Krag 2017.
15. Parlasca 1987; 2000. See also Cussini 2000; Krag and Raja 2019.
16. Yon 2002.
17. Yon 2002, 166–174.
18. Cussini 1995; 2004; 2005; 2012.
19. See Cussini 2004; 2005; 2012; 2017.
20. See the contribution by Kaizer in this volume.
21. Funerary portraiture, for example, see Ingholt 1935; 1938; 1970; Abdul-Hak 1952; Michałowski 1960; 1962; 1963; 1964; 1966; Gawlikowski 1984; Saliby 1992; Hicughi and Izumi 1994; Sadurska and Bounni 1994; Higuchi and Saito 2001; Henning 2013. Inscriptions, for example, see Hillers and Cussini 1996; Yon 2002; 2012; 2013.
22. See Heyn 2010; Krag and Raja 2016; Krag 2018, 67-93.

Fig. 1: Loculus bust relief depicting a father and his two children; an adult son and a young daughter, 150-200 CE. Ny Carlsberg Glyptotek, IN 1027 (Courtesy of Ny Carlsberg Glyptotek, photo by Palmyra Portrait Project).

The most abundant material from Palmyra, which offers an insight into the life of women and children, stems from the funerary buildings. The funerary buildings are distributed on four necropolei surrounding the city and include tower tombs, temple or house tombs and hypogea.[23] These buildings were constructed by families and used as a resting place for members of these families; sections of the buildings could be sold to other families for these to use.[24] The earliest of these buildings stem from the late first century BCE and they continued to be constructed into the third century CE.[25] Inside the buildings, it was common for family groups to be portrayed in banqueting scenes, however, also loculus bust reliefs, loculus stelae, wall paintings and freestanding statues portray family groups (fig. 1).[26] The banqueting scenes portray extended families with up to seven individuals partaking in the banquet.[27] These scenes served to include a display of the family within the funerary buildings emphasising the prominent role the family unit held in society. In many of the scenes, men are reclining with their wives seated at their feet and children, both young and adult, are depicted in the background or standing next to the reclining men (fig. 2). Thus, marriage and offspring was highlighted in these scenes; besides the large reclining men taking the centre stage. However, not only the funerary portraits themselves underlined matrimony. In addition, inscriptions accompanying the portraits can record the married status of the women, also when they are not portrayed together with their husbands.[28]

The foundation inscriptions located externally on the funerary buildings can, sometimes record the marriage between certain individuals, and inscriptions found out of their original contexts record that women could even be co-founders of the buildings together with their husbands, although this is rare.[29] However, in general the dynamics between husbands

23. On funerary buildings in Palmyra, see Gawlikowski 1970; 2005; Schmidt-Colinet 1992; Henning 2013.
24. See Gawlikowski 1970; Cussini 1995; 2005.
25. See Gawlikowski 1970; 2005; Schmidt-Colinet 1992; Henning 2013.
26. See Colledge 1976; Parlasca 1984; 1998; Sadurska 1994; 1995; 1996; Sadurska and Bounni 1994; Heyn 2010; Krag and Raja 2016; 2017; Krag 2018, 67-93.
27. al-As'ad 2013, 19, fig. 9.
28. For example, see Sadurska and Bounni 1994, 190-191; Audley-Miller 2016, 558; Krag 2018.
29. Cussini 1995; 2005.

Fig. 2: Sarcophagus from the tomb of Yarḥaî, 237–255 CE. National Museum of Damascus (© Palmyra Portrait Project, Ingholt Archive at Ny Carlsberg Glyptotek, PS 890, 892).

and wives in the funerary buildings is not well understood. Agnes Henning explores the evidence for matrimony found in the Palmyrene tower tombs in Chapter 1. By examining epigraphy, internal décor as well as portrait reliefs that can be ascribed to their original locations inside the tombs, or at least the tomb to which they originally belonged, Henning traces the role matrimony played in the tower tombs. The contribution provides a broader discussion of the internal and external appearance of tower tombs, and these appear to have served to communicate different aspects. This is also true in terms of how matrimony was represented in the tombs. Henning underlines that an emphasis on matrimony was by far larger inside the tower tombs than on their outside. This is a very important observation, as it provides a more nuanced understanding of the power dynamics in the funerary sphere as well as the role matrimony held in the internal and external display. The chapter therefore provides a deeper understanding of matrimony represented internally and externally on tower tombs.

In situ funerary material is not only found in the tower tombs; a rather large amount of portraits are preserved in situ also in temple or house tombs, but the majority are found in the underground hypogea. In fact, portraits can be ascribed to more than 60 funerary buildings from Palmyra.[30] The combination of

30. For example, see Cantineau 1929; Gabriel 1929; Ingholt 1935; 1938; 1970; Abdul-Hak 1952; Michałowski 1960; 1962; 1963; 1964; 1966; Gawlikowski 1970; 1984; Makowski 1983; Saliby 1992; Higuchi and Izumi 1994; Sadurska and Bounni 1994; Higuchi and Saito 2001; Henning 2013.

Fig. 3: Portrait of a woman wearing several pieces of jewellery, 200–273 CE. Ny Carlsberg Glyptotek, IN 1073 (Courtesy of Ny Carlsberg Glyptotek, photo by Palmyra Portrait Project).

Fig. 4: Portrait of a priest wearing a brooch, 150–200 CE. Ny Carlsberg Glyptotek, IN 1031 (Courtesy of Ny Carlsberg Glyptotek, photo by Palmyra Portrait Project).

foundation inscriptions, cession texts, funerary epigraphy, portrait reliefs and the location of portraits inside the buildings can offer a different insight into family structures in Palmyra. In Chapter 2, Signe Krag surveys three underground hypogea from the city to see what these might reveal about family burial patterns in the city. It can be observed that women could be buried either with their marital family or with their biological family (even when the women were married). The family burial practices in the city are therefore more dynamic than previously thought as suggested by the funerary in situ material from the three tombs. Krag further explores marriage customs and the organisation of different families inside the buildings. How did new families gain access to the funerary buildings and how were marriages structured? The chapter thus offers insight into the organisation of families in a few funerary buildings in Palmyra as well as marital customs.

Inside the funerary buildings women compose no less than approximately 40% of the portrait reliefs and sculptures produced during the late first century BCE to the third century CE.[31] In this sphere of the city, representations of women played a significant role. A quite common and characteristic feature of the Palmyrene female portraits is that women are portrayed wearing different items of jewellery; the quantity differs between portraits (fig. 3).[32] Men can also wear jewellery, the most common item is the finger ring and priests also often wear a brooch (fig. 4).[33]

In funerary banquet scenes, children are often

31. The information is from the Palmyra Portrait Project database, December 2017. See also Krag 2018, 68.
32. On jewellery in Palmyra, see also Mackay 1949; Gawlikowski 1966; El-Chehadé 1972; Colledge 1976; Deppert-Lippitz 1987; Schenke 2003; 2004; Palmieri 2010; Zenoni 2010; Krag 2017.
33. See Stucky 1973; Raja 2016; 2017a; 2017b, 2017c.

standing behind their reclining fathers, and sometimes brothers, as well as their seated mothers. They occur together with their relatives also on loculus stelae, loculus reliefs and wall paintings (figs. 1 and 2).[34] Furthermore, individual portraits of children occur on loculus stelae where they are depicted in full figure.[35] Skeletal material from the funerary buildings reveal that children were buried both in the loculi placed in horizontal and vertical rows in the walls of the buildings as well as in pit graves situated in the floor of the buildings.[36] Children were therefore often included in the funerary display in iconography and buried alongside their relatives: both in loculi and in pit graves. In fact, around 7% of the Palmyrene funerary portraits are of children.[37] Still, very little is known of the roles which children held in the Palmyrene society and how childhood was perceived. Sara Ringsborg at the workshop addressed representations of Palmyrene children. Her contribution, which unfortunately is not included in this volume, especially focused on representations of children with other family members as the majority of the children's depictions stem from group constellations. Ringsborg examined the iconography of children, the large variety of constellations in which they are depicted and the epigraphy belonging to the portraits together with aspects of age and gender in order to reveal the role of children in the funerary representations. She pointed out, that even though children most frequently are portrayed as accompanying other individuals in portraiture, they were far from anonymous in the Palmyrene funerary representations. This is, amongst other things, underlined by the elaborate jewellery and clothing worn by children together with the frequent prominent positions of children in the depictions highlighting these in the display, and the frequent inclusion of children in general, she argued.

A large amount of epigraphy is preserved from Palmyra and the majority of this stems from the funerary buildings.[38] Epigraphy analysed together with funerary portraiture can provide a more detailed understanding of the lives of the Palmyrenes according the aspects highlighted in their funerary portraits. This is something that is rarely done in research; most often iconography and epigraphy are separated in publications. In Chapter 3, Eleonora Cussini examines the epigraphical material from the city, especially from the funerary contexts, and what this can reveal about relationships between women and their relatives. In her contribution, Cussini points out that the professions of women are rarely recorded in epigraphy (and only a few professions were available to women). Instead, women are often addressed as daughters but also other roles are included such as wives, mothers and granddaughters. Cussini includes several funerary portraits and addresses the ways in which women were portrayed and how this links to the preserved epigraphy. She finds, that it is only possible to truly understand the role of women in Palmyra by combining all sources available to us, such as epigraphy and portraiture. Interestingly, Cussini states that the portraiture and their individual stories in Palmyra are not simple, but she finds a large complexity, which is discussed and presented in her contribution.

Part II: Women, children and the family in civic and religious spheres

Outside of the funerary buildings, in the religious and civic spheres in the city, the material providing an insight into the roles of women and children in Palmyra is rather fragmented when it comes to reliefs and sculptures, but the epigraphy is abundant.[39] However, the evidence from these areas shows a much larger focus on men.[40] Because the evidence from the

34. See Krag and Raja 2016; Ringsborg 2017; Krag 2018, 67-93.
35. See Pierson 1984; Ringsborg 2017.
36. On pit graves, for example, see Higuchi and Izumi 1994; Higuchi and Saito 2001; Saito 2005.
37. The information is from the Palmyra Portrait Project database, December 2017. See also Ringsborg 2017.
38. See Hillers and Cussini 1996; Yon 2012; 2013.
39. Epigraphy, see Hillers and Cussini 1996; Yon 2002; 2012; 2013.
40. See Cussini 1995; 2004; 2005; 2012; 2017; Kaizer 2002; Yon 2002.

religious and civic spheres in the city is much more fragmented than that from the funerary buildings, it offers several methodological issues: what can be said about Palmyrene women and children in the civic and religious spheres based on such small material? What was their involvement in the civic and religious life of Palmyra?

In religious dedications, children frequently act as the receivers alongside the gods: whether these were young or adult children is unknown.[41] However, it underlines the great importance importance of children and the continuation of the lineage in Palmyra, which was important to emphasise also in the civic and religious display. Outside the funerary buildings, portrait reliefs and sculptures are likewise discovered. Either these are honorific statues of both men and women, or they are religious reliefs such as votive plaques and reliefs on altars.[42] Rarely children are included on religious reliefs.[43] When children do occur, they are depicted in family constellations as can also be observed in the funerary buildings; but never alone. In fact, group constellations are rather frequent on the religious reliefs and played a significant role in the public display; not only through epigraphy but also iconography. In Chapter 4, Ted Kaizer examines family connections and religious life at Palmyra expressed through public and religious reliefs, wall paintings and epigraphy. He examines how family connections might have effected the way in which patterns of worship were constructed in the city. The contribution by Kaizer includes not only material from Palmyra, but also Palmyrene material evidence from other regions or cities, such as Dura Europos, where family connections are represented in several wall paintings found in the city: in this case inside temples and private houses. He points out how evidence from private spheres stand in strong contrast to evidence from the public and religious spheres. When portrayed in public monuments women are by-standers, which they are not in the private spheres. His contribution therefore interestingly explores families' connections in religion at Palmyra.

Evidence of a lively religious life is documented in Palmyra. In the city, priesthood was connected to different families; some of the families can at times be connected to specific temples and gods.[44] Religious banquets are well documented; small tesserae providing access to such banquets have been found in large quantities from the city.[45] Priestesses have so far not been documented in the city; although Sadurska claimed a funerary portrait of a woman holding a skyphos and twig did in fact represent a priestess.[46] However, more likely the woman is engaged in a funerary ritual and cannot with certainty be argued a priestess, as also pointed out by other scholars.[47] Thus, only men had access to priesthood in the city and were dominant partakers in the religious life. But what role did the families of the priests hold in the lives of priests? In Chapter 5, Rubina Raja examines priests from Palmyra and their families. She offers an analysis a discussion of the representational categories of the images of Palmyrene priests, which are so plentiful in the corpus of portraits stemming from the funerary sphere. Through having brought together the immense amounts of priestly representations, Raja offers considerations on the meaning of Palmyrene priesthood within the wider societal structure of Palmyra and Palmyrene families in general.

Scholars such as Cussini, Heyn, Sadurska and Yon have brought attention to the roles played by women in the construction and sale of funerary property and in religion in the Palmyrene society.[48] Cussini has published several important articles on the role of women in legal affairs and has importantly demonstrated

41. See Hillers and Cussini 1996; Yon 2012; 2013.
42. For example, see al-Hassani and Starcky 1953; 1957; Drijvers 1976; Tanabe 1986; Balty 2005.
43. For example, see Katzumi Tanabe (1986, 265, pl. 132) for a votive relief with a representation of a boy and Finn Ove Hvidberg-Hansen and Gunhild Ploug (1993, 160, no. 129) for an altar with a representation of a boy.
44. See Milik 1972; Stucky 1973; Kaizer 2002; Yon 2002; Raja 2016; 2017a; 2017b.
45. Ingholt et al. 1955; Raja 2015.
46. Sadurska 1990–1991.
47. Kaizer 2002, 237, n.134; Yon 2002, 169, n. 28.
48. See Sadurska 1990–1991; Cussini 1995; 2004; 2005; 2012; 2017; Yon 2002; Heyn 2010; 2016.

Fig. 5: Honorific statue of a woman found in the Agora, 175–225 CE. National Museum of Damascus, C4022 (© Palmyra Portrait Project, Ingholt Archive at Ny Carlsberg Glyptotek).

how Palmyrene women were fully capable of selling and buying sections of funerary buildings as well as erect the buildings together with men as previously mentioned.[49] Thus, Palmyrene women had important social roles in the funerary sphere, where they could manage property. Furthermore, Cussini, Klaas Dijkstra and Yon have examined the roles of women in the religious life of the city. In the public spheres of the city, only a few women were involved in erecting honorific sculpture or buildings, but women could more often dedicate smaller altars around the city (fig. 5).[50] In Chapter 6, Sanne Klaver addresses the fragmented, but nonetheless highly important, evidence from the civic and religious spheres in Palmyra to highlight the participation of Palmyrene women in the religious life of the city. In her contribution, Klaver discusses the reliefs portraying women partaking in religious processions and sacrificial events as well as dedications by women (altars, honorific sculptures and architectural dedications). She points out, that it was socially accepted for women to be part of the religious life in the city, however, their degree of participation was small compared to men in these matters. Stimulatingly, Klaver suggests that not only the upper class in society had access to smaller religious dedications, but that most of these were in fact dedicated by individuals belonging to the middle class. Therefore, the material offers an insight into not only the upper class of society but also the broader middle class, and Klaver's contribution thus offers a more nuanced understanding of the material.

It appears that the only woman in Palmyra to hold a public powerful role was Queen Zenobia. However, much of our knowledge of Zenobia stems from ancient literary sources not originating from Palmyra.[51] Over time, several publications on Zenobia have appeared; most are based on the descriptions found in the ancient literary sources.[52] In Chapter 7, Nathanael J. Andrade offers a quite different and captivating take on Zenobia, as he examines the burial of Odainath, the husband of Zenobia, and the role she might have played in this event. He suggests, that as the husband of Zenobia, Odainath had no adult living male relatives when he died and that it is probable, that Zenobia was in charge of arranging his burial. Andrade reconstructs the funeral of Odainath including speculations on how his funerary portrait might have appeared and how the

49. See Cussini 1995; 2004; 2005; 2012.

50. Dijkstra 1995; Yon 2002; Cussini 2004; 2005; 2012; 2017.

51. See esp. Hartmann 2001.

52. For example, see Stoneman 1992; Equini Schneider 1993; Southern 2008; Bland 2011; Sartre 2016; Sartre and Sartre 2014.

building, in which he was buried, looked. Thus, the funerary ceremony of Odainath is interestingly explored in the contribution discussing the role Zenobia played in the event. This provides an understanding of the events that occurred in the late 260s when Zenobia lost her husband and power in Palmyra was transferred to her.

Part III: Comparative aspects

A final aspect addressed at the workshops, was how the life of women and children in Palmyra was compared to women and children in other areas of the Roman world. By comparing the Palmyrene material to other regions, the material is placed in a broader perspective in this last part. This in turn allows for a better understanding of the nature of the material. Was the life of women and children in Rome similar to that in Palmyra, or can certain differences be observed? Are the representations of Roman Imperial women similar to those observed in Palmyra?

In Chapter 8, Mary T. Boatwright presents the model families in Imperial Roman and Palmyra. Boatwright presents the representations of families over time with an emphasis on Rome. Interestingly, she examines the material from Rome in relation to the three chronological groups into which Ingholt divided the Palmyrene material (50–150 CE; 150–200 CE and 200–273 CE) finding changes in the material. She, for example, underlines how the roles of women as mothers is emphasised in portraiture in Rome especially from the middle of the second century CE, which does also appear to have manifested more strongly in Palmyrene portraiture around this time. Boatwright's contribution provides an important comparative timeline of core Roman portraiture to which the Palmyrene portraits can be compared. This is highly useful in future examinations of the circulation of influences between Palmyra and Rome, and the circulation of ideas in the Roman Empire in general.

As previously addressed, the material from Palmyra testifying to the childhood and the religious participation of children in the city is rather poor. Only a few reliefs depicting children are found outside of the funerary sphere; however, inside the tombs children are more well represented. Moreover, children are often referred to in epigraphy (whether young or adult) underlining the great importance of children and the continuation of lineage in society. In Chapter 9, Ville Vuolanto addresses the children's portraits from Palmyra by comparing these to the material and knowledge on childhood from elsewhere in the Roman world. The contribution seeks to reveal aspects of the roles of children in religious affairs, both civic as well as those private in character. Vuolanto examines several aspects of children's portraits such as the necklaces resembling the Roman *bulla,* a protective amulet, underlining that the meaning of this type of necklace in the Palmyrene funerary representations is unclear. Even though the Palmyrene evidence on children and childhood is scarce, some interesting and new results are brought forward in his contribution.

The contributions in this volume sheds light on important aspects of women, children and in a broader sense the family in Palmyra and its status. By looking at both iconography and epigraphy from the city, further aspects are added through this volume to our understanding of woman and children and how they were perceived in Palmyra as well as the identity aspects included in their portraiture and the written evidence that also informs us about them.

Bibliography

Abdul-Hak, S. 1952, L'hypogée de Taai à Palmyre, *AAS* 2, 1–2, 193–251.
Albertson, F. C. 2000, Three Palmyrene reliefs in the Colket collection, University of Wyoming, *Syria* 77, 159–168.
Andrade, J. 2013, *Syrian Identity in the Greco-Roman World*, Cambridge.
al-As'ad, W. 2013, Some tombs recently excavated in Palmyra, *Studia Palmyreńskie* 12, 15–24.
Audley-Miller, L. 2016, The Banquet in Palmyrene Funerary Contexts, in C. M. Draycott and M. Stamatopoulou (eds.), *Dining and Death: Interdiciplinary Perspectives on the 'Funerary Banquet' in Ancient Art, Burial and Belief*, Leuven, Paris and Bristol, 553–590.
Balty, J-C. 2005, La sculpture, in C. Delplace and J.

Dentzer-Feydy (eds.), *L'Agora de Palmyre*, Bordeaux, 321–341.

Bland, R. 2011, The Coinage of Vabalathus and Zenobia from Antioch and Alexandria, *NC* 171, 133–186.

Cantineau, J. 1929, Fouilles à Palmyre, *Mélanges de l'Institut Français de Damas* 1, 1–15.

El-Chehadeh, J. 1972, *Untersuchungen zum antiken Schmuck in Syrien*, unpublished PhD Thesis, Freie Universität Berlin.

Colledge, M. A. R. 1976, *The Art of Palmyra*, London.

Cussini, E. 2017, The Pious Butcher and the Physicians. Palmyrene Professions in Context, in T. Long and A. H. Sørensen (eds.) *Positions and Professions at Palmyra*, Palmyrene Studies 2, Copenhagen, 84–96.

Cussini, E. 2016, Reconstructing Palmyrene Legal Language, in A. Kropp and R. Raja (eds.), *The World of Palmyra*, Palmyrene Studies 1, Copenhagen, 42–52.

Cussini, E. 2012, What Women Say and Do (in Aramaic Documents), in G. B. Lanfranchi, D. M. Bonacossi, C. Pappi and S. Ponchia (eds.), *Leggo! Studies Presented to Prof. Frederick Mario Fales on the Occasion of his 65th Birthday*, Wiesbaden, 161–172.

Cussini E. 2005, Beyond the Spindle: Investigating the Role of Palmyrene Women, in E. Cussini (ed.), *A Journey to Palmyra: Collected Essays to Remember Delbert R. Hillers*, Leiden and Boston, 26–43.

Cussini, E. 2004, Regina, Martay and the Others. Stories of Palmyrene Women, *Orientalia* 73, 235–244.

Cussini, E. 2000. Palmyrene Eunuchs? Two Cases of Mistaken Identity, in E. Rova (ed.), *Patavina orientalia selecta*, Padova, 279–290.

Cussini, E. 1995, Transfer of Property at Palmyra, *ARAM periodicals* 7, 233–250.

Dentzer-Feydy, J. and J. Teixidor 1993, *Les antiquités de Palmyre au Musée du Louvre*, Paris.

Deppert-Lippitz, B. 1987, Die Bedeutung der palmyrenischen Grabreliefs für die Kenntnis römischen Schmuck, in E. Ruprechtsberger (ed.), *Palmyra: Geschichte, Kunst und Kultur der syrischen Oasenstadt*, Linz, 179–192.

Dijkstra, K. 1995, *Life and Loyalty: A Study in the Socio-Religious Culture of Syria and Mesopotamia in the Graeco-Roman Period based on Epigraphical Evidence,* Leiden, New York and Cologne.

Dirven, L. 1999, *Palmyrenes of Dura-Europos: A Study of Religious Interaction in Rome Syria, Leiden, Boston and Cologne.*

Drijvers, H. J. W. 1976, *The religion of Palmyra*, Iconography of religion XV.15, Leiden.

Equini Schneider, E. 1993, *Septimia Zenobia Sebaste*, Rome.

Finlayson, C. S. 2008, *Mut'a* Marriage in the Roman Near East: The Evidence from Palmyra, Syria, in B. A. Nakhai (ed.), *The World of Women in the Ancient and Classical Near East*, Newcastle-upon-Tyne, 99–138.

Finlayson, C. S. 2002–2003, Veil, Turban and Headpiece: Funerary Portraits and Female Status at Palmyra, *AAAS* 45–46, 221–235.

Finlayson, C. S. 1998, *Veil, Turban, and Headpiece: Funerary Portraits and Female Status at Palmyra*, unpublished PhD Thesis, University of Iowa.

Gabriel, A. 1929, Recherches archéologiques à Palmyre, *Syria* 7, 71–92.

Gawlikowski, M. 2005, The City of the Dead, in E. Cussini (ed.), *A Journey to Palmyra: Collected Essays to Remember Delbert R. Hillers*, Leiden and Boston, 44–73.

Gawlikowski, M. 1984, *Les principia de Dioclétien, Temples des Enseignes*, Warsaw

Gawlikowski, M. 1974, *Recueil d'inscriptions palmyréniennes provenant de fouilles syriennes et polonaises récentes à Palmyre,* Paris.

Gawlikowski, M. 1970, *Monuments funéraires de Palmyre*, Warsaw.

Gawlikowski, M. 1966, Remarques sur l'usage de la fibule à Palmyre, in M. L. Bernhard (ed.), *Mélanges offerts à Kazimierz Michalowski*, Warsaw, 411–419.

Hartmann, U. 2001, *Das Palmyrenische Teilreich*, Stuttgart.

al-Hassani, D. and J. Starcky 1957, Autels palmyréniens découverts prés de la source Efca (suite), *AAS* 7, 95–122.

al-Hassani, D. and J. Starcky 1953, Autels palmyréniens découverts prés de la source Efca, *AAS* 2, 154–164.

Henning, A. 2013, *Die Turmgräber von Palmyra. Eine lokale Bauform im kaiserzeitlichen Syrien als Ausdruck kultureller Identität,* Rahden/Westf.

Heyn, M. K. 2016, Status and Stasis: Looking at Women in the Palmyrene Tomb, in A. Kropp and R. Raja (eds.), *The World of Palmyra*, Palmyrene Studies 1, Copenhagen, 194–206.

Heyn, M. K. 2010, Gesture and Identity in the Funerary Art of Palmyra, *AJA* 114, 4, 631–661.

Higuchi. T. and T. Izumi (eds.) 1994, *Tombs A and C: Southeast Necropolis, Palmyra Syria: Surveyed in 1990–92*, Nara.

Higuchi, T. and K. Saito (eds.) 2001, *Tomb F – Tomb of BWLH and BWRP: Southeast Necropolis, Palmyra, Syria*, Nara.

Hillers, D. R. and E. *Cussini.* 1996, *Palmyrene Aramaic Texts*, Baltimore.

Hvidberg-Hansen, F. O. and G. Ploug 1993, *Katalog: Palmyra samlingen, Ny Carlsberg Glyptotek,* Copenhagen.

Ingholt, H. 1970, The sarcophagus of Beʿelai and other sculptures from the tomb of Malkû, Palmyra, *MélBeyrouth* 45, 173–200.
Ingholt, H. 1938, Inscriptions and Sculptures from Palmyra, II, *Berytus* 5, 93–140.
Ingholt, H. 1935, Five Dated Tombs from Palmyra, *Berytus* 2, 57–120.
Ingholt, H. 1928, *Studier over Palmyrensk Skulptur*, Copenhagen.
Ingholt, H., H. Seyrig and J. Starcky 1955, *Recueil des tessères de Palmyre*, Paris.
Kaizer, T. 2002, *The Religious Life of Palmyra: A Study of the Social Patterns of Worship in the Roman Period*, Stuttgart.
Krag, S. 2018, *Funerary Representations of Palmyrene Women: From the First Century BC to the Third Century AD*, Studies in Classical Archaeology, Turnhout.
Krag, S. 2017, Changing Identities, Changing Positions: Jewellery in Pamyrene Female Portraits, in T. Long and A. H. Sørensen (eds.), *Positions and Professions in Palmyra*, Palmyrene Studies 2, Copenhagen, 36–51.
Krag, S. and R. Raja 2019, Unveiling Female Hairstyles: Markers of Age, Social Roles, and Status in the Funerary Sculpture from Palmyra, *Zeitschrift für Orient-Archäologie* 11, 243-277.
Krag, S. and R. Raja 2017, Representations of Women and Children in Palmyrene Banqueting Reliefs and Sarcophagus Scenes, *Zeitschrift für Orient-Archäologie* 10, 196-227.
Krag, S. and R. Raja 2016, Representations of Women and Children in Palmyrene Funerary *Loculus* Reliefs, *Loculus Stelae* and Wall Paintings, *Zeitschrift für Orient-Archäologie* 9, 134–178.
Mackay, D. 1949, The Jewellery of Palmyra and Its Significance, *Iraq* 11, 2, 160–187.
Makowski, K. C. 1983, Recherches sur le tombeau de Aʿailamî et Zebîdâ, *DM* 1, 175–187.
Michałowski, K. 1966, *Palmyre: Fouilles polonaises 1963 et 1964*, Warsaw.
Michałowski, K. 1964, *Palmyre: Fouilles polonaises 1962*, Warsaw.
Michałowski, K. 1963, *Palmyre: Fouilles polonaises 1961*, Warsaw.
Michałowski, K. 1962, *Palmyre: Fouilles polonaises 1960*, Warsaw.
Michałowski, K. 1960, *Palmyre: Fouilles polonaises 1959*, Warsaw.
Milik, J. T. 1972, *Dedicaces faites par des Dieux (Palmyre, Hatra, Tyr) et des thiases sémitiques à l'époque romaine*, Paris.
Millar, F. 1993, *The Roman Near East, 31 BC – AD 337*, Cambridge, Massachusetts and London.
Palmieri, L. 2010, Il lusso privato in Oriente: analisi comparata dei gioielli delle signore di Palmira, *Bollettino di Archaeologia online*, 34–44.
Parlasca, K. 2000, Ein syrischer Kopf der römischen Kaiserzeit in Mariemont, *DM* 12, 135–139.
Parlasca, K. 1998, Palmyrenische Sarkophage mit Totenmahlreliefs - Forschungsstand und ikonographische Probleme, in G. Koch (ed.), *Akten des Symposiums: 125 Jahre Sarkophag-Corpus. Marburg, 4.–7. Oktober 1995*, Mainz am Rhein, 311–317.
Parlasca, K. 1987, Ein antoninischer Frauenkopf aus Palmyra in Malibu, in J. Frel, A. A. Houghton and M. True (eds.), *Ancient Portraits in the J. Paul Getty Museum*, vol. I, Malibu, 107–114.
Parlasca, K. 1984, Probleme der palmyrenischen Sarkophage, in B. Andreae (ed.), *Symposium über die Antiken Sarkophage. Pisa, 5.–12. September 1982*, Marburg, 283–297.
Pierson, F. 1984, Recherches sur le costume des enfants dans l'iconographie palmyrénienne, *RALouvain* 17, 95–111.
Raja, R. 2017a, Networking beyond death: Priests and their family networks in Palmyra explored through the funerary sculpture, H. F. Teigen and E. H. Seland (eds.), *Sinews of Empire: Networks in the Roman Near East and Beyond*, Oxford, 121–135.
Raja, R. 2017b. "You can leave your hat on": Priestly representations from Palmyra between visual genre, religious importance and social status, in R. Gordon, G. Peitridou and J. Rüpke (eds.), *Beyond Priesthood: Religious Entrepreneurs and Innovators in the Roman* Empire, Berlin, 417–442.
Raja, R. 2017c, To be or not to be depicted as a priest in Palmyra: A matter of representational spheres and societal values, in T. Long and A. H. Sørensen (eds.), *Positions and Professions in Palmyra,* Palmyrene Studies 2, Copenhagen, 115–130.
Raja, R. 2016, Representations of Priests in Palmyra: Methodological Considerations on the meaning of the Representations of Priesthood in Roman Period Palmyra, *Religion in the Roman Empire* 2, 125–146.
Raja, R. 2015, Staging 'private' religion in Roman 'public' Palmyra. The role of the religious dining tickets (banqueting *tesserae*), in J. Rüpke (ed.), *Public and Private in Ancient Mediterranean Law and Religion*, Berlin, 165–186.
Ringsborg, S. 2017, Children's portraits from Palmyra, in R. Raja (ed.), *Palmyra: Pearl of the Desert*, Aarhus, 66–75.
Sadurska, A. 1996, L'art et la société. Recherches ico-

nologiques sur la sculpture funéraire de Palmyra, in *AAAS* 42, 285–288.

Sadurska, A. 1995, La famille et son image dans l'art de Palmyre, *Arculiana*, 583–589.

Sadurska, A. 1994, L'art et la société: Recherches iconologiques sur l'art funéraire de Palmyre, *Archeologia-War* 45, 11–23.

Sadurska, A. 1990–1991, Le role des femmes dans le culte à Palmyre (recherche iconographique), *Vox patrum* 11–12, 101–104.

Sadurska, A. 1983, Le modèle de la semaine dans l'imagerie palmyrénienne, *ÉtTrav* 12, 24, 151–156.

Sadurska, A. and A. Bounni 1994, *Les sculptures funéraires de Palmyre*, Rome.

Saliby, N. 1992, L'hypogée de Sassan fils de Malê à Palmyre (with a bibliography appendix by Klaus Parlasca), *DM* 6, 267–292.

Saito, K. 2005, Palmyrene Burial Practices from Funerary Goods, in E. Cussini (ed.), *A Journey to Palmyra: Collected Essays to Remember Delbert Hillers*, Leiden and Boston, 150–165.

Sartre, M. 2016, Zénobie dans l'imaginaire occidental, in A. Kropp and R. Raja (eds.), *The World of Palmyra*, Palmyrene Studies 1, Copenhagen, 207–221.

Sartre, M., tr. C. Porter and E. Rawlings, with J. Routier-Pucci 2005, *The Middle East under Rome*, Cambridge, Massachusetts.

Sartre, A. and M. Sartre 2014, *Zénobie: de Palmyre à Rome*, Paris.

Sartre, M. 2001, *D'Alexandre à Zénobie: Histoire du Levant antique, IVe siècle avant J.-C.–IIIe siècle après J.-C.*, Paris

Schenke, G. 2004, Zum Schmuckgebrauch an palmyrenischen Grabreliefs, *DM* 14, 83–90.

Schenke, G. 2003, Frühe palmyrenische Grabreliefs: Individuelle und kulturelle Identität durch Selbstdarstellung im Sepulkralbereich, in K. S. Freyberger, A. Henning and H. von Hesberg (eds.), *Kulturkonflikte in Vorderen Orient and der Wende vom Hellenismus zur römischen Kaiserzeit*, Rahden, 109–116.

Schmidt-Colinet, A. 1992, *Das Tempelgrab Nr. 36 in Palmyra: Studien zur palmyrenischen Grabarchitektur und ihrer Ausstattung*, 2 vols., Mainz am Rhein.

Seland, E. H. 2016, *Ships of the Desert and Ships of the Sea: Palmyra in the World Trade of the First Three Centuries CE*, Wiesbaden.

Smith, A. M. 2013, *Roman Palmyra: Identity, Community, and State Formation*, Oxford.

Southern, P. 2008, *Empress Zenobia: Palmyra's Rebel Queen*, London and New York.

Stoneman, R. 1992, *Palmyra and Its Empire: Zenobia's Revolt against Rome*, Ann Arbor.

Stucky, R. A. 1973, Prêtres syriens. 1. Palmyre, *Syria* 50, 1–2, 163–180.

Tanabe, K. 1986, *Sculptures of Palmyra I*, Tokyo.

Will, E. 1992, *Les palmyréniens: La Venise des sables*, Paris.

Yon, J.-B. 2013, L'épigraphie palmyrénienne depuis *PAT*, 1996–2011, *Studia Palmyreńskie* 12, 333–379.

Yon, J.-B. 2012, *Inscriptions grecques et latines de la Syrie, Tome 17, Fascicule 1: Palmyre,* Beirut.

Yon, J.-B. 2002, *Les notables de Palmyre,* Beirut.

Zenoni, G. 2010, Modelli e mode fra Oriente e Occidente: le collane delle signore de Palmira, *Bollettino di Archaeologia Online,* 45–54.

CHAPTER I

The representation of matrimony in the tower tombs of Palmyra

Agnes Henning

SCI.DAN.H.4.10 · WOMEN, CHILDREN AND THE FAMILY IN PALMYRA
THE ROYAL DANISH ACADEMY OF SCIENCES AND LETTERS · 2019

Introduction

As hardly any other place in antiquity, the funerary monuments of Palmyra with their specific features offer an abundance of information on family and social structures of the deceased. This is due to the numerous reliefs and particularly the detailed inscriptions as well as the spatial arrangements of the monument's different forms of representation and their relation to each other. This also applies to the tower tombs that, in addition to the hypogea and temple tombs, belong to one of the three main groups of funerary monuments in the Syrian oasis town (fig. 1).[1] Therefore, although the evidence is little, matrimonial relations between persons buried in the tower tombs can be revealed.

The archaeological remains of the tower tombs are mostly of architectural nature only. Some of the monuments were still preserved to a height of 25 meters with several stories (fig. 2).[2] Their decorations in the form of reliefs and portraits, however, are mostly lost since the tower tombs were open for many centuries and their decor thus either robbed or destroyed. Nevertheless, some reliefs, inscriptions, wall paintings and graffiti were documented in the tower tombs that offer an approximate reconstruction of the original decor of the tombs. Furthermore, fragments of sculptures and inscriptions from the archives of the museums of Palmyra and other museums could be re-associated with specific towers. Based on this material, it is possible to observe a basic structure concerning the decor of the monuments, which is important for understanding the mechanisms of specific forms of representation within the tower tombs. Only in consideration of these collectively recognized structures for imparting knowledge on social configurations in ancient Palmyra, is it possible to comprehend the different statements and representation forms of matrimony in the tower tombs.

Tower tombs and their forms of representation

With about 180 discernible structures, the tower tombs are the largest group of the monumental tombs in the necropoleis of Palmyra.[3] Their architectural design is specific to Palmyra and is unparalleled in other necropoleis of the ancient Mediterranean. While there was a tradition of tower tombs in the larger Syrian region, as examples in the Euphrates area demonstrate, the particular architectural design in Palmyra is unique.[4]

As many other monuments in Palmyra, numerous

1. I would like to thank the two organizers of this meeting, Signe Krag and Sara Ringsborg as well as Rubina Raja for giving me the opportunity to present my results in Aarhus and publish them here. Generally on the funerary monuments of Palmyra, see Watzinger and Wulzinger 1932; Gawlikowski 1970a; Schmidt-Colinet 1992; Higuchi and Izumi 1994; Higuchi and Saito 2001. Specifically on the tower tombs, see Henning 2013a; 2013b.
2. The documentation of the described tower tombs was conducted until 2005. Meanwhile, the well-preserved and high-standing towers were destroyed during armed conflicts in the summer of 2015.

3. Henning 2013a.
4. Henning 2013a, 101–116.

Fig. 1: Palmyra, western necropolis, view of the tower tombs along the northeastern slopes of Umm el-Qais, nos. 71, 70, 69, 68, 67, 65, 64, 63 and 51, from left to right (© author).

tower tombs are securely dated, therefore a robust chronological framework for their temporal development can be deduced.[5] It has been established that the tower tombs were constructed from the mid-first century BCE to the mid-second century CE and were in continuous use until the third century CE. Architecturally, there is a prevailing base form that was consequently applied to nearly all tower tombs (fig. 3). First, there is the stepped base on which the actual shaft is erected. Over a revolving cornice the superstructure continues in a step-like fashion. Most likely there was a flat roof. With the exception of three to four canonical decorative elements, the outer walls were mostly not decorated. The mentioned decorative elements include the door, which could have been architecturally framed or adorned with a pediment (fig. 15), the tabula with the foundation inscription (fig. 9) and a relief alcove and the revolving cornice (fig. 2).

5. Currently this includes fourteen towers, see the actual compilation in Henning 2013a, 23–25. See also Gawlikowski 2005, 44–51, 58 (without tower no. 21). Inside the tower no. 206, on a stone sarcophagus box, the date 128 CE is preserved, see al-As'ad 2013, 16. This date is only a terminus ante quem for the construction of the tower, which should have been built due to its architectural details during the second half of the first century CE. The before-mentioned sarcophagus box as well as two additional boxes were placed approximately half a century later. Tower no. 206 should not be included into the group of securely dated towers as wrongly done by Henning 2013b, 160.

Fig. 2: Palmyra, western necropolis, tower tomb no. 71. View of the façade (© author).

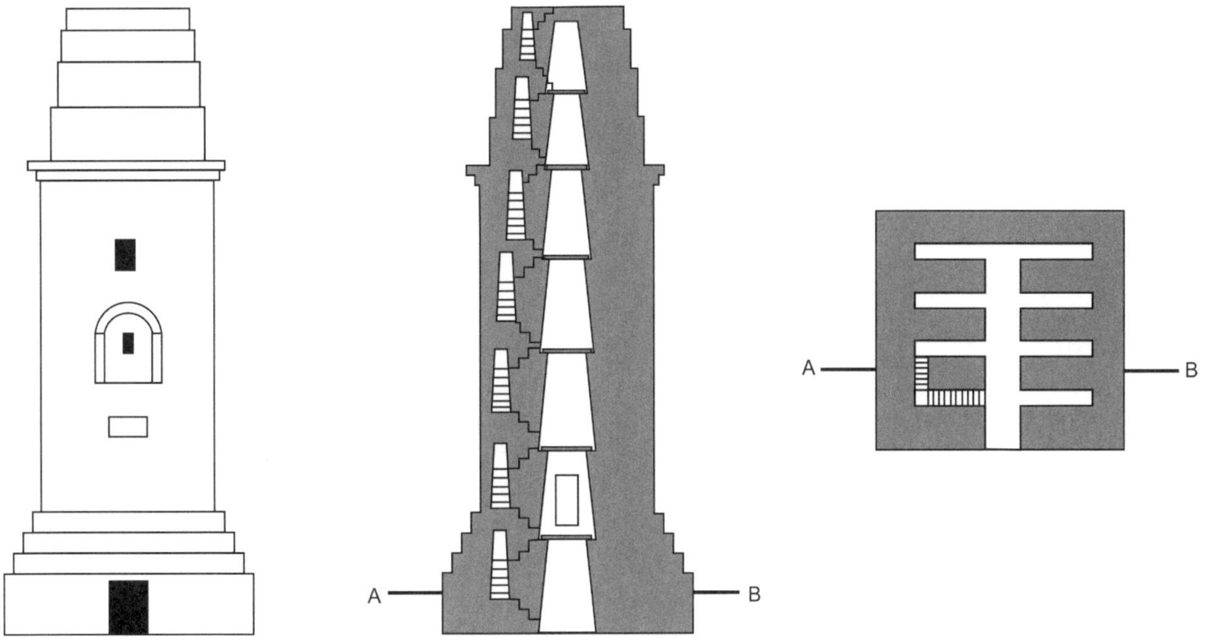

Fig. 3: Schematic reconstruction of a tower tomb. Façade, sectional view and ground plan (© author).

Often, undecorated windows were set into the walls as well. The decorative elements were almost exclusively concentrated on the façade towards the viewer standing in front of the tomb. Thus, there were no revolving decorations as known from other ancient freestanding funerary monuments, where friezes ran along all sides or columns adorned the entire monument. Principally, the decorative elements of Palmyrene tower tombs were focused on one main view and there are only very few examples that deviate from this scheme. An essential element of the exterior design was the relief alcove and its architectural frame in which the tomb founder was displayed banqueting together with further family members (fig. 13).[6] The interior of the towers was structured by several burial chambers on different levels, which could be accessed by a staircase (fig. 3). The actual burial shafts with the loculi were placed on both sides of the burial chamber. While in earlier tombs, the ground plans of the chambers were often still irregular, later examples, c. from the mid-first century CE onwards, regularly showed similar ground plans.[7]

As on the exterior façades, the decoration in the interior of the monuments was reduced to only a few but distinct elements. Originally, the tombs' interior showed no signs of decorations at all. Instead, individual design possibilities were chosen, such as wall paintings that either adorned central parts of the monument or individual burial places only (fig. 4).[8] Before the loculi in the interior of the tower tombs were sealed with portrait slabs of the deceased from the mid-first century CE onwards, the openings were closed with simple quarry stones and plaster.[9] Occasionally, short inscriptions were written into the plaster when it was

6. Will 1951; Gawlikowski 1970a; 2005, 44-51; Henning 2013a, 14, 50-51, 98-99; 2013b, 160.

7. Gawlikowski 1970a, 52-106, Henning 2013a, 33-34.

8. Wall paintings that adorned interior central parts of the monuments, for example, see the vault in tower no. 19; Henning 2013a, 73-77, 162, 311-312, pl. 31; 2013b, 161-162, 174, fig.14. Wall paintings that adorned individual burial places only, for example, see individual burial shafts or loculi in towers A, no. 22, no. 62, no. 67. See also Henning 2013a.

9. Earliest dated portrait slab, see Ingholt 1930; Ploug 1995, 35-36, cat. no. 1.

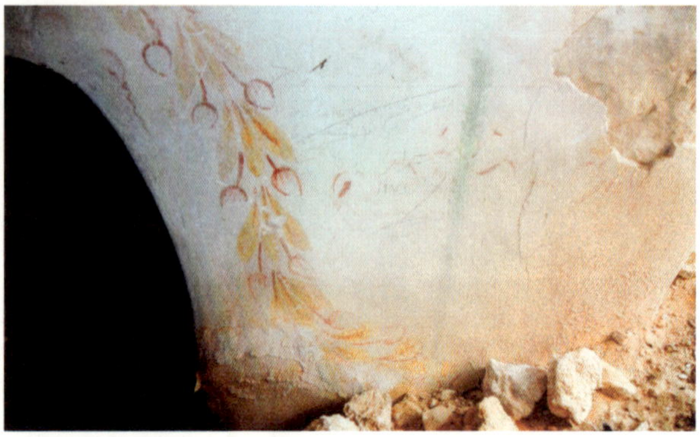

Fig. 4: Palmyra, western necropolis, tower A. Wall paintings between two loculus shafts (© author).

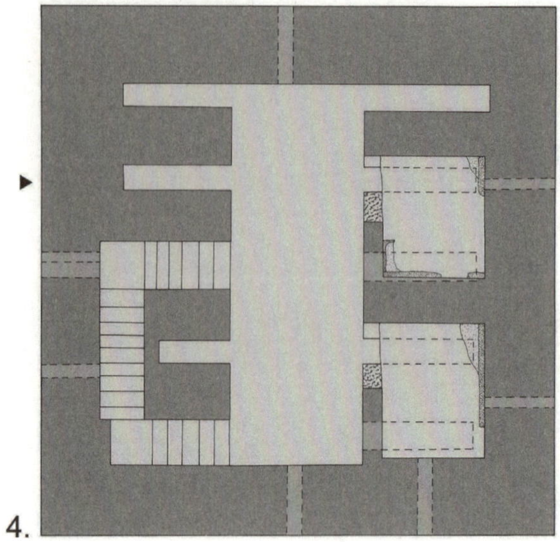

Fig. 5: Palmyra, western necropolis, tower tomb of Elahbel (no. 13). Ground plan of the fourth floor with sarcophagus chamber (© author).

still moist.[10] With the emergence of the portrait slabs came also a change in the decoration of the tower tombs' chambers. Structural ornamentation now emphasized specific elements of the chambers. These particularly included pilasters between the loculi shafts, cornices above the capitals of the pilasters, panelled ceilings as well as more reliefs (fig. 7 and 17).[11] Even though burials in loculi saved space, it can be observed that from the second half of the first century CE onwards, specific areas were designed that claimed quite more space for the deceased.[12] Sarcophagi were placed in these chambers, which I refer to as sarcophagus chambers (fig. 5). However, these were constructed by individual stone slabs and plaster since monolithic sarcophagus boxes could not be carried up the narrow staircases (fig. 6). The sarcophagi were probably adorned with the typical Palmyrene banquet scenes, which were placed on the built sarcophagi in the same manner as on monolithic sarcophagus boxes (fig. 27).[13]

Fig. 6: Palmyra, western necropolis, tower tomb of Elahbel (no. 13). Remains of built sarcophagi (© author).

10. Henning 2013a, 68, pl. 42c.
11. Henning 2013a, 61-63; 2013b, 162-164.
12. Henning 2013a, 35; 2013b, 164.
13. The preserved banquet reliefs in the tower of Elahbel can be dated only to the end of the second century and the first half of the third century CE, see Henning 2013a, 35, 69-71; 2013b, 164. Although in Palmyra several monolithic sarcophagus boxes from the first half of the second century CE are preserved, we do not know any belonging to banquet scenes, Colledge 1976, 77. For sarcophagi of the first half of the second century and later, see Colledge 1976, 77-78; Makowski 1985; Wielgosz 1997.

Concerning the perceptive strategies of these canonically recurring decorative elements, certain regularities can be detected. This can be particularly observed by the fact that the exterior of the towers addressed a different target group than the interior.[14] Within the necropoleis of Palmyra, the tower tombs and their façades were deliberately placed in order to be perceived by travellers along the main routes to and from the city (fig. 1).[15] The foundation inscriptions attest to this particularly well. While they were exclusively written in Palmyrene Aramaic until the mid-first century CE, from then on a Greek version of the text was also added (fig. 9).[16] The bilingual character of these inscriptions had several social reasons, one of which was certainly their 'international' comprehensibility. Therefore, inserted into the exterior façade, both the inscription as well as the relief alcove very much brought the tombs' founders into focus. Within the necropolis with its numerous funerary monuments, they were perceived as prominent personalities within an urban community.

In contrast, the decorative elements in the interior of the tower tombs were much more oriented towards a local target group: most of the inscriptions on the loculus slabs and reliefs were written in Palmyrene Aramaic (fig. 18, 19 and 26).[17] The tomb founder was represented here as well, but together with his entire family. The many loculus reliefs in the chambers seem very much like a family album depicting the tomb founder with his nearest relatives, as is also known from the context of the partly still in situ hypogea.[18] Here, the individual moved more into the background, thus emphasizing the representation of the entire family. Generally, the decorative elements were kept comparatively economical so that, during new burials, visitors perceived them only superficially. It can be observed, that while particularly the ground floor chambers of the towers were still luxuriously decorated (fig. 7), the decorative opulence decreased in the upper floors (fig. 8). It may therefore be assumed that the Palmyrenes speculated that visitors sojourned mostly on the ground floor only, perhaps on the first and second floor as well. It thus seems that the first impression counted.

Fig. 7: Palmyra, western necropolis, tower tomb of Iamlikû (no. 51). Architectural structure of the ground floor (© author).

Particularly the differences between the tombs' interior and exterior played a central role for the forms of representing spouses. The perceptive strategies were strongly normative and there were rarely deviations from the specific formal norms. Differentiating these norms is an important prerequisite for comprehending these representative forms. This, however, can be generalized: for our understanding of Palmyrene reliefs it is immensely crucial to know their immediate context, the target groups they addressed,

14. See also Henning 2013a, 98-99.
15. Gawlikowski 1970a, 165; 2005, 44; Henning 2013a, 11, 93.
16. Yon 2002, 222-226; Henning 2013a, 94.
17. Yon 2002, 223-224.
18. See also for example Dentzer-Feydy and Teixidor 1993, 68-69.

Fig. 8: Palmyra, western necropolis, tower tomb of Iamlikû (no. 51). Walls of the chamber in the fifth floor (© author).

how they communicated with them and what message they aimed to transmit. I am of course well aware of the fact that, for most of the Palmyrene reliefs, this is no longer possible. However, there are nevertheless a few contexts allowing us to delve deeper into iconographical interpretations.

Representations of matrimony on the exterior façades of the tower tombs

For compiling the few preserved examples of depicted spouses in the tower tombs, it is important to differentiate between the already defined categories of exterior and interior representations. Therefore, let us focus first on the façade of the towers. An important source of information on Palmyrene family structures are the inscription tabluae in which the foundation of the monument is documented. A particularly impressive example is the bilingual inscription of the tower of Iamlikû (no. 51) in the western necropolis dating to 83 CE (fig. 9).[19] It follows a typical structure: the founder of the tomb is named first (although also several people are evidenced to have sponsored tower tombs), followed by a listing of his family lineage.[20] It is then specified who is allowed to further make use of the tomb and finally the construction or induction date is given (including the year and month). Normally, the Palmyrene Aramaic and Greek versions of the inscriptions share the same content. Only in a very few cases does the content deviate between the two versions:

Fig. 9: Palmyra, western necropolis, tower tomb of Iamlikû (no. 51). Inscription tabula (© author).

> Μνημεῖον αἰώνιον γ(έ)ρας ᾠκοδόμ|ησεν Ιαμλιχος Μοκειμου τοῦ και | Ακκαλεισου τοῦ Μαλιχου εἴς τε | ἑαυτὸν καὶ υἱοὺς καὶ ἐγγόνους ἔτους δϙτ´ | μηνὶ Ξανδικῷ. Byrḥ nysn šnt 394 | qbrʾ dnh bnʾ ymlkw br mqymw ʾqlyš br mlkw | ʾbnyt br blʿqb br mykʾ br mtʾ tdmryʾ lh | wbnwhy wlbny bnwhy lyqrhn ʿd ʿlmʾ.

(This) eternal monument of honour was built by Iamlichos, son of Mokimos, called Akkaleisos, son of Malichos, for himself and for his children and their

19. Gawlikowski 1970a, 84-87; Henning 2013a, 192-195. The numbering of the funerary monuments is based on Watzinger and Wulzinger 1932.
20. Frequently they are several brothers, for example, see the tower of Elahbel (no. 13) below.

descendants, in the year 394 (AD 83), in the month of Xandikos, (Greek). In the month of Nîsan year 394 (83 CE), this tomb was built by Iamlikû, son of Moqîmû Aqalîš, son of Malikû Obnît, son of Belʿaqab, son of Mîkâ, son of Mattâ, from Tadmôr, for himself and for his children and the children of his children, in their honour, in eternity, (Palmyrene Aramaic).[21]

Without exception, the founder of a tower tomb is always male. There are no women, thus also no wives, listed as tower tomb founders.[22] Only brothers could appear as tomb founders together.[23] Following the name of the tomb founder, his filiation is listed. Only the father and not the mother is mentioned, which is not unusual in antiquity. In their inscriptions, Palmyrene women normally also refer to their fathers only. After the listing of the family lineage, the persons to be buried in the tomb in the future are mentioned. Here, not only the sons, but the children in general are listed; therefore female descendants as well. Whether these children were potentially also married and whether their families were allowed to be buried in the tomb as well, is not known. Only the children of the mentioned children of the tomb founder can follow, which may imply a marriage. It may therefore be concluded that the foundation inscription did not function as a platform for representing matrimony. Although, considering the various family relations, information on marriages can be deduced. However, they are not mentioned directly. Despite the strong presence of the tomb founder, his wife played no role in the foundation text.

However, this is not the case for the inscription in the relief alcove of the tower of Kithôt (no. 44).[24] In order to properly contextualize this Palmyrene Aramaic text, it is important to note that the text is actually not directly associated with the foundation inscription of the tower tomb. The tower of Kithôt is an exception. The alcove is not situated on the tomb's southern side (fig. 10) with the entrance to the ground floor chamber and opening to the route through the western necropolis, as is usually the case. Instead, the relief is oriented towards the east (fig. 11) and therefore visible from a pathway that leads from the city to the tomb (fig. 12).[25]

The actual foundation inscription was above the entrance inscribed into a slab of the lintel and is now lost.

Fig. 10: Palmyra, western necropolis, tower tomb of Kithôt (no. 44). View of the southern side (© author).

21. CIS 4123bis; Cantineau 1930, 6-7, no. 6; Hillers and Cussini 1996, PAT 0473; Yon 2012, 317-318, no. 405.
22. Usually women do not appear as tomb founders of other tomb types either. However, some inscriptions mention women to be actively involved in the selling of certain sections of the tomb to other families, see e.g. Tower no. 70. See also Cantineau 1930, no. 1; Gawlikowski 1970a, 173; Cussini 1995, 246, and for other examples and exceptions, see Cussini 2005, 30-37. More on actively involved women in Palmyrene inscriptions, see Cussini 1995; 2005; Yon 2002, 165-174, 180-181.
23. See also the tower of Elahbel (no. 13) below.
24. Will 1951; Gawlikowski 1970a, 71-77; Henning 2013a, 185-186.
25. Gawlikowski 1970a, 155-157.

Fig. 11: Palmyra, western necropolis, tower tomb of Kithôt (no. 44). View of the eastern side (© author).

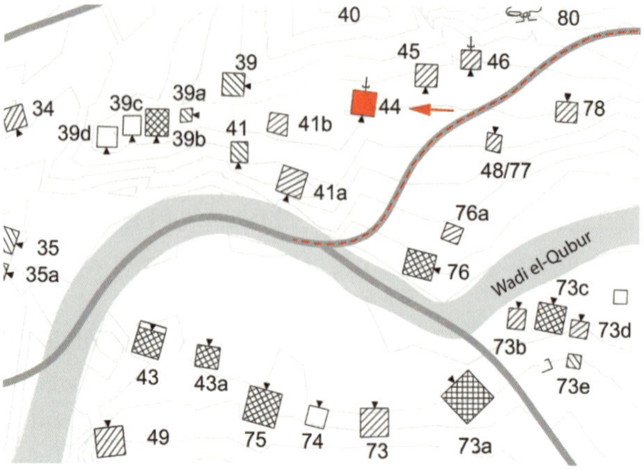

Fig. 12: Palmyra, western necropolis. Pathways in the area of the tower of Kithôt (no. 44) (© author).

However, based on previous documentation, it could be reconstructed without any mentioning of wives:

> Byrḥ sywm šnt 3[...] qbrʾ dnh dy kytwt | br tymrṣw br kytwt br tymʾ rbʾ dy mn pḥd bny | [mt]bwl dy ʿbd lh wlbnwhy lʿlmʾ.

In the month of Siwan, year 3.., this is the tomb of Kithôt, son of Taimarṣû, son of Kithôt, son of Taimiša the elder from the bene [Maththa]bôl, which he built for himself and his children, in eternity.[26]

Due to the various orientations of the tomb's sides, it was nevertheless necessary that the relief alcove was inscribed as well:

> [Byrḥ sywn] šnt 351 | [ṣlmyʾ ʾln] dy kytwt br | [tymrṣw wdy myš]ʾ brt | [mlkw ʾtt]h wdy lšmš | [brh wdy šlmn] brh wdy | mlkw ʿlymh.

[In the month of Siwan] year 351 (40 CE), (these are) [the images] of Kithôt, son of [Taimarṣû, and of Maiš]a, daughter of [Malikû, his wife] and Lišamš, [his son and Šalman], his son, and Malikû his servant.[27]

This short text clearly mentions the wife of Kithôt. It is Maiša, whose father was a certain Malikû. Her listing in the inscription is also mirrored in her representation in the relief alcove (fig. 13).[28] Behind the lying central figure, which is most likely Kithôt himself, are three further figures. To the right there is a woman, who most likely is Maiša, next to whom the two sons are standing. Only the mentioned servant is not represented. Although it is possible that he may be reconstructed in the destroyed part of the relief.[29] Thus, in contrast to the actual foundation inscription above the tomb entrance the wife of the tomb founder is named in the text of the relief alcove. However, this text is not the foundation inscription. Instead, it describes the representa-tion of the family in the alcove and is therefore deliberately placed there.

26. Transcription from Hillers and Cussini 1996, PAT 0463. See also CIS 4115; Cantineau 1930, 18-19, no. 18.

27. Transcription and translation from Hillers and Cussini 1996, PAT 0464. See also CIS 4115bis.

28. Will 1951; Gawlikowski 1970a, 72; Henning 2013a, 185-186.

29. Gawlikowski 1970a, 72.

Fig. 13: Palmyra, western necropolis, tower tomb of Kithôt (no. 44). Relief alcove (© author).

Fig. 14: Palmyra, southeastern necropolis, tower tomb of Ogeilû (no. 194). Relief alcove (Courtesy of the Institut Français du Proche-Orient Damascus, neg. no. 5274).

Such an inscription of the relief alcove is also evidenced by a further example. The relief of the tower tomb of ʿOgeilû (no. 194) in the south-eastern necropolis is documented only by older photographs (fig. 14), the quality of which is unfortunately not particularly satisfying.[30] The tomb itself is also nearly completely destroyed.[31] However, the relief's inscription is documented.

> slmyʾ ʾln dy ʿgylw br ʿhʾ br mqymw | br ḥdwdn wdy ʾmtḥʾ brt bwnʾ ʾtth | tdmry[ʾ] wdy ʿgʾ brh dy bnʾ [b]ḥywhy lyqrh | wly[qr b]nwhy dy bt ʿlmʾ byrḥ nysn šnt | 384.

(These are) the images of ʿOgeilû, son of ʿOggâ, son of Moqîmû, son of Ḥaddûdan, and of Amataḥâ, daughter of Bonnê, his wife, from Tadmôr, and of ʿOggâ, his son, which he built during his lifetime, in his honour and in the honour of his children, this house of eternity in the month of Nîsan, year 384 (73 CE).[32]

The wife of the tomb founder is also mentioned here, namely Amataḥâ, daughter of Bonnê. She is also clearly represented in the relief as well as her son Oggâ. However, Amataḥâ is not mentioned in the following lines of the inscription, which mention the construction of the tomb and future burials. It can be assumed that Amataḥâ was represented in the upper part of the heavily destroyed relief; possibly in a similar fashion as in the relief of Kithôt, thus behind the lying main figure since the stereotypical representation of women sitting at the feet of the men was not established yet in the

30. Photograph, by courtesy of the Institut Français du Proche-Orient Damascus, neg. no. 5274. See also Will 1951, 83-84, fig. 3; Gawlikowski 1970b, fig. 13; Wielgosz 1997, 74, pl. X,1; Henning 2013, pl. 81c.

31. See Watzinger and Wulzinger 1932, 70; Will, 1951, 84, note 2; Henning 2013a, 286.

32. Transcription from Hillers and Cussini 1996, PAT 0549. See also CIS 4193.

first century CE.[33] The wife thus played a role in the pictorial representation of the family, however not in the context of the tomb foundation.

Unfortunately, only the architectural frames for inserting the relief alcoves of especially the larger and later tower tombs such as the towers of Elahbel (no. 13) (fig. 16) and Iamlikû (no. 51) (fig. 1) are preserved. Since no inscriptions are evidenced, no information on the represented individuals can be given. However, wives were not always depicted in the alcoves. This is evidenced by a fragmentary text inscribed on the lintel of the tower tomb of the sons and grandsons of Elahšâ (no. 69), situated in the vicinity of the tower of Iamlikû and therefore also in the western necropolis (fig. 1).[34] The alcove itself and the actual relief, however, are lost. The Greek version of the bilingual text is more intelligible:

> Αἱ ἐν ψαλίδι εἰκόνες Μ[οκειμου καὶ Θαιμισα καὶ Ζεβειδα υἱῶν] Ελασσα τοῦ Σαεδει τοῦ Ελ[ασσα καὶ] Ελασσα καὶ Ογηλου καὶ Σαεδε[ι τούτου τοῦ Μοκειμου] καὶ Ελασσα τούτου τοῦ Θαι[μισα...] [...] ΕΝΟΥ [καὶ] Μοκειμου [τούτου τοῦ Ζεβειδα φυλῆς Μαθθαβω]λιων μηνὸς Δείου τοῦ η[..]΄ ἔτου[ς].

The images in the alcove (are those of) Mokimos and Thaimes and Zebeidas, sons of Elassas, son of Saedei, son of Elassas and of Elassa and Ogelos and Saedei, sons of the same Mokimos and Elassas, sons of the same Thaimes, and Rabbelos and ... and of Moqîmû, son of the same Zebeidas, from the bene Maththabôloi, in the month of Deios, year..8.[35]

Fig. 15: Palmyra, western necropolis, tower tomb of Nebuzabad (no. 83a). Pediment with portrayal of a priest, 120 CE (© author).

Thus, exclusively men were listed here; namely three brothers together with their sons. The respective wives play no role, although they must have existed. Potential daughters are also not mentioned. This case therefore demonstrates how male family members had precedence over the wives. It is assumed that the three named and represented brothers issued the construction of the tomb together as is evidenced by various other foundation inscriptions.[36] Therefore, it was important that all three tomb founders were also depicted in the relief. Due to lack of space, only men were chosen as motive in this case.

In addition to the foundation inscription and the relief alcove, there was another visual medium in the façade of the tower tombs: the pediments. These could be placed above the entrance of the façade.[37] Such pediments appear in the course of the second half of the first century CE, some depicting only one person: they are bust reliefs of men in priestly attire (fig. 15).[38] The depiction of women or wives is not documented.

Let us recapitulate what we know about the representations of matrimony on the tombs' exterior. In the official foundation inscription, which was placed in the tower's façade for all to see, the wife of the tomb founder is not mentioned. Here the tomb founder and his family lineage clearly stands out. He also specified the

33. The early banquet scenes of the first century CE do not present sitting women, for example, see in the towers of Kithôt (no. 44) and Hairan (no. 67), see Will 1951; Gawlikowski 1970b, 81-85, fig. 12; Colledge 1976, 73, fig. 39; Henning 2013a, pls. 41, 59a, and in the hypogeum of Aštôr, see Sadurska and Bounni 1994, 16-17, cat. nos. 5-8, figs. 208-214. For first examples of the first half of the second century CE including sitting women, for example, see Sadurska and Bounni 1994, 134-135, cat. no. 181, fig. 218, 138-139, cat. no. 184, fig. 221.

34. Gawlikowski 1970a, 99-100; Henning 2013a, 212-215.

35. Transcription and translation from Yon 2012, 344-345, no. 449. See also Cantineau 1930, 2-3, no. 2

36. See e.g. the tower of Elahbel (no. 13) below.

37. Still preserved in the towers nos. 39, 51, 74, 83a, 164.

38. Towers nos. 39, 74, 83a. See also al-As'ad and Schmidt-Colinet 2005, 38-41; Henning 2013a, 53, 64-66, pl. 38b.

future burials of his children. Here as well, the wife is not mentioned. In the pictorial representation of the family in the relief alcove, however, the wife as well as the sons could appear. It is possible that there were only male descendants of those families from whom reliefs and inscriptions are preserved. Conspicuously, however, there are no pictorial representations of daughters. Generally, it seems that male family members had precedence in being listed by name and represented pictorially. In the tower tombs, wives are included in the family groupings or family constellations during the first century CE (there is no evidence for the later periods) and are mentioned by name in the inscriptions. In the reliefs, together with their sons, they fall into the background behind their husbands. Thus, this is not an image of a harmonious couple. Instead, the wife symbolizes a part of the tomb founder's family. This relation may be differently weighted in the later reliefs, in which the woman sits at the feet of the husband.[39]

The pediments above the entrances with the priest portraits emphasize the fact that the tomb founder was the focus of the exterior representation. With the relief, he indicates that he was embedded in a family structure and clearly sees himself as the head of that family in a socially, highly regarded role as a priest. As the great majority of other funerary monuments with similar representative concepts also show, the male tomb founders clearly aimed at standing out in Palmyrene society. They defined themselves by different media and various roles, although the family had a major part in their self-portrayal. Particularly marriage as a family bond and legal institution was insignificant in this perceptive strategy.

Representations of matrimony on the interior of the tower tombs

Due to the tower tombs' poor state of preservation, we only have little evidence on forms of representation of matrimony from the interior of the monuments. Only very few loculus reliefs are preserved that can securely be associated with specific tower tombs.[40] Nevertheless, none of these positively represent spouses.[41]

However, a particularly important context for the representation of wives and spouses can be found in the tower of Elahbel (no. 13) (fig. 16).[42] Reliefs of wom-

Fig. 16: Palmyra, western necropolis, tower tomb of Elahbel (no. 13). View of the façade (© author).

39. See note 33.

40. See also Henning 2013a, 66–68.

41. In a fragmentary inscription from the tower no. 69, the wife of a certain Moqîmû is mentioned. See CIS 4189, pl. 34. One slab from the tower of the Bene Baa (no. 68) possibly shows a family constellation, which may also only represent a mother with her two sons. One of the depicted is surely a child as he is standing with the attributes typically associated with children, namely a bunch of grapes and a bird. See also Gawlikowski 1970b, 93, fig. 4; Henning 2013a, 211, pl. 60a.

42. See also Gawlikowski 1969. Generally on the tower of Elahbel, see Gawlikowski 1970a, 87–91; Henning 2013a, 152–154.

Fig. 17: Palmyra, western necropolis, tower tomb of Elahbel (no. 13). View into the ground floor chamber with portraits on the front side (© author).

Fig. 18: Palmyra, western necropolis, tower tomb of Elahbel (no. 13). Portraits above the entrance to the staircase (© author).

Fig. 19: Palmyra, western necropolis, tower tomb of Elahbel (no. 13). Portraits on the front side, detail (© author).

en were inserted into the walls of the ground floor chamber as a fixed construction element of the monument (fig. 17). There were no burials behind the reliefs and there were probably never any burials planned. Therefore, the reliefs are not associated with any loculi. The reliefs are placed in two rows at the front side of the chamber (fig. 17) and along the left side above the entrance to the staircase (fig. 18). In total there are thirteen portraits, nine of which are set on the frontal side and the remaining four (among them also one man) are above the staircase. Twelve of the portrayed are named and their filiations as well as the names of their husbands are listed (fig. 19, 20 and 21).[43] We can thus

43. Cantineau 1930, no. 27m-x; Gawlikowski 1969, 55; Hillers and Cussini 1996, PAT 0497-0508.

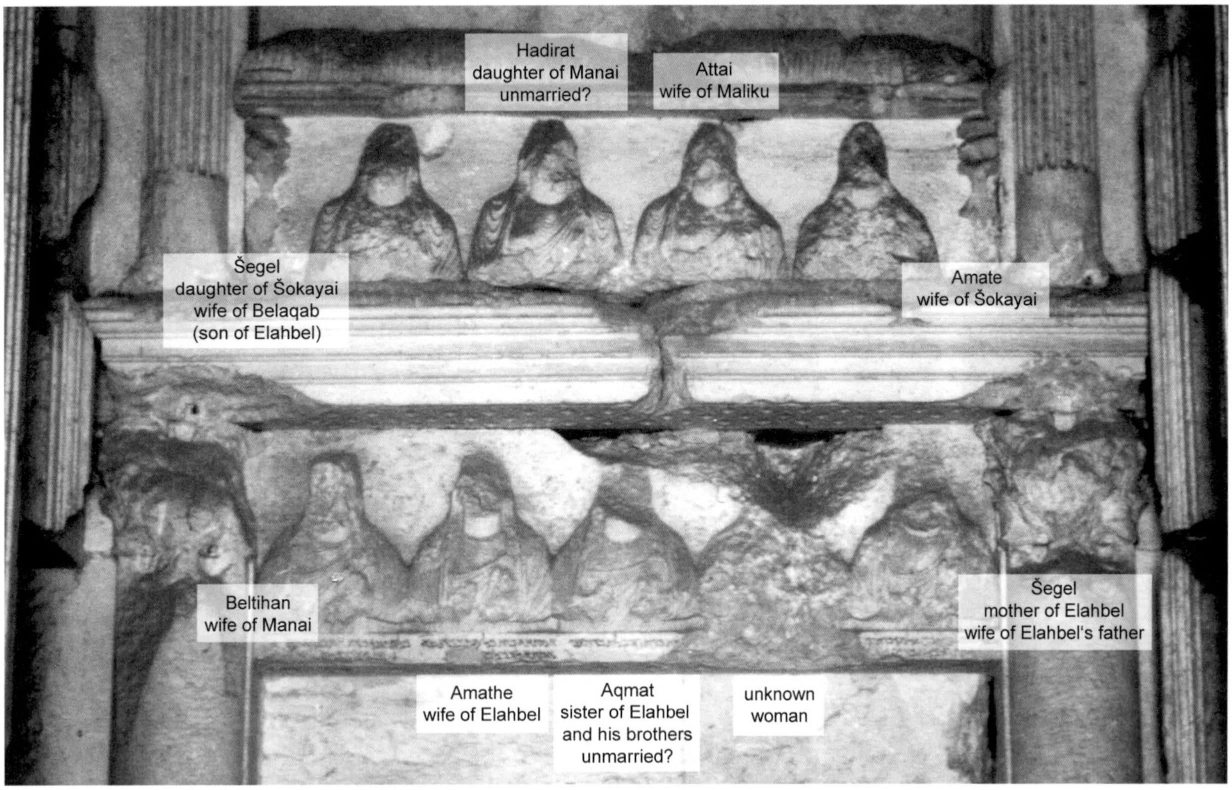

Fig. 20: Palmyra, western necropolis, tower tomb of Elahbel (no. 13). Portraits on the front side, names (© author).

identify several wives of three generations.[44] It should be noted, that not only women are portrayed in the ground floor chamber. The men of the family (in total ten individuals) appear in inscriptions on the architrave of the chamber.[45] It is not entirely clear who exactly is meant by these listings. Some of them were probably represented in the pictorial decoration of the ceiling.[46] Also, there must have been reliefs of banqueting men in the ground floor chamber that were set into the frontal side of the room (fig. 17).[47]

For the understanding of the family structures depicted in the portraits of women and their associated inscriptions, it is crucial to know that the so-called tower of Elahbel was constructed by four brothers in 103 CE, Elahbel, Maʿnai, Šokhaîaî and Malikû, as evidenced by the foundation inscription on the façade of the tower.[48] The Palmyrene Aramaic text states:

> Q̱brʾ dnh bnʾ ʾlhbl wmʿny wškyy | wmlkw bny whblt br mʿny ʾlhbl | lhwn wlbnyhwn byrḥ nysn šnt 414.

This tomb was built by Elahbel and Maʿnaî Šokaîaî and Malikû, sons of Wahballat, son of Maʿnaî Elahbel, for themselves and for their children, in the month of Nîsan, year 414 (103 CE).[49]

44. See the family trees in Milik 1972, 246; Gawlikowski 1969, 52; Yon 2002, 279.
45. Cantineau 1930, no. 27c-l; Gawlikowski 1969, 53.
46. The paneled ceiling was painted with twelve portraits, including at least eight men. See also Henning 2013a, pls. 14, 84.
47. See also Henning 2013a, pl. 13a.
48. The family of Elahbel played a significant role in the social life of Palmyra, see Yon 2002, 81-87, 204-206. Based on all inscriptions of the family, a comprehensive family tree could be reconstructed, see Milik 1972, 246; Yon 2002, 279.
49. Transcription from Hillers and Cussini 1996, PAT 0486. See also CIS 4134; Yon 2012, 319-320, no. 407.

Fig. 21: Palmyra, western necropolis, tower tomb of Elahbel (no. 13). Portraits above the entrance to the staircase, names (© author).

The portraits of the women in the ground floor are revealing in many aspects. First, their uniformity is striking. Although the faces are destroyed, the torsos are absolutely identical. They wear an embroidered garment under a cloak that covers the head. In the right hand, they hold the end of a cloak and spinning utensils (namely three distaffs) can be identified in their left hand. It is therefore not possible to differentiate between the women, and it is questionable whether this would change if their faces were preserved. Individualization is therefore only made possible by the inscriptions. However, it is also questionable whether these were readable at a height between 4 and 6 meters. Although they were painted over in red, they were probably not particularly well visible. Nevertheless, the Palmyrene Aramaic inscriptions help us to understand who was represented. On the frontal side, the four wives of the founding brothers are depicted. In addition, there is the mother and the sister of the four brothers as well as the daughters of two of the brothers (fig. 20 and 25). Above the staircase, there are further depictions of four more daughters of the tomb founders. Most of the depicted women, however, are listed as wives (fig. 22 and 23, marked in green). Those women, who are not named as wives, were probably not married (yet) at the time when the relief was inserted (marked in red). No differentiation in terms of representation or arrangement between the married and unmarried women could be made. Generally, the composition is very complex demonstrating the extremely close family-related marriages in Palmyra (compare fig. 24). In the generation of the children of Elahbel and his brothers, at least three men were married to their respective cousins.

Additionally, this find offers insights into the workmanship of the sculptors. They obviously received the order to produce a certain amount of reliefs depicting women. The inscription was then inserted subsequently. Possibly, a sequence for associating the inscriptions with the portraits may be deduced (compare fig. 25). First, the mother of the four founding brothers, Šegel, appears in the lower right of the frontal side of the tomb, followed by a destroyed and therefore unknown portrait (compare fig. 20 and 25). Next to that, the sister of the four brothers is depicted.[50] The last two women of that row, as well as the

50. It may therefore be assumed that the destroyed relief possibly depicted another sister.

Fig. 22: Palmyra, western necropolis, tower tomb of Elahbel (no. 13). Portraits on the front side. Markings of married (green) and unmarried (red) women (© author).

Fig. 23: Palmyra, western necropolis, tower tomb of Elahbel (no. 13). Portraits above the entrance to the staircase. Markings of married (green) and unmarried (red) women (© author).

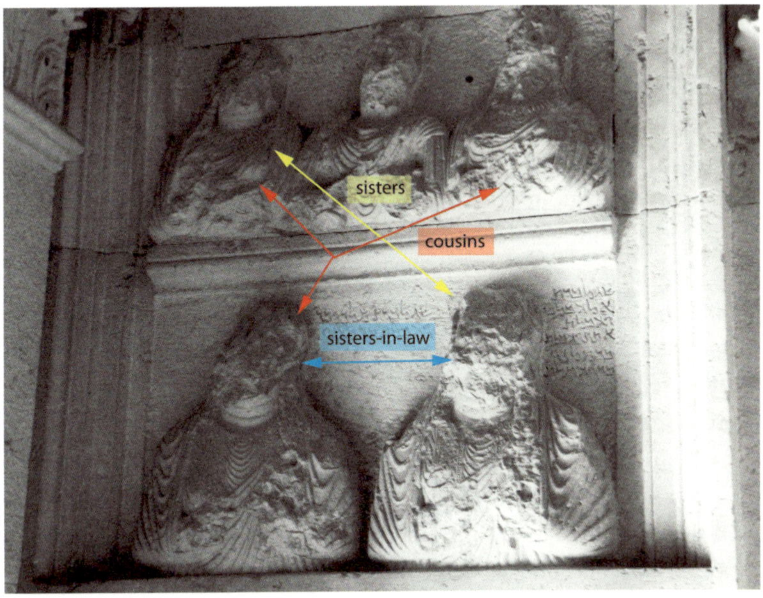

Fig. 24; Palmyra, western necropolis, tower tomb of Elahbel (no. 13). Portraits above the entrance to the staircase, family-related connections (© author).

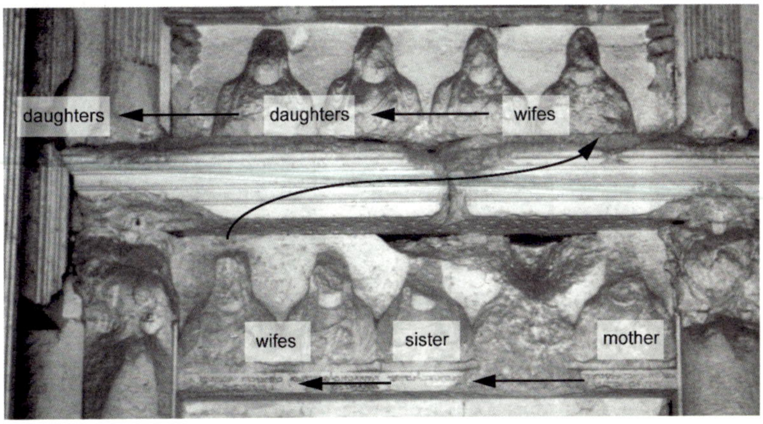

Fig. 25: Palmyra, western necropolis, tower tomb of Elahbel (no. 13). Portraits on the front side. Hierarchical structure of depictions (© author).

two on the right of the upper row, are the wives of the brothers. Subsequently, two daughters of the founding brothers follow. Four more daughters are depicted above the entrance to the staircase. Based on this arrangement, a hierarchy in inscribing the reliefs can be assumed: first came the mother, then the sister, followed by the wives and finally the daughters.

However, we would like to ask what these depictions tell us about the significance of matrimony. While it was particularly important which woman was married to which man, this information was given after the mentioning of filiation. It is, however, more a definition by name and association with the husband and the family than an actual representation of a privileged matrimonial status. Husband and wife are not depicted together. For the ancient viewer, not familiar with the complex structure of this family, it must have been impossible to comprehend who was married to whom. The depictions of the women and the listing of their names as well as those of their husbands had one main purpose: demonstrating the size of the family. The mere mass alone should impress. Together with the now lost, but surely once existing, loculus reliefs with the portraits of the deceased, a huge family album was created. The arrangement of the ground floor chamber is unique among the tower tombs. There are no other examples known where such a large amount of portraits were placed already during the construction of the monument.[51]

An important methodological aspect to be considered is the fact that, as already mentioned, the representations of women do not mark burials. Instead, since the portraits as well as the inscriptions were inserted into the monument during its construction, the portraits mirror the then current family relations. For example, we do not know whether the two unmarried daughters of Elahbel and Malikû, Hadîrat and Šegel, were later married and, if so, to whom. Additionally, we do not know whether all these persons were actually buried in the tower tomb of Elahbel and his brothers.

Fig. 26: Palmyra, western necropolis, tower tomb of Elahbel (no. 13). Pediment of Maʿnaî and Beltîḥan in the second floor (© author).

Certainly, the tower was designed for them. However, assuming that the two daughters were later actually married into another family, they may have been buried in the family tomb of their husbands. No male in-law is mentioned in the inscriptions of the tower of Elahbel.

In order to evaluate who of the depicted women was actually buried in the tower of Elahbel, an inscription of the second floor may help. Here, Beltîḥan and her husband Maʿnaî, one of the four founding brothers, are mentioned in a small pediment above the entrance to a so-called sarcophagus chamber (fig. 26). While the ground floor chamber only holds loculus shafts as a burial form, the second floor includes two small chambers on its eastern side where the remains of built sarcophagi were preserved. Furthermore, several reliefs of banqueting figures were dispersed over the individual floors, which must have once stood on these built sarcophagi.[52] The entrances to these sarcophagus chambers are adorned with small pediments. One of these pediments on the second floor has the following inscription:

> Byrḥ tšry šnt 433 ywm 30 ḥbl mʿny br ʾḥd mn |
> ʾrbʿʾ ʾḥyʾ dy bnw qbrʾ dnh wbltyḥn brt ʾtpny br
> mlkw | ʿtršwry ʾtth.

51. While the general structure with pilasters and reliefs is similar in comparable tower tombs (e.g. tower nos. 51 and 164), they do not show this abundance of portraits.

52. See also Henning 2013a, 69–71; 2013b, 164.

In the month of Tišri, year 433 (121 CE), on the 30th day, alas, Maʿnaî, son of Wahballat Maʿnaî, one of the four brothers, who built this tomb, and Beltîḥan, daughter of Etpenîn, son of Malikû Attašuri, his wife.[53]

According to the text, on 30 October, 121 CE, it was determined that Maʿnaî and his wife should be buried here. Whether this is the actual day of death or merely a decree, we do not know. With the sarcophagus chamber, the spouses received a privileged place within the tower tomb. Possibly, similar places were also reserved for the three other brothers, but their burial places are not secured. Both husband and wife are deliberately mentioned here and thus considered as a unity in order to be buried together. However, the inscription does not attest to an emotional, but rather to a family unity. It can be assumed that either two reliefs or one depicting husband and wife together were placed in the sarcophagus chamber.[54]

A similar form of representing matrimony can also be found in the formerly well-preserved tower of Iamlikû (no. 51). Here, reliefs that must have once stood on built sarcophagi as well were also documented in the upper floors of the monument. One depicts a banqueting man with a woman seated at his feet (fig. 27).[55] The relief is conspicuously compressed, which may suggest that it was once placed in a small sarcophagus chamber with little space.

Unfortunately, we do not know who is depicted since the relief has no inscription. Chronologically, however, it belongs to the late second century CE, thus giving evidence that the tower was still used as a burial place at that time.[56] However, it is assumed that the tower, or at least parts of it, was no longer used by

53. Transcription and translation from Hillers and Cussini 1996, PAT 0510. See also CIS 4158; Cantineau 1930, no. 27y.
54. Whether the loculus reliefs or the reclining figures of Maʿnaî and Beltîḥan are preserved among the few sculptural remains in the tower of Elahbel is speculative. See also Henning 2013a, 67–69, 71.
55. Henning 2013a, 194, pl. 52b.
56. See also Henning 2013a, 194.

Fig. 27: Palmyra, western necropolis, tower tomb of Iamlikû (no. 51). Relief depicting banqueting spouses (© author).

the founding family, as evidenced by other inscriptions.[57]

Generally, the evidence for matrimony within the tower tombs is very limited. The few examples nevertheless clearly demonstrate the importance of considering the reliefs and the inscriptions in their contexts. The main focus was on representing the extended family. The more portraits were observed at first glance, the better. This may explain the many portraits in the tower of Elahbel. Although the inscriptions indicate that real women were meant to be depicted, the reliefs of the tower depicting women show that individual persons are not represented pictorially, instead they appear rather stereotypical.

In the ground floor, men and women were obviously depicted separately from each other. Spouses do not appear together. It also seems that the depiction of wives did not follow any particular form of representation in terms of dress or other attributes. In order to further emphasize the family relations, the mentioning of the husband played an important role when wives are named. Despite these rather 'matter-of-fact' forms of representation, spouses were never-

57. Another banquet scene names two men that did not belong to the family of Iamlikû. See also Gawlikowski and al-As'ad 1997, 32–33, pl. 5,2.

theless buried together. In this context, they could also be depicted together. This is confirmed in the hypogeum C, where close family ties can be observed for the burials.[58]

Conclusion

This contextual analysis leads to the following conclusions:

For external representations within Palmyrene society, marriage played only a subordinate role. It was certainly important for the social life as shown by the intra-family marriages and the labelling of women as wives. In the external funerary representation, wives took over the role as symbolizing 'family' as shown by the relief alcoves. The moment that men are included in the reliefs because there are several tomb founders, women play no role anymore. Only in the smallest family unit, namely at individual burials, could there be a deliberate choice to be represented as spouses. However, in the masses of portraits these matrimonial relations were pushed to the background for the sake of representing the larger, more extended family. This is further indicated by the generally small number of portrait reliefs with depictions of men and women together.[59]

Although women were or should have been buried together with their husbands, we do not know whether this applied to all women. The tower tombs give no evidence for what happened when a daughter, who was supposed to be buried in her family's funerary monument – as it can be observed in the tower of Elahbel – married later in life. Nor can we reconstruct what happened to women who remained childless during their marriage, that were divorced or whose husbands died.[60] Here, the hypogea and the better preserved loculus reliefs and inscriptions offer valuable information.[61]

Distinct symbols of marriage played no role in funerary representations in Palmyra.[62] Also, no emotional ties can be observed, which, in reality, certainly and hopefully existed.[63] When evaluating certain social aspects, for example marriage, we thus always have to reconsider the context of such depictions and ask who actually saw these images and keep in mind which social aspects we cannot grasp anymore. Such examples can help to develop a better and more detailed understanding of these complex social structures.

Abbreviations

CIS J.-B. Chabot (ed.) 1926, *Corpus Inscriptionum Semiticarum, Pars secunda, Tomus III: Inscriptiones palmyrenae,* Paris.
PAT D. R. Hillers and E. Cussini 1946, *Palmyrene Aramaic Texts,* Baltimore.

Bibliography

al-As'ad, W. 2013, Some tombs recently excavated in Palmyra, *Studia Palmyreńskie* 12, 15–24.
al-As'ad, K. and A. Schmidt-Colinet 2005, Kulturbegegnung im Grenzbereich, in A. Schmidt-Colinet (ed.), *Palmyra: Kulturbegegnung im Grenzbereich*, Mainz am Rhein, 36–62.
Cantineau, J. 1930, *Inventaire des inscriptions de Palmyre: La vallée des tombeaux,* vol. IV, Beirut.
Colledge, M. A. R. 1976, *The Art of Palmyra*, London.
Cussini, E. 2005, Beyond the Spindle: Investigating the

58. Saito 2005, 33, 35.
59. For example, see Dentzer-Feydy and Teixidor 1993, 200–201, no. 199; Sadurska and Bounni 1994, 62, cat. no. 80, fig. 20, 131, cat. no. 174, fig. 42; Ploug 1995, 101–103, no. 29, 103–105, no. 30.
60. The anthropological analyses in the hypogea have shown a relatively balanced ratio between men and women. However, there are some conspicuous exceptions. This led Kiyohide Saito to the assumption, that childless women were not buried together with their husbands. Instead, based on modern funerary practices in Palmyra, he deduces that they may have been buried in their actual family's tombs (2013, 290–292).
61. See also the contribution of Signe Krag in this volume.
62. We of course know the deliberate choice in antiquity to depict matrimony (for example the freedmen reliefs from Rome, see Zanker 1975). The possibility to marry was a privilege and represented by distinct symbols such as the wedding ring or the dextrarum iunctio.
63. Only in one relief, now in the Louvre in Paris, does the woman touch her husband, therefore creating a certain emotional relation between the two (Dentzer-Feydy and Teixidor 1993, 212–213, no. 209).

Role of Palmyrene Women, in E. Cussini (ed.), *A journey to Palmyra: Collected Essays to Remember Delbert R. Hillers*, Leiden and Boston, 26-43.

Cussini, E. 1995, Transfer of Property at Palmyra, *ARAM periodicals* 7, 233-250.

Dentzer-Feydy, J. and J. Teixidor 1993, *Les antiquités de Palmyre au Musée du Louvre*, Paris.

Gawlikowski, M. 2005, The City of the Dead, in E. Cussini (ed.), *A journey to Palmyra: Collected Essays to Remember Delbert R. Hillers*, Leiden and Boston, 44-73.

Gawlikowski, M. 1970a, *Monuments funéraires de Palmyre*, Warsaw.

Gawlikowski, M. 1970b, Palmyrena, *Berytus* 19, 65-94.

Gawlikowski, M. 1969, Rodzina Elahbela, *Studia Palmyreńskie* 3, 47-58.

Gawlikowski, M. and K. al-As'ad 1997, Inscriptions de Palmyre nouvelles et revisitées, *Studia Palmyreńskie* 10, 23-38.

Henning, A. 2013a, *Die Turmgräber von Palmyra. Eine lokale Bauform im kaiserzeitlichen Syrien als Ausdruck kultureller Identität,* Rahden/Westf.

Henning, A. 2013b, The tower tombs of Palmyra: chronology, architecture and decoration, *Studia Palmyreńskie* 12, 159-176.

Higuchi. T. and T. Izumi, (eds.) 1994, *Tombs A and C: Southeast Necropolis, Palmyra Syria: Surveyed in 1990-92*, Nara.

Higuchi, T. and K. Saito (eds.) 2001, *Tomb F - Tomb of BWLH and BWRP: Southeast Necropolis, Palmyra, Syria*, Nara.

Ingholt, H. 1930, The oldest known grave-relief from Palmyra, *ActaArch* 1, 191-194.

Makowski, K. C. 1985, La sculpture funéraire palmyrénienne et sa fonction dans l'architecture sépulcral, *Studia Palmyreńskie* 8, 69-116.

Milik, J. T. 1972, *Dedicaces faites par des dieux (Palmyre, Hatra, Tyr) et des thiases sémitiques à l'époque romaine*, Paris.

Ploug, G. 1995, *Catalogue of the Palmyrene Sculptures: Ny Carlsberg Glyptotek*, Copenhagen.

Sadurska, A. and A. Bounni 1994, *Les sculptures funéraires de Palmyre*, Rome.

Saito, K. 2013, Female burial practices in Palmyra: some observations from the underground tombs, *Studia Palmyreńskie* 12, 287-298.

Saito, K. 2005, Die Arbeiten der japanischen Mission in der Südost-Nekropole, in A. Schmidt-Colinet (ed.), *Palmyra: Kulturbegegnung im Grenzbereich*, Maiz am Rhein, 32-35.

Schmidt-Colinet, A. 1992, *Das Tempelgrab Nr. 36 in Palmyra: Studien zur palmyrenischen Grabarchitektur und ihrer Ausstattung*, 2 vols., Mainz am Rhein.

Watzinger, C. and K. Wulzinger 1932, Die Nekropolen, in T. Wiegand (ed.), *Palmyra: Ergebnisse der Expedition von 1902 und 1917*, 2 vols., Berlin, 44-76.

Wielgosz, D. 1997, Funeralia Palmyrena, *Studia Palmyreńskie* 10, 69-77.

Will, E. 1951, Le relief de la tour de Kithot et le banquet funéraire à Palmyre, *Syria* 28, 70-100.

Yon, J.-B. 2012, *Inscriptions grecques et latines de la Syrie, Tome 17, Fascicule 1: Palmyre,* Beirut.

Yon, J.-B. 2002, *Les notables de Palmyre*, Beirut.

Zanker, P. 1975, Grabreliefs römischer Freigelassener, *JdI* 90, 267-315.

CHAPTER 2

Palmyrene funerary buildings and family burial patterns

Signe Krag

Introduction

More than three hundred funerary buildings have so far been discovered surrounding the ancient city of Palmyra.[1] Inside these tombs, the Palmyrene inhabitants buried their deceased family members. The bodies were often placed inside loculi - deep shelves arranged in horizontal and vertical rows and sealed with a plaque bearing a portrait - or in sarcophagi, which were also embellished with portrait sculpture. A large number of funerary portraits have either been preserved in situ or have their original tomb context documented.[2] Many of these portraits are accompanied by inscriptions, naming the deceased and their genealogy. Foundation inscriptions recording the families who owned the tombs, as well as the so-called cession texts - detailed recordings of the sale of sections within the funerary buildings - are also preserved in some contexts.[3] However, the majority of these contexts were unfortunately disturbed before legal excavations of the tombs took place. Thus, portrait reliefs are frequently lacking from the funerary buildings, or are only partially preserved.[4] Even so, detailed information about family lineages and marriages can be inferred from the various types of inscriptions preserved in the tombs (foundation inscriptions, cession texts, and funerary inscriptions). This article will explore burial patterns in Palmyra, and specifically how families were organised within their tombs. The funerary contexts, the portraits and the accompanying epigraphy will be evaluated to gain a broader understanding of family burial patterns in Palmyra.

Funerary contexts

The funerary buildings of Palmyra comprise tower tombs, temple or house tombs and underground hypogea. Of these, the tower tombs were the first to come into use, with the earliest dated to 9 BCE; the earliest hypogeum is dated to 87 CE, and the earliest temple tomb to 143 CE.[5] The tombs are distributed over the north necropolis, the western necropolis and the southern necropolei, to both south-west and south-east. The less careful methods used during the early excavations left the material rather poorly documented, and many contexts have simply never been published.[6] Slightly more than 60 funerary buildings,

1. I would like to thank Rubina Raja for including me in the Palmyra Portrait Project, in which I was previously employed as Assistant Professor, and for access to the project database. The project is generously funded by the Carlsberg Foundation since 2012. For more information on the project, see: Kropp and Raja 2014; 2015; http://projects.au.dk/palmyraportrait/. I would further like to thank Jean-Baptiste Yon for revising several of the inscriptions included in the catalogue. For funerary buildings, see Schnädelbach 2010, Annex.

2. For example, see Ingholt 1935; Abdul-Hak 1952; Saliby 1992; Higuchi and Izumi 1994; Sadurska and Bounni 1994; Higuchi and Saito 2001.

3. See Gawlikowski 1970; Cussini 1995; 2005; Hillers and Cussini 1996.

4. For example, see Saliby 1992, 268; Higuchi and Izumi 1994; Sadurska and Bounni 1994; Higuchi and Saito 2001.

5. Funerary tower from 9 BCE, see Gawlikowski 1970, 45, 184, no. 1; 2005, 47; Henning 2013a, 14; hypogeum from 87 CE, see Gawlikowski 1970, 48, 189, no. 19; 2005, 51; funerary temple from 143 CE, see Gawlikowski 1970, 51, 196, no. 49; 2005, 55.

6. Gawlikowski 2005, 51.

SCI.DAN.H.4.10 · WOMEN, CHILDREN AND THE FAMILY IN PALMYRA
THE ROYAL DANISH ACADEMY OF SCIENCES AND LETTERS · 2019

to which portraits can be ascribed, are documented.[7] In their 1994 book on the funerary sculpture of Palmyra, Anna Sadurska and Adnan Bounni brought together a collection of many of the underground hypogea whose funerary sculpture has been excavated and documented.[8] They included a total of fifteen hypogea in their book, although more than 30 of these with funerary sculpture have been documented.[9] To these, more than 30 tower tombs and temple or house tombs, to which funerary sculpture can be ascribed, can be added; but the tower tombs and temple or house tombs and their portraits tend to be poorly preserved, with only a few portraits ascribed to each tomb.[10] While this is also true for the underground hypogea, because the tower tombs and temple or house tombs are located above ground, they have suffered a great deal of destruction, which makes it difficult to explore family relations within these tombs in broader terms.[11] Both foundation inscriptions, located on the exterior of the funerary buildings, and cession texts, located on both exterior and interior, are frequently still preserved in situ. Both types of text record the founder or founders, the date of construction of the tombs and that of the transfer of ownership of sections within them.[12] The tombs could be owned by a single family, or several families could own different sections of the same tomb. Especially during the late second century and into the third century CE, it became common practice to sell sections of tombs to other branches of the same genealogy, or to entirely different families.[13]

The present study focuses on those funerary contexts where a relatively high proportion of the funerary portraits have preserved epigraphy. These tombs are also recorded in Sadurska and Bounni's publication. They include the hypogea of the families of Sasan and Maṭṭaî, the Bôlḥâ family and the Artaban family.[14] The material has been grouped in a catalogue to present the reader with an overview of the material, but see the publication by Sadurska and Bounni from 1994 for a full overview of the material. The Palmyra Portrait Project database numbers are provided in the catalogue. Only hypogea are investigated, because these are the contexts that are best documented and best preserved. The study required epigraphy as a precondition for identifying the relationships between the individuals portrayed, but also the carved portraits of the individuals concerned as a precondition of documenting their actual presence in the funerary buildings. Several of the published reconstructions of Palmyrene family genealogies include all the names given in inscriptions; but the inscriptions of individual portrait reliefs sometimes list several generations of family members, including husbands, wives and children, not all of whom were necessarily portrayed or buried in the same tombs.[15] Therefore, a study of the actual individuals portrayed in the tombs

7. For example, see Ingholt 1928; 1932; 1935; 1936; 1938; 1962; 1966; 1970; 1974; Cantineau 1929; Will 1948; 1949; Abdul-Hak 1952; Bounni and Saliby 1957; Michałowski 1960; 1962; 1963; 1964; 1966; Kraeling 1961–1962; al-As'ad and Taha 1965; 1968; Gawlikowski 1970; Sadurska 1977; Makowski 1983; Saliby 1992; Schmidt-Colinet 1992; Higuchi and Izumi 1994; Sadurska and Bounni 1994; Fortin 1999; Dunant and Stucky 2000; Higuchi and Saito 2001; al-As'ad 2013; al-Hariri 2013; Henning 2013a; 2013b; Raja and Sørensen 2015; Saito 2016; Miyashita 2016.
8. Les Sculptures Funéraires de Palmyre, 1994.
9. See Ingholt 1928; 1932; 1935; 1936; 1938; 1962; 1966; 1970; 1974; Abdul-Hak 1952; Bounni and Saliby 1957; Michałowski 1960; 1962; 1963; 1964; 1966; Kraeling 1961–1962; al-As'ad and Taha 1965; 1968; Gawlikowski 1970; Sadurska 1977; Saliby 1992; Higuchi and Izumi 1994; Sadurska and Bounni 1994; Fortin 1999; Dunant and Stucky 2000; Higuchi and Saito 2001; al-As'ad 2013; al-Hariri 2013; Saito 2016; Miyashita 2016.
10. Funerary towers, see Will 1948; 1949; Michałowski 1960; 1962; 1963; 1964; 1966; Gawlikowski 1970; Witecka 1994; al-As'ad 2013; Henning 2013a; 2013b; funerary temples or houses, see Cantineau 1929; Gawlikowski 1970; Makowski 1983; Schmidt-Colinet 1992; Raja and Sørensen 2015. See also Watzinger and Wulzinger 1932, most of the pieces documented in their publication are, however, lost today.
11. For example, see Gawlikowski 1970; Schmidt-Colinet 1992; Henning 2013a.
12. For example, see Ingholt 1935; 1938; Gawlikowski 1970; Cussini 1995; Hillers and Cussini 1996.
13. Cussini 1995; 2005; Gawlikowski 2005, 53.
14. al-As'ad and Taha 1968; Sadurska and Bounni 1994, 23–90, cat. nos. 19–121.
15. For example, see Sadurska and Bounni 1994; Yon 2002. See cat. nos. 2–5, 33–34, 37, 60, 66.

is likely to yield a better understanding of burial patterns and family organisation inside the tombs. Moreover, sometimes several individuals were inhumed together in loculi; therefore, only individuals whose portrait reliefs survive in the tombs and are accompanied by epigraphy can properly be identified and used to reconstruct genealogies and burial patterns.[16] Nevertheless, it is important to stress that not every individual buried in the tombs received their own funerary portrait; this study emphasises the portraits of the individuals chosen for the funerary display. In what follows, I will examine the funerary portraits whose epigraphy is preserved in the three chosen funerary buildings. On the basis of this evidence, I will explore whether and which patterns of funerary practice can be deduced.

Hypogeum of the Sasan and Maṭṭaî families

The hypogeum of the Sasan and Maṭṭaî families was excavated in 1958 by Nasib Saliby and Obeid Taha, and is located in the south-east necropolis.[17] The results of the excavation were published in 1992 by Saliby.[18] During the excavations, the in situ door was found to be still closed and this was accessed by a dromos.[19] The hypogeum has six galleries carved out with loculi, and the portraits are divided primarily between five of these galleries.[20] Unfortunately, no foundation inscription is preserved.[21] However, from the funerary epigraphy it can be inferred that two branches of a large family - that of Sasan and Maṭṭaî - occupied the largest space of the hypogeum. A third branch belongs to another Sasan, son of Bôrrefâ, and a fourth to a certain Lishamsh. The latter is poorly preserved and does not allow for further reconstruction of a genealogy as stated by Sadurska and Bounni.[22] The present investigation includes only the two branches that can be traced back to the first Sasan and to Maṭṭaî. Fifty-one portrait reliefs ascribed to this hypogeum are preserved, distributed between six loculus stelae and forty-four loculus bust reliefs, and one male portrait probably originating from a sarcophagus lid.[23] Of the fifty-one portrait reliefs, thirty belonging to the Sasan and Maṭṭaî families have epigraphy preserved, allowing for genealogies to be reconstructed (see catalogue, part I). The earliest portraits are dated to around the end of the first century CE, while the latest are from the late second century CE.[24] Thus, the hypogeum was used by the two families for a period stretching slightly over one hundred years.

In the Maṭṭaî branch, the earliest portraits are of Malkû and Berenike, portrayed together in a loculus bust relief. In the epigraphy they are identified as husband and wife (see table 1).[25] The lineage can be traced back to Malkû's father, Maṭṭaî.[26] Maṭṭaî may have been the founder of the hypogeum, or perhaps, as no portrait is ascribed to Maṭṭaî, this may have been Malkû himself.[27] Two female portrait reliefs depict two daughters of Malkû and Berenike: Amatâ and Shalmat.[28] Portraits of two sons of Shalmat - Malkû and Zebîdâ - are also found in the hypogeum.[29] The only ancestor mentioned in the epigraphy of Malkû and Zebîdâ is their father. Shalmat's inscription mentions her marriage to the father of Malkû and Zebîdâ, Taîm'amed, and allows her to be identified as their mother.[30] Amatâ, the other daughter of Malkû and

16. For example, see Higuchi and Izumi 1994; Higuchi and Saito 2001.
17. Saliby 1992, 267; Sadurska and Bounni 1994, 41.
18. L'hypogée de Sassan fils de Malê à Palmyre, 1992.
19. Saliby 1992, 268.
20. Saliby 1992, 267-284; Sadurska and Bounni 1994, 41.
21. Sadurska and Bounni 1994, 41.
22. Sadurska and Bounni 1994, 41, 44.
23. Sadurska and Bounni 1994, 43.
24. Earliest dated, 80-120 CE, cat. nos. 1-2. Latest, 170-200 CE, cat. nos. 28-30.
25. Cat. no. 1. In tables with genealogies, a '(P)' indicates that a portrait was included of the individual.
26. Sadurska and Bounni 1994, 43.
27. Sadurska and Bounni (1994, 43) suggest that Malkû was either the founder of the hypogeum or of the gallery in which he was buried.
28. Cat. nos. 3-4.
29. Cat. nos. 7-8.
30. Cat. no. 4.

Berenike, was married to Belshûrî, son of Sasan, in the other branch of the family buried in the hypogeum.[31] It is highly plausible that Belshûrî and his family gained access to the tomb through the marriage.[32] Perhaps Belshûrî bought a section of the building or was given access to the tomb by marriage without having to purchase the property and could thereafter add additional sections to the hypogeum. Belshûrî and Amatâ's daughter is Nabî, who is also buried in the tomb; her burial close to Sasan, father of Belshûrî, identifies her as daughter of Belshûrî and Amatâ, and the stylistic features of her portrait further support this, dating it in the early first century CE.[33] There is also a portrait relief of Aqamat, married to Belshûrî, another son of Maṭṭaî.[34] A portrait relief also depicts the grandson of Aqamat and Belshûrî.[35]

The portrait of Aqmê bears two inscriptions that identify her as the daughter of Sîgâ and also of Belshûrî and suggests that Belshûrî may have married twice.[36] Jean-Baptiste Yon does not agree with this interpretation. He suggests that the 'and' added by Sadurska and Bounni in their reading of the two inscriptions, 'Aqmê daughter of Sîgâ and daughter of Belshûrî', should be removed and that it is therefore Sîgâ who is the daughter of Belshûrî.[37] Thus, he claims that the inscription on the right side of the relief is a continuation of the one on its left side. Inscriptions on both left and right side of loculus and stelae portraits are not common in Palmyra; there are only about forty examples.[38] Usually, two inscriptions are included in portraits which are dated by the epigraphy, with one inscription stating the genealogy and the other the year of death.[39] In other cases, the inclusion of two inscriptions often records different aspects: bilingual inscriptions, patrons, genealogies of fathers and husbands and so forth.[40] The inclusion of two inscriptions was primarily, therefore, to include two different aspects; in a few instances the two inscriptions record the same name, but do not form a continuous text.[41] So far, there is only one example of an inscription continuing on both sides of the head, a loculus stele from the Palmyra museum depicting Bat-Malê, and here the lack of space certainly left the carver of the inscription with no choice but to use both sides of the re-

31. Cat. no. 3. Sadurska and Bounni 1994, 43.

32. Sadurska and Bounni 1994, 43.

33. Cat. no. 6. Sadurska and Bounni 1994, 47.

34. Cat. no. 2.

35. Cat. no. 9.

36. Cat. no. 5. Sadurska and Bounni 1994, 59; Yon 2002, 175-176.

37. Yon 2002, 175-176.

38. Numbers are from the Palmyra Portrait Project Database, August 2017.

39. For example, see American University Museum, Beirut, inv. 2739 (PAT 0610; Chabot 1922, 128; Ingholt 1928, 69-73, PS 43, pl. XIII,3; Colledge 1976, 260); Archaeological Museum, Istanbul, inv. 3840 (PAT 0977; Ingholt 1928, 34-35, PS 11, pl. IV,1; Colledge 1976, 250); Freer Gallery of Art, Washington D.C., inv. F1908.236 (PAT 0821; Ingholt 1928, 87-89, PS 54, pl. XVI,3; Colledge 1976, 263); Ny Carlsberg Glyptotek, Copenhagen, inv. IN 1155 (PAT 0603; Chabot 1922, 117, 121, no. 47, pl. XXX,5; Ingholt 1928, 58-59, PS 34, pl. XI,1; Colledge 1976, 257, pl. 84; Hvidberg-Hansen and Ploug 1993, 45-46, no. 4; Ploug 1995, 43-44, no. 4; Hvidberg-Hansen 1998, 29-30, no. 4); The Metropolitan Museum of Art, New York, inv. 02.29.3 (PAT 0614; Arnold 1905, 104-106, no. I, pl. I; Chabot 1922, 113, pl. XXVII,2; Ingholt 1928, 62-63, PS 37, pl. XI; Colledge 1976, 256).

40. For example, see bilingual inscriptions, Musée du Louvre, Paris, inv. AO 1556 (PAT 0761; Colledge 1976, 69, 225, pl. 144; Dentzer-Feydy and Teixidor 1993, 162, no. 166; Yon 2012, 413, no. 551); Private collection, Lebanon (Abousamra 2015, 229-233, no. IV, figs. 11-13); Palmyra Museum, Palmyra, inv. B 1783/6606 (PAT 1824; Bounni and Saliby 1957, 45, no. 7, pl. II,2; Bounni 1961-1962, 154, no. 10; Gawlikowski 1974, 19, no. 33; Colledge 1976, 247; Tanabe 1986, 319, pl. 288; Sadurska and Bounni 1994, 155-156, cat. no. 202, fig. 57; al-As'ad and Gawlikowski 1997, 28, no. 33, fig. 33; Yon 2012, 329, no. 426); patrons, Archaeological Museum, Istanbul, inv. 3818 (PAT 0966; Chabot 1922, 125, no. 28; Colledge 1976, 259); Berkshire Museum, Pittsfield, inv. 1903.7.5 (PAT 0839; Ingholt 1928, 138, PS 415; 1938, 131, pl. XLVIII,4; Colledge 1976, 259); genealogy of husband, Ny Carlsberg Glyptotek, Copenhagen, inv. IN 1057 (PAT 0712; Ingholt 1928, 52-54, PS 30, pl. X,1; Colledge 1976, 255-256; Hvidberg-Hansen and Ploug 1993, 43, no. 2; Ploug 1995, 37-39, no. 2; Hvidberg-Hansen 1998, 26-27, no. 2); individuals buried in the loculus, State Hermitage Museum, St Petersburg, inv. DV-8840 (PAT 0649; Ingholt 1928, 40, 111, PS 19, pl. VI,2; Colledge 1976, 250-251).

41. One example is in Musée d'Art et d'Histoire, Genève, inv. 008194 (PAT 4309-4310; Deonna 1923, 232, no. 5, pl. XXXII,5; Ingholt 1928, 121, PS 263; Chamay and Maier 1989, 92-93, no. 118, pl. 103,1).

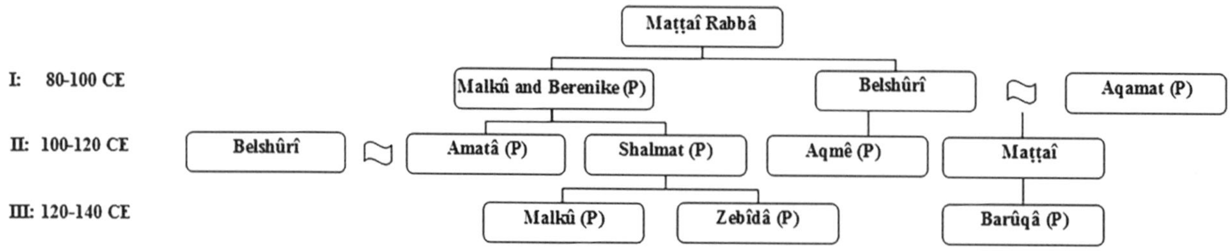

Table 1: The Maṭṭaî branch, hypogeum of the Sasan and Maṭṭaî families (based on Sadurska and Bounni 1994, 42).

lief.[42] This is not the case with the portrait of Aqmê, where the two inscriptions should be understood as separate; documenting Aqmê's mother in one inscription and her father in the other. Furthermore, Yon suggests that Sîgâ was instead the daughter of Belshûrî and Aqmê.[43] This would move the dating of Aqmê's portrait from 100–120 CE to 140–160 CE, some twenty to sixty years later. However, Aqmê's portrait is older than the portraits dating to 140–160 CE in the hypogeum. Thus, Aqmê's genealogy should not be changed, and the inscriptions belonging to her portrait are to be understood as two separate inscriptions recording two different aspects. The possiblilty that Belshûrî was married twice should therefore not be rejected.

The other branch in the tomb is traced back to Sasan, the father of Belshûrî, who is married to Amatâ from the Maṭṭaî branch (see tables 2 and 3). The next member portrayed is Sasan, a nephew of Belshûrî.[44] Four of his children are portrayed: M..., Amatâ, Yarḥibôlâ and ʿOggâ.[45] Yarḥibôlâ is portrayed with his own son Yarḥaî, but no wife is mentioned.[46] Three further children of Yarḥibôlâ are also portrayed with epigraphy mentioning only Yarḥibôlâ as predecessor.[47] Sasan's daughter Amatâ is portrayed with her own daughter, but a husband is not recorded.[48] Another son of Sasan, ʿOggâ, is portrayed, as well as four of his children: Malkat, Maflûn, Malê and Nabî.[49] Barqê is a fifth child of ʿOggâ's, but no portrait ascribed to him is found and instead his two children, Malê and Malaftâ, are portrayed together in one loculus bust relief.[50] Sadurska and Bounni suggest that ʿOggâ's wife and the mother of his five children is Ḥalî, whose portrait is located in the same section as ʿOggâ's: this is because Ḥalî's father is not mentioned in other inscriptions in the tomb and because her portrait resembles that of ʿOggâ's daughter Malkat.[51] The portraits of Amatâ and of Nabî – Amatâ is the sister of ʿOggâ and Nabî is his niece – also resemble Ḥalî's portrait.[52] Thus, the location of Ḥalî's portrait close to ʿOggâ's is not sufficient evidence to prove that she is his wife: she may have been wife to ʿOggâ, to one of his brothers, to one of his children, or to the child of one of ʿOggâ's siblings. Zabdibôl is another son of Sasan, and his two sons are portrayed.[53] A last son of Sasan, Belshûrî, is not portrayed, but his son ʿOggâ is.[54] Sasan also had a brother named ʿOggâ, and the son of this ʿOggâ is portrayed, as are his three grandsons and a great-grandson.[55] Finally, Moqîmû and Amatâ, probably two grandchildren of another son of ʿOggâ, are portrayed.[56] Thus, numerous generations from the two families are buried in the hypogeum.

42. Palmyra Museum, Palmyra, inv. B 2211 (PAT 1973; Michałowski 1966, 46–48, no. 1, fig. 55; 115, no. 8; Gawlikowski 1974, 96, no. 191).
43. Yon 2002, 176.
44. Cat. no. 10.
45. Cat. nos. 11–14.
46. Cat. no. 13.
47. Cat. nos. 17–19.
48. Cat. no. 12.
49. Cat. nos. 14–15, 20–23.
50. Cat. no. 28.
51. Sadurska and Bounni 1994, 50.
52. Cat. nos. 12 and 17.
53. Cat. no. 24.
54. Cat. no. 25.
55. Cat. nos. 26–27.
56. Cat. nos. 29–30. Sadurska and Bounni 1994, 57–58.

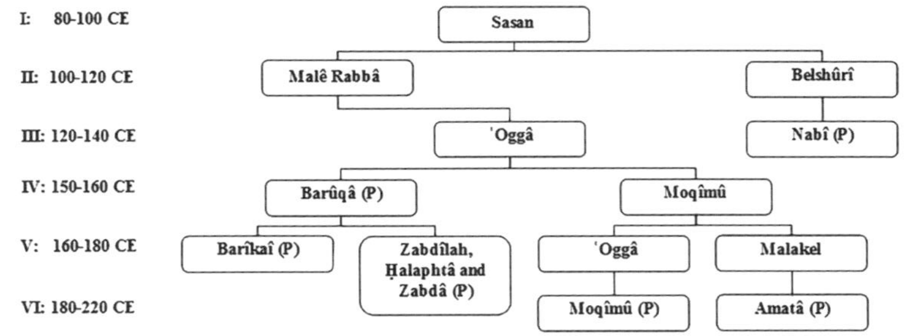

Table 2: The Sasan Branch, hypogeum of the Sasan and Maṭṭaî families, part 1 (based on Sadurska and Bounni 1994, 42).

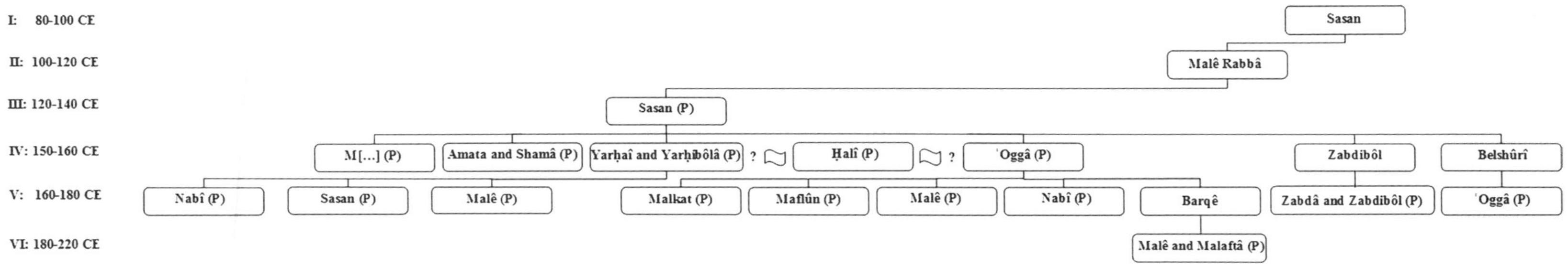

Table 3: The Sasan Branch, hypogeum of the Sasan and Maṭṭaî families, part 2 (based on Sadurska and Bounni 1994, 42).

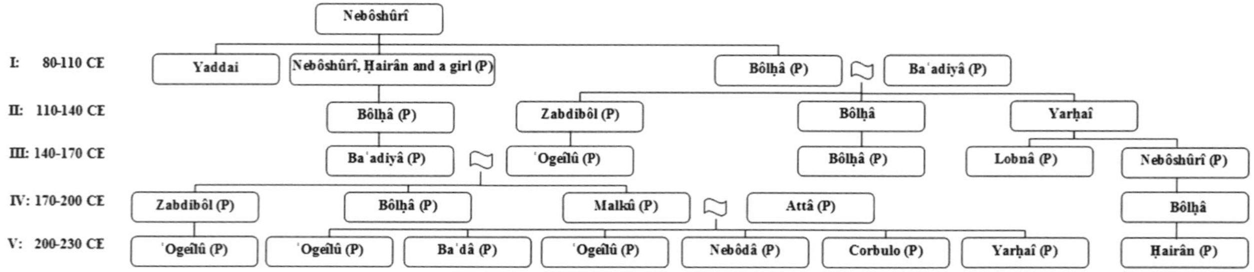

Table 4: The Bôlḥâ family, part 1 (based on Sadurska and Bounni 1994, 70-72).

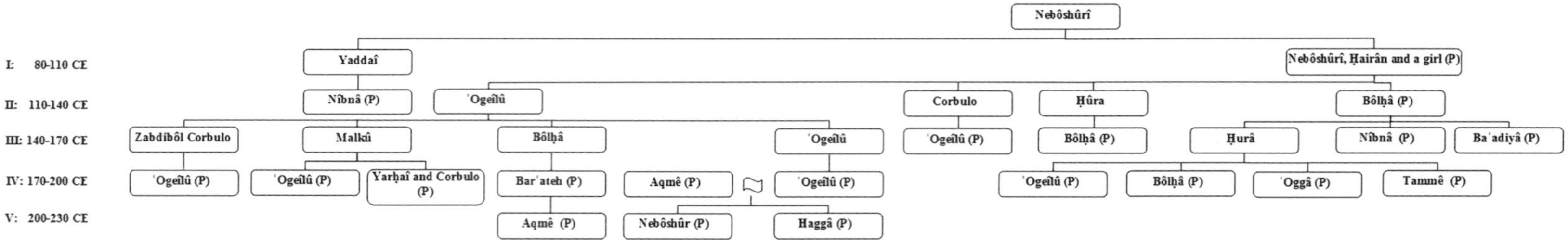

Table 5: The Bôlḥâ family, part 2 (based on Sadurska and Bounni 1994, 70-72).

Hypogeum of Bôlḥâ

The hypogeum of Bôlḥâ was excavated in 1958 by Taha and Kheir. It is located in the south-east necropolis.[57] The results of the excavation were published in 1968 by Khaled and Taha.[58] The hypogeum has three galleries and is entered through a dromos with a door found in situ.[59] The foundation inscription on the external door lintel records:

BT ʿLMʾ DNH ʿBD BWLḤʾ BR NBWŠWRY
LH WLBNWHY LʿLMʾ BʾB ŠNT 4.100

This house of eternity was made by Bôlḥâ son of Nebôshûrî for himself and for his children in eternity in Ab year 40 (89 CE).[60]

Twenty-nine portrait reliefs from the Bôlḥâ family are found in the hypogeum, divided among the three galleries of the tomb.[61] They comprise six loculus stelae, nineteen loculus bust reliefs, three relief plaques depicting sarcophagi and one sarcophagus.[62] Twenty-three portrait sculptures, including the four banqueting scenes (see catalogue, part II), can also be included in the reconstruction of the genealogy. The hypogeum was in use from 70 to 89 CE to the beginning of the third century CE.[63] Thus, the families used the hypogeum to bury their deceased ancestors for close to a hundred and fifty years.

One of the earliest portraits from the hypogeum is a loculus stele depicting Nebôshûrî, brother of the founder of the hypogeum. He is depicted with the two children of his niece Nîbnâ (see tables 4 and 5).[64] The inscriptions belonging to Nîbnâ's two children and that of her own portrait reveal that she was married to a certain Bôlḥâ, son of Zabdibôl.[65] Bôlḥâ, the founder, and his wife are portrayed, as are one of their children, six of their grandchildren, three of their great-grandchildren, and seven of their great-great-grandchildren.[66] Sadurska and Bounni suggest that a certain Ḥairân is grandchild to Nebôshûrî - Nebôshûrî himself being grandchild to the founder, Bôlḥâ - but this is not completely certain.[67] Furthermore, Hermes, a freedman of Malkû, son of ʿOgeîlû, is portrayed reclining in a banqueting scene with Malkû's seated mother and two sons.[68] Therefore, in this tomb, a freedman of the family is portrayed and was probably buried here as well. Nebôshûrî, brother to the founder, had four children; a portrait is preserved of one son, Bôlḥâ, and of four grandchildren.[69] One of his granddaughters, Baʿadiyâ, married the grandchild of Bôlḥâ.[70] Ten of Nebôshûrî's great-grandchildren and three of his great-great-grandchildren are also buried in the tomb.[71] Moreover, Nîbnâ, the daughter of Yaddaî (another brother to Bôlḥâ), is buried in the tomb.[72] Sadurska and Bounni suggest that Tammê was wife to Bôlḥâ's great-grandchild, Zabdibôl; however, as nothing can securely support this or even connect Tammê to any individuals in the tomb, her portrait and that of her son are not included here.[73] Sadurska and Bounni further claim that a great-grandchild of Nebôshûrî', Barʿateh, was married to a certain Bat-Abdai, but this too is not supported.[74]

57. al-As'ad and Taha 1968; Sadurska and Bounni 1994, 70. For a recent examination of the tomb, see Audley-Miller 2016, 572–584.
58. Madfan Bûlhâ al-Tadmurî (The Tomb of Bôlḥâ), 1968.
59. al-As'ad and Taha 1968; Sadurska and Bounni 1994, 70.
60. PAT 1867; al-As'ad and Taha 1968; Gawlikowski 1974, 37, no. 75; Sadurska and Bounni 1994, 70, 72. Transcription is from Hillers and Cussini (1996, PAT 1867).
61. al-As'ad and Taha 1968; Sadurska and Bounni 1994, 70.
62. al-As'ad and Taha 1968; Sadurska and Bounni 1994, 72.
63. Earliest, 70–89 CE, cat. no. 31; latest, 180–230 CE, cat. nos. 39–40, 48, 52–53.
64. Cat. no. 31. Sadurska and Bounni 1994, 70.
65. Cat. nos. 31 and 34.
66. Founder and wife, cat. nos. 32–33; son of founder, cat. no. 36; grandchildren of founder, cat. nos. 31 (2), 40–43; great-grandchildren, cat. nos. 40 and 52 (2); great-great-grandchildren, cat. nos. 39 (2), 40 (4), 52.
67. Cat. no. 53. Sadurska and Bounni 1994, 79.
68. Cat. no. 39. Sadurska and Bounni 1994, 71, 89.
69. Nebôshûrî, cat. no. 31; son, cat. no. 35; grandchildren, cat. nos 37–39, 44.
70. Cat. nos. 39–40.
71. Great-grandchildren, cat. nos. 40, 45 (2), 46–48 (2), 49–51; great-great-grandchildren, cat. no. 48 (3).
72. Cat. no. 34.
73. Sadurska and Bounni 1994, 71. See cat. no. 40.
74. Sadurska and Bounni 1994, 72, 82.

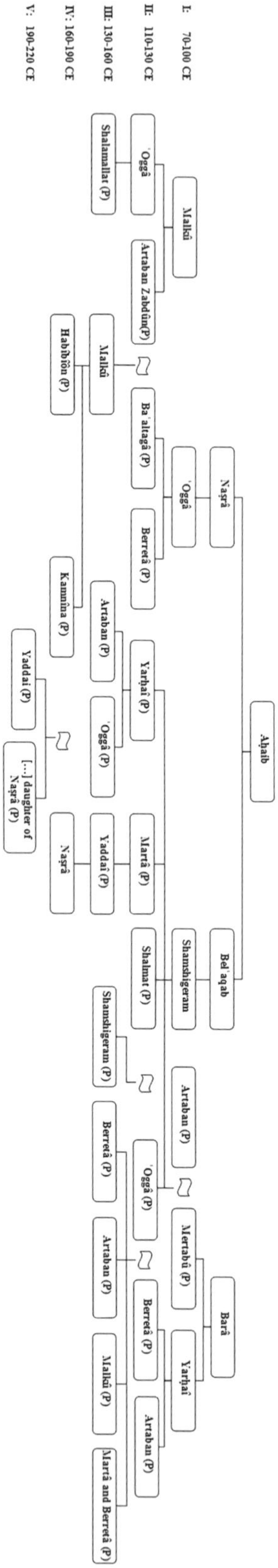

Table 6: The Artaban family (based on Sadurska and Bounni 1994, 23-24).

Hypogeum of Artaban

The last hypogeum is that of Artaban. This was excavated in 1958 by Taha and Kheir and, like the two previous hypogea, it is located in the south-east necropolis.[75] The hypogeum has five galleries, and the tomb is accessed by a dromos.[76] The foundation inscription is missing, but an inscription on a relief plaque depicting a sarcophagus belonging to ʿOggâ records:

> ʿGʾ BR ʾRṬBN BR | ʿGʾ ḤBL DY LʾBWHY | WLʾḤWHY ʿL ḤYWHY

ʿOggâ son of Artaban son of | ʿOggâ alas (he made) this for his father | and for his brother in his lifetime.[77]

Thus, the inscription reveals that the family of Artaban were probably the owners of the tomb.[78] The tomb has twenty-five portrait reliefs: twenty-two loculus bust reliefs, one relief plaque depicting a sarcophagus, one relief plaque depicting a sarcophagus box and one loculus stele.[79] Of the twenty-five preserved sculptures, twenty-two have the epigraphy preserved. Fifteen portrait sculptures, including the relief plaque displaying a sarcophagus, can be ascribed to the Artaban family (see catalogue, part III). The earliest dated portrait reliefs are from the beginning of the second century CE, and the latest is from the beginning of the third century CE.[80] It seems then that the Artaban family used the hypogeum for approximately one hundred years.

One of the earliest portrait reliefs from the tomb is a large relief plaque depicting a sarcophagus (see table 6). Here, ʿOggâ (who, as mentioned, commissioned the relief) is portrayed.[81] Sadurska and Bounni suggest that ʿOggâ's father, Artaban, was the founder of the hypogeum, but it may be more plausible that ʿOggâ himself founded the hypogeum and included portraits of his parents in his own funerary display.[82] The relief includes portraits of himself, his wife Berretâ, his wife's brother, two of their children and his parents. ʿOggâ's brother and his two sons are included as a single relief with three portrait busts, situated directly above the relief plaque depicting a sarcophagus.[83] Martâ, sister to ʿOggâ, is also buried in the tomb, as is her son, Yaddaî.[84] Interestingly, the inscription belonging to Yaddaî's portrait mentions only that he is Martâ's son.[85] Martâ's grandson Naṣrâ was married to a certain Kamnîn, and Kamnîn and Naṣrâ's son and daughter, Martâ's great-grandchildren, are also buried in the tomb.[86] With his wife, Berretâ, ʿOggâ had four children - or at least, four of their children are depicted in the tomb.[87]

According to Sadurska and Bounni, ʿOggâ was also married to another woman, Shalmat, and they had one son together, Shamshigeram.[88] Sadurska and Bounni do not specify why they come to this conclusion. It might be due to the proximity of Shalmat's burial location to Berretâ, or to the fact that the name of ʿOggâ's son, Shamshigeram, is also that of Shalmat's father, following the common practice in Palmyra of naming a child after its grandfather, as pointed out by Yon.[89] The name Shamshigeram cannot be traced in the family of ʿOggâ, and this may be no coincidence. Still, it can be debated whether ʿOggâ was married to two women. The family of Shalmat - a second family branch - are also buried in the tomb, including Berretâ and Baʿaltagâ, grandchildren of Shalmat's grandfather's brother.[90] Sardurska and Bounni argue that Baʿaltagâ was married to Artaban, the third family branch represented in the tomb.[91] The burials of Baʿaltagâ and Arta-

75. Sadurska and Bounni 1994, 23.
76. Sadurska and Bounni 1994, 23.
77. PAT 2664-2673; Sadurska and Bounni 194, 37-39. Transcription is from Hillers and Cussini (1996, PAT 2664).
78. Sadurska and Bounni 1994, 25.
79. Sadurska and Bounni 1994, 25.
80. Earliest, 100-150 CE, cat. nos. 54-57, 59, 61; latest, 220-220 CE, cat. no. 68.
81. Cat. no. 54.
82. Sadurska and Bounni 1994, 25.
83. Cat. no. 54.
84. Cat. nos. 58 and 62.
85. Cat. no. 62.
86. Kamnîn, cat. no. 66; children, cat. nos. 67-68.
87. Berretâ, cat. nos. 54 and 61; children, cat. nos. 54 (2), 61, 64.
88. Shalmat, cat. no. 59; Shamshigeram, cat. no. 63. Sadurska and Bounni 1994, 33; Yon 2002, 175.
89. Yon 2002, 175. See also Sadurska and Bounni 1994, 33.
90. Cat. nos. 56-57.
91. Cat. no. 55. Sadurska and Bounni 1994, 25, 27-28.

ban are in the same section and even in the same loculus, which Sardurska and Bounni use as an argument for their marriage.[92] Artaban's grandchild is called Naṣraî and was probably named after Baʿaltagâ's father, supporting the hypothesis of a marriage between Baʿaltagâ and Artaban.[93] Artaban's nephew, Shalamallat, was also buried in the tomb.[94] Artaban and Baʿaltagâ's two grandchildren are also portrayed: their granddaughter is Kamnîn, who married Naṣrâ from the family of Artaban, and their grandson is Habîbîôn.[95] These are all the individuals who can be ascribed to the Artaban family through the epigraphy.

Family burial patterns

In what follows, some general observations on the burial patterns in the three hypogea are made. Of the individuals portrayed in the tombs, ninety-eight belong to extended families or to larger lineages brought together in the tombs: for example, in the hypogeum of the Sasan and Maṭṭaî families, the two families were joined in the hypogeum by the marriage between Amatâ, daughter of Malkû (son of Maṭṭaî), and Belshûrî, son of Sasan. Only six of the individuals portrayed are neither related to the owners of the tombs nor introduce their own extended genealogies; these six individuals are all women.[96] Of the total of 104 individuals portrayed, identified through the epigraphy and ascribed to the lineages in the three tombs, sixty-one are men, thirthy-five are women, seven are young boys, and one is a young girl.[97] Portraits of women thus account for 36.5% of adult portraits - which does, more or less, correspond to the 40% share of women in the adult funerary portraiture of Palmyra.[98] Children make up close to 8% of the portraits. In fact, in the tombs belonging to the families of Sasan and Maṭṭaî and of Artaban, women represent between 41 and 46% of the portraits, but in the tomb of Bôlḥâ only around 29%. In the Bôlḥâ family, therefore, fewer women were included in the funerary display.

Marriage

Women were more likely to be buried in the tombs of their husbands' bloodline without bringing their own extended families with them, as seen in six instances in the three tombs.[99] In three cases in these tombs, men also used the tomb belonging to the women's bloodlines: Belshûrî in the hypogeum of the Sasan and Maṭṭaî families, Bôlḥâ in the hypogeum of Bôlḥâ, and Artaban Zabdûn in the hypogeum of Artaban. All, however, brought their own descent with them.[100] In all the tombs documented in Sadurska and Bounni's book, there are four cases of men marrying into families without bringing their own descent to the tombs but they are not among the individuals portrayed here.[101] One of the four is Taîmʿamed, married to Shalmat from the hypogeum of the Sasan and Maṭṭaî families; another is Bôlḥâ, married to Nîbnâ from the hypogeum of Bôlḥâ; and in fact Bôlḥâ dedicated the portrait of Nîbnâ.[102] A possibility is that these men were not actually buried in their wives' families' tombs, but elsewhere, perhaps in those of their own descent. In the three tombs included in the present contribution, around 83% of the women are found in the tomb of their own descent or brought their own bloodline with them into the tombs, including brothers, uncles, nieces and other relatives. Furthermore, in the hypogeum of the Bôlḥâ family, a portrait of Hermes, a freedman of Malkû, is included in the funerary display in a banqueting scene, reclining

92. Sadurska and Bounni 1994, 25, 27-28.
93. Cat. no. 65.
94. Cat. no. 60.
95. Cat. nos. 65-66.
96. Sadurska and Bounni 1994, 43. Cat. nos. 1-2, 15, 33, 40, 48.
97. Boys, cat. nos. 8-9, 27, 31, 46, 51, 54; girl, cat. no. 31.
98. Information from the Palmyra Portrait Project database, August 2017. See Krag and Raja 2016; Krag 2018, 68.
99. Cat. nos. 1-2, 15, 33, 40, 48.
100. Belshûrî, no portrait is preserved of him, see table 1; Bôlḥâ, no portrait is preserved of him, see cat. no. 34 and table 5; Artaban Zabdûn, cat. no. 55, see table 6.
101. Hypogeum of Shalamallat, Sadurska and Bounni 1994, 164-165, cat. no. 218, fig. 205; hypogeum of the Sasan and Maṭṭaî families, cat. no. 4; hypogeum of the Bôlḥâ family, cat. no. 34.
102. See cat. nos. 4 and 34.

next to Malkû's mother and sons.[103] This is a rare example of a freedman being buried with the family he had once served.

Inscriptions on ten portraits of women mention their marriages, but in four instances, the fact that they are married is revealed by epigraphy belonging to other portraits, or by location of the portraits in the tomb and/or a resemblance to other portraits in the tomb. This is observed in the portrait of Ḥalî from the hypogeum of the Sasan and Maṯṯaî families, as her portrait resembles several others in the tomb. In nine of these instances, portraits of husbands are also found; who Ḥalî's husband was is uncertain.[104] It is evident that an identity aspect such as marriage could be represented in the portraits through epigraphy. However, of the thirthy-five adult women portrayed and identified through epigraphy in the three tombs, twenty-one - approximately 60% - are not identified as married.[105] They can thus be placed in the genealogies only as daughters or sisters, rather than wives. The question that arises is why so many women do not refer to husbands, or are not buried with them. Were all these women unmarried, and did they die before they reached marriageable age? Or was it simply a free choice whether women were buried inside the family tomb belonging to their fathers' bloodline or that of their husbands? It cannot be assumed that all the portraits of their husbands have simply been lost: that would be quite a large number of portraits from the three contexts and specifically those of the husbands. It does, however, appear to indicate that there was a general knowledge of marriages within the families and that this did not necessarily have to be recorded in epigraphy.[106] The visitors to the tombs would have known this. Thus, the lack of references to marriages in epigraphy could simply be due to a reliance on knowledge of marriages shared between family members. Furthermore, men are often documented only as sons or brothers, with no reference to marriage or wives; in general, men do not refer to their wives in epigraphy, the only exception being when a wife dedicated the funerary portrait.[107] Some of the men and women might indeed have been unmarried because they died young. Two women from the hypogeum of the Sasan and Maṯṯaî families are depicted with short-cropped hair, which, it is argued, signifies their adolescence.[108] The two are therefore adolescent daughters who were not yet married. One of the women, Malaftâ, is instead portrayed with her brother.[109]

The portrayal of children with their parents in loculus bust reliefs raises the question of whether the marriage could be emphasised in other ways in portraiture. The portrait of Amatâ from the hypogeum of Sasan and Maṯṯaî, for example, depicts her with her daughter Shamâ, and it is therefore reasonable to assume that Amatâ was married.[110] However, her husband is not portrayed in the tomb. This is also the case with Amatâ's brother, Yarḥibôlâ, who is depicted with his son, and no wife is portrayed.[111] In fact, only one parent is portrayed; five women and eight men are portrayed alone with their children.[112] It might therefore be deduced that for both women and men, the paternal line remained just as important as the new branch of lineage created with a husband or wife. It could have been a matter of individual choice for a woman whether to be buried with her husband or with her father's family. In fact, it appears that it was more usual to choose the father's decent.[113]

In ten instances, the husbands of the women identified as married are also portrayed, as mentioned above:

103. Cat. no. 39.
104. Cat. nos. 1, 32, 40 (2), 48, 52, 54 (2), 55; Ḥalî, cat. no. 15.
105. Cat. nos. 5-6, 12 (2), 17, 20, 23, 28, 30, 34, 42, 40 (2), 48 (2), 54, 57-59, 61, 68.
106. See also Krag 2015, 105.
107. There is only one known example, Archaeological Museum, Istanbul, inv. 3748 (PAT 0877; Ingholt 1928, 101, PS 102; Colledge 1976, 247).
108. Cat. nos. 23 and 28. Parlasca 1987a; Cussini 2000; Krag and Raja 2019.
109. Cat. no. 28.
110. Cat. no. 12.
111. Cat. no. 13
112. Men, cat. nos. 10, 13, 16, 31, 36, 47, 52, 54; women, cat. nos. 3-4, 12, 58, 66.
113. Krag and Raja 2016, 143-144.

two couples are related, eight are not.[114] Intermarriage between relatives could be an explanation for why women and men are often buried with their own families. A focus on marriage within the family would reduce the need to include additional families in their genealogy. In the hypogeum of Bôlḥâ, one large family shares the tomb; in the other two hypogea, the tombs are shared by multiple families. In the hypogeum of the Sasan and Maṭṭaî families and also in that of Artaban, the families were united through marriage. As previously stated, Belshûrî married into the family and likely gained access to the tomb by so doing, and it is thus likely that the key to purchasing access to a tomb was marriage.[115] Simply put, the marriage granted the new family access to the funerary space.

Remarriage

Another observation, which can be made based on the material from the three hypogea, concerns the phenomenon of remarriage in Palmyra.[116] This is observable in the hypogeum of the Sasan and Maṭṭaî families, and perhaps also in the hypogeum of Artaban. In the Sasan and Maṭṭaî family hypogeum, the inscription belonging to the relief of Aqmê records that she was the child of Belshûrî and Sîgâ.[117] This reveals that Belshûrî was married to two women, the other being Aqamat, whose inscription records that she was married to Belshûrî.[118] ʿOggâ, from the Artaban hypogeum may also have been married to two women: Shalmat and Berretâ.[119] ʿOggâ is depicted with Berretâ on a relief plaque depicting a sarcophagus, and she is recorded in the epigraphy as his wife.[120] As previously mentioned, the location of Shalmat's burial close to Berretâ together with the name of ʿOggâ's son, Shamshigeram (perhaps named after Shalmat's father) could be grounds for inferring that Shalmat was the mother and therefore an additional wife of ʿOggâ.[121] Furthermore, Sadurska and Bounni underline that the resemblance between the portraits of Berretâ and Shalmat indicates that they were probably produced by the same workshop.[122] Perhaps Shalmat died early and ʿOggâ subsequently married Berretâ, as only one son of Shalmat and ʿOggâ is portrayed, whereas four children of Berretâ and ʿOggâ are depicted.[123] The extended families of both wives were also buried in the hypogeum. This situation might have been the same with Sîgâ and Belshûrî. As discussed elsewhere, such instances are more likely evidence of remarriage than of polygamy.[124] This is for example evidenced by Shalmat and ʿOggâ having only one child portrayed, whereas Berretâ and ʿOggâ have four, suggesting that Shalmat died and that ʿOggâ then remarried.

Multiple representations

In the hypogeum of Artaban, Berretâ (married to ʿOggâ, who commissioned the banqueting relief) is depicted both on the banqueting relief, and with her daughter in a loculus bust relief.[125] Berretâ is thus included in two different group constellations within the tomb; one with her extended family, and one with only her daughter. It is relevant briefly to address the few cases in which more than one portrait of the same individual survives, in this instance of women.[126] The

114. Not related, cat. nos. 1, 32-33, 40, 48, 54-56, 59; Ḥalî is married into the family and she might be married to ʿOggâ, identity of husband is unsure, cat. nos. 14-15; relatives, cat. nos. 54, 39-40.
115. Belshûrî, see table 1 and 2.
116. See also Yon 2002, 175-176.
117. Cat. no. 5.
118. Cat. no. 2.
119. Cat. nos. 54, 59, 61.
120. Cat. no. 54. Her inscription records: BRTʾ BRT | YRḤY BRʾ | ʾTTH; Berretâ daughter of | Yarḥaî (son of) Barâ | his wife (transcription is from Hillers and Cussini (1996, PAT 2667)).
121. Cat. nos. 59 and 63. See Yon 2002, 175.
122. Sadurska and Bounni 1994, 33.
123. Shalmat and ʿOggâ, cat. no. 63; Berretâ and ʿOggâ, cat. nos 54 (2), 61, 64. See Yon 2002, 175.
124. Krag and Raja 2017; Krag 2018, 83.
125. Cat. nos. 54 and 61.
126. Arnold 1905, 107; Colledge 1976, 62, n.185; Parlasca 1985, 350-351; Heyn 2010, 640; Kropp and Raja 2014, 404; Krag 2016, 189-190; Raja 2017, 338. See also contribution by Cussini in this volume.

Fig. 1: Loculus relief depicting ʿAlâ. Ny Carlsberg Glyptotek, Copenhagen, inv. IN 1079, 113/114 CE (Courtesy of Ny Carlsberg Glyptotek, photo by Palmyra Portrait Project).

Fig. 2: Loculus relief depicting ʿAliyat. The Metropolitan Museum of Art, New York, inv. 02.29.5, 150–200 CE (© The Metropolitan Museum of Art, www.metmuseum.org).

well-known portraits of ʿAlâ, one in the Ny Carlsberg Glyptotek and one in the British Museum, depict the same woman, and the year of her death is recorded in both portraits.[127] The Louvre has two reliefs depicting Haîdrâ, and the epigraphy reveals that in one image she is portrayed with her husband and in the other with her son.[128] In the Metropolitan Museum, two portraits of ʿAliyat are preserved: one individual loculus bust relief and one group constellation with her father and siblings.[129] It has been suggested that the two portraits of ʿAlâ originated from two different tombs, one belonging to her husband and one to her

127. British Museum, London, inv. BM 125695 (PAT 0732; Chabot 1922, 127, no. 20, pl. XXXII,4; Ingholt 1928, 55–57, PS 31, pl. X,2; Colledge 1976, 62, 70, 256, pl. 63); Ny Carlsberg Glyptotek, Copenhagen, inv. IN 1079 (PAT 0733; Chabot 1922, 121, no. 46, pl. XXXII,3; Ingholt 1928, 57–58, PS 32, pl. X,3; Colledge 1976, 62, 70, 255–256, pl. 64; Hvidberg-Hansen and Ploug 1993, 44, no. 3; Ploug 1995, 39–42, no. 3; Hvidberg-Hansen 1998, 28, no. 3).

128. Musée du Louvre, Paris, inv. AO 2000 (PAT 0862; Chabot 1922, no. 11, pl. XXXII,12; Ingholt 1928, 96, PS 73; Colledge 1976, 62, pl. 61; Dentzer-Feydy and Teixidor 1993, 172–173, no. 175); inv. AO 2093 (PAT 0863; Chabot 1922, 122, no. 12, pl. XXXII,13; Ingholt 1928, 96, PS 74; Colledge 1976, 62, pl. 62; Dentzer-Feydy and Teixidor 1993, 178–179, no. 180).

129. The Metropolitan Museum of Art, New York, inv. 02.29.1 (PAT 0615; Arnold 1905, 104–107, no. II, pl. II; Chabot 1922, 112–113, pl. XXVII,11; Ingholt 1928, 95–96, PS 67; 1954, no. 6); inv. 02.29.5 (PAT 0616; Arnold 1905, 107, no. III, pl. III; Chabot 1922, 113, pl. XXVII,7; Ingholt 1928, 139, PS 420; Colledge 1976, 259).

Fig. 3: Banqueting relief depicting ʿAliyat, standing in the right side of the relief, together with her siblings and reclining father. The Metropolitan Museum of Art, New York, inv. 02.29.1, 140–180 CE (© The Metropolitan Museum of Art, www.metmuseum.org).

father's line of descent (see fig. 1).[130] Such an instance of an individual being buried in two tombs would strengthen the impression that strong relationships to both the father's bloodline and the new family branch begun by husband and wife (as observed in the three hypogea) could be upheld and maintained. This could perhaps have been the solution in a few instances. The same could be the case with ʿAliyat, except for William R. Arnold's suggestion that if ʿAliyat received her own funerary portrait at her death subsequent to her inclusion in her father's funerary display, then both ʿAliyat's portraits could have been located in the same tomb (see figs. 2 and 3).[131] Haîdrâ's two portraits were probably situated in the same tomb, and here the bond stressed is not only that between husband and wife, but also between mother and son, as with Berretâ and her daughter (see figs. 4 and 5).[132] Another possibility, is that her son erected his own funerary building and that his mother was included in this display as it is not uncommon for adult sons to stress a bond with their mothers in portraiture. Moreover, Berretâ's daugher is one of the few instances in which the child is depicted smaller than the adult, yet wearing an adult costume.[133] Thus, both are portrayed as adult and married women.

Location

No clear patterns emerge in the spatial organisation of the portraits within the tombs. In the tomb of Bôlḥâ, the portraits are spread across the tomb, and close and distant relatives are buried next to one an-

130. Colledge 1976, 62, n.185; Heyn 2010, 640. See also Kropp and Raja 2014, 404; Krag and Raja 2016; Krag and Raja 2019.
131. Arnold 1905, 107; Heyn 2010, 640. See also Colledge 1976, 62, n.185.

132. See also Colledge 1976, 62, n.185.
133. Krag and Raja 2016, 140–141.

Fig. 4: Banqueting relief depicting Haîdrâ and her reclining husband. Musée du Louvre, Paris, inv. AO 2000, 200–273 CE (© Palmyra Portrait Project, Ingholt Archive at Ny Carlsberg Glyptotek, PS 73).

Fig. 5: Banqueting relief depicting Haîdrâ and her reclining son. Musée du Louvre, Paris, inv. AO 2093, 200–273 CE (© Palmyra Portrait Project, Ingholt Archive at Ny Carlsberg Glyptotek, PS 74).

other.[134] In the hypogea, the location of burial places can be more mixed between the families.[135] In the hypogeum of Sasan and Maṯṯaî, for example, Nabî, daughter of Belshûrî (the brother of Sasan), is buried right between her uncle Sasan and her cousin, his son.[136] Uncles are thought to have had a close relationship to nephews and nieces, and relationships between siblings and cousins in Palmyra also seem to be underlined as strong.[137] Also in the Sasan and Maṯṯaî hypogeum, Ḥalî and ʿOggâ (perhaps husband and wife) were both buried in section 9, while ʿOggâ's children were buried close to them in sections 10 to 12.[138] In these instances, close family members were buried right next to one another. While the locations of the portraits in the tombs show no consistent pattern in the distribution of family members and different lineages, in general it can be said that members of the same family appear to be grouped somewhat more closely within the funerary buildings, and only in the sections they owned.

Conclusion

The evidence from Palmyrene in situ contexts sheds only a dim light on the organisation of families within the funerary buildings. However, from the better preserved material it is clear that a range of different burial patterns were followed within the tombs and that different marriage strategies could be practised. Sons, or men, tend to be buried in their paternal family tombs, whereas women could be buried in the family tombs of their husbands - marrying into the family, but not bringing their own family with them. However, most of the women, not recorded as married, are buried in the family tombs belonging to their fathers. This can partly be ascribed to intermarriage between relatives. In these three tombs, it can be observed that intermarriage was often limited to a small number of families who came to share the tomb over time, so that these lineages would become the genealogy for the entire tomb. The present study has focused on individuals represented through portraiture; however, it is also evident that additional individuals could be referred to in the epigraphy, with husbands or wives represented through their names only. This tendency displays the importance of recording descent, and wives could refer to their husbands epigraphically even if they were not buried in the same tomb. From the evidence it thus appears that the organisation of families within funerary buildings was, unsurprisingly, to a great extent controlled by the paternal line, and partly by controlled intermarriage between families, which united them in the tombs and thus also controlled access to these.

Catalogue

Part I: Hypogeum of the Sasan and Maṯṯaî families, south-east

The Maṯṯaî branch

1. Database number: PM189
Loculus bust relief depicting Berenike and Malkû
Date: 80-120 CE (Sadurska and Bounni 1994)
References: Colledge 1976, 258; Sadurska 1983, 153, fig. 2; 1995, 585-586, fig. 7; Tanabe 1986, 399, pl. 368; Parlasca 1988, 219-220, n.41; Saliby 1992, 280, no. 37, taf. 54a; Piersimoni 1994, 311-312, no. 42; Sadurska and Bounni 1994, 62, cat. no. 80, fig. 20; al-As'ad and Gawlikowski 1997, 42-43, no. 56, fig. 56; Heyn 2010, app. 3, cat. nos. 22a-22b; Krag 2018, 169, cat. no. 24.
Inscription: PAT 1047
Between their heads: ḤBL | MLKW BR | MṬY | Wʾ BRNYQ | BRT RBʾL | ʾTT<H> ḤBL; Alas | Malkû son of | Maṯṯaî | and Berenike| daughter of Rabbel | [his] wife alas

2. Database number: PM169
Loculus bust relief depicting Aqamat
Date: 80-120 CE (Sadurska and Bounni 1994)
References: Saliby 1992, 279, no. 33, taf. 53a; Sadurska and

134. See Sadurska and Bounni 1994, 70-90. See also al-As'ad and Taha 1968.
135. See Sadurska and Bounni 1994, 23-40, 41-69. See also Saliby 1992.
136. Nabî, cat. no. 6; Sasan, cat. no. 10; Sasan's son, cat. no. 11.
137. Sadurska and Bounni 1994, 190-191; Finlayson 2008, 117, 125, n.77 (Finlayson uses examples from tombs); Heyn 2010, 639-640.
138. Ḥalî, cat. no. 15; ʿOggâ, cat. no. 14; children, cat. nos. 20-23.

Bounni 1994, 60, cat. no. 76, fig. 131; Krag 2018, 168, cat. no. 19.
Inscription: PAT 1043
On her left: ʾQMT | BRT BRWQ[ʾ] | BR TYMŠʾ | ʾTT BLŠWRY | BR MṬY RBʾ | ḤBL; Aqamat | daughter of Barûq[â] | son of Taîmshâ | wife of Belshûrî | son of Maṭṭaî the elder | alas

3. Database number: PM172
Loculus bust relief depicting Amatâ
Date: 100-130 CE (Sadurska and Bounni 1994)
References: Saliby 1992, 278, no. 30, taf. 52b; Sadurska and Bounni 1994, 58-59, cat. no. 73, fig. 146; Zenoni 2010, 49, fig. 7; Krag 2018, 192, cat. no. 94.
Inscription: PAT 1040
On her left: ḤBL | ʾMTʾ | BRT | MLKW | ʾTT | BLŠWRY | BR SSN; Alas | Amatâ | daughter of | Malkû | wife of | Belshûrî | son of Sasan

4. Database number: PM171
Loculus bust relief depicting Shalmat
Date: 100-130 CE (Sadurska and Bounni 1994)
References: Saliby 1992, 179, no. 34, taf. 53b; Sadurska and Bounni 1994, 60-61, cat. no. 77, fig. 145; Krag 2018, 182, cat. no. 62.
Inscription: PAT 1044
On her right: ḤBL | ŠLMT | BRT | MLK[W] | MṬY | ḤBL; Alas | Shalmat | daughter of | Malkû (son of) | Maṭṭaî | alas
On her left: ŠLM[T] | ʾTT | TYMʿ|MD | BR | ZBYDʾ; Shalma[t] | wife of | Taîmʿamed | son of | Zebîdâ

5. Database number: PM166
Loculus bust relief depicting Aqmê
Date: 100-120 CE (Sadurska and Bounni 1994).
References: Saliby 1992, 278, no. 31, taf. 52c; Sadurska and Bounni 1994, 59, cat. no. 74, fig. 144; Krag 2018, 180, cat. no. 56.
Inscription: PAT 1041
On her right: ḤBL | ʾQMʾ |BRT | SYGʾ; Alas | Aqmê | daughter of | Sîgâ
On her left: BRT | BLŠ|WRY; Daughter of | Belsh|ûrî

6. Database number: PM168
Loculus bust relief depicting Nabî
Date: 110-130 CE (Sadurska and Bounni 1994)
References: Saliby 1992, 270-271, no. 5, taf. 46a; Sadurska and Bounni 1994, 46-47, cat. no. 48, fig. 147; Krag 2018, 182, cat. no. 65.
Inscription: PAT 1018
On her left: NBY | BRT | BLŠWRY | ḤBL; Nabî | daughter of | Belshûrî | alas

7. Database number: PM147
Loculus stele depicting Malkû
Date: 120-140 CE (Sadurska and Bounni 1994)
References: Saliby 1992, 279-280, no. 35, taf. 53d; Sadurska and Bounni 1994, 61, cat. no. 78, fig. 10.
Inscription: PAT 1045
On his left: MLKW BR | TYMʿMD | ḤBL; Malkû son of | Taîmʿamed | alas

8. Database number: PM149
Loculus stele depicting Zebîdâ
Date: 120-140 CE (Sadurska and Bounni 1994)
References: Saliby 1992, 280, no. 38, taf. 54b; Sadurska and Bounni 1994, 62-63, cat. no. 81, fig. 9.
Inscription: PAT 1048
On his left: ZBYDʾ | BR TY MʿM | DW ZBY | Dʾ | ḤBL; Zebîdâ | son of Taî|mʿamed (son of) Zebî|dâ | alas

9. Database number: PM148
Loculus stele depicting Barûqâ
Date: 110-130 CE (Sadurska and Bounni 1994)
References: Saliby 1992, 280, no. 36, taf. 53d; Sadurska and Bounni 1994, 61-62, cat. no. 79, fig. 8.
Inscription: PAT 1046
On his left: ḤBL | BRWQʾ | BR | MṬY BR | BLŠ | WRY; Alas | Barûqâ | son of | Maṭṭaî son of | Belsh|ûrî

The Sasan branch

10. Database number: PM175
Loculus bust relief depicting Sasan
Date: 140-160 CE (Sadurska and Bounni 1994)
References: Saliby 1992, 271, no. 6, taf. 46b; Sadurska and Bounni 1994, 47, cat. no. 49, fig. 60.
Inscription: PAT 1019
On his left: ḤBL | SSN | BR | MLʾ | RBʾ; Alas | Sasan | son of | Malê | Rabbâ

11. Database number: PM181
Loculus bust relief depicting M…
Date: 150-200 CE (Sadurska and Bounni 1994)
References: Saliby 1992, 270, no. 4, taf. 45d; Sadurska and Bounni 1994, 46, cat. no. 47, fig. 69.
Inscription: PAT 1017
On his right: ḤB[L] | M[…] | BR […] | S[SN]; Ala[s] | M[…] | son of […] | S[asan]

12. Database number: PM188
Loculus bust relief depicting Shamâ standing behind the shoulder of her mother Amatâ
Date: 140–160 CE (Sadurska and Bounni 1994)
References: Colledge 1976, 259; Tanabe 1986, 371, pl. 340; Saliby 1992, 274, no. 23, taf. 50c; Piersimoni 1994, 308–309, no. 30; Sadurska and Bounni 1994, 55, cat. no. 66, fig. 170; al-As'ad and Gawlikowski 1997, 44, no. 59, fig. 59; al-As'ad and Yon 2001, 40, no. 7; Heyn 2010, app. 4, cat. no. 42; Krag and Raja 2016, 160–161, cat. no. 11 ; Krag 2018, 228, cat. no. 231.
Inscription: PAT 1034
On her left: ḤBL | ʾMTʾ | BRT | SSN | ŠMʾ | BRTH; Alas | Amatâ | daughter of | Sasan | Shamâ | her daughter

13. Database number: PM164
Loculus bust relief depicting Yarḥaî and his father Yarḥibôlâ
Date: 140–160 CE (Sadurska and Bounni 1994)
References: Tanabe 1986, 326, pl. 295; Saliby 1992, 272, no. 14, taf. 48b; Piersimoni 1994, 302–304, no. 10; Sadurska and Bounni 1994, 50–51, cat. no. 57, fig. 53; Sadurska 1995, 584, fig. 3; al-As'ad and Gawlikowski 1997, 37, no. 46, fig. 46.
Inscription: PAT 1026
Between their heads: ḤBL | YRḤY | BRH; Alas | Yarḥaî | his son
On the left: ḤBL | YRḤBWLʾ | BR SSN; Alas | Yarḥibôlâ | son of Sasan

14. Database number: PM177
Loculus bust relief depicting ʿOggâ
Date: 140–160 CE (Sadurska and Bounni 1994)
References: Gawlikowski 1987, 296–297, fig. 16; Parlasca 1987b, 280, cat. no. 16; Saliby 1992, 271–272, no. 11, taf. 47c; Sadurska and Bounni 1994, 49, cat. no. 54, fig. 52.
Inscription: PAT 1023
On his right: ḤBL | ʿGʾ | BR SSN | BR MLʾ; Alas | ʿOggâ | son of Sasan | son of Malê

15. Database number: PM167
Loculus bust relief depicting Ḥalî
Date: 140–160 CE (Sadurska and Bounni 1994)
References: Saliby 1992, 272, no. 12, taf. 47d; Sadurska and Bounni 1994, 49–50, cat. no. 55, fig. 168; Krag 2018, 228, cat. no. 230.
Inscription: PAT 1024
On her left: ḤBL | ḤLY | BRT | YMLʾ; Alas | Ḥalî | daughter of | Yamlâ

16. Database number: PM179
Loculus bust relief depicting Barûqâ
Date: 120–140 CE (Sadurska and Bounni 1994)
References: Saliby 1992, 274, no. 24, taf. 50d; Sadurska and Bounni 1994, 55, cat. no. 67, fig. 24.
Inscription: PAT 1035
On his right: BRWQʾ | BR ʿGʾ | BR MLʾ | ḤBL; Barûqâ | son of ʿOggâ | son of Malê | alas

17. Database number: PM192
Loculus bust relief depicting Nabî
Date: 140–160 CE (Sadurska and Bounni 1994)
References: Saliby 1992, 274, no. 22, taf. 50b; Sadurska and Bounni 1994, 54–55. cat. no. 65, fig. 169; Krag 2018, 228, cat. no. 232
Inscription: PAT 1033
On her left: NBY | BRT | YRḤBWLʾ | ḤBL; Nabî | daughter of | Yarḥibôlâ | alas

18. Database number: PM158
Loculus bust relief depicting Sasan
Date: 160–190 CE (Sadurska and Bounni 1994)
References: Tanabe 1986, 331, pl. 300; Saliby 1992, 273–274, no. 21, taf. 50a; Piersimoni 1994, 302–304, no. 15; Sadurska and Bounni 1994, 54, cat. no. 64, fig. 101; al-As'ad and Gawlikowski 1997, 41, no. 53, fig. 53; Albertson 2000, 166, n.31.
Inscription: PAT 1032
On his left: SSN | BR | YRḤBWLʾ | ḤBL; Sasan | son of | Yarḥibôlâ | alas

19. Database number: PM174
Loculus bust relief depicting Malê
Date: 140–160 CE (Sadurska and Bounni 1994)
References: Saliby 1992, 271, no. 10, taf. 47b; Sadurska and Bounni 1994, 48–49, cat. no. 53, fig. 51.
Inscription: PAT 1022
On his right: ḤBL | MLʾ | BR | YRḤBWLʾ | SSN; Alas | Malê | son of | Yarḥibôlâ | (son of) Sasan

20. Database number: PM193
Loculus bust relief depicting Malkat
Date: 150–170 CE (Sadurska and Bounni 1994)
References: Saliby 1992, 273, no. 19, taf. 49c; Sadurska and Bounni 1994, 53, cat. no. 62, fig. 164; Krag 2018, 249, cat. no. 307.
Inscription: PAT 1031
On her left: ḤBL | MLKT | BRT ʿGʾ | BR SSN; Alas | Malkat | daughter of ʿOggâ | son of Sasan

21. Database number: PM143
Loculus bust relief depicting Maflûn
Date: 170-190 CE (Sadurska and Bounni 1994)
References: Saliby 1992, 271, no. 6, taf. 48d; Piersimoni 302-304, no. Sadurska and Bounni 1994, 51-52, cat. no. 59, fig. 114.
Inscription: PAT 1028
On his left: MPLWN | BR ʿGʾ | SSN | ḤBL; Maflûn | son of ʿOggâ | (son of) Sasan | alas

22. Database number: PM163
Loculus bust relief depicting Malê
Date: 150-200 CE (Sadurska and Bounni 1994)
References: Tanabe 1986, 327, pl. 296; Saliby 1992, 272-273, no. 15, taf. 48c; Piersimoni 1994, 302-304, no. 11; Sadurska and Bounni 1994, 51, cat. no. 58, fig. 75; al-As'ad and Gawlikowski 1997, 37-38, no. 47, fig. 47.
Inscription: PAT 1047
On this right: ḤBL | MLʾ BR | ʿGʾ BR | SSN; Alas | Malê son of | ʿOggâ son of | Sasan

23. Database number: PM186
Loculus bust relief depicting Nabî
Date: 150-200 CE (Sadurska and Bounni 1994)
References: Saliby 1992, 273, no. 18, taf. 49b; Piersimoni 1994, 308-309, no. 33; Sadurska and Bounni 1994, 52-53, cat. no. 61, fig. 165; al-As'ad and Gawlikowski 1997, 45, no. 62, fig. 62; Krag 2018, 304, cat. no. 509.
Inscription: PAT 1030
On her left: NBY BRT | ʿGʾ SSN | ḤBL; Nabî daughter of | ʿOggâ (son of) Sasan | alas

24. Database number: PM151
Loculus bust relief depicting Zabdâ and Maflûn
Date: 181/182 CE (dated by inscription)
References: Colledge 1976, 249; Tanabe 1986, 401, pl. 370; Saliby 1992, 272, no. 13, taf. 48a; Piersimoni 1994, 311-312, no. 44; Sadurska and Bounni 1994, 50, cat. no. 56, fig. 99; Sadurska 1995, 287, fig. 10; al-As'ad and Gawlikowski 1997, 44, no. 58, fig. 58.
Inscription: PAT 1025
Between their heads: ZBDʾ BR | ZBDBWL | BR SSN ḤBL | MPLWN BR | ZBDBWL BR SSN | ḤBL ŠNT 4.100|+82+10+3; Zabdâ son of | Zabdibôl | son of Sasan alas | Maflûn son of | Zabdibôl son of Sasan | alas year 493 (181/182 CE)

25. Database number: PM165
Loculus bust relief depicting a priest, ʿOggâ
Date: 160-190 CE (Sadurska and Bounni 1994)
References: Saliby 1992, 273, no. 17, taf. 49a; Sadurska and Bounni 1994, 52, cat. no. 60, fig. 87; Heyn 2010, app. 5, cat. no. 34.
Inscription: PAT 1029
On his left: ʿGʾ BR | BLŠWRY | SSN ḤBL; ʿOggâ son of | Belshûrî | (son of) Sasan alas

26. Database number: PM153
Loculus bust relief depicting Barîkaî
Date: 140-160 CE (Sadurska and Bounni 1994)
References: Tanabe 1986, 336, pl. 305; Saliby 1992, 275, no. 25, taf. 51a; Sadurska and Bounni 1994, 56, cat. no. 68, fig. 67; al-As'ad and Gawlikowski 1997, 41, no. 52, fig. 52.
Inscription: PAT 1036
On his left: ḤBL BRYKY | BR BRW[Qʾ]; Alas Barîkaî | son of Barû[qâ]

27. Database number: PM191
Loculus bust relief depicting Zabdîla, Ḥalaphtâ and Zabdâ
Date: 140-170 CE (Sadurska and Bounni 1994)
References: Colledge 1976, 250; Tanabe 1986, 402, pl. 371; Saliby 1992, 275-276, no. 26, taf. 51b; Piersimoni 1994, 311-312, no. 45; Sadurska and Bounni 1994, 56-57, cat. no. 69, fig. 56; Sadurska 1995, 584, fig. 2; al-As'ad and Gawlikowski 1997, 43, no. 57, fig. 57.
Inscription: PAT 1037
On the plinth: ḤBL ZBDʾ ḤLPTʾ; Alas Zabdâ (son of) Ḥalaphtâ
Between their heads, left: ḤBL | ḤLPTʾ | BRWQʾ; Alas | Ḥalaphtâ (son of) | Barûqâ
Between their heads, right: ḤBL | ZBDLʾ | BRWQʾ; Alas | Zabdîlah (son of) | Barûqâ

28. Database number: PM150
Loculus bust relief depicting Malê and Malaftâ
Date: 180-200 CE (Sadurska and Bounni 1994)
References: Colledge 1976, 260-261; Tanabe 1986, 400, pl. 369; Saliby 1992, 278-279, no. 32, taf. 52d; Piersimoni 1994, 311-312, no. 43; Sadurska and Bounni 1994, 59-60, cat. no. 75, fig. 103; Sadurska 1995, 585-586, fig. 8; al-As'ad and Gawlikowski 1997, 42, no. 55, fig. 55; Cussini 2002, 89, fig. 4; Heyn 2010, app. 3, cat. nos. 21a-21b; Krag 2018, 302, cat. no. 506.
Inscription: PAT 1042

Next to the man: ḤBL | ML' BR BRQ' | BR 'G' SSN; Alas | Malê son of Barqê | son of 'Oggâ (son of) Sasan
Next to the woman; ḤBL | MLPT' | BT BRQ' | 'G' | SSN; Alas | Malaftâ | daughter of Barqê | (son of) 'Oggâ | (son of) Sasan

29. Database number: PM162
Loculus bust relief depicting Moqîmû
Date: 170–200 CE (Sadurska and Bounni 1994)
References: Tanabe 1986, 329, pl. 298; Saliby 1992, 276, no. 27, taf. 51c; Piersimoni 1994, 302–304, no. 13; Sadurska and Bounni 1994, 57, cat. no. 70, fig. 102; al-As'ad and Gawlikowski 1997, 38, no. 49, fig. 49; Albertson 2000, 167, n.44.
Inscription: PAT 1038
On his left: MQYMW | BR | 'G' | MQYMW | ḤBL; Moqîmû | son of | 'Oggâ (son of) | Moqîmû | alas

30. Database number: PM185
Loculus bust relief depicting Amatâ
Date: 170–200 CE (Sadurska and Bounni 1994)
References: Colledge 1976, 259; Tanabe 1986, 371, pl. 341; Saliby 1992, 276, no. 28, taf. 51d; Piersimoni 1994, 308-309, no. 31; Sadurska and Bounni 1994, 57-58, cat. no. 71, fig. 184; al-As'ad and Gawlikowski 1997, 44, no. 60, fig. 60; Finlayson 2002–2003, 222, pl. I; Palmieri 2010, 39, fig. 6; Krag 2018, 286, cat. no. 443.
Inscription: PAT 1039
On her left: 'MT' | BRT | MLK'L | MQYMW | ḤBL; Amatä | daughter of | Malakel | (son of) Moqîmû | alas

Part II: Hypogeum of the Bôlḥâ family, south-east

31. Database number: InSitu070
Loculus stele depicting Bôlḥâ together with his sister and their uncle Nebôshûrî
Date: 70–89 CE (Sadurska and Bounni 1994)
References: Ingholt Archive, PS 1372; al-As'ad and Taha 1968, 94, no. 2, pl. III; Gawlikowski 1974, 37–38, no. 77, pl. III; Tanabe 1986, 250, pl. 217; Sadurska and Bounni 1994, 74, cat. no. 96, fig. 2; Sadurska 1995, 583, fig. 1.
Inscription: PAT 1869
On the plinth: NBWŠRY BR NBWŠRY | Nebôshûrî son of Nebôshûrî
Above the boy: ḤBL ḤYRN BLḤ'; Alas Ḥairân (son of) Bôlḥâ
Above the girl: BN NY | BN'; Child of Nîbnâ
Above the girl: BRT | BLḤ' | ḤBL; Daughter of | Bôlḥâ | alas

32. Database number: InSitu065
Loculus bust relief depicting Bôlḥâ
Date: 103/104 CE (dated by inscription)
References: Ingholt Archive, PS 1351; al-As'ad and Taha 1968, 94, no. 4, pl. I; Gawlikowski 1974, 39, no. 79; Tanabe 1986, 232, pl. 199; Sadurska and Bounni 1994, 75, cat. no. 98, fig. 21; Taylor 2001, 211, n.51.
Inscription: PAT 1871
On his right: BWLḤ | BR NBWŠWRY RB' | ḤBL; Bôlḥâ | son of Nebôshûrî the elder | alas
On his left: ŠNT | 15; Year | 15 (AD 103/104)

33. Database number: InSitu072
Loculus bust relief depicting Ba'adiyâ
Date: 110–130 CE (Sadurska and Bounni 1994)
References: al-As'ad and Taha 1968, 95, no. 6, pl. I; Gawlikowski 1974, 39, no. 81; Tanabe 1986, 231, pl. 198; Sadurska and Bounni 1994, 76, cat. no. 100, fig. 143; Krag 2018, 180, cat. no. 57.
Inscription: PAT: 1873
On her right: B'DY' | BRT ḤYRN | ḤŠŠ | 'TT | BWLḤ' | NBWŠWRY | ḤBL; Ba'adiyâ | daughter of Ḥairân | (son of) Ḥashash | wife of | Bôlḥâ | (son of) Nebôshûrî | alas

34. Database number: InSitu061
Loculus bust relief depicting Nîbnâ
Date: 110–140 CE (Sadurska and Bounni 1994)
References: Ingholt Archive, PS 1366; al-As'ad and Taha 1968, 95, no. 5, pl. III; Gawlikowski 1974, 39, no. 80, pl. III; Tanabe 1986, 250, pl. 217; Sadurska and Bounni 1994, 75–76, cat. no. 99, fig. 142; Krag 2018, 183, cat. no. 69.
Inscription: PAT 1872
On her left: ḤBL NYBN' | BRT YDY BR | NBWŠWR DY 'BD | LH BWLḤ' BR | ZBDBWL B'LH; Alas Nîbnâ | daughter of Yaddaî son of | Nesbôshûr it was made | for her by Bôlḥâ son of | Zabdibôl her husband

35. Database number: InSitu032
Loculus bust relief depicting Bôlḥâ
Date: 110–140 CE (Sadurska and Bounni 1994)
References: Ingholt Archive, PS 1353; al-As'ad and Taha 1968, 99, no. 18, pl. VI; Gawlikowski 1974, 43, no. 92; Sadurska and Bounni 1994, 82, cat. no. 112, fig. 27.
Inscription: PAT 1884
On her right: BLḤ' | BR | NBWŠWR | ḤBL; Bôlḥâ | son of | Nebôshûrî

36. Database number: InSitu036
Loculus bust relief depicting Zabdibôl

Date: 110-140 CE (Sadurska and Bounni 1994)
References: Ingholt Archive, PS 1357; al-As'ad and Taha 1968, 96, no. 10, pl. II; Gawlikowski 1974, 40, no. 85; Tanabe 1986, 227, pl. 194; Sadurska and Bounni 1994, 78, cat. no. 104, fig. 26.
Inscription: PAT 1884
On his right: ZBDBWL | BR BWLḤ' | NBWŠWR; Zabdibôl | son of Bôlḥâ | (son of) Nebôshûrî

37. Database number: InSitu033
Loculus bust relief depicting Bôlḥâ
Date: 160/161 CE (dated by inscription)
References: Ingholt Archive, PS 1366; al-As'ad and Taha 1968, 97, no. 13, pl. III; Gawlikowski 1974, 41, no. 88; Tanabe 1986, 238, pl. 205; Sadurska and Bounni 1994, 79, cat. no. 107, fig. 73.
Inscription: PAT 1877
On his left: BWLḤ' BR | ḤWR' NBWŠWR | ḤBL DY 'BD | LH ḤWR' BRH | BŠNT 472; Bôlḥâ son of | Hûrâ (son of) Nebôshûrî | alas, (this) was | made by Hûrâ his son | year 472 (160/161 CE)

38. Database number: InSitu062
Loculus bust relief depicting Nîbnâ
Date: 150-180 CE (Sadurska and Bounni 1994)
References: Ingholt Archive, PS 1369; al-as'ad and Taha 1968, 100-101, no. 24, pl. V; Gawlikowski 1974, 44, no. 97; Sadurska and Bounni 1994, 85, cat. no. 118, fig. 174; Krag 2018, 252, cat. no. 315.
Inscription: PAT 1889
On her left: NYBN' BRT | BLḤ' | BR NBWŠWR | ḤBL; Nîbnâ daughter of | Bôlḥâ | son of Nebôshûr | alas

39. Database number: InSitu060
Relief plaque depicting a sarcophagus. The relief depicts Hermes, Ba'adiyâ, 'Ogeîlû and Yarḥaî
Date: 180-220 CE (Sadurska and Bounni 1994)
References: al-As'ad and Taha 1968, 101-106, no. 29; Gawlikowski 1974, 45-47, no. 102; Tanabe 1986, 226, pl. 193; Sadurska and Bounni 1994, 86-88, cat. no. 120, figs. 234, 236; Audley-Miller 2016, 575, 579-580, fig. 9; Krag 2018, 317, cat. no. 565.
Inscription: PAT 1894
ṢLM HRMS BR ḤRY MLKW WBLḤ' 'ḤWH; Image of Hermes freedman of Malkû and of Bôlḥâ his brother
ṢLMT B'DY' BRT BWLḤ' | NBWŠWR 'TT 'GYLW BR ZBDBWL; Image of Ba'adiyâ daughter of Bôlḥâ | (son of) Nebôshûr wife of 'Ogeîlû son of Zabdibôl
'GYLW | BR MLKW | BR 'GYLW | ḤBL; 'Ogeîlû | son of Malkû | son of 'Ogeîlû | alas
YRḤY BR | MLKW BR | 'GYLW | ḤBL; Yarḥaî son of | Malkû son of | 'Ogeîlû | alas

40. Database number: InSitu075
Relief plaque depicting a sarcophagus. The relief depicts Attâ, Malkû, 'Ogeîlû, Nebô'dâ, 'Ogeîlû, Corbulo, Ba'dâ and Tammê
Date: 180-220 CE (Sadurska and Bounni 1994)
References: al-As'ad and Taha 1968, 101-106, no. 28; Gawlikowski 1974, 45-47, no. 101; Makowski 1985, 102-103, fig. 14; Tanabe 1986, 221-224, pls. 188-191; Sadurska 1994, 15, fig. 9; Sadurska and Bounni 1994, 86-88, cat. no. 120, figs. 231-232; Audley-Miller 2016, 575, 579-580, fig. 7; Krag 2018, 317, cat. no. 566.
Inscription: PAT 1893
ṢLMT 'T' BRT NBWD' | BR MQY 'TT MLKW; Image of Attâ daughter of Nebô'dâ | son of Maqqaî wife of Malkû
ṢLM' DNH DY MLKW BR'GYLW BR ZBDBWL BR BWLḤ' NBWŠWR; This image is that of Malkû son of 'Ogeîlû son of Zabdibôl son of Bôlḥâ (son of) Nebôshûr
ṢLM 'GYLW BR ZBDBWL BR | BWLḤ' NBWŠWR ḤBL; Image of 'Ogeîlû son of Zabdibôl son of | Bôlḥâ (son of) Nebôshûr alas
ṢLM | NBWD' | BR MLKW BR | 'GYLW; Image of | Nebô'dâ | son of Malkû son of | 'Ogeîlû
ṢLM 'GYLW | BR MLKW BR | 'GYLW; Image of 'Ogeîlû | son of Malkû son of | 'Ogeîlû
QRBL' | BR MLKW | BR 'GYLW; Corbulo | son of Malkû | son of 'Ogeîlû
ṢLMT B'D' | BRT MLKW BR | 'GYLW; Image of Ba'dâ | daughter of Malkû | son of 'Ogeîlû
ṢLMT TM' | BRT ḤWR' BR | BWLḤ' ḤBL; Image of Tammê | daughter of Ḥûrâ son of | Bôlḥâ alas

41. Database number: InSitu071
Loculus stele depicting Bôlḥâ
Date: 125-150 CE (Sadurska and Bounni 1994)
References: Ingholt Archive, PS 1363; al-As'ad and Taha 1968, 94, no. 3, pl. III; Gawlikowski 1974, 38, no. 78; Parlasca 1982, 236, taf. 24,3; Tanabe 1986, 230, pl. 197; Sadurska and Bounni 1994, 74-75, cat. no. 97, fig. 13.
Inscription: PAT 1870
On his left: ḤBL | BWLḤ' | BR | BWLḤ' | BR | BWLḤ'; Alas | Bôlḥâ | son of | Bôlḥâ | son of | Bôlḥâ

42. Database number: InSitu030
Loculus bust relief depicting a man and Lobnâ
Date: 140-170 CE (Sadurska and Bounni 1994)

References: Ingholt Archive, PS 1368; al-As'ad and Taha 1968, 97, no. 11, pl. II; Gawlikowski 1974, 41, no. 86; Tanabe 1986, 228, pl. 195; Sadurska and Bounni 1994, 78-79, cat. no. 105, fig. 163; Krag and Raja 2016, 161, cat. no. 12; Krag 2018, 265, cat. no. 368.
Inscription: PAT 1878
On her left: LBN' | BRT YRḤY | BLḤ' | ḤBL; Lobnâ | daughter of Yarḥaî | (son of) Bôlḥâ | alas

43. Database number: InSitu024
Loculus bust relief depicting Nebôshûr
Date: 130-150 CE (Sadurska and Bounni 1994)
References: al-As'ad and Taha 1968, 95, no. 7, pl. II; Gawlikowski 1974, 40, no. 82; Tanabe 1986, 233, pl. 200; Sadurska and Bounni 1994, 76-77, cat. no. 101, fig. 40.
Inscription: PAT 1874
On his right: NBWŠWR | BR YRḤY | BR BWLḤ | ḤBL; Neboshûr | son of Yarḥaî | son of Bôlḥâ | alas

44. Database number: InSitu026
Loculus bust relief depicting 'Ogeîlû
Date: 170-190 CE (Sadurska and Bounni 1994)
References: Ingholt Archive, PS 1355; al-As'ad and Taha 1968, 100, no. 23, pl. VII; Gawlikowski 1974, 44, no. 96; Tanabe 1986, 246, pl. 213; Sadurska and Bounni 1994, 84-85, cat. no. 117, fig. 105
Inscription: PAT 1888
On his left: ḤBL 'GYLW | BR ZBDBWL | BY MTQR' QRBL' | BR NBWŠWRY; Alas 'Ogeîlû | son of Zabdibôl | who is named | Corbulo | son of Nebôshûrî

45. Database number: InSitu027
Loculus bust relief depicting 'Ogeîlû and together with his cousin 'Ogeîlû
Date: 170-200 CE (Sadurska and Bounni 1994)
References: Ingholt Archive, PS 1356; al-As'ad and Taha 1968, 100, no. 22, pl. VII; Gawlikowski 1974, 43, no. 95; Tanabe 1986, 248, pl. 215; Sadurska and Bounni 1994, 84, cat. no. 116, fig. 104.
Inscription: PAT 1887
On the right: ṢLM | 'GYLW | BR | QRBL' | 'GYLW ḤBL; Image of | 'Ogeîlû | son of | Corbulo (son of) | 'Ogeîlû
On the left: ṢLM | 'GYLW | BR | MLKW | 'GYLW | ḤBL; Image of | 'Ogeîlû | son of Malkû (son of) | 'Ogeîlû | alas

46. Database number: InSitu073
Loculus stele depicting Yarḥaî together with brother Corbulo
Date: 170-200 CE (Sadurska and Bounni 1994)
References: Ingholt Archive, PS 1373; al-As'ad and Taha 1968, 101, no. 6, pll. VII; Gawlikowski 1974, 44-45, no. 99, pl. IV; Tanabe 1986, 247, pl. 214; Sadurska and Bounni 1994, 85-86, cat. no. 119, fig. 19; Albertson 2000, 162, n.17.
Inscription: PAT 1891
On his right: YRḤY | BR MLKW | 'GYLW | ḤBL; Yarḥaî | son of Malkû | (son of) 'Ogeîlû | alas
On the pedestal: QRBL' BR | MLKW 'GYLW | ḤBL; Corbulo son of | Malkû (son of) 'Ogeîlû | alas

47. Database number: InSitu034
Loculus bust relief depicting a priest, Bar'ateh
Date: 170-200 CE (Sadurska and Bounni 1994)
References: Ingholt Archive, PS 1365; al-As'ad and Taha 1968, 99-100, no. 20, pl. VI; Gawlikowski 1974, 43, no. 94; Tanabe 1986, 246, pl. 213; Sadurska and Bounni 1994, 83, cat. no. 114, fig. 94.
Inscription: PAT 1886
On his left: BR'TH | BR BWLḤ' | 'G[W]<Y>LW | NBWŠWR | ḤBL; Bar'ateh | son of Bôlḥâ | (son of) 'Ogeîlû | (son of) Nebôshûrî | alas

48. Database number: InSitu074
Sarcophagus depicting 'Ogeîlû, Nebôshûr, Aqmê, Aqmê, and Haggâ
Date: 200-230 CE (Sadurska and Bounni 1994)
References: Ingholt Archive, PS 1374; al-As'ad and Taha 1968, 106-108, no. 30; Tanabe 1986, 242-245, pls. 209-212; Gawlikowski 1974, 47-48, no. 103; Sadurska and Bounni 1994, 89-90, cat. no. 121, fig. 246; Audley-Miller 2016, 575, 577, fig. 10; Krag 2018, 390-391, cat. no. 843.
Inscription: PAT 1895
ṢLM 'GYLW BR | 'GYLW BR 'GYLW | DY 'B<D> LH NBWŠWR | BRH BTR MWTH | ŠNYN ŠTYN; Image of 'Ogeîlû son of | 'Ogeîlû son of 'Ogeîlû | who made (this) for him Nebôshûr | his son after his death | at the age of 60
ṢLM NBWŠWR | BR 'GYLW BR | 'GYLW; Image of Nebôshûr | son of 'Ogeîlû son of | 'Ogeîlû
ṢLM 'QM' | BT BR'TH; Image of Aqmê | daughter of Bar'ath
ṢLMT 'QM' BT | 'G' 'GML | 'MH DY | NBWŠWR; Image of Aqmê daughter of | 'Oggâ (son of) Aqqamal | mother of | Nebôshûr
ṢLMT HG' | BT 'GYLW; Image of Haggâ | daughter of 'Ogeîlû

49. Database number: InSitu067
Loculus stele depicting ʿOgeîlû
Date: 160–180 CE (Sadurska and Bounni 1994)
References: Ingholt Archive, PS 1364; al-As'ad and Taha 1968, 98, no. 15, pl. III; Gawlikowski 1974, 42, no. 90, pl. IV; Tanabe 1986, 241, pl. 208; Sadurska and Bounni 1994, 80–81, cat. no. 109, fig. 16.
Inscription: PAT 1882
On his left: ḤBL ʿGYLW | BR ḤWRʾ BR | BWLḤʾ | NBWŠWRY; Alas ʿOgeîlû | son of Ḥûrâ son of | Bôlḥâ | (son of) Nebôshûrî

50. Database number: InSitu038
Loculus bust relief depicting Bôlḥâ
Date: 170–200 CE (Sadurska and Bounni 1994)
References: Ingholt Archive, PS 1359; al-As'ad and Taha 1968, 97–98, no. 14, pl. III; Gawlikowski 1974, 41, no. 89; Tanabe 1986, 240, pl. 207; Sadurska and Bounni 1994, 80, cat. no. 108, fig. 106; Albertson 2000, 166, n.31.
Inscription: PAT 1881
On his left: BWLḤʾ | BR | ḤWRʾ | ḤBL; Bôlḥâ | son of | Ḥûrâ | alas

51. Database number: InSitu069
Loculus stele depicting ʿOggâ
Date: 140–170 CE
References: Ingholt Archive, PS 1372; al-As'ad and Taha 1968, 93, no. 1, pl. III; Gawlikowski 1974, 37, no. 76, pl. III; Tanabe 1986, 250, pl. 217; Sadurska and Bounni 1994, 73–74, cat. no. 95, fig. 15.
Inscription: PAT 1868
On this right: ḤBL ʿG[ʾ] | BR ḤWRʾ | BR BWLḤʾ | NBWŠWRY; Alas ʿOgg[â] | son of Ḥûrâ | son of Bôlḥâ | (son of) Nebôshûrî

52. Database number: InSitu076
Relief plaque depicting a sarcophagus. The relief depicts Bôlḥâ, Zabdibôl and ʿOgeîlû
Date: 180–220 CE (Sadurska and Bounni 1994)
References: al-As'ad and Taha 1968, 101–106, no. 27; Gawlikowski 1974, 45–47, no. 100; Tanabe 1986, 225, fig. 192; Sadurska and Bounni 1994, 86–88, cat. no. 120, fig. 235.
Inscription: PAT 1892
ṢLM BWLḤʾ BR ʿGYLW BR ZBDBWL | NBWŠWR ḤBL; Image of Bôlḥâ son of ʿOgeîlû son of Zabdibôl | (son of) Nebôshûr alas
ṢLM ZBDBWL Q̮RBLʾ BR ʿGYLW | BR ZBDBWL NBWŠWRY ḤBL; Image of Zabdibôl Corbulo son of ʿOgeîlû son of | Zabdibôl Nebôshûrî alas
ʿGYLW | BR ZBDBWL | Q̮RBLʾ | ḤBL; ʿOgeîlû | son of Zabidbôl | Corbulo | alas

53. Database number: InSitu063
Loculus bust relief depicting Ḥairân
Date: 200–230 CE (Sadurska and Bounni 1994)
References: Ingholt Archive, PS 1362; al-As'ad and Taha 1968, 97, no. 12, pl. III; Gawlikowski 1974, 41, no. 87, pl. III; Tanabe 1986, 221, pl. 188; Sadurska and Bounni 1994, 79, cat. no. 106, fig. 127.
Inscription: PAT 1879
On his left: ḤYRN BR | BWLḤʾ | NBWŠWRY | ḤBL; Ḥairân son of | Bôlḥâ | (son of) Nebôshûrî

Part III: Hypogeum of the Artaban family, south-east

54. Database numbers: InSitu086 and InSitu087
Relief depicting Yarḥaî, Artban and ʿOggâ; Relief plaque depicting a sarcophagus. The relief depicts Berretâ, ʿOggâ, Artaban, Berretâ, Artaban, Mertabû and Artaban
Date: 100–150 CE (Sadurska and Bounni 1994)
References: Tanabe 1986, 262–265, pls. 229–232; Parlasca 1987b, 279–281, abb. 3; 1995, 67–68, fig. 10; Sadurska 1994, 15, fig. 8; Sadurska and Bounni 1994, 37–39, cat. no. 41, figs. 222–224; Heyn 2010, 641, fig. 8; Krag 2018, 244, cat. no. 289.
Inscription: PAT 2664–2673
Loculus bust relief: ḤBL | YRḤY | BR ʾRṬBN | BR ʿGʾ; Alas | Yarḥaî | son of Artaban | son of ʿOggâ
ḤBL | ʾRṬBN BR | YRḤY BRH; Alas | Artaban son of | Yarḥaî his son
ḤBL ʿGʾ | BR YRḤY | ʾRṬBN BRH; Alas ʿOggâ | son of Yarḥaî | (son of) Artaban his son
Banqueting scene: ʿGʾ BR ʾRṬBN BR | ʿGʾ ḤBL DY LʾBWHY | WLʾḤWHY ʿL ḤYWHY; ʿOggâ son of Artaban son of | ʿOggâ alas (he made) this for his father | and for his brother in his lifetime
BRTʾ BRT | YRḤY BRʾ | ʾTTH; Berretâ daughter of | Yarḥaî (son of) Barâ | his wife
ʾRṬBN BR | YRḤY BRʾ; Artaban son of Yarḥaî | (son of) Barâ
BRTʾ BRT | ʿGʾ BR[T]H; Berretâ daughter of | ʿOggâ his daughter
ʾRTBN BR | ʿGʾ BRH; Artaban son of | ʿOggâ his son
On box:
ḤRTBW BRT | BRʾ ʾMH; Mertabû daughter of | Barâ his mother
[ʾRT]BN BR | [ʿGʾ ʾ]BWHY; [Arta]ban son of | [ʿOggâ] his father

55. Database number: InSitu020
Loculus bust relief depicting Artaban Zabdûn
Date: 110–140 CE (Sadurska and Bounni 1994)
References: Tanabe 1986, 268, pl. 235; Sadurska 1994, 21, fig. 15; Sadurska and Bounni 1994, 27, cat. no. 21, fig. 32; Albertson 2000, 164, n.21.
Inscription: PAT 2644
On his right: ʾRṬBN DY | MTQRʾ ZBDWN | BR MLKW BR YRḤY | NYQʾ ʾPKLʿ ṬBʾ | DY ʿGLBWL WMLKBL; Artaban who | is named Zabdûn | son of Malkû son of Yarḥai | (son of) Nîdâ the good priest | of Aglibol and Malakbel

56. Database number: InSitu023
Loculus bust relief depicting Baʿaltagâ
Date: 100–130 CE (Sadurska and Bounni 1994)
References: Tanabe 1986, 267, pl. 234; Sadurska 1994, 18, fig. 11; Sadurska and Bounni 1994, 27–28, cat. no. 22, fig. 151; Krag 2018, 206, cat. no. 145.
Inscription: PAT 2645
On her right: ḤBL BʿLTGʾ | BRT ʿGʾ BR | NṢRʾ ḤBL; Alas Baʿaltagâ | daughter of ʿOggâ son of | Naṣrâ alas

57. Database number: InSitu084
Loculus bust relief depicting Berretâ
Date: 100–130 CE (Sadurska and Bounni 1994)
References: Tanabe 1986, 366, pl. 233; Sadurska 1994, 16, fig. 2; Sadurska and Bounni 1994, 33, cat. no. 33, fig. 136; Krag 2018, 181, cat. no. 59.
Inscription: PAT 2656
On her right: BRTʾ | ʿGʾ NṢRY; Berretâ | (daughter of) ʿOggâ (son of) Naṣraî

58. Database number: InSitu081
Loculus bust relief depicting Martâ
Date: 130–150 CE (Sadurska and Bounni 1994)
References: Sadurska and Bounni 1994, 31–32, cat. no. 30, fig. 152; Krag 2018, 198, cat. no. 114.
Inscription: PAT 2653
On her left: MRTʾ | ʾRṬBN | ḤBL; Martâ (daughter of) | Artaban | alas

59. Database number: InSitu083
Loculus bust relief depicting Shalmat
Date: 100–130 CE (Sadurska and Bounni 1994)
References: Tanabe 1986, 266, pl. 233; Sadurska and Bounni 1994, 33, cat. no. 32, fig. 135; Krag 2018, 181, cat. no. 58.
Inscription: PAT 2655
On her right: ŠLMT BRT | ŠMŠGRM BR | BLʿQB ʾḤYB; Shalmat daughter of | Shamshigeram son of | Belʿaqab (son of) Ahiba

60. Database number: InSitu019
Loculus bust relief depicting a priest, Shalamallat
Date: 150–200 CE (Sadurska and Bounni 1994)
References: Sadurska and Bounni 1994, 28–29, cat. no. 23, fig. 70; Heyn 2010, app. 5, cat. no. 28.
Inscription: PAT 2646
On this right: ṢLMʾ DH DY ŠLMLT | BR ʿGʾ MLKW | DY ʿBD LH ! | ŠLMLT BR | ʿBDLT! (?) BTR | DY MYT LYQRH; This image (is) of Shalamallat | son of ʿOggâ (son of) Malkû | who (made this) ʿAbdelâ (son of) | Shalamallat son of | ʿAbdelâ after | (his) death in his honour

61. Database number: InSitu082
Loculus bust relief depicting Berretâ and her daughter Martâ
Date: 100–130 CE (Sadurska and Bounni 1994)
References: Sadurska and Bounni 1994, 32, cat. no. 31, fig. 134; Heyn 2010, app. 1, cat. no. 10, app. 4, cat. no. 35; Krag and Raja 2016, 159, cat. no. 2; Krag 2018, 189, cat. no. 54.
Inscription: PAT 2654
On her left: ḤBL | BRTʾ | BRT YRḤY | MRTʾ | BRTH | ḤBL; Alas | Berretâ | daughter of Yarḥaî | Martâ | her daughter | alas

62. Database number: InSitu001
Loculus bust relief depicting Yaddaî
Date: 130–160 CE (Sadurska and Bounni 1994)
References: Sadurska and Bounni 1994, 35–36, cat. no. 38, fig. 30.
Inscription: PAT 2661
On his right: ḤBL YDY | BR MRTʾ; Alas Yaddaî | son of Martâ

63. Database number: InSitu010
Loculus bust relief depicting Shamshigeram
Date: 120–150 CE (Sadurska and Bounni 1994)
References: Tanabe 1986, 267, pl. 234; Sadurska and Bounni 1994, 26–27, cat. no. 20, fig. 29.
Inscription: PAT 2643
On his left: ŠMŠGRM BR | ʿGʾ BR ʾRṬBN | ḤBL; Shamshigeram son of | ʿOggâ son of Artaban | alas

64. Database number: InSitu015
Loculus bust relief depicting Malkû
Date: 140–170 CE (Sadurska and Bounni 1994)

References: Sadurska 1994, 20, fig. 12; Sadurska and Bounni 1994, 30, cat. no. 27, fig. 71.
Inscription: PAT 2650
On his right: ḤBL | MLKW | BR ʿGʾ | ʾRṬBN; Alas | Malkû | son of ʿOggâ | (son of) Artaban

65. Database number: InSitu018
Loculus bust relief depicting Habîbîôn
Date: 150–170 CE (Sadurska and Bounni 1994)
References: Sadurska and Bounni 1994, 29, cat. no. 24, fig. 59; Yon 2012, 398, no. 532.
Inscription: PAT 2647; Yon 2012, no. 532
On his left: ḤBYBYWN DY | MTQRʾ | NṢRY BR | MLKW | ʾRTBN | ḤBL; Ḥabîbîôn who | is named | Naṣraî son of | Malkû | (son of) Artaban | alas
On his right: Αβειβιωνα | τὸν καὶ Νασ|ραιον Μαλ|χου τοῦ | Αρταβανου | μνήμης | χάριν; Abibiôn | called Nas|raios (son of) Mal|chos | (son of) Artabanos | in his memory

66. Database number: InSitu123
Loculus bust relief depicting Kamnîn
Date: 160–190 CE (Sadurska and Bounni 1994)
References: Sadurska and Bounni 1994, 30–31, cat. no. 28, fig. 175; Yon 2002, 262; 2012, 399, no. 533; Krag 2018, 275, cat. no. 404.
Inscription: PAT 2651; Yon 2012 , no. 533
On her left: ḤBL KMNYN BRT MLKW | ʾRṬBN ʾTTH NṢR; Alas Kamnîn daughter of Malkû | (son of) Artaban wife of Naṣrâ
On the her right: [...] Καμνυνα | Μαλιχου | Αρταβανου [σύμβιος] Νασρ | δκ´;; [...] Kamnya | daughter of Malichos son of | Artabanos [wife of] Nasr | [...] 24 (years?)

67. Database number: InSitu021
Loculus bust relief depicting a priest, Yaddaî
Date: 150–200 CE (Sadurska and Bounni 1994)
References: Tanabe 1986, 269, pl. 236; Sadurska and Bounni 1994, 26, cat. no. 19, fig. 83; Heyn 2010, app. 5, cat. no. 27.
Inscription: PAT 2642
On his left: ḤBL YDY | BR NṢR | BR YDY; Alas Yaddaî | son of Naṣrâ | son of Yaddaî

68. Database number: InSitu022
Loculus bust relief depicting ..., daughter of Nasrai
Date: 200–220 CE (Sadurska and Bounni 1994)
References: Sadurska and Bounni 1994, 34–35, cat. no. 36, fig. 178; Krag 2018, 325, cat. no. 596.
Inscription: PAT 2659
On her left: [...] | [...]NṢRY | [...] | [...] | ḤBL; [...] | (daughter of) Nasrai | [...] | [...] | alas

Abbreviations

PAT D. R. Hillers and E. Cussini 1996, *Palmyrene Aramaic Texts,* Baltimore.

Bibliography

Abdul-Hak, S. 1952, L'Hypogée de Taai à Palmyre, *AAS* 2, 1–2, 193–251.

Abousamra, G. 2015, Palmyrene Inscriptions on Seven Reliefs, *Semitica* 57, 217–242.

Albertson, F. C. 2000, Three Palmyrene reliefs in the Colket collection, University of Wyoming, *Syria* 77, 159–168.

Arnold, W. R. 1905, Additional Palmyrene Inscriptions in the Metropolitan Museum of Art, New York, *JAOS* 26, 105–112.

al-As'ad, K. and M. Gawlikowski 1997, *The Inscriptions in the Museum of Palmyra: a catalogue,* Palmyra and Warsaw.

al-As'ad, K. and O. Taha 1968, Madfan Bûlhâ al-Tadmurî (The Tomb of Bôlḥâ), *AAS* 18, 83–108.

al-As'ad, K. and O. Taha 1965, Madfan Zabd-ʿAtah al-Tadmurî (The Tomb of Zabdʿateh), *AAS* 15, 29–46.

al-As'ad, K. and J.-B. Yon 2001, *Inscriptions de Palmyre: promenades épigraphiques dans la ville antique de Palmyre,* Beirut, Damascus and Amman.

al-As'ad, W. 2013, Some tombs recently excavated in Palmyra, *Studia Palmyreńskie* 12, 15–24.

Audley-Miller, L. 2016, The Banquet in Palmyrene Funerary Contexts, in C. M. Draycott and M. Stamatopoulou (eds.), *Dining and Death: Interdiciplinary Perspectives on the 'Funerary Banquet' in Ancient Art, Burial and Belief,* Leuven, Paris and Bristol, 553–590.

Bounni, A. 1961–1962, Inscriptions palmyréniennes inédites, *AAS* 11–12, 145–162.

Bounni, A. and N. Saliby 1957, Madfan šalam allât (The Tomb of Shalamallat), *AAS* 7, 25–52.

Cantineau, J. 1929, Fouilles à Palmyre, *Mélanges de l'Institut Français de Damas* 1, 1–15.

Chabot, J.-B. 1922, *Choix d'inscriptions de Palmyre,* Paris.

Chamay, J. and J.-L. Maier 1989, *Art romain. Sculptures en pierre du Musée de Genève. Tome II,* Mainz am Rhein.

Colledge, M. A. R. 1976, *The Art of Palmyra,* London.

Cussini, E. 2005, Beyond the Spindle: Investigating the Role of Palmyrene Women, in E. Cussini (ed.), *A Journey to Palmyra. Collected Essays to Remember Delbert R. Hillers,* Leiden and Boston, 26–43.

Cussini, E. 2000, Palmyrene Eunuchs? Two Cases of Mistaken Identity, in E. Rova (ed.), *Patavina orientalia selecta*, Padova, 279–290.

Cussini, E. 1995, Transfer of Property at Palmyra, *ARAM periodicals* 7, 233–250.

Dentzer-Feydy, J. and J. Teixidor 1993, *Les antiquités de Palmyre au Musée du Louvre,* Paris.

Deonna, W. 1923, Monuments orientaux du Musée de Genève, *Syria* 4, 3, 224–233.

Dunant, C. and R. A. Stucky 2000, *Le sanctuaire de Baalshamîn à Palmyre: The Sculpturesm Bibliotheca Helvetica Romana. Le Sanctuaire de Baalshamîn à Palmyre, Mission archéologique Suisse en Syrie, 1954-1966, vol. IV,* Rome.

Finlayson, C. S. 2008, *Mut'a* Marriage in the Roman Near East: The Evidence from Palmyra, Syria, in B. A. Nakhai (ed.), *The World of Women in the Ancient and Classical Near East,* Newcastle-upon-Tyne, 99–138.

Finlayson, C. S. 2002–2003, Veil, Turban and Headpiece: Funerary Portraits and Female Status at Palmyra, *AAS* 45–46, 221–235.

Fortin, M. 1999, *Syrien. Wiege der Kultur,* Mainz am Rhein.

Gawlikowski, M. 2005, The City of the Dead, in E. Cussini (ed.), *A Journey to Palmyra. Collected Essays to Remember Delbert R. Hillers,* Leiden and Boston, 44–73.

Gawlikowski, M. 1987, Objektbeschreibungen, nr. 1–76, in E. M. Ruprechtsberger (ed.), *Palmyra: Geschichte, Kunst und Kultur der syrischen Oasenstadt,* Linz, 287–339.

Gawlikowski, M. 1974, *Recueil d'inscriptions palmyréniennes provenant de fouilles syriennes et polonaises récentes à Palmyre,* Paris.

Gawlikowski, M. 1970, *Monuments funéraires de Palmyre,* Warsaw.

al-Hariri, K. 2013, The tomb of ʿAqraban, *Studia Palmyreńskie* 12, 149–157.

Henning, A. 2013a, *Die Turmgräber von Palmyra. Eine lokale Bauform im kaiserzeitlichen Syrien als Ausdruck kultureller Identität,* Rahden/Westf.

Henning, A. 2013b, The tower tombs of Palmyra: chronology, architecture and decoration, *Studia Palmyreńskie* 12, 159–176.

Heyn, M. K. 2010, Gesture and Identity in the Funerary Art of Palmyra, *AJA* 114, 4, 631–661.

Heyn, M. K. 2008, Sacerdotal Activities and Parthian Dress in Roman Palmyra, in C. S. Colburn and M. K. Heyn (eds.), *Reading a Dynamic Canvas: Adornment in the Ancient Mediterranean World,* Newcastle, 170–193.

Higuchi. T. and T. Izumi (eds.) 1994, *Tombs A and C: Southeast Necropolis, Palmyra, Syria, Surveyed in 1990–92,* Nara.

Higuchi, T. and K. Saito (eds.) 2001, *Tomb F – Tomb of BWLH and BWRP, Southeast Necropolis, Palmyra, Syria,* Nara.

Hillers, D. R. and E. Cussini 1996, *Palmyrene Aramaic Texts,* Baltimore.

Hvidberg-Hansen, F. O. 1998, *The Palmyrene Inscriptions, Ny Carlsberg Glyptotek,* Copenhagen.

Hvidberg-Hansen, F. O. and G. Ploug 1993, *Katalog, Palmyra Samlingen, Ny Carlsberg Glyptotek,* Copenhagen.

Ingholt, H. 1974, Two unpublished Tombs from the Southwest Necropolis of Palmyra, Syria, in D. K. Kouymjian (ed.), *Near Eastern Numismatics, Iconography, Epigraphy and History. Studies in Honor of George C. Miles,* Beirut, 37–54.

Ingholt, H. 1970, The sarcophagus of Beʿelai and other sculptures from the tomb of Malkû, Palmyra, *MélBeyrouth* 45, 173–200.

Ingholt, H. 1966, Some Sculptures from the Tomb of Malkû at Palmyra, in M.-L. Bernhard (ed.), *Mélanges offerts à Kazimierz Michałowski,* Warsaw, 457–476.

Ingholt, H. 1962, Palmyrene Inscriptions from the Tomb of Malkû, *MélBeyrouth* 38, 101–119.

Ingholt, H. 1954, *Palmyrene and Gandharan Sculpture,* Yale.

Ingholt, H. 1938, Inscriptions and Sculptures from Palmyra, II, *Berytus* 5, 93–140.

Ingholt, H. 1936, Inscriptions and Sculptures from Palmyra, I, *Berytus* 3, 83–125.

Ingholt, H. 1935, Five Dated Tombs from Palmyra, *Berytus* 2, 58–120.

Ingholt, H. 1932, Quelques fresques récemment découvertes à Palmyre, *ActaArch* 3, 1–20.

Ingholt, H. 1928, *Studier over Palmyrensk Skulptur,* Copenhagen.

Kraeling, C. H. 1961–1962, Color Photographs of the Paintings in the Tomb of the Three Brothers at Palmyra, *AAS* 11–12, 13–18.

Krag, S. 2018, *Funerary Representations of Palmyrene Women. From the First Century BC to the Third Century AD,* Studies in Classical Archaeology, Turnhout.

Krag, S. 2016, Females in Group Portraits in Palmyra, in A. Kropp and R. Raja (eds.), *The World of Palmyra,* Palmyrene Studies 1, Copenhagen, 180–193.

Krag, S. 2015, The Secrets of the Funerary Buildings in Palmyra during the Roman Period, in E. Mortensen and S. G. Saxkjær (eds.), *Revealing and Concealing in Antiquity. Textual and Archaeological Approaches to Secrecy,* Aarhus, 105–118.

Krag, S. and R. Raja 2019, Unveiling Female Hairstyles: Markers of Age, Social Roles, and Status in the Funerary Sculpture from Palmyra, *Zeitschrift für Orient-Archäologie* 11, 243-277.

Krag, S. and R. Raja 2017, Representations of Women and Children in Palmyrene Banqueting Reliefs and Sarcophagus Scenes, *Zeitschrift für Orient-Archäologie* 10, 196-227.

Krag, S. and R. Raja 2016, Representations of Women and Children in Palmyrene Funerary *Loculus* Reliefs, *Loculus* Stelae and Wall Paintings, *Zeitschrift für Orient-Archäologie* 9, 134–178.

Kropp, A. and R. Raja. 2015, The Palmyra Portrait Project, in Á. Martínez, T. N. Bassarrate and R. de Lianza (eds.), *Proceedings of the XVIIIth International Congress of Classical Archaeology, II: Centre and Periphery,* Mérida, 1223–1226.

Kropp, A., and R. Raja 2014, The Palmyra Portrait Project, *Syria* 91, 393–405.

Makowski, K. C. 1985, La sculpture funéraire palmyrénienne et sa fonction dans l'architecture sépulcrale, *Studia Palmyreńskie* 8, 69–117.

Makowski, K. C. 1983, Recherches sur le tombeau de A'ailamî et Zebîdâ, *DM* 1, 175–187.

Michałowski, K. 1966, *Palmyre. Fouilles polonaises 1963 et 1964,* Warsaw.

Michałowski, K. 1964, *Palmyre. Fouilles polonaises 1962,* Warsaw.

Michałowski, K. 1963, *Palmyre. Fouilles polonaises 1961,* Warsaw.

Michałowski, K. 1962, *Palmyre. Fouilles polonaises 1960,* Warsaw.

Michałowski, K. 1960, *Palmyre. Fouilles polonaises 1959,* Warsaw.

Miyashita, S. 2016, The Vessels in Palmyrene Banquet Scenes: Tomb BWLH and BWRP and Tomb TYBL, in J. C. Meyer, E. H. Seland and N. Anfinset (eds.), *Palmyrena: City, Hinterland and Caravan Trade between Orient and Occident. Proceedings of the Conference held in Athens, December 1–3, 2012,* Oxford, 131–146.

Palmieri, L. 2010, Il lusso privato in Oriente: analisi comparata dei gioielli delle signore di Palmira, *Bollettino di Archaeologia online,* 34–44.

Parlasca, K. 1995, Some Problems of Palmyrene Plastic Art, *ARAM periodicals* 7, 59–71.

Parlasca, K. 1988, Ikonographische Probleme palmyrenischer Grabreliefs, *DM* 3, 215–221.

Parlasca, K. 1987a, Ein antoninischer Frauenkopf aus Palmyra in Malibu, in J. Frel, A. A. Houghton and M. True (eds.), *Ancient Portraits in the J. Paul Getty Museum, Volume I,* Malibu, 107–114.

Parlasca, K. 1987b, Aspekte der palmyrenischen Skulpturen, in E. M. Ruprechtsberger (ed.), *Palmyra: Geschichte, Kunst und Kultur der syrischen Oasenstadt,* Linz, 276–282.

Parlasca, K. 1985, Das Verhältnis der palmyrenischen Grabplastik zur römischen Porträtkunst, *RM* 92, 343–356.

Parlasca, K. 1982, *Syrische Grabreliefs hellenistischer und römischer Zeit. Fundgruppe und Probleme,* Mainz am Rhein.

Piersimoni, P. 1994, New Palmyrene Inscriptions: Onomastics and Prosopography, *Annali di Archeologia e Storia Antica* 53–54, 298–316.

Ploug, G. 1995, *Catalogue of the Palmyrene Sculptures, Ny Carlsberg Glyptotek,* Copenhagen.

Raja, R. 2017. Powerful images of the Deceased: Palmyrene funerary portrait culture between local, Greek and Roman representations, in D. Boschung and F. Queyrel (eds.), *Bilder der Macht. Das griechische Porträt und seine Verwendung in der antiken Welt,* Paderborn, 319–348.

Raja, R. and A. H. Sørensen 2015, The "Beauty of Palmyra" and Qasr Abjad (Palmyra): new discoveries in the archive of Harald Ingholt, *JRA* 28, 1, 439–450.

Sadurska, A. 1995, La famille et son image dans l'art de Palmyre, in F. E. Koenig and S. Rebetez (eds.), *Arculiana. Ioanni Boegli anno sexagesimoQuinto feliciter peracto amici discipuli college socii dona dederunt A.D. XIIII Kalendas Decembris MDCCCCLXXXXV,* Avenches, 583–589.

Sadurska, A. 1994, L'art et la société: recherches iconologiques sur l'art funéraire de Palmyre, *Archeologia-War* 45, 11–23.

Sadurska, A. 1983, Le modèle de la semaine dans l'imagerie palmyrénienne, *ÉtTrav* 12, 24, 151–156.

Sadurska, A. 1977, *Palmyre VII. Le Tombeau de Famille de 'Alainê,* Warsaw.

Sadurska, A. and A. Bounni 1994, *Les sculptures funéraires de Palmyre,* Rome.

Saito, K. 2016, Excavation of No. 129-b House Tomb at the North Necropolis in Palmyra, in J. C. Meyer, E. H. Seland and N. Anfinset (eds.), *Palmyrena: City, Hinterland and Caravan Trade between Orient and Occident. Proceedings of the Conference held in Athens, December 1–3, 2012,* Oxford, 115–130.

Saliby, N. 1992, L'hypogée de Sassan fils de Malê à Palmyre (with a bibliography appendix by Klaus Parlasca), *DM* 6, 267–292.

Schmidt-Colinet, A. 1992, *Das Tempelgrab Nr. 36 in Palmyra. Studien zur palmyrenischen Grabarchitektur und ihrer Ausstattung,* 2 vols. Mainz.

Schnädelbach, K. 2010, *Topographia Palmyrena I: Topography,* Damascus.
Tanabe, K. 1986, *Sculptures of Palmyra I,* Tokyo.
Taylor, D. G. K. 2001, An Annotated Index of Dated Palmyrene Aramaic Texts, *JSS* 46, 2, 203-219.
Watzinger, C. and K. Wulzinger 1932, Die Nekropolen, in T. Wiegand (ed.), *Palmyra: Ergebnisse der Expedition von 1902 und 1917*, 2 vols. Berlin, 44-84.
Will, E. 1949, La tour funéraire de Palmyre, *Syria* 26, 1-2, 87-116.
Will, E. 1948, La tour funéraire de Palmyre, *CRAI* 92, 2, 184-187.
Witecka, A. 1994, Catalogue of jewellery found in the tower-tomb of Atenatan at Palmyra, *Studia Palmyreńskie* 9, 71-91.
Yon, J.-B. 2012, *Inscriptions grecques et latines de la Syrie, Tome 17, Fascicule 1: Palmyre,* Beirut.
Yon, J.-B. 2002, *Les Notables de Palmyre,* Beirut.
Zenoni, G. 2010, Modelli e mode fra Oriente e Occidente: le collane delle signore de Palmira, *Bollettino di Archaeologia Online,* 45-54.

CHAPTER 3

Daughters and wives: Defining women in Palmyrene inscriptions

Eleonora Cussini[1]

SCI.DAN.H.4.10 · WOMEN, CHILDREN AND THE FAMILY IN PALMYRA
THE ROYAL DANISH ACADEMY OF SCIENCES AND LETTERS · 2019

The funerary relief of Marcus Julius Maximus Aristeides, from an unknown tomb, portrays a bearded man (fig. 1). His receding hairline and wrinkles that mark his forehead speak to his mature age. A bilingual epitaph in Greek and Aramaic records that he was from Beirut, and the father of a woman named Lucilla, wife of Pertinax (PAT 0761):

1. Μάρκος / 2. Ἰούλιος / 3. Μάξιμος / 4. Ἀριστείδης / 5. κολῶν / 6. Βηρύτιος / 7. πατὴρ Λου- / 8. κίλλης γυ- / 9. ναικὸς Περ- / 10. τίνακος

mrqws ywlyws mksmws / ʾrsṭyds qwlwn / brtyʾ ʾb<w>h dy / lwqlʾ ʾtt prtnks

"Marcus Julius Maximus Aristeides of the colony of Beirut, father of Loukilla, wife of Pertinax."

The Greek epitaph is inscribed on a book roll placed on a pilaster to his left, while the four line Aramaic text is written vertically in cursive script, above his right shoulder, in the background portion of the relief. Aristeides was a foreigner in Palmyra, where we assume he had moved and later died. The findspot of the relief and when it was removed from the tomb are unknown and we only know that in 1887 it was acquired by the

Fig. 1: Marcus Julius Maximus Aristeides (PAT 0761). Musée du Louvre, Paris, inv. AO 1556 (Ph. © Palmyra Portrait Project, Ingholt Archive at Ny Carlsberg Glyptotek, PS 1010).

1. I wish to thank the organizers of the workshop Representations of Women and Children in Roman Period Palmyra: Family Structures in Palmyra, held at Aarhus University on October 3rd, 2016 for their invitation, and especially Rubina Raja, Director of the Palmyra Portrait Project and Editor of this volume.

Louvre Museum.[2] The reason why Aristeides had moved away from Beirut, his profession, and other information concerning his life and career are unavailable.[3] The sculpted book roll could point to literacy as a symbol of status, or might indicate he was professionally involved with writing or administration. What concerns us here is the fact that both versions of his epitaph, in addition to name and provenance, cite his daughter Lucilla, wife of Pertinax.

Daughters are frequently mentioned in their parents' epitaphs and may be portrayed with them. What is unique to this epitaph is the fact that he is defined as the *father* of Lucilla, and not just as Aristeides from Beirut. The epitaph was certainly commissioned by Lucilla, and this would account for the emphasis on reference to her. The funerary reliefs of Lucilla and her husband are not known. On the basis of this inscription, the only existing evidence, Lucilla's father Aristeides had moved to Palmyra. We do not know whether he had purchased burial spaces of his own or was buried in the family tomb of his son-in-law Pertinax. That family tomb, however, has not been located. A man named Pertinax is cited in two other texts. An inscription of 243 CE, honoring Yarhay Agrippa head of the symposium, mentions his sons Pertinax and Malchusa (PAT 2743).[4] Another occurrence of the name Pertinax is found on a tessera, that bears the rather effaced image of a banqueting priest on the obverse, while the name Pertinax is written below the kline (PAT 2547).[5] This tessera was an entrance token to a banquet organized by Pertinax. The lack of other identifying elements makes it impossible to say whether these three Pertinax were one and the same person.

Although nothing else is known about her, Lucilla was certainly an elite woman, who could afford to commission a funerary relief for her father. The scarcity of information on her personal story is not surprising. A reconstruction of the lives and role of Palmyrene women is based on fragmentary information gleaned from the available sources: epigraphs and visual representations.

Having studied the capacity of Palmyrene women to sell, buy and inherit immovable property, their active role as legal guardians and tomb owners, and the fact they could dedicate inscriptions, columns, altars and ex-voto to gods,[6] I would like to concentrate here on designations of women and on the manners in which the relationships between women and their family members are expressed in the epigraphic sources.

Female professions are almost never recorded nor represented. An exception is the mention of prostitutes found in the Tariff, the long Greek-Palmyrene inscription recording the Fiscal Law of Palmyra, of 137 CE. That text contains a reference to taxes imposed on prostitutes, referred to as *znyt'* and *'lymh*.[7] Another type of designation is the hard-to-pinpoint social group of the *bt ḥry* (and the male form *br ḥry*). The status of these women was probably comparable to that of manumitted slaves, if one follows the correspondence *liberta bt ḥry* found in the Latin-Palmyrene epitaph of Regina, wife of Bar'ate.[8] An in-depth study of that group of women and of the meaning of their designation cannot be undertaken here. For the sake of the present discussion, it should be noted that women defined *bt ḥry* (and men *br ḥry*) are mentioned in different

2. Dentzer-Feydy and Teixidor 1993, 162, no. 166.
3. Colledge 1976, 225: 'Marcus Julius Maximus Aristeides, who had exchanged the humidity of Beirut for the dryer atmosphere of Palmyra, received a funerary relief bust of early third-century type'.
4. Connected to the same family is another Yarhay son of Yarhay, who is portrayed on his funerary stele as a learned man, or as someone who used writing in his profession. He is accompanied by a youth, a pupil or a servant, who holds a codex and a capsa. PAT 0679: 'Yarhay, son of Yarhay, son of Yarhay (son of) Yadi'bel (son of) Ya'ut'.
5. Ingholt et al. 1955, 106, no. 806.
6. Cussini 2004; 2005; 2012; 2016a.
7. PAT 0259 line 47: '... In addition, the tax-collector shall collect tax from the prostitutes (*znyt'*) ...) and line 125: (... the tax on prostitutes (*'lymt'*) ...'.
8. PAT 0246: Latin, 'To the D(eparted) S(pirits). To Regina, freedwoman (*liberta*) and wife of / Barates, the Palmyrene, who was of the tribe / of the Catuvellauni, at age 30'. Aramaic 'Regina, freedwoman (*bt ḥry*) of Bar'ate. Alas!' On this inscription and the relief of Regina, Cussini 2004.

text-types and they built tombs, bought and sold tomb portions, had funerary reliefs made and dedicated ex-voto altars.[9] Finally, one finds the royal title 'queen' designating Zenobia in two honorific inscriptions and on tesserae and coins.[10]

Overall, ethnonyms or toponyms are rarely found in the Palmyrene epigraphic corpus and the adjective 'Palmyrene' is attested mainly in inscriptions found outside the city (e.g. epitaphs of Palmyrenes buried abroad).[11] From Palmyra, besides Aristeides from Beirut, there are few other examples.[12] Two epitaphs define two women, respectively as 'the Egyptian' and 'the Greek'. Apart from those notations, their poses and representations, their names, or the structures of the epitaphs and the types of script employed, do not stand out as unique, or *foreigner* as the two adjectives could lead one to think and the reliefs were certainly produced in local workshops. The first epitaph (PAT 0908) accompanies a second century relief. It is written in cursive script to the woman's left: 'Shagal / daughter of Boropa / an Egyptian woman'. The woman wears a himation, on her head a frontlet and turban, the right hand clasps her veil, while in the left hand, she holds the spindle and distaff (fig. 2).[13] The other epitaph is on a third century relief of a woman, flanked by a child who clasps her veil. The woman's chin rests on her left hand, and she touches her cheek with the index finger (fig. 3). She wears a finely embroidered long-sleeved tunic, three necklaces, a bracelet and rings. Her himation, decorated by wool tassels, is fastened by a round brooch. The four-line epitaph to her left is in formal script and does not cite the child: 'Alas! / Amata / daughter of Zubaida / a Greek woman' (PAT 0907).

The great majority of references of women are found in funerary inscriptions, mostly in epitaphs. Feminine names also occur in the cession texts, other significant text-types from the funerary context. They are monumentalized excerpts from original legal contracts now lost, that record the sale of burial spaces and, among sellers and buyers, we also find women.[14] Women also dedicated inscriptions and altars. In a small number of extant honorific inscriptions, they were celebrated by their fathers and mothers or husbands.[15]

Women are obviously identified by female names. Certain personal names, however, can be used either for men or women: an example is Shalma'. This truncated form or hypocoristicon designates a man, for example in the epitaph on a bust-relief (PAT 0018), or in a 267 CE honorific inscription on a column (PAT 0289). In other instances, it occurs as a female name, in funerary reliefs (PAT 0576, or PAT 0647 and other examples). Therefore, when the relief is lost or when a visual representation was not there to begin with, the apposition 'son of' or 'daughter of' followed by the patronym, is the distinctive element indicating gender. In the past, an interpretation stemming from the analysis of iconographic features resulted in misleading conclusions with regard to two inscribed female funerary portraits.[16] They are the relief of a woman flanked by a female mourning figure, a well-known

9. Cussini 2005; with regard to dedicatory inscriptions also Cussini (forthcoming).

10. PAT 0293, 271 CE: 'Statue of Septimia Batzabbay, the magnificent and righteou[s] / queen ...'; PAT 0317: '... and for / the life of Septimia Batzabbay, the illustrious queen, mother of the king of kings ...'. Two lead tesserae with the Greek legend 'Sep(timia) Zenobia the queen': Seyrig 1937 and PAT 2827. du Mesnil du Buisson 1962, 755-758. For examples of coins of Zenobia in Turin, Barello 2002, 112-115.

11. PAT 0246, 0250, 0253, 0255, 0257; Yon 2013, no. 184; from Palmyra: PAT 0271, 0312, 0535, 1078 (Dura Europos), 1366, 1376, and other examples.

12. Another ethnonym referred to a man is found in a dedicatory text on altar of 132 CE, PAT 0319: 'Ubaidu, son of 'Anamu / [son of] Shu'adallat, the Nabataean, the Ruhaea[n]'.

13. On this symbol and the reconstruction of the role of Palmyrene women, see Cussini 2005.

14. Cussini 1995; 2012; 2016a.

15. Cussini 2004. See also Milik 1972, 163 (=Yon 2013 no. 14) for a daughter, on a column-bracket; Gawlikowski and As'ad 1997, 5, 26 (=Yon 2013 nos. 27, 63) for a wife, on a column shaft; Bounni 2004, no. 13 (=Yon 2013 no. 129) offered to a daughter, on a column-bracket; al-As'ad and Yon 2007, no. 8 (=Yon 2013, no. 169) altar offered by a woman.

16. For a critical discussion of the interpretations offered by Colledge (1976, 72, 264) and Hvidberg-Hansen and Ploug (1993, 129), see Cussini 2000.

Fig. 2: Shagal, daughter of Boropa (PAT 0908). Yale University Art Gallery, New Haven, inv. 1954.30.02 (Ph. © Courtesy of the Yale University Art Gallery).

Fig. 3: Amata, daughter of Zubaida (PAT 0907). Musée Archéologique, Strasbourg (Ph. © Palmyra Portrait Project, Ingholt Archive at Ny Carlsberg Glyptotek, PS 480).

scene documented by other funerary reliefs, and the bust of a girl. Curiously, they have both been interpreted as representations of eunuchs, although the female portraits are accompanied by well-preserved epitaphs indicating they were women: Hagar, daughter of Zubayda (PAT 0804), and Batti, daughter of Yarhay (PAT 0743), and the reliefs do not show iconographic elements allowing for a different interpretation.

Besides female names, that may sometimes be ambiguous, the key element designating women in the majority of Palmyrene inscriptions is the apposition *brt* or, less frequently *bt* 'daughter of', followed by the patronym (PN *daughter of* + father's name, sometimes with previous generations).[17] The patronym also defines men, according to a pattern that illustrates the local social structure. In rarer instances, one finds matronyms: in two funerary busts, the first from the hypogeum of Ta'ai: 'Barate, daughter of (*bt*) Modalla daughter of (*bt*) Mokimu' (PAT 1806). The second, from the hypogeum of Shalamallat: 'Statue of / Ba'a, daughter of (*brt*) 'Ate'akab / daughter of (*bt*) Haumal (or: member of the Haumal clan). Alas!' (PAT 1833).

The inscriptions may also record information concerning women's status. The fact they were married is

17. The less frequent *bt* PN is found in a number of instances: PAT 0067, 194 CE, PAT 0102, 0211, 0317, 0426, 0657, 226 CE, PAT 0670, 0739, 0769, 0773, 0804, 1042, 1221, 1314, 1806, 1833, 1875, 2683 and other examples. A group of texts cite the same woman, Batmalku daughter of Zabdibol: PAT 0528, 0529, 0540.

expressed by the noun *'nth* 'wife' in construct state with the husband's name. The common noun 'wife' also occurs following the husband's name, with a suffix pronoun: 'So-and-so, his wife'. In some cases, a woman may be defined 'daughter of (+ patronym) and wife' of someone. References to daughters also occur in tomb foundation texts, in provisions regarding future use and presumably the inheritance of funerary properties: 'In his (own) honor, made by Hairan, son of Yadday, son of Hairan Hannate, for himself and for his daughters. In the year (4)18' (PAT 0002, 106 CE), or: 'This tomb was made by Male, son of Sa'iday, son of Male, for himself and for his sister[18] / and for his sons and for his daughters and for his grandsons, forever' (PAT 2776, 142 CE).

Other designations illustrate kin-relations. Women are frequently defined as someone's mother. Less frequently, we find the noun sister (*'ḥh,* about ten occurrences),[19] niece (*bt 'ḥh,* found once, 'daughter of PN's sister', PAT 0252), (female) cousin (found once, [PN] *bt ḥlh* 'PN, daughter of her uncle', PAT 0562, 234 CE), daughter-in-law (*klh*, found once, on a banquet relief of 188 CE, where it designates Barbarah daughter of Hairan),[20] step-sister (once, 'PN daughter of Yad'u, my father, Alas!').[21] In one rare occurrence, unparalleled so far, in her son's epitaph, a mother mother is called 'the unfortunate one', (*byšt gd'*) to express her grief (PAT 0847).[22] Another unique term designating a woman, is the noun *wršh,* possibly 'heiress', painted on the plastered walls of a tomb, referred to Batmalku, who was the last descendant of the tomb builders and current owner of part of the original family property (e.g. PAT 0528).[23] Finally, the noun 'grandchildren' (indicating both male and female descendants) is frequently found, especially in tomb foundations and cession texts, for example: 'PN ceded to / Julia Aurelia Amata, daughter of Bolhazay (son of) Mokimu, for her and for her children's children. In their honor, forever' (PAT 0057, 263 CE). Mentions of granddaughters, referred to as one's daughter's daughter, may be found in banquet groups, as that of Ba'alai son of Dayyon: 'Ramay, daughter of Nabay / his granddaughter'.[24]

With regard to the study of designations of women, funerary reliefs and frescoes are also significant. In fact, in addition to what is recorded by the epitaphs, the visual representations of the deceased offer additional insights, for example a perception of their age. Taking into account the visual evidence provided by the portraits, it is sometimes possible to see whether the epitaphs mention children, adolescents or adults. On the other hand, conclusions drawn from the visual element only may sometimes be misleading. The relief of a woman and a child, standing to her left, may be interpreted as that of a mother and her child. The epitaph, however, shows that the child is the woman's granddaughter, while the child's mother is not mentioned: '[S]tatue of / Shalmat / wife of / Akiba. / Alas! / And Tema / daughter of / her / daughter. / Alas!'[25]

The Tariff has preserved a term indicating 'girls' meaning prostitutes.[26] The noun girl, however, is never found elsewhere, and in epitaphs we never find specific terms to define girls or unmarried young women. Signs of aging may sometimes appear on the sculp-

18. Note the problematic *l'dth* 'for his Lady' (?), perhaps more likely *l'ḥth* 'for his sister', see PAT, Glossary, 335.

19. In numerous cases, the kin-relation may be inferred from the text, for example PAT 0167: ''Attay and Shabhay, daughters of Shahra', therefore sisters, or the fact that a woman is someone's sister is expressed by the noun 'brother', PAT 0641: 'Attay daughter of / 'Atenatan. / Alas! (This is) what / was made for her by / Yarhay / her brother', and other examples.

20. From the banquet group of Ba'alai son of Dayyon: 'Barbarah, daughter of Hairan / wife of Dayyon, his daughter-in-law'. The woman's bust is sculpted below the kline (al-As'ad and Gawlikowski 1997, no. 73).

21. al-As'ad et al. 2012, 167, no. 9.

22. PAT 0847: the same four-line epitaph is sculpted on two stelae found in Qaryatein. In one case, the epitaph is carved above a hanging curtain, with rosettes and palm-branches on each side. On the other stele, the inscription only.

23. PAT 0528: 'Batmalku, daughter of Zabdibol / son of Zabdibol, son of Sa'iday / heiress of house and tomb'. On the inscriptions of Batmalku and the term 'heiress', see Cussini 2016a, 50-51.

24. al-As'ad and Gawlikowski 1997, no. 73d, 188 CE. See also the epitaph of Shalmat wife of Akiba discussed below.

25. Meischner and Cussini 2003, 102.

26. PAT 0259, see above, n.7.

tures as noted above with regards to the relief of Aristeides. Age, however, is very rarely recorded in the inscriptions. The Latin version of the epitaph of Regina wife of Barʿate (PAT 0246) specifies she was thirty years old, whereas the Palmyrene part does not mention that piece of information. The epitaph of Hanna, daughter of Barikay and the wife of another Barikay records she was twenty-three years old upon her death (PAT 1830).[27] As we have seen, the greatest majority of Palmyrene inscriptions define women according to their name and patronym only.

The top part of a banquet scene portrays a reclining woman, in the foreground.[28] An inscription to her right records her name and genealogy: 'Statue of Bolya, daughter of / ʿOga, son of Boropa' (PAT 1802). Next to her, is a reclining man holding a drinking cup. In the inscription between their heads, his name and the same genealogy indicating that he was her brother: 'Statue of Male / son of ʿOga / (son of) Boropa'. The hanging curtain behind his shoulders symbolizes that he was dead.[29] In contrast, the woman was still living when the relief was executed and perhaps she had commissioned it.[30] The lavishness of her jewellery and the huge wooden jewelry box sculpted to her right indicate her affluent status. Her physical features may suggest she was middle aged. Perhaps she was married and had children, although this information is not recorded in the inscription.

Over four hundred inscriptions mention women. They are inscribed on funerary reliefs and banquet groups portraying women, girls and children. This figure also includes fragments, with the inscription only. Other texts were not always accompanied by visual representations; they are inscriptions on stone slabs, on architectural elements and altars. The inscriptions record women's names and patronyms: 'PN, daughter of + patronym'. The patronym is never found when women are defined *bt ḥry* for reasons connected to the peculiarity of that social group.[31]

More than one hundred inscriptions mention married women. The Palmyrene epigraphic corpus does not provide information regarding the type of contract issued nor indications concerning the ceremony performed. Our only source, the monumental inscriptions, record the noun 'wife' in construct state with the husband's name or as an apposition, following women's names, 'PN, his wife'.

The corpus has not preserved other examples of inscriptions comparable to the epitaph of Aristeides 'father of Lucilla', with mention of a man as a woman's husband. When the noun 'husband' *bʿl* appears in the inscriptions, it nearly always defines the man who performs the action: a dedication, a construction or the like. Three inscriptions illustrate how husbands commemorated their wives by offering funerary reliefs or a column. The first epitaph simply mentions the woman's husband, with no record of his name: '[Statue of ...] / daughter of Warag / made by / her husband. Alas!' (PAT 0211). In another case, the relief of a woman flanked by her son Shuraiku and her daughter Batahu, her husband Bonnuri specifies she had honored his brother and children: 'Alas! Akme / daughter of Maliku, son of Dionys, made for her by Bonnuri / her husband, in her honor, because she honored Maliku, his brother / and his children' (PAT

27. For male epitaphs, see PAT 1316, Zabda, nine-year old, portrait lost; PAT 1895, ʿOgailu, sixty upon his death.
28. Damascus National Museum, inv. 18802. For an image, Charles-Gaffiot et al. 2001, 314, fig. 255 (=Gabucci 2002, 92, fig. 105).
29. On interpretations of the hanging curtain Colledge 1976, 157 with reference to previous bibliography.
30. The presence of a curtain behind the shoulders, in the literature dorsalium or parapetasma, symbolizes the passage to the netherworld. Found in double or single portraits, it may also be placed before the deceased, as in PAT 1211, the funerary stele of standing man (al-Asʿad and Gawlikowski 1997, no. 99). Other stelae have the curtain alone and no bust-relief, e.g. PAT 1193, PAT 1192 (al-Asʿad and Gawlikowski 1997, nos. 93, 95). Living female mourners or other female or male relatives, sometimes accompany a dead relative, as Bolya in this banquet relief. Another relief with a mourning woman embracing a deceased male relative portrayed before a hanging curtain, was excavated in the Northern wall area (al-Asʿad et al. 2012, 172, no. 27).
31. E.g.: PAT 1266, 175 CE: 'Shagal / freedwoman of Yarhay. / Alas! / The year / 487'.

0879). We may conclude that Maliku (same name of Akme's father) was Akme's first husband, and the two children portrayed next to her were Akme's and Maliku's. This seems to be the sense of the dedication offered by Bonnuri, her second husband and formerly, her brother-in-law. Another funerary relief, from the hypogeum of Bolaha, was dedicated by the tomb's eponym to his wife, with no additional details, concerning her age or the date of her death (PAT 1872: 'Alas! Naibanay / daughter of Yadday, son of / Nabushur, that which was made / for her by Bolaha, son of / Zabdibol, her husband'). Finally, one last example mentioning a woman's husband is a 170 CE honorific inscription on a column shaft, offered by Sewira to his wife Shallum: 'This statue is of Shallum, daughter of / Belhazay, son of Sewira, wife of Sewira, / son of Yarhay, (son of) Edipus (?) which was erected for her by / [Sewi]ra, son of Yarhay, her husband, after her d[eath] / in her honor. In the month of Shebat, the year 480/481'.[32]

Two dedications offered by wives to their husbands are an ex-voto on an altar (PAT 0373, 230 CE) and a foundation inscription. According to this last text, a woman, whose name is not preserved, built and dedicated a tomb to her husband. The limestone slab, without any visual representation as is customary with this type of texts, was found in the hypogeum of Bolaha, its secondary findspot and refers to an earlier tomb: 'This monument is that which was mad[e by ...] / Habbata, daughter of [... son of] / Hanaina, (son of) Asoray for Malik[u, son of ...] / (son of) Halkash, her husband and for Malik[u, son of Maliku], her son and for their *br ḥry*' (PAT 1896).[33] The uninscribed fragmentary relief of a man and a woman, apparently his widow, from an unknown tomb, may be a comparable example of a relief offered by a woman.[34] The scene, framed by an entwined grape-and-vine motif, portrays a standing woman, next to a man before a hanging curtain. She is not featured nor dressed as a mourning figure, but she clasps the curtain with her left hand in a gesture that was probably meant to express their tie and one last connection.[35] An inscription, that probably accompanied this relief, may have recorded their names and perhaps indicated their relationship, defining the woman as his wife, or a sister, as in the banquet relief of Bolya and her brother discussed above (PAT 1802). A woman's husband is cited in a cession text of 171 CE from Bazuriyye. In that case, the text records that the wife acted 'in the place of her husband', probably because he was unable to participate to that transaction, the sale of part of a tomb (PAT 1791).[36]

The pattern of epitaphs of married women is: PN, *daughter of* + patronym, *wife of* PN (followed by the husband's genealogy). In other cases, we find: 'PN (of husband and his genealogy) and PN, *his wife*'. As an example, the epitaph on a second century relief of a woman, who holds the spindle and distaff, records her name and patronym and specifies she is Mattanay's wife: 'Tema, daughter of / Harsha / wife of Mattanay / son of Nurbel / (son of) Mahuy' (PAT 0483). Despite the fact that her husband and his genealogy figure prominently in her epitaph, the woman is portrayed alone on a relief that sealed her burial niche. There are additional examples of single reliefs of married women portrayed in a medallion. For instance, the relief of a woman with a long epitaph dated 125 CE that records her genealogy and defines her as the wife of Bareʿa ('Alas! Hada / daughter of Bolaha / son of Zabdila, / wife of Bareʿa / (son of) Zabdaʿate. The year / 437', PAT 0603).[37] The second epitaph of 145 CE accompanies the fragmentary bust of her daughter

32. al-As'ad and Gawlikowski 1986-1987, no. 9; with a corrected and improved reading, Gawlikowski and al-As'ad 1997, 26.

33. It seems likely that this earlier inscription was transferred from an unknown funerary tower (as the term *npšʾ* indicates, PAT, Glossary, 390) to the hypogeum of Bolaha by the builder's descendants when the tower tomb was abandoned, perhaps because it was in ruins. On this Gawlikowski 1974, 48.

34. Formerly, Museum of Palmyra. For an image, Gabucci 2002, 87, pl. 100.

35. Note a comparable gesture of affection, a child clasps his mother's veil, PAT 0907, see fig. 3.

36. Cussini 2016a.

37. Not a 'girl' as Colledge 1976, pl. 84.

Shalmat, also in a medallion. Prosopography shows that they are mother and daughter: '[Ala]s! Shalma[t] / daughter of Bareʿa, (son of) / Zabdaʿateh / wife of / Nabula (son of) / Nabuza. / [In the month of] / Tishri, the year / 457' (PAT 0605).

Married women were often portrayed with their husbands in double bust-reliefs and in banquet groups. The banqueting scenes depict families centred around a reclining man. In these family groups, the wife usually sits on a chair or on cushions placed at the end of the banquet bed. There are reliefs featuring two or more men or rare examples of reclining women as in the relief of Bolya and her brother (PAT 1802).[38] Bolya, however, does not hold banquet vessels, as customary. When preserved, the inscriptions record the names of each member, sometimes with specifications of kin-relations. They are not always epitaphs, since they often portray living family members, as is the case of Bolya and of a girl named Alayyat, featured in her family banquet relief (PAT 0615).[39]

Turning to examples of double reliefs, Anna Sadurska and Adnan Bounni called attention to the secondary role of the wife in her representation in a double bust-relief from the hypogeum of Shalamallat.[40] The couple's epitaph is now lost and was perhaps comparable to the ones already examined with both names and genealogy and the apposition 'wife of'. The man is in the foreground, his left shoulder leaning against his wife's right shoulder behind him. Perhaps the construction of this scene did not necessarily imply hierarchy as the editors indicated. A comparable example of double relief from the hypogeum of Sassan, shows two brothers before a hanging curtain. The bearded one is in the foreground, his brother, beardless and younger looking, is behind him, their bodies slightly overlapping. Their epitaph, of 181 CE is incised in the space between their heads: 'Zabda, son of / Zabdibol / son of Sassan. Alas! / Kephalon (?) son of / Zabdibol, son of Sassan. / Alas! The year 493' (PAT 1025). Having the younger one in the background, could speak in favour of a hierarchic interpretation of this type of scene, although the inscription does not contain information on their age. The beard could be an age indicator; the bearded, older looking brother in the foreground and the younger and beardless in the background. I suggest that the slightly overlapping construction of these scenes resulted from the need to fit two figures in the reduced space offered by a loculus slab, perhaps with no hierarchic meaning attached.

Other double portraits show men and women side by side. A relief from an unknown tomb portrays a man and his wife: 'Haggay / daughter of / Haddudan. / Alas! / Zabdibol / son of Shulman. / Alas!' (PAT 0831). The couple, Zabdibol and his wife Haggay, is identified by two epitaphs in cursive script written between their heads and to the man's right. Following the woman's name is her patronym only, and the epitaph does not define her as Zabdibol's wife. Another couple, Valens and his wife Tadmor, is portrayed side by side on a relief from the hypogeum of Zabdʿateh (PAT 1855). Tadmor holds their child in her left hand. The six-line epitaph records their names, and defines her as Valens' wife.[41]

Married couples were also portrayed in banquet groups. When represented below the kline, in medallions or bust-reliefs, they were relatives or the reclining man's parents. In these cases, the pattern of representation does not seem hierarchic, and husbands and wives are usually portrayed symmetrically, one next to the other.[42] A fragment of the lower register of a banquet scene displays the busts of a man and a woman in round medallions (fig. 4). The extant portion of the inscription below the woman's bust, records her patronym and the apposition 'his wife' (PAT 0770).[43] Be-

38. For other uninscribed reliefs of reclining women, Cussini 2016b.

39. On Alayyat, her representations and inscriptions, PAT 0615 and PAT 0616, Cussini 2018.

40. Sadurska and Bounni 1994, 161-162, cat. no. 212, fig. 126.

41. PAT 1855: 'Valens, son of / Marcus. / Alas! And Tadmor / his wife. Alas! / Marcus, his son. Alas!'

42. For an uninscribed parallel, see also a man and his wife side by side in medallions, on an architectural relief (Ny Carlsberg Glyptotek, IN 1148), Colledge 1976, pl. 97, and other examples.

43. '[... daughter of ...] Timaios, his wife'.

Fig. 4: PAT 0770. Musée du Louvre, Paris, inv. AO 2630 (Ph. © Palmyra Portrait Project, Ingholt Archive at Ny Carlsberg Glyptotek, PS 854).

low the man's bust, there is no inscription. We may conclude that he was her husband, although there may have been other portraits, now lost, to the right. In another case, in the lower part of a banquet group, we see the busts of a couple; the parents of the reclining man. The woman's epitaph records her name and indicates she was Mokimu's wife, who is also portrayed next to her (PAT 0005, 148 CE).[44]

In these and numerous other cases, women do not appear in what Sadurska and Bounni considered a secondary position. In banquet scenes, the centrality of the husband is unquestionable. In the main scene, on the top part of reliefs or sarcophagi, women sit on high backed chairs at the end of the mattress or on cushions and, as we saw, do not actively participate in the banquet. Quite often, they are smaller in scale, when compared to the reclining figure. In two reliefs from the same unknown tomb, the inscriptions identify Hadira, who sits at the end of the kline. In one case, she is with her reclining husband, in the other relief with her son, in the same pose. In both cases, her name is not followed by a patronym, but she is simply referred to as 'wife of' or 'mother of'.[45] The reclining man's mother is featured in another banquet

44. PAT 0005: (By male bust) 'Alas! / Mokimu / the master craftsman / son of Nurbel / son of Zabda'. (By female bust) 'Alas! / Tadmor / wife of / Mokimu / son of Nurbel / son of Zabda / the master craftsman'. (Left of female bust) 'Died / the 29th day / in (the month of) Siwan / the year 459'. On this text, the upper banquet scene and other funerary reliefs of members of the same family, see Cussini 2018.

45. PAT 0862: 'Statue of Maliku, son of Hagigu, son of / Maliku, the eldest of / the community. Alas! And Hadira / his wife. Alas!'; PAT 0863: 'Statue of Taime, son of Maliku, son of / Hagigu. Alas! And Hadira / his mother. Alas!.

Fig. 5: Tabnan, daughter of Hagigu (PAT 0864). Musée du Louvre, Paris, inv. AO 1998 (Ph. © Palmyra Portrait Project, Ingholt Archive at Ny Carlsberg Glyptotek, PS 409).

Fig. 6: Habba, daughter of ʿOga (PAT 0899), Musée du Louvre, Paris, inv. AO 4147 (Ph. © Palmyra Portrait Project, Ingholt Archive at Ny Carlsberg Glyptotek, PS 512).

group, which portrays a man and his three brothers. The inscription has preserved her name and genealogy and the apposition 'his mother' (PAT 0587).[46] No information concerning the status or role of women may be found in the inscriptions accompanying these reliefs. The epitaphs simply record their names, or sometimes specify that they were married, although the fact that a woman was someone's wife is not always recorded as a rule, also in double reliefs that clearly portray a man and his wife.

Quite often, the epitaphs accompanying the busts of mothers and their children, do not mention they were married. They only record their names and sometimes the children's name. An illustration is the relief of Tabnan, daughter of Hagigu, (son of) Maliku, shown with her baby child in her arm (fig. 5). The epitaph to her left does not mention her husband nor the child's name, only her name and genealogy (PAT 0864). However, the child's name might have been inscribed in the missing part to the right. Comparable examples are the relief of Habba, daughter of ʿOga, in the same pose (PAT 0899) (fig. 6), or that of Habba, daughter of Male (PAT 0874). Her epitaph specifies she is the daughter of 'the physician'.[47] Her child behind her right shoulder is not identified and next to him is an abbreviated version of Habba's epitaph: 'Habba daughter of / Male. Alas!' Perhaps these reliefs with children not identified by their names could be explained as conventional representations of wom-

46. PAT 0587, at the end: 'ʿAtema [daughter of] / Mokimu / (son of) Gaddibol, his mother'.

47. Cussini 2017.

en as mothers. Moreover, the husband's name was not always recorded in inscriptions of presumably married women, probably because their burial niches were located next to their husbands' in their family tomb, or were placed right behind the couple's double-portrait. In the private family context of the tombs who-is-who explanations were probably unnecessary, as were references to one's profession or occupation, which were only seldom recorded.[48]

A fairly long epitaph on a limestone slab unravels a complicated family matter (PAT 1220). The inscription commemorates a man, Taimassa, and his three sons Zabdaʿateh, Taime and ʿAteʿakab.[49] There are no portraits to accompany the inscription and it is impossible to know if they were children, adolescents or adults. Two women are mentioned: Akamat, daughter of Taime, who is referred to as 'their mother'. Although it is not specified, she must have been Taimassa's wife. The second woman, Shalmat, is defined *their foster-mother* (*mrbythwn*). That term, probably better understood as 'tutor', indicates women or men who had legal responsibility for the upbringing of children.[50] Perhaps Shalmat came into the picture because Taimassa, the father, had died or because both parents were unable to care for their children. The inscription does indicate the dedicant's name and does not offer additional information to shed light on that situation.[51] It seems likely that all those mentioned were dead, and the inscription was dedicated to their memory by another family member who was not mentioned. The occurrence of the noun *mrbyh* in another text provides interesting details of another woman. The inscription accompanies a group, portraying two women, a boy and a child (PAT 2813). The two women, placed to either sides of the boy, hold a cup containing the dome-shaped cake or bread associated to mourning rituals also found in other funerary reliefs.[52] The woman to the boy's left embraces him in the typical comforting gesture. Three brief inscriptions identify them: 'Zaktaratay / their *foster-mother*. 'Alaisha and Belshuri / sons of Taime. Alas! 'Attay, daughter of / 'Alaisha, their mother'. The curtain hanging behind the adolescent, 'Alaisha, leads us to think that he had died, while his younger brother, placed slightly offside next to his mother, was still living. The inscription, however, with the exclamation of grief following their names, indicates they were both dead. Their mother's name is followed by her patronym, but there is no reference to the children's father, apart from the patronym Taime. The mention of a woman referred to as their tutor, suggests that their mother was a widow. Therefore, Zaktaratay probably played a key role in their upbringing, including legal responsibilities. As the relief shows, the boys' mother was alive, but she was probably unable to provide for her children's needs and profited from Zaktaratay's intervention before her children's death.[53] Her comforting embrace may also symbolize the protection provided as their *mrbyh*.

The definition of women as 'mothers' occurs in epitaphs and in other text-types throughout the corpus, although as we saw, it is not always recorded in portraits of women and children. It occurs as an apposition, following the woman's name: 'PN, his/her/their mother'. Frequently in funerary epitaphs: 'Zubaida, son of / Yadi'bel. / Alas! / Ummabi / daughter of ʿOgailu, his mother. Alas!' (PAT 0021), or 'Stat-

48. In addition to the reference to the physician (PAT 0874), there are other rare instances. On this Cussini 2017.

49. PAT 1220: 'Alas! Taimassa, son of / Zabda'ateh, (son of) Kaisa / and his sons: that is, Zabda'ateh / his son, and alas! Taime / his son, and alas! 'Ate'akab / his son, and alas! Akamat / daughter of Taime, their mother, and alas! Shalmat, their fostermother'.

50. Cussini 2016a, 49-50.

51. In other cases, women defined as tutor or fostermother dedicate the relief and inscription, see PAT 0840, 1767. For the funerary relief of a woman designated *brt ḥry* and *mrbyt*, PAT 2695.

52. Cussini 2017, 88, with previous bibliography.

53. Differently Colledge 1976, pl. 72: 'Early second-century funerary stele with three children and their nurse in relief'. As the inscriptions indicate, the relief portrays two children, their mother, and their foster-mother. The lack of patronym does not indicate that Zaktaratay was a servant, or a person of humble origin. As I argued elsewhere, men and women defined as such were not nurses, but rather legal tutors, Cussini 2016a, 49-50.

ue of Akamat / daughter of Shu'aday, our mother' (PAT 0035) and further examples.[54] Mention of one's mother also occurs in dedicatory texts, as in the inscription that records the construction of a cultic structure by five brothers. Among the dedicatees, there is 'Bolhay, daughter of 'Amaru, their mother' (PAT 0257, 146 CE), or in tomb foundations: 'This eternal home was made by Mattanay, son of Nurbel, son of Malku / son of Taimahe, for Nurbel, his father and for Nabay, his mother, in their honor' (PAT 0482, 95 CE). In two cession texts, there is probably a reference to the inheritance rights of two brothers, who are defined the 'sons of the (same) mother' (PAT 0072, 186 CE and PAT 0073). Reference to the same mother, while the father was different, occurs in a tomb foundation text (PAT 1134, 67 CE). It records the construction of a tower tomb with annexed hypogeum by Yadi'bel son of Taimahe, who dedicated it to his father and mother and to his three half-brothers, who were his mother's sons. The genealogy indicates that they were born from the woman's previous marriage to Yadi'bel's great-uncle.[55] In other cases, especially in ex-voto inscriptions on altars, the reference to one's mother or daughter is not always accompanied by the woman's name. In those inscriptions, the dedication is extended to other family members and may also include one's mother or daughter.[56]

The specification 'mother of' is found in the honorific inscription of Zenobia, with obvious reference to her son Wahaballat: 'Septimia Batzabbay, the illustrious queen, mother of the king of kings' (PAT 0317). In funerary epitaphs, it specifies the relation between the dead and her offspring, be they children or adults: 'Akamat / [dau]ghter of / Hairan, son of / Bonnur. / Alas! / The mother of / Nabuzabad / (son of) Barikay' (PAT 1828). In one case, the epitaph identifies a woman, records her daughter's name and also indicates her daughter's burial place, above her niche: 'Alas! [Ha]da / daughter of Mokimu / son of Sa'iday, mother of / Akamat / who lies above' (PAT 0546). The apposition 'mother of' may sometimes illustrate a more complex situation, such as that of Haggat, daughter of Bolaha, and her children she had from two different fathers: Akme, daughter of Dionys, and 'Ate'akab, son of Sa'iday. The woman had married two different men, Dionys, and Sa'iday, although the epitaph does not allow us to know who was the first, and who was the second husband: 'Alas! Haggat / daughter of Bolaha / (son of) 'Atenatan / (son of) Ahitur / mother of Akme / daughter of Dionys / (son of) Sa'iday, and mother of / 'Ate'akab / son of Sa'iday' (PAT 0644). It seems likely that the two men came from the same family, although a further discussion of their connection is hindered by the lack of patronym of Sa'iday, the father of her son 'Ate'akab.[57]

Three epitaphs from the tomb of Zabda illustrate the similar story of a woman called Beltihan. The first

54. Note also the epitaph ''Ala / daughter of / Aieda'an / son of Yarhay (son of) / Makkay. Her mother / and her father / are here. / Alas!' (PAT 1595) containing a unique indication of the parents' presence (perhaps at the funeral rite, or buried near her).

55. PAT 1134, a Greek-Palmyrene inscription: (Greek) 'The hypogeum and the monument above it were built by / Iedeibelos, son of Thaimaes, son of Aggodomos, of the tribe of the Chomarenoi, at his own expense, for Thaimaes / his father and Maisa, daughter of Thaimisas, his mother and Ogelos Thaimaes and / Atthaias, his brothers by the same mother, as an everlasting honor. In the year 378'. (Aramaic) 'This monument and hypogeum were made by Yadi'bel, son of Taimahe, son of Yadi'bel, son of 'Abd'ateh / (son of) Aggudum for Taimahe, his father and for Maisha, daughter of Taimsha, son of Yadi'bel (son of) Timon, his mother / and for 'Ogailu and Taimahe and 'Attay, the sons of Hairan, son of 'Abd'ateh (son of) Aggudum, his brothers, sons of the same Maisha / who is of the Bani Komara tribe in their honor, forever. In the month of Tebet, the year 378'.

56. See numerous examples, PAT 0360, 207 CE 'For Blessed-Be-His-Name-Forever / the Good and Merciful, this altar / was made by Makki, daughter of / 'Oga, wife of Male, son of / Maliku, for her life and the life of / her daughter. In the month of Tebet / the year 518', PAT 0370, 228 CE '(For) Blessed-Be-His-Name-Forever / made in thanksgiving / Mokimu, son of Gay / for his life and the life of / his mother and his brothers. / In the month of Ab / the year 539'. In other cases, daughters' names may be recorded, as in PAT 0404.

57. One possibility is that her second husband Dionys was a son of her first husband Sa'iday. However, he could also be another relative, a member of another branch of that family.

inscription is on a slab that portrays a reclining man. It reads: 'These statues are of Zabda, son of Mokimu, (son of) Bakray and of / Beltihan, daughter of Atepanay, his wife, who made this eternal dwelling / and the building which is above it. And they are buried behind / these statues' (PAT 1812). In the main burial chamber of that tomb, another portion of that banquet scene was found, showing a woman sitting on a chair with the inscription: 'Beltihan / his wife' (PAT 1813).[58] Beltihan, daughter of Atepanay is also known from other inscriptions: an epitaph on a funerary relief (PAT 0504), and a foundation inscription of 121 CE, from the tomb of Elahbel (Tower 13).[59] In both texts, she is referred to as the wife of Maʿanay, son of Wahaballat. Beltihan had married two different and quite affluent men, who both owned monumental tombs decorated with finely carved reliefs.[60] She was also the mother of a distinguished Palmyrene who in 130 CE held the position of chief of the *marzeaḥ*, as mentioned on a tessera: 'Atepanay (son of) Maʿanay, (son of) Wahaballat, chief of the *marzeaḥ*. The year 442'.[61] The elements gleaned from the available inscriptions, including chronology, suggest that Zabda was her first husband, while Maʿanay the second and the father of Atepanay and her other children.[62] It is not known whether she had other children from her first husband Zabda. As her funerary relief indicates, she was buried with her second husband Maʿanay and the rest of their family in their family tomb and not in the tomb of Zabda, as her first husband had planned and written in the inscription on his sarcophagus.[63]

As the epigraphic records indicate, women in Palmyra are defined according to a limited number of lexical items: daughter, wife, mother, sister, niece, granddaughter. Their definition, as I stated at the outset, mainly centers on family and kin-relations. To a lesser degree, other less attested designations indicate social groups and legal roles or a profession and, with regard to Zenobia, one finds the royal title 'queen'. The existing sources do not allow for a deeper understanding of the role of women in their families and in the broader context of Palmyrene society. The women mentioned in the inscriptions or portrayed in the reliefs belonged to the wealthier segment of the population.[64] As such, the monumental inscriptions do not provide information on Palmyrene women from all social classes and, for example, nothing is known on designations of female workers. Elite women had an active role outside their home; they could buy or sell properties on their own like their male relatives did. Nonetheless, they are never portrayed with documents in their hands, or book rolls and writing tools, although they could certainly write and signed contracts of sale. When portrayed with their husbands or in banquet scenes, Palmyrene women do not always appear in a secondary position.

A careful analysis of inscriptions mentioning women, also of apparently repetitive epitaphs, sometimes unveils the complexity of ties and of individual life events. That of Shalmat and other women who

58. Michałowski 1960, 166–168, pls. 184, 186; al-Asʿad and Gawlikowski 1997, no. 69, Beltihan's relief.

59. PAT 0510, 'In the month of Tishri, the year 433, the 30th day. Alas! Maʿanay, son of Wahaballat, (son of) Maʿanay, one of / the four brothers who built this tomb, and Beltihan, daughter of Atepanay, son of Malku / (son of) ʿAttarshuri, his wife'. That tomb was originally built in 103 CE by Maʿanay and his three brothers as we read on a stone tablet (PAT 0486). Eighteen years later, in 121 CE, Maʿanay felt the need to add another foundation text on the door lintel that mentioned his wife Beltihan.

60. Michałowski 1960, 168 'Le relief de Zabdâ et de sa femme Bêltiḥân se distinguent au contraire par un travail plus artistique, une touche plus personelle de l'artiste qui se laisse remarquer surtout dans la finesse de modelé de la tête de Bêltiḥân'. Michałowski suggests to date the relief 'de la fin de la première période de la sculpture palmyrénienne, c. à. d. de la fin de la première moitié du IIe siècle de notre ère'.

61. Schmidt-Colinet 2011.

62. From the same tomb, the funerary reliefs of her sons and daughter: the already mentioned Atepanay (PAT 0487), her daughter Hadirat (PAT 0499), her other sons Wahaballat (PAT 0496) and Maʿanay the younger (PAT 0491). On the complex genealogy reconstructed thanks to inscriptions from this tomb, see Chabot 1926, 269.

63. The possibility that Beltihan of PAT 1812 is the same woman of PAT 0504 and PAT 0486 was mentioned by Gawlikowski 1974, 13.

64. Presumably, with the exception of prostitutes, on whose background and social origin nothing is known.

had the role of (legal) tutors of somebody else's children, or that of Haggat and her children from two different marriages (PAT 0644) and the other examples examined. Drawing a conclusion on the secondary role of Palmyrene women focusing only on the pattern of their visual representations could be misleading. Images of women in the context of their family should be analyzed vis-à-vis the evidence brought by the epigraphic records with special attention to actions they performed and their legal capacities. When the archaeological context is preserved, it offers additional information and provides interesting insights, as the story of a woman who had dedicated an earlier tomb to her husband, which we may reconstruct thanks to an inscription found in its secondary placement in the hypogeum of Bolaha. Or that of Beltihan, whose two spouses had both prepared dignified burials for her, including a monumentalized mention of her name on the door lintel of one of the tombs. The picture resulting from the analysis of the visual and epigraphic sources show that Palmyrene women were defined and represented almost exclusively in the framework of their families, while additional designations pertaining to other spheres, religious or professional, illustrating a role other than that of mothers, daughters and wives, have not survived.

Abbreviations

PAT D. R. Hillers and E. Cussini 1996, *Palmyrene Aramaic Texts,* Baltimore.

Bibliography

al-As'ad, K. and M. Gawlikowski 1997, *The Inscriptions in the Museum of Palmyra: a catalogue*, Palmyra and Warsaw.

al-As'ad, K. and M. Gawlikowski 1986-1987, New honorific inscriptions in the Great Colonnade of Palmyra, *AAS* 36-37, 164-171.

al-As'ad, K., M. Gawlikowski and J.-B. Yon 2012, Aramaic Inscriptions in the Palmyra Museum. New Acquisitions, *Syria* 89, 163-184.

al-As'ad, K. and J.-B. Yon 2007, Nouveaux textes palmyréniens, *Semitica* 52-53, 101-110.

Barello, F. 2002, Le monete di Zenobia, in A. Gabucci (ed.), *Zenobia: Il sogno di una regina d'Oriente*, Milano, 111-115.

Bounni, A. 2004, *Le sanctuaire de Nabū à Palmyre: Texte*, Beirut.

Chabot, J.-B (ed.) 1926, *Corpus inscriptionum semiticarum. Pars secunda, Tomus III: Inscriptiones palmyrenae*, Paris.

Charles-Gaffiot J., H. Lavagne and J.-M. Hofman (eds.) 2001, *Moi, Zénobie Reine de Palmyre*, Paris, Rome and Milan.

Colledge, M. A. R. 1976, *The Art of Palmyra*, London.

Cussini, E. 2018, Out of a Palmyrene Family. Notes on the Metropolitan Museum of Art Palmyrene Collection in J. Arvz (ed.), *Palmyra Mirage in the Desert*, The Metropolitan Museum of Art Symposia, New York, 90-99.

Cussini, E. 2017, The Pious Butcher and the Physicians. Palmyrene Professions in Context, in T. Long and A. H. Sørensen (eds.) *Positions and Professions at Palmyra*, Palmyrene Studies 2, Copenhagen, 84-96.

Cussini, E. 2016a, Reconstructing Palmyrene Legal Language, in A. J. M. Kropp and R. Raja, (eds.), *The World of Palmyra*, Palmyrene Studies 1, Copenhagen, 42-52.

Cussini, E. 2016b, Family Banqueting at Palmyra. Reassessing the Evidence, in P. Corò, E. Devecchi, N. De Zorzi and M. Maiocchi (eds.), *Libiamo ne' lieti calici: Ancient Near Eastern Studies Presented to Lucio Milano on the Occasion of his 65th Birthday by Pupils, Colleagues and Friends*, Alter Orient und Altes Testament, Münster, 139-159.

Cussini, E. 2012, What Women Say and Do (in Aramaic Documents), in G. B. Lanfranchi, D. Morandi Bonacossi, C. Pappi and S. Ponchia (eds.), *Leggo! Studies Presented to Prof. Frederick Mario Fales on the Occasion of his 65th Birthday*, Wiesbaden, 161-172.

Cussini, E. 2005, Beyond the Spindle: Investigating the Role of Palmyrene Women, in E. Cussini (ed.) *A Journey to Palmyra: Collected Studies to Remember Delbert R. Hillers*, Leiden and Boston, 26-43.

Cussini, E. 2004, Regina, Martay and the Others. Stories of Palmyrene Women, *Orientalia* 73, 235-244.

Cussini, E. 2000, Palmyrene Eunuchs? Two Cases of Mistaken Identity, in E. Rova (ed.) *Patavina orientalia selecta*, Padova, 279-290.

Cussini, E. 1995, Transfer of Property at Palmyra, *ARAM* 7, 233-250.

Cussini, E. (forthcoming), Images of Individual Devotion in Palmyrene Sources, in R. Raja (ed.), *Revisiting the Religious Life of Palmyra*.

Dentzer-Feydy, J. and J. Teixidor 1993, *Les antiquités de Palmyre au Musée du Louvre*, Paris.

Gabucci, A. (ed.), 2002, *Zenobia: Il sogno di una regina*

d'Oriente, Milano.

Gawlikowski, M. and K. al-As'ad 1997, Inscriptions de Palmyre nouvelles et revisitées, *Studia Palmyreńskie* 10, 23-38.

Gawlikowski, M. 1974, *Recueil d'inscriptions palmyréniennes provenant de fouilles syriennes et polonaises récentes à Palmyre*, Paris.

Hvidberg-Hansen, F. O. and G. Ploug 1993, *Katalog: Palmyra Samlingen, Ny Carlsberg Glyptotek*, Copenhagen.

Ingholt, H., H. Seyrig and J. Starcky 1955, *Recueil des tessères de Palmyre*, Paris.

Meischner, J. and E. Cussini 2003, Vier Palmyrenische Grabreliefs im Museum von Antakya, *AA* 2, 97-105.

du Mesnil du Buisson, R. 1962, *Les tessères et les monnaies de Palmyre: Une art, une culture et une philosophie grecs dans les moules d'une cité et d'une religion sémitiques. Inventaire des collections du Cabinet des Médailles de la Bibliothèque Nationale*, Paris.

Michałowski, K. 1960, *Palmyre: Fouilles polonaises 1959*, Warsaw.

Milik, J. T. 1972, *Dédicaces faites par des dieux (Palmyre, Hatra, Tyr) et des thiases sémitiques à l'époque romaine*, Paris.

Sadurska, A. and A. Bounni 1994, *Les sculptures funéraires de Palmyre*, Rome.

Schmidt-Colinet, A. 2011, Priester beim festmahl: Etpeni, Symposiarch 130/31 n. Chr. und andere palmyrenische tesserae, in C. Lippolis and S. de Martino (eds.), *Un impaziente desiderio di scorrere il mondo: Studi in onore di Antonio Invernizzi per il suo settantesimo compleanno*, Firenze, 161-167.

Seyrig, H. 1937, Antiquités syriennes, *Syria* 18, 1-4.

Yon, J.-B., 2013, L'épigraphie palmyrénienne depuis PAT, 1996-2011, *Studia Palmyreńskie* 12, 333-379.

CHAPTER 4

Family connections and religious life at Palmyra

Ted Kaizer

Introduction

This paper aims to focus on the way in which family connections among cult participants played a role in the construction of patterns of worship at Palmyra.[1] Visual evidence from the funerary sphere for family relations is of course plentiful. A number of funerary reliefs depict a woman holding a child, and the large banqueting reliefs are representations of whole families. An example is a relief now in the Metropolitan Museum of Art in New York, datable according to the prosopography to the second half of the second century CE and coming from a tomb built by three brothers in the southwest necropolis, with four separate Aramaic inscriptions identifying the figures: the main person reclining is 'Zabdibol, son of Moqimu, son of Nurbel, son of Zabda, son of Abday Zabdibol'; the girl nearest to him is 'Tadmor his daughter'; the boy in the middle is 'Moqimu his son'; and the girl on the left is 'Aliyyat his daughter'.[2] Another example, from the hypogeum of Ta'ai in the southeast necropolis from the late second century CE, depicts a man and a woman who, according to their respective genealogy, are brother and sister; he is Male son of Oga Borpa, whereas she is Bolaya daughter of Oga Borpa.[3] The numbers provided by the Palmyra Portrait Project are certainly striking: roughly 40% of funerary sculpture concerns group portraits, 40% are representations of women, and 8% are children, so it is clear that depictions of women and children formed a substantial part of funerary imagery.[4] But when it comes to cultic activities outside the necropoleis, the ritual act is in the large majority of cases performed only by one person, and in fact mostly by one male. A few examples will suffice. On a relief of 154 CE from Khirbet Semrine in the Palmyrena, two mounted deities (Abgal and 'Ashar) are approaching the worshipper (Maqqay son of Azizu) and his altar in the middle;[5] a relief of five Palmyrene deities is dedicated in 225 CE in the steppe outside Palmyra by the *stratègos* of Ana and Gamla jointly with his lieutenant, although only the leading dedicant is depicted;[6] someone identifying himself as a 'servant of Odaenathus the consul' offered a relief to Abgal, the good god, depicting himself in the ritual act;[7] and in the inscription below a relief from the temple of Allat, depicting a worshipper

1. I am grateful to Signe Krag and Sara Ringsborg for the invitation, to Rubina Raja for discussion and some references, and to all participants in the workshop in February 2017 for their helpful comments. I also owe many thanks to Lisa Brody of the Yale University Art Gallery for helping me to find the unpublished images of the wall paintings from Dura-Europos in the archives at West Campus in New Haven during a visit, funded by the Leverhulme Trust, in September 2017. Finally, I am obliged to the Leverhulme Trust for the award of a Major Research Fellowship during which this article was written.

2. Whelchel et al. 2012, 36 (collection no. 02.29.1), with PAT 0615. For the family, see Piersimoni 1995, II, 618, no. 75.

3. PAT 1802, with Charles-Gaffiot et al. 2001, 367–368 (entry by J.-B. Yon) with 314 no. 255.

4. These percentages are based on information provided by Signe Krag and Sara Ringsborg in their conference invitation.

5. Drijvers 1976, pl. LXIII,2; Tanabe 1986, pl. 136; with the accompanying inscription PAT 1670.

6. Drijvers 1976, pl. IX,2; Tanabe 1986, pls. 103–105; with the accompanying inscription PAT 2757.

7. Gross 2005, 94–97, no. 2 with fig. 2; with Yon 2013, 360, no. 157, for the accompanying inscription.

offering to four deities, Samga son of Yarhai stated how he 'made these images during his presidency of the confraternity'.[8]

Depictions of family in cultic contexts

Visual evidence for family connections outside the funerary sphere is rather limited, although there are a few examples that ought to be mentioned. Firstly, a relief from the temple of Bel, dedicated 'to the Gad of the gardens and to Arsu and Rahim', shows an adult worshipper with a smaller figure to the right of an altar, with one of the deities standing on its other side.[9] The relief is said to have been made by a certain 'Yarhibola son of ʾ[.]bʾ Bana and Balo his son', but the final bit of that information, 'and Balo his son' (*wb'lw brh*), is actually inscribed separate from the rest of the inscription, namely next to the head of the smaller figure within the relief section. Interestingly, the boy is placed on a pedestal, with both his hands raised in the common prayer gesture. Does this mean that Yarhibola's son was not actually present at the performance of the sacrifice, since he was represented in statue format?[10] In any case, the appearance of children as statues in funerary contexts does not necessarily mean that they were deceased too.[11] Secondly, a relief dated to 138 CE from a private collection in Beirut, depicts the god Munʿim on horseback with three worshippers standing by an altar.[12] Their names are only partly preserved in the Aramaic, and even less so in the damaged Greek, and the epigraphy is not helpful with regard to their relation to each other. However, since the figure on the right is substantially smaller than the other two, it has been suggested that he is the son of one of the larger figures.[13] Jean Starcky, futhermore, suggested that the two adults were brothers.[14] Unusually, the two figures on the right put their arms around the shoulder of the person standing to their right, and the peculiar posture may hint at a different place of origin of the relief than the city of Palmyra itself.[15] Thirdly, a small altar to 'He whose name is blessed for ever', now in the Ny Carlsberg Glyptotek, shows a woman with her hands raised standing below what seems to be an arch, alongside a small child who also has its hands raised in worship. The accompanying inscription records that it was 'made by [A/Ra]mallah and Hurmuz, for the life of her son' (*'bd[t ʾ/r]mlh whrmz 'l ḥyʾ brh*).[16] Unusually, as has re-

8. PAT 1128, with Kaizer 2002, 230 for an improved reading, and for the relief see Ruprechtsberger 1987, 309, no. 31.
9. PAT 1621, with Drijvers 1976, pl. LII,2; Tanabe 1986, 165, pl. 132; Kaizer 2002, 119. Since Arsu and Rahim are male deities, the female figure depicted left of the altar is supposed to be the Gad of the gardens. The two gods must have been placed on the part of the relief that has been broken off.
10. See Starcky 1961, 124, who does not comment on the representation but simply describes it as follows: 'Le fils a les deux mains levées dans l'attitude de l'orant. Il est plus petit et se tient sur un piédestal'. For figures standing or sitting on pedestals or benches on reliefs from northern Syria (though very different from the relief here under discussion), see Blömer 2014, 259-260, no. B.II.5 with pl. 66,1; 269, no. B. II.20, pl. 71,1; 269-271, no. B.II.21, pl. 70,1; 271, no. B.II.22, pl. 71,2; 273, no. B.II.25, pl.72, 1. A female figure on a pedestal is also depicted on a previously unknown Palmyrene relief from the American Academy in Rome, now published by Hutton and Klein 2018, 35-38, fig. 3-4. I am grateful to Jeremy M. Hutton for showing this to me ahead of publication.
11. I am grateful to Rubina Raja and Sara Ringsborg for their advice on this point. Sara Ringsborg was preparing a dissertation on representations of children in funerary portraiture, see briefly Ringsborg 2017. See Krag and Raja 2016, 145. A relief of an adult man standing between two children is particularly interesting, since one of the children stands while the other is seated and on a pedestal. The latter boy has his head touched by the adult. The repetition of *ḥbl*, 'alas' in the accompanying inscription strongly suggest that both children are deceased, in which cases differences in representation (seated or standing, on a pedestal or not) cannot be taken as clear guidance. Sadurska and Bounni 1994, 74, cat. no. 96, fig. 2; Tanabe 1986, 250, pl. 217. For the inscription, see PAT 1869.
12. Drijvers 1976, pl. LXIX; Teixidor 1979, pl. XXV,1; with the accompanying inscription PAT 2625.
13. As suggested by Starcky 1972, 57.
14. Starcky 1972, 61: 'deux frères (?)'.
15. I owe this observation to Rubina Raja.
16. PAT 0420; Dijkstra 1995, 145; Hvidberg-Hansen 1998, 81, no. 129. Gunhild Ploug (1995, 260) unconvincingly suggested that the depiction of the arch implied that the ritual act took place in a temple.

cently been emphasised by Aleksandra Kubiak-Schneider, the beneficiary of the 'for the life of' formula seems therefore depicted alongside the dedicant.[17]

The sacrifice by Konōn's family on a painting from Dura-Europos

There are some more examples,[18] but there is no sacrificial relief scene with a family gathering that can match the famous wall painting of Konōn from the temple commonly known as that 'of Bel' (or - in its later phase - 'of the Palmyrene gods') at Dura-Europos.[19] Since the Dura-Europos painting helps to draw attention to what we lack at Palmyra itself, it is worth attention in this context. The sacrificial scene covered the side (south) wall of the naos, the most sacred room in the sanctuary. It must be emphasised that this painting (and also that of the main cult image, mostly lost, which had originally decorated the west wall of this room)[20] predates the period in which the temple came to be frequented by Palmyrenes. The priests presiding over the burning of incense (two on the main panel, and one on the part of the wall, which sticks out between the naos and the pronaos) are clearly not Palmyrene priests. As has often been observed, with their tall conical headgear they match more readily the description of the priestly attire in Hierapolis - according to Lucian's *On the Syrian Goddess* (42) and supported by visual evidence.[21] The figure on the left is identified through a memento (Μ(νησθῆ)) inscription as 'Konōn son of Nikostratos'. On the other side of the two priests, stands a woman elaborately dressed, wearing an ostentatious head cloth and with sumptuous jewellery. She is identified by an inscription painted on her dress as 'Bithnanaia daughter of Konōn'.[22] To the right stand four men identically depicted, all wearing purple undergarments with a white overgarment. They are identified as follows: 'Diogenēs son of Konōn', 'Lysias son of Konōn', 'Patroklos son of Konōn', and 'Konōn son of Patroklos', in other words three of Konōn's sons and a grandson. In the foreground, stand three children, one boy in the middle, and a girl and a boy towards the right. Of those, the boy to the right is the only of the three children on whose clothes an inscription has been traced to identify him, 'X (possibly Nikostratos?) son of Konōn', which makes him either another son of the *paterfamilias*, the Konōn on the far left, or a son of the Konōn son of Patroklos (son of Konōn), i.e. the great-grandson of the *paterfamilias* (in which case we are dealing with five generations according to the epigraphy, the elder Konōn's own father Nikostratos included). It is worth noticing that the priests are all depicted as much taller than any of the family members. Especially the contrast with the *paterfamilias* Konōn is stark. The latter stands on the far left of the scene (and thus furthest away from the cult image on the western wall), but impressions may deceive: he is not necessarily smaller than his daughter (although her headcloth gives that impression), his sons and grandson. If the painting creates that sense, it is only because he is positioned more to the front than the others.

Palmyrene banqueting scenes on paintings from Dura-Europos

In contrast to the sacrifice by Konōn and his family, another relevant wall painting from Dura-Europos, from the south wall of a house in block M7 ('the house of the banquet'), *is* actually connected to the Palmyrene

17. Kubiak-Schneider 2016, 96-97, 193-194, no. CLXXXVIII. For the role of women in the cult of 'He whose name is blessed for ever' in general, see Kubiak-Schneider 2016, 76-77.
18. See Colledge (1976, 40) for some descriptions and further references, and for further discussion see especially the contribution by Klaver in this volume.
19. Cumont 1926, 41-73 with pls. XXXI-XLI.
20. For a discussion of the lost painting from the western wall, see Kaizer 2016.
21. Lightfoot 2003, 479-486.

22. The painting was in fact initially known as 'the wall of Bithnanaia', in the words of Breasted 1924, 76: 'after the gorgeous lady who is so prominent in the painting'. Documentation in the Cumont archives of the Academia Belgica in Rome shows how Cumont initially took over the designation before ceasing to use it, e.g. Inv. no. 2560/35, where 'mur de Bithnanaïa' received a strikethrough and was replaced with 'Tableau I' (see Cumont 1926, pl. XXXVIII).

Fig. 1: Right half of a wall painting with hunting scene from Dura-Europos (cf. fig. 2), now in the Louvre (© Ted Kaizer).

inhabitants of the small Euphrates town. It concerns a combination of two scenes, now divided between the Louvre and the Yale University Art Gallery.[23] On the right (now in Paris), is a hunting scene with a Palmyrenean Aramaic inscription on the side, which dates it to 194 CE (fig. 1).[24] It records a request for remembrance and blessing for 'the men who have been painted here' (*'nšy' dṣy[ryn] tn[n]*) 'before Bel and Yarhibol and Aglibol and Arsu'. Both the script and especially the divine names make the Palmyrene setting of course undisputable. The figure of the mounted hunter overlaps with an Eros figure (identified as such by a Greek inscription)[25] which in a way bridged the hunting scene with the banquet scene depicted on the left (now in New Haven). Here, one can recognise at least five men, reclining on a couch and one female figure seated on a chair (fig. 2). The names of the reclining men that are legible, are in Greek and can all be explained with the help of Palmyrene onomastics.[26] The seated female is not accompanied by an inscription. The relation of the men to each other, or indeed to the woman, remains unknown. The adjacent west wall of the same room had two panels similarly showing banquets, which depict Palmyrenes as well. The first shows three men reclining (fig. 3).[27] These are identified by Greek and Palmyrenean inscriptions, but there is again nothing that can be said about possible familial connections. The second one, next to that of the three men, is a poorly preserved painting which - uniquely - seems to depict a group of three women enjoying a banquet, supposedly flanked by female servants. Two women seated on a couch are hardly visible, and the third woman is sitting on a chair, while being served by the woman standing and holding a bowl. The parallel setting with the

23. Rostovtzeff et al. 1936, 151-155, with pl. XLII,1; Dirven 1999, 291-292 with pl. XI. It remains unclear how half of the scene ended up in the Louvre.

24. PAT 1091; Dirven 1999, 282-284; Bertolino 2004, 36-37, no. A.M 7.01.

25. Rostovtzeff et al. 1936, 153 and 171, no. 692 (Ἔρως).

26. Rostovtzeff et al. 1936, 155 and 172, nos. 693-694.

27. Rostovtzeff et al. 1936, 147-149, pl. XLII,2; Dirven 1999, 292-293. The preliminary report only published a black and white drawing of this panel. Fig. 3 is the water colour drawn in the 1930s by Van W. Knox, jr., which is reproduced here with kind permission by the Yale University Art Gallery.

Fig. 2: Left half of a wall painting with banquet scene from Dura-Europos (cf. fig. 1), now in the Yale University Art Gallery (Photo courtesy YUAG).

Fig. 3: Water colour reproduction of wall painting showing men's banquet from Dura-Europos (drawn in the 1930s by Van W. Knox, jr. Courtesy YUAG).

reclining males next to this scene leaves no doubt that the ladies are similarly enjoying a banquet (figs. 4-5).[28] Their names are mostly written in both Greek and Palmyrenean Aramaic, but again their relation to each other remains unknown. The two panels on the west wall obviously formed a pair, and it is most telling that they represent two secluded events, one for men and one for women only. As Jen Baird put it, 'commensality would have allowed for the articulation of social groups within and between households'.[29] There are of course many tesserae depicting reclining priests, and family banqueting scenes on funerary sculpture (on sarcophagus lids and on reliefs), but these concern our only securely identifiable paintings of banquets by Palmyrenes.

28. Rostovtzeff et al. 1936, 149-151; Dirven 1999, 292. No photo or drawing of this panel was published in the preliminary report. Fig. 4 is the water colour drawing by Van W. Knox, jr., and fig. 5 is a photo of the scene in situ. Both are reproduced here with kind permission by the Yale University Art Gallery.

29. Baird 2014, 254. On the paintings, see Baird 2014, 74-75, n.155.

Fig. 4: Water colour reproduction of wall painting showing women's banquet from Dura-Europos (cf. fig. 5) (drawn in the 1930s by Van W. Knox, jr. Courtesy YUAG).

Fig. 5: Photo of wall painting showing women's banquet from Dura-Europos (cf. IV) in situ (with part of the men's banquet visible, cf. fig. 3) (Courtesy YUAG).

Women attending public religious ceremonies

A painting of a women's banquet in a domestic context stands in sharp contrast with the evidence from the public and religious spheres, where women are playing a much less visible role than men. The two times that women are depicted prominently on a public monument depicting a religious scene, they seem to be by-standers and are represented in what is nowadays perceived as a subservient fashion. A famous relief on one of the beams from the peristyle of the temple of Bel shows two groups of veiled women attending a sacred procession centred around a camel (with a covered item on its back) and a donkey.[30] A number of male attendants are raising their hands in prayer gesture, whereas the women have their heads bowed submissively and hold on to their veils in order to make sure their face is covered. It is interesting to note that

30. Drijvers 1976, pl. V; Tanabe 1986, 87–89, pls. 42–44.

the veiled women in the top left corner of the relief are seemingly looking in the wrong direction, away from the action. Lucinda Dirven has argued that the relief represents the investiture of Allat at Palmyra, since a fragment from the temple of that goddess suggests the depiction of a similar scene.[31] The fact that the women needed to be veiled must be explained by reference to a specific ceremonial context, as the little evidence there is makes clear that women did not need to have their faces covered in public and religious life in general. We have already seen a woman on the little altar dedicated to 'He whose name is blessed for ever' - a cultic practice that seems to have entered in the religious life of Palmyra only from the second century CE onwards - but women also appear not completely draped in the veil on a much older item, a relief in archaic style, found in the agora (but doubtless from a sanctuary, perhaps the nearby shrine of Rabaseire, which has now been located immediately south of the agora?).[32] The relief shows two cloaked females on the right, carrying a cup and perfume burner, respectively, then a male figure holding a wreath and to the left a priest casting incense over a small altar.[33] The man stands closer to the altar and to the priest, than the two women. In any case, there is, as far as I am concerned, still no evidence for women occupying sacerdotal positions themselves in Palmyrene society.[34]

Priesthoods, genealogies and ancestral deities

Only a few comments need to be made here about family connections in the context of priesthood.[35] The question of whether Palmyrene priesthood in general was hereditary is, in principle, a valid one. The key item here is the well-known relief from the temple 'of Nebu' that depicts three generations of priests, all neatly identified, including their familial link. ZBD'TH 'NQYR is seated in the middle, with GRYMY his son (*brh*) standing on his right and MTN' his grandson (*br brh*) on the left, the latter in the act of crowning his grandfather with a laurel wreath.[36] To what degree this implies that specific families actually monopolised specific priesthoods is another matter. The family group known as the Bene Taimarsu identified themselves on one honorific inscription as 'the priests of Baaltak the goddess'.[37] I have argued elsewhere that if prosopographical research shows that certain families produced generations of priests, this does not necessarily need to be interpreted within the context of a traditional and 'closed' system of hereditary succession, but that it could also be explained through the assignment of priesthood to benefactors of a cult, and henceforward to their descendants.[38] This would of course have led to an uncontrolled growth of the number of priests, but perhaps that was not as problematic for the Palmyrenes as it may appear to us.[39] In any case, the phenomenon provides context for a bilingual inscription from the second half of the second century CE, which records the setting up of a statue by someone in honour of his brother, because the latter had taken on him the expenses for his nephew to become a priest.[40] The best evidence for sons succeeding their fathers in temple-related positions comes in the form of two inscriptions, from May 272 CE and May 273 CE, respectively. Both texts are dated to the presidency of the *marzeah* of Bel of Hadudan the senator, and both texts present

31. Dirven 1999, 81-86. For the relief from the temple of Allat, see Ruprechtsberger 1987, 314, no. 37; Tanabe 1986, 188-189, pls. 155-156; Charles-Gaffiot et al. 2001, 346 (entry by J.-B. Yon) with 267 no. 159.

32. For the discovery of the temple of Rabaseire, see Gawlikowski 2012.

33. Tanabe 1986, 168, pl. 135; Ruprechtsberger 1987, 308, no. 30.

34. Kaizer 2002, 237; contra Sadurska 1994, 18-19.

35. For discussion, see Raja 2017a and her contribution in this volume.

36. Bounni 2004, 88-89, no. 32; Bounni et al. 1992, fig. 108; Tanabe 1986, 206, pl. 173. For the inscription, see Bounni 2004, 73, no. 42; Yon 2013, 344, no. 38.

37. PAT 2750, with Kaizer 2002, 237, n.131 for references to the various readings.

38. Kaizer 2002, 240.

39. See the discussion in Raja 2017b, who also emphasised that c. one in ten funerary reliefs represents a priestly figure, and one in five reliefs of men.

40. PAT 1372; IGLS XVII.1, no. 262.

a nearly identical list of functionaries in the temple.[41] Michał Gawlikowski has shown that the men who are listed in the second inscription are the sons of the men listed a year earlier. It seems unlikely to have been the result of a rigorous hereditary system - if so, then why did Hadudan remain in his position? - and it should rather be explained in the context of the peculiar political circumstances at the time.[42]

There is no doubt that the family held a pivotal role in Palmyrene society as far as the emphasis on genealogy is concerned. In inscriptions, often three or four generations, occasionally more, are listed to identify a dedicant or honorand - always following the male line. The way family groupings, clans, are commonly referred to is another case in point, *bene* X, 'the sons of X'.[43] From the epigraphy, it is also clear that specific families could play a prominent role in particular sanctuaries and cults, such as the Bene Nurbel in the temple of Allat, the Bene Maʿziyan in the temple of Baal-Shamin, and the Bene Mattabol in the cult of Arsu. But if certain family groupings were notably visible in specific cultic contexts - through dedications or priesthoods - that is not to say that they held a monopoly on the patterns of worship in the relevant sanctuaries. Jean-Baptiste Yon has shown that, surprisingly, the two families whose presence can be detected in the so-called temple of Nebu did not actually use their clan designation in the context of that temple (it is only from funerary inscriptions that we know that benefactors to the temple belonged to these families). Whereas the Belshuri family first and foremost seems to have had a 'cultic' interest in the sanctuary, for the family of Elahbel, it served more as a 'lieu de représentation'.[44] The question remains why it was deemed unnecessary only in this particular temple to mention family connections explicitly, but it is most likely that this 'new mode in which social realities found expression'[45] ought to be explained in terms of a development over time of Palmyrene society at large.

If genealogical lists link the dedicant to his family, there is one particular, and popular, divine epithet that links him to his family's deity: πατρῷος means literally 'from one's father' or 'inherited from one's father'. Commonly translated as 'ancestral', it has been argued by Ramsay MacMullen that it was utilised - in the Roman empire at large - by worshippers either to express a protecting quality attributed to the deity or in a migrant's tribute to a deity known from one's far-away homeland.[46] At Palmyra, the label often remains untranslated in bilingual inscriptions, but when it *is* rendered in Palmyrenean-Aramaic, as in a text from 140 CE, the dedication πατρῴοις θεοῖς has as its counterpart 'for the good gods' (*lʾlhyʾ ṭbyʾ*).[47] It suggests, indeed, that the epithet was in the first place applied to assert a special rapport between the worshipper and his deity, because Palmyrenean clearly had the means to express that the cult of a specific god or goddess was hereditary.[48] In fact, an Aramaic formula used in an inscription from 85 CE can be considered as the missing equivalent. The dedicants of an altar to Shamash refer to him as 'the god of the house of their fathers' (*ʾlh ʾbyt ʾbwhn*).[49] MacMullen's second explanation, namely that the term could be applied by a migrant in tribute to a set of deities known from his homeland, also has a clear example as regards Palmyra: an often discussed Latin inscription from Sarmizegetusa in Dacia, which records a dedication by P. Aelius Theimes, a Palmyrene migrant (though not necessarily first-generation, as Nathanael Andrade has explained).[50] Theimes, who had made it to the top of his local society as one of the two *duumviri*, built a

41. PAT 1358 and 2812, respectively, with Gawlikowski 1971, 412-421.
42. See Kaizer 2002, 233: 'it is suspicious that ... all ... were replaced by their sons simultaneously and at precisely this moment, whereas it is physically impossible that hereditary succession took place annually'.
43. Note how a woman could be referred to as belonging to the '*Banot* X' rather than the '*Bene* X', as in PAT 0168, mentioning someone 'who is from the *Banot* (daughters of) *MYT*'' (*dy mn bnt myt*').
44. Yon 2002, 84.
45. Yon 2002, 85: 'nouveau mode d'expression des réalités sociales'.
46. MacMullen 1981, 3-4.
47. PAT 0273; IGLS XVII.1, no. 306.
48. Kaizer 2004, 179.
49. PAT 0324.
50. CIL III S 7954, with Kaizer 2002, 111-112; see Andrade (forthcoming).

temple 'for the ancestral gods' (*DIIS PATRIIS* being the Latin equivalent of πατρῴοις θεοῖς). Bel-Hammon and Manawat formed an established constellation in Palmyra itself, and Malakbel was one of the most popular deities in Palmyrene contexts abroad.[51] The problem is that Theimes got some of the details rather embarrassingly wrong: *BEBELLAHAMON* seems to be a mixture between the divine names Bel and Bel-Hammon, and the unknown *BENEFAL* is commonly thought to be an error for Fenebal, one of the great goddesses in the older Phoenician pantheon who is not otherwise attested in Palmyrene settings. It is very hard indeed to explain the epithet as truly meaning that the deities are 'inherited from one's father' if the dedicant does not actually know how they are named correctly!

Family and the 'for the life of' inscriptions

Finally, in a discussion of family connections and religious life at Palmyra, the formula 'for the life of' (*'l ḥyy*), so popular in Palmyrenean dedicatory inscriptions, deserves discussion.[52] This formula links the dedicant with either one or (usually) a number of beneficiaries, in the form of persons 'for whose life' the dedication (for example of a temple structure, or of an altar) was made to a certain deity. The formula was widespread also elsewhere in the Roman Near East, but whereas in Nabataean inscriptions dedications were made nearly without exceptions 'for the life of the king', and in Hatra the formula was used to establish (or deepen) a relationship between patron and client, the epigraphic material from Palmyra always lists family members, mostly sons and brothers, but occasionally sisters, parents and sometimes the dedicant's household as a whole (*bny byth*, *bny byth klhn*, or *byth klh*).[53] In this manner, part of the prestige realised by the dedicant through his dedication was shifted on, and shared with those family members who found themselves favoured by means of the formula, thus strengthening the social (familial) relation between dedicant and formulaic beneficiary.[54] As Klaas Dijkstra has shown, 'the beneficiaries of major dedications in Palmyra ... are without exception the dedicant's *sons and brothers*'.[55] The one exception would be a dedication by two brothers for the life of themselves only – as they were undertaking the dedication jointly as two brothers for themselves, there was obviously no need to add the formula 'for their brothers' if they had no other brothers.[56] In contrast to the major dedications (parts of temples, columns, reliefs), the beneficiaries of the formula accompanying minor dedications (mostly small altars) consist of a more wide-ranging family network, including mother, wife, daughters, sisters, uncles and nephews – in addition to sons and brothers, who remain significant beneficiaries also in this context.[57] It should be noted that on a few occasions, a Greek text or fragment without Aramaic counterpart uses a more gender-neutral term (ὑπὲρ σωτηρίας ... τέκνων), though in bilingual inscriptions this is used as the equivalent of the masculine Aramaic word for 'sons'.[58]

51. Bel-Hammon and Manawat at Palmyra, see Kaizer 2002, 108–116; Malakbel abroad, see Dirven 1999, 170–183.
52. For a comprehensive analysis of the formula, see the important book by Dijkstra 1995.
53. E.g. PAT 0379, 0382, and 0355, respectively. The Palmyrene tendency to focus on family in the modern sense of the word makes it perhaps unlikely that at the oasis the conception of the 'household' (bt) included slaves in the same way that domus (or, even more so, familia) did in the Roman world. On the Latin terminology, see Saller 1984. Note that Kubiak-Schneider 2016, 89–91, has argued that the appearance of emancipated slaves among dedicants in the cult of 'He whose name is blessed for ever' hints at a non-official, private character' of this form of worship.
54. Thus Dijkstra 1994, 190. It may be relevant to note that what goes on in these dedications to a deity by one human for the life of another human is, in a way, not too dissimilar from what goes on in the well-known group of dedications made by the gods themselves (mostly of statues of human benefactors). On the latter category, see Milik 1972, passim, and for a different interpretation, see Kaizer 2004, 172–175. In both cases, a network of relations is being created or maintained.
55. Dijkstra 1995, 290 (original italics).
56. PAT 2749, with Dijkstra 1995, 94.
57. Dijkstra 1995, 148–149.
58. E.g. PAT 0344; IGLS XVII.1, no. 130: *'l ḥywhy wḥyy bnwhy w'ḥwhy* ~ [ὑπὲρ] ὑγείας αὐτοῦ καὶ τέκνω[ν αὐτοῦ καὶ] ἀδελφῶν; PAT 1571; IGLS XVII.1, no. 324: *'l ḥywhy wḥyy bnwhy* ~ ὑπὲρ ρίασ[ςωτη αὐτοῦ καὶ τῶ]ν τέκνων. See IGLS XVII.1, no. 163, 319, 323 for Greek only.

A brief look at five different examples of the formula *ʿl ḥyy* will serve to shed further light on the role of family connections in cultic contexts.[59] Firstly, a dedication from 132 CE of two altars by a Nabataean in Palmyrene military service follows the common Palmyrenean pattern only in part.[60] The beneficiaries of the formula are his two brothers and his son: *ʿl ḥywhy wḥyy mʿyty wʿbdw ʾḥwhy wšʿdlt brh* ('for the life of himself and the life of Meaiti and Abdu his brothers, and Shadilat his son'). However, all three are named, which is in contrast to the more shorthand formula commonly applied in Palmyrenean epigraphy. If it is remarkable that the dedicant identifies himself as 'a Nabataean of the Rawwaha' (*nbṭyʾ rwḥyʾ*) twenty-six years after the Nabataean kingdom had ceased to exist in 106 CE, the end of his ancestral realm meant that the common older Nabataean habit to dedicate something 'for the life of the king' could not have been adhered to anyway. The dedicant also mentions a host and friend with Palmyrene names for the full genealogy: *wdkyr zbydʾ br [š]mʿwn br blʿqb gyrh wrḥmh* ('may Zebaida son of Shimeon son of Belaqab, his host and friend, be remembered'), but not in the 'for the life of' formula, but with the formula *dkyr*, 'may be remembered', instead – thus following the Palmyrene habit of limiting the recipients of the *ʿl ḥyy* formula to family members only. Secondly, a column set up by five brothers in Nazala, about 120 km southwest of Palmyra in the direction of Damascus, 'for the life of themselves and for the life of their sons and for the life of Belhay, daughter of Imru, their mother' (*ʿl ḥyyhn wḥ[yy] bnyhn wḥyy blḥy brt ʾmrw ʾmhn*).[61] Either the five brothers had moved to Nazala themselves with their own families, or – perhaps more plausible – they are second-generation migrants who were taken to Nazala by their father. The dedication to the great god of Nazala (*lʾlhʾ rbʾ dnzly*) shows their attempts at integration, but they still identify themselves explicitly as 'Tadmoreans who are in Nazala' (*tdmryʾ [dy] bnzly*).[62] The beneficiaries of the formula are their sons, but obviously not their brothers, and also – 'most unusual in Palmyrene epigraphy, where major dedications are concerned'[63] – their mother. If Dijkstra is right that the 'for the life of' inscriptions are about life at present (unlike funerary texts, which are about eternity), it must mean that the family's matriarch is still alive, while the father had died.[64] Thirdly, another inscription which names the mother of the two dedicants as a beneficiary: *ʿl ḥyy[hwn] wḥyy ʾmhwn wbnyhwn* ('for the life of themselves and the life of their mother and their sons').[65] This time, the explanation may be sought in the fact that we are apparently dealing with two half-brothers who according to their patronyms only share their mother: *ydy br h[...] [w]lšmš br š[...] ʾ[ḥ]wh* ('Yaddai, son of H[...], and Lishamsh son of Š[...], his brother').[66] In order to emphasise their mutual relationship, the half-brothers do not list their respective fathers (although these might of course both have been deceased) but the mother whom they share. Fourthly, one of the few bilingual texts that applies the formula, on the well-known relief from Rome depicting Aglibol and Malakbel.[67] Whereas the Greek lists as beneficiaries the dedicant himself, his wife and

59. In addition to the examples discussed in the main text, I mention here the ingenious but speculative restoration of PAT 0404 by Milik 1972, 181–182, who interpreted the inscription as referring to the healing of a paralysed daughter. See Dijkstra 1995, 141.

60. PAT 0319, with Dijkstra 1995, 108–110.

61. PAT 0257, with Dijkstra 1995, 135–136; Dirven 1999, 125, n. 100.

62. Kaizer 2015, 21.

63. Dijkstra 1995, 136.

64. PAT 0334, a dedication by a woman, is made 'for the life of herself and the life of her sons and her brother(s)' (*ʿl ḥyyh wḥyy bnyh wʾḥyh*), which would, according to this logic, mean that her husband was no longer alive. It is then relevant to note that she is still identifying herself as 'wife of' (*ʾtt*). Unsurprisingly, self-identification in Palmyra is never as 'widow of' a deceased husband, which would fit well with what has been claimed about the classical world, namely that there was no specific terminology applied to express posthumous spousal connections. The available words in Latin (*vidua*) and Greek (*χήρα*) 'were used for a semantic field that differed significantly from today's use'. See Jussen 2015, 34.

65. PAT 0402.

66. Dijkstra 1995, 146.

67. PAT 0247, with Dijkstra 1995, 138, and for the relief see Drijvers 1976, pl. XXXVIII.

their children (ὑπὲρ σωτηρίας αὐτοῦ καὶ τ(ῆς) συμβίου καὶ τ(ῶν) τέκνων), the Aramaic only lists the dedicant himself and this sons (*ʿl ḥywhy wḥy ʾbnwhy*), thus snubbing the wife.[68] Fifthly, a dedication from 52 CE by a woman (Amtallat daughter of Baraa son of Etnatan who is from the Banot [*sic*] Mita, wife of Taimi son of Belhazai son of Zabdibel who is from the tribe of the Bene Maziyan) 'for her life and the life of her sons and brothers' (*ʿl ḥyyh wḥyy bnyh w ʾḥyh*).[69] The woman's sons (and she herself, through her marriage) will have belonged to another clan than the one to which her brothers still belonged and in which she grew up herself. As Dijkstra puts it, 'dedications of women, then, involuntarily establish social relationships between members of different families, clans or tribes. At the same time, they bear witness to the importance of the bond siblings tend to develop with each other'.[70]

Dijkstra has suggested that the difference in beneficiaries between major and minor dedications can, in part, be explained by the fact that the major ones mostly date from the period until the first half of the second century CE, whereas the minor ones are chiefly from the third century CE, and that this ought to be linked with the process that Palmyra underwent under Roman influence, in which 'the frame of reference of the Palmyrene inhabitants … was directed away from the tribal group to the city':[71] 'Concomitantly, the household came into prominence as the social and economic unit to the detriment of the clan or tribe. As a subdivision it was more appropriate for the needs of the city as main frame of reference'.[72] If the family undoubtedly continued to play a pivotal role throughout the remainder of Palmyra's glorious civilization, its role and functioning in society then nevertheless underwent a development, from male-dominated tribal links to a more inclusive, holistic *domus* set-up. In both cases, however, the choice of beneficiaries in the inscriptions served to register the social (whether 'tribal' in the sense of clan-related, or 'familial' in the sense of household-related) identity of the dedicant in civic documentation and in this manner helped to confirm his or her affiliations to blood- and other relatives.[73]

68. On the formula ὑπερ σωτηρίας, which is also the Greek rendering of 'for the life of' in another bilingual text (PAT 1571; IGLS XVII.1, no. 324), see above all Moralee 2004. Note that in another, heavily damaged bilingual, the Aramaic formula does not seem to have a counterpart in the Greek text, see PAT 2770; IGLS XVII.1, no. 152, with Dijkstra 1995, 120. With regard to the relief from Rome, it is perhaps also possible that mention of the wife was deleted from the Aramaic due to lack of space, as Rubina Raja suggests to me.

69. PAT 0168.

70. Dijkstra 1995, 118-119 (also with regard to PAT 0167) and 129. Both the woman's and her husband's tribe may also have been mentioned together to add weight to her own social position, or to emphasise social alliance between the different familial groupings. See Yon 2002, 180. On dedications of statues by and for women in general, see also the contribution in this volume by Klaver.

71. Dijkstra 1995, 152.

72. Dijkstra 1995, 152.

73. See Dijkstra 1995, 166 on the relative emphasis of vertical and horizontal kinship in inscriptions containing the formulae 'for the life of' (*ʿl ḥyy*) or 'in honour of' (*lyqr*). Note that two words both conventionally translated as 'foster mother', *mrbyth* and *mprnsyt*', appear in Palmyra in a funerary context, but not in combination with the 'for the life of' formula, see PAT 0840 and 0095, respectively.

Abbreviations

IGLS XVII.1 J.-B, Yon 2012, *Inscriptions grecques et latines de la Syrie, Tome 17, Fascicule 1: Palmyre,* Beyrouth.

PAT D. R. Hillers and E. Cussini 1996, *Palmyrene Aramaic Texts,* Baltimore.

Bibliography

Andrade, N. J. (forthcoming), Palmyrene military expatriation and its religious transfer at Roman Dura-Europos, Dacia, and Numidia, in R. Raja (ed.), *Palmyra and the Mediterranean*, Cambridge.

Baird, J. A. 2014, *The Inner Lives of Ancient Houses: An Archaeology of Dura-Europos*, Oxford.

Bertolino, R. 2004, Corpus des inscriptions sémitiques de Doura-Europos, *Supplemento n. 94 agli ANNALI (Sez. Orientale)* 64, Naples.

Blömer, M. 2014, *Steindenkmäler römischer Zeit aus Nordsyrien. Identität und kulturelle Tradition in Kyrrhestike und Kommagene,* Bonn.

Bounni, A. 2004, *Le sanctuaire de Nabū à Palmyre. Texte,* Beirut.

Bounni, A., J. Seigne and N. Saliby 1992, *Le sanctuaire de Nabū à Palmyre. Planches,* Paris.

Breasted, J. H. 1924, *Oriental Forerunners of Byzantine Painting. First-Century Wall Paintings from the Fortress of Dura on the Middle Euphrates*, Chicago.

Charles-Gaffiot, J., H. Lavagne and J.-M. Hofman (eds.) 2001, *Moi, Zénobie: Reine de Palmyre*, Paris, Rome and Milan.

Colledge, M. A. R. 1976, *The Art of Palmyra*, London.

Cumont, F. 1926, *Fouilles de Doura-Europos (1922–1923)*, Paris.

Dijkstra, K. 1995, *Life and Loyalty: A Study in the Socio-Religious Culture of Syria and Mesopotamia in the Graeco-Roman Period Based on Epigraphical Evidence,* Leiden, New York and Cologne.

Dijkstra, K. 1994, Aramese votiefteksten en votiefgeschenken uit Hatra, *Phoenix* 40, 184–194.

Dirven, L. 1999, *The Palmyrenes of Dura-Europos: A Study of Religious Interaction in Roman Syria,* Leiden, Boston and Cologne.

Drijvers, H. J. W. 1976, *The religion of Palmyra*, Iconography of religions XV.15, Leiden.

Gawlikowski, M. 2012, Le tarif de Palmyre et le temple de Rabʿasirê, *CRAI* 2, 765–780.

Gawlikowski, M. 1971, Inscriptions de Palmyre, *Syria* 48, 407–426.

Gross, A. D. 2005, Three New Palmyrene Inscriptions, in E. Cussini (ed.), *A Journey to Palmyra. Collected Essays to Remember Delbert R. Hillers,* Leiden and Boston, 89–102.

Hutton, J. M. and K. M. Klein (2018), Two Palmyrene funerary stelae in the collection of the American Academy in Rome, *Journal of Northwest Semitic Languages* 44.

Hvidberg-Hansen, F. O. 1998, *The Palmyrene inscriptions, Ny Carlsberg Glyptotek*, Copenhagen.

Jussen, B. 2015, Posthumous Love as Culture. Outline of a Medieval Moral Pattern, in B. Jussen and R. Targoff (eds.), *Love after Death: Concepts of Posthumous Love in Medieval and Early Modern Europe*, Berlin, 27–54.

Kaizer, T. 2016, Revisiting the "Temple of Bêl" at Dura-Europos: A Note on the Fragmentary Fresco from the Naos, in M. K. Heyn and A. I. Steinsapir (eds), *Icon, Cult, and Context: Sacred Spaces and Objects in the Classical World*, Los Angeles, 35–46.

Kaizer, T. 2015, 'Familiar Strangers': Gods and Worshippers away from Home in the Roman Near East, in M. Blömer, A. Lichtenberger and R. Raja (eds.), *Religious Identities in the Levant from Alexander to Muhammed: Continuity and Change,* Turnhout, 19–32.

Kaizer, T. 2004, Religious mentality in Palmyrene documents, *Klio* 86, 165–184.

Kaizer, T. 2002, *The Religious Life of Palmyra: A Study of the Social Patterns of Worship in the Roman Period*, Stuttgart.

Krag, S. and R. Raja. 2016, Representations of Women and Children in Palmyrene Funerary *Loculus* Reliefs, *Loculus Stelae* and Wall Paintings, *Zeitschrift für Orient-Archäologie* 9, 134–178.

Kubiak-Schneider, A. 2016, *«Celui dont le nom est béni pour l'éternité». Une étude des dédicaces votives sans théonyme proper de Palmyre*, unpublished PhD Thesis, University of Warsaw.

Lightfoot, J. L. (ed.), 2003, *Lucian: On the Syrian Goddess,* Oxford.

MacMullen, R. 1981, *Paganism in the Roman Empire*, New Haven and London.

Milik, J. T. 1972, *Dédicaces faites par des dieux (Palmyre, Hatra, Tyr) et des thiases sémitiques à l'époque romaine,* Paris.

Moralee J. 2004, *'For Salvation's Sake': Provincial Loyalty, Personal Religion, and Epigraphic Production in the Roman and Late Antique Near East*, New York and London.

Piersimoni, P. 1995, *The Palmyrene Prosopography,* 2 vols., unpublished PhD Thesis, University College London.

Ploug, G. 1995, *Catalogue of the Palmyrene Sculptures, Ny Carlsberg Glyptotek*, Copenhagen.

Raja, R. 2017a, Networking beyond death: Priests and their family networks in Palmyra explored through the funerary sculpture, in H.F. Teigen and E. H. Seland (eds.), *Sinews of Empire: Networks in the Roman Near East and Beyond*, Oxford, 121–135.

Raja, R. 2017b, To be or not to be depicted as a priest in Palmyra: A matter of representational spheres and societal values, in T. Long and A. H. Sørensen (eds.), *Positions and Professions in Palmyra,* Palmyrene Studies 2, Copenhagen, 115–130.

Ringsborg, S. 2017, Children's portraits from Palmyra, in R. Raja (ed.), *Palmyra: Pearl of the Desert*, Aarhus, 66–75.

Rostovtzeff, M. I., A R. Bellinger, C. Hopkins and C. B. Welles 1936, *Preliminary Report of Sixth Season of Work, October 1932 – March 1933, The Excavations at Dura-Europos Conducted by Yale University and the French Academy of Inscriptions and Letters*, New Haven.

Ruprechtsberger, E. M. (ed.) 1987, *Palmyra: Geschichte, Kunst und Kultur der syrischen Oasenstadt*, Linz.

Sadurska, A. 1994, L'art et la société: recherches iconologiques sur l'art funéraire de Palmyre, *Archeologia-War* 45, 11–23.

Sadurska, A. and A. Bounni 1994. *Les sculptures funéraires de Palmyre,* Rome.

Saller, R. P. 1984, 'Familia, Domus', and the Roman Conception of the Family, *Phoenix* 38, 336-355.

Schlumberger, D. 1951, *La Palmyrène du nord-ouest: villages et lieux de culte de l'époque impériale: recherches archéologiques sur la mise en valeur d'une région du désert par les Palmyréniens,* Paris.

Starcky, J. 1972, Relief dédié au dieu Mun'îm, *Semitica* 22, 57-65.

Starcky, J. 1961, Deux inscriptions palmyréniennes, *Mél-Beyrouth* 38, 121-139.

Tanabe, K. 1986, *Sculptures of Palmyra I*, Tokyo.

Teixidor, J. 1979, *The Pantheon of Palmyra,* Leiden.

Whelchel, H., M. Aspinwall and E. Urbanelli 2012, *The Metropolitan Museum of Art: Guide*, New York, New Haven and London.

Yon, J.-B. 2013, L'épigraphie palmyrénienne depuis *PAT*, 1996-2011, *Studia Palmyreńskie* 12, 333-379.

Yon, J.-B. 2002, *Les notables de Palmyre,* Beirut.

CHAPTER 5

It stays in the family: Palmyrene priestly representations and their constellations[1]

Rubina Raja

Introduction

The religious life of Palmyra has long been a topic of research.[2] While much is known about the pantheon of the city - the roles, which the different deities played, the religious festivals and processions, including religious banquets and the organization of the tribal sanctuaries - the knowledge about the priesthoods of Palmyra remain obscure.[3] Not many written or epigraphic sources have been handed down to us, which speak to us about the organization of Palmyrene priesthoods or the role of the priests in the different cults.[4] Furthermore, although we know that extended families (usually termed 'tribes' in scholarship) stood at the centre of the societal structure of Palmyra and that some of the Palmyrene sanctuaries were connected to these families, we know little about the ways in which such family structures worked in reality and how the organization of the sanctuaries might have been influenced by the Palmyrene priests.[5] The knowledge that we have about Palmyrene priests in fact largely comes from the funerary sphere, where families were represented in family tombs and where children, mothers, fathers, grandparents, nieces and nephews, aunts and uncles were depicted together with their immediate and extended family in large grave galleries, which would have filled up over the years and generations.[6] Among these representations

1. I would like to thank the Carlsberg Foundation for the generous funding, which they have granted me since 2012 to conduct the Palmyra Portrait Project. More can be read about the project on the following webpage: http://projects.au.dk/palmyraportrait/. Furthermore, I would like to thank the three diligent research assistants working on the Palmyra Portrait Project together with me and who have helped compile information for this article: Olympia Bobou, Nathalia Breintoft Kristensen and Rikke Randeris Thomsen. Without their competent help and eye for the detail the project would not be what it is.

2. See Kaizer 2002 for an important contribution on the religious life also summing up earlier research on the religious life of the city as well as further references. Also, see the following for earlier important research on the religious life of Palmyra (the list is in no way exhaustive): Drijvers 1976; Gawlikowski, 1979-1980; Gawlikowski 1990; Dirven 1999; Gawlikowski 2015.

3. Kaizer (2002, 234) states that in comparison to other descriptions of the role priests in the Near East the representations of the priests from Palmyra and our knowledge in general about them is a disappointment. Kaizer Kaizer (2002, 234-235) also neatly sums up what earlier scholars have written about the Palmyrene priests, their roles, their clothing and attributes, much of which is now outdated in the light of the findings made within the Palmyra Portrait Project. See for example: Raja 2017a for the most up to date tackling of the evidence related to what earlier has been termed the 'former priests'.

4. Again Kaizer 2002 remains a crucial source also for further references. In particular, Kaizer 2002, 234-242 sums up much of the evidence available to us, but also underlines its scarcity and the large lacunae that the evidence presents.

5. It has been extensively discussed how many tribes there were in Palmyra. According to Piersimoni, we can count fourteen tribes (Piersimoni 1995a, 252-253; 1995b, II, 532-541). See Kaizer 2002, 48-51 for an extensive discussion of the available evidence and debates. As we know from the epigraphic evidence Palmyrene society seems to have been organized on four tribes at some point by the second century CE (Kaizer 2002, 47-48). What this indeed meant to the overall structure of the Palmyrene society we do not know. Also see Gawlikowski 2003.

6. Raja 2016a; Raja 2017b. These publications deal with

were numerous priests as well. The tombs, mostly tower tombs or underground tombs (hypogea) were usually founded by a family father, which we know from founder's inscriptions placed on the facades of some of these graves.[7] The Palmyrene funerary portraiture was produced from the early first century CE until the sack of Palmyra in 273 CE by the emperor Aurelian and his troops; this tight chronological span combined with the immense amounts of material now collected within the framework of the Palmyra Portrait Project makes this unique group of material extremely important for understanding wider issues of representational values in the ancient world in general.[8]

Within the visual material from the funerary sphere, representations of priests make up a significant group, which because of its sheer number is incomparable to priestly representations from all other places in the ancient world. However, the immense amount of representations also allows us to investigate in detail aspects of visual continuity and change within one group of material, which is a unique situation in the ancient world. These priestly representations from the Palmyrene funerary sphere firmly underline, through their amount alone, that holding a priesthood was one way of underlining elite and social standing in Palmyrene society and that priests, on the one hand, were shown together with their families and, on the other hand, were shown alone.[9] So while we know that priests were plentiful in Palmyra, we know little about what that actually meant in a societal context and little about the importance or lack thereof that the immediate family played to these priests within the context of their status as priests.

This contribution, therefore, brings together and tackles material stemming from the funerary sphere, which relates to the representations of Palmyrene priests and their immediate families. It aims at analyzing and discussing in which ways this visual evidence might enhance our understanding of Palmyrene priesthood in general as well as the societal implications of holding a priesthood, and in which ways families might or might not have played a role when displaying ones Palmyrene priesthood in the funerary sphere. This paper aims at tackling the funerary representations of Palmyrene priests in the context of what we know about the societal structure of Palmyra and more specifically within the context of the Palmyrene family, which remained at the heart of the city's life and which the funerary representations attest so vividly to, but about which we know little from the archaeological and epigraphic evidence.

Palmyrene funerary portraiture in general and the priests in particular.

7. See Henning 2013. Furthermore, see Sadurska and Bounni 1994. The only known founder's relief, which includes an image is the following: InSitu043 (database number of Palmyra Portrait Project): date: 40 CE (dated by inscription). Further references: Will 1949, 94-95, fig. 8; 1951, 70-71, fig. 1, pls. 7, 8; Morehart 1956-1957, 65-68, cat. 24, fig. 22; Gawlikowski 1970, 71-72, fig. 36; Colledge 1976, 83, 101, 114, 120, 131, 136, 146-147, 158, 209-210, 233, 239, fig. 37; Parlasca 1984, 284; Tanabe 1986, 29, pl. 177; Ruprechtsberger 1987, 112, fig. 95; Schmidt-Colinet 1996, 366-367, cat. 62, fig. 198; Wielgosz 1997, 74, pl. 9.2; Gawlikowski 2005, 46, 48, 53-54, fig. 6; Henning 2013, 312-313, cat W 8, pl. 41.a-b; Wielgosz-Rondolino 2016, 74, fig. 11. Inscription: Will 1951, 70, n.1; de Vogüe 1868, 29, cat. 33.

The inscription reads: [In the month of] Sîwan year 352, [images] of Kîtôt son of [Taîmarṣû and of Maîsh] â daughter of [Malkû, his wife], and of Lishamsh [his son and of Shalman] his son and of Malkû his servant. (References: CIS 4115bis; PAT 0464).

8. Kropp and Raja 2015; Kropp and Raja (eds.) 2016. For more up to date publications reporting on the project status see: Raja 2016a; Raja 2017c.

9. Raja 2016b; Raja 2017a; Raja 2017b; Raja 2017d; Raja 2017e. See the above for the most recent contributions to the study of the iconography of the Palmyrene priests and further references. The publications have clearly shown that further methodological studies of the priestly representations add to our knowledge and understanding of the role of Palmyrene priesthoods. Earlier scholarship includes the important contributions by Gawlikowski 1966; Stucky 1973; Heyn 2008. These publications, however, were based on a much smaller amount of material than now available.

The Palmyrene priests and their iconography

Palmyrene priests are recognized through their distinct iconography. They are always displayed with a priestly hat or with the priestly hat next to them (catalogue nos. 1-10, figs. 1-10).[10] Furthermore, they carry tunics often displaying embroidery and often decorated cloaks. They also usually hold a small pitcher and a bowl in their hands. From the banqueting tesserae, which we know were used as entrance tickets to religious banquets held in the sanctuaries in Palmyra, and some of which are inscribed and give us information about Palmyrene priests, we know that such dress went hand in hand with priesthood in Palmyra.[11] In the funerary sphere, however, none of the numerous representations are signified as priests through the accompanying inscription.[12] The representations obviously spoke for themselves and were unmistakenly understood to be images of Palmyrene priests.

Representations of Palmyrene priests make up a significant amount of the complete corpus of funerary representations. 365 priests are included in the corpus until this date out of 3698 portraits (10 percent).[13] Out of these, 29 representations have the priestly hat located next to them.[14] The representations of men shown with their priestly hats next to them have been dealt with in detail in an earlier publication (catalogue nos. 11-41, figs. 11-24).[15] Out of a total of 1941 male portraits, the priests make up a total of 19 percent, so almost 1/5. This must be said to be a significant number and completely unique for the classical ancient world.

The priestly representations were divided across the various types of funerary representations. These divisions are important to understand, since some of the groups and the iconographic styles displayed on these would have had more to do with the shapes and forms and their limitations than the representation itself. This was the case with the loculus reliefs for example. Other groups, such as the banqueting scenes, both those of the so-called banqueting reliefs, but in particular those displayed on the sarcophagi lids as well as the sarcophagi reliefs, allowed for much more variation in turn, therefore, also displayed a wider range of choice made by the customers and craftsmen.

The divisions of the priestly representations on the loculus reliefs, banqueting reliefs as well as sarcophagi are the following: 88 loculus reliefs displaying Palmyrene priests are compiled in the Palmyra Portrait Project database. Loculus reliefs were the most common type of representation found in the Palmyrene tombs. These rectangular slabs carved of the local limestone would partly have been prefabricated. They come in fairly specific measures showing that the limestone slabs would have been precarved - not least to fit - more or less the burial niches, which they were intended to cover. Most often they depict one individual. However, there are also numerous examples, more than 150, of loculus reliefs displaying two or even three or four individuals. The division of priestly representations in the loculus re-

10. Raja 2017a for the most up to date contribution on the representations of the men displayed with their priestly hats next to them.

11. Raja 2015a; Raja 2015b; Raja 2016a for recent contributions on the so-called banqueting tesserae of Palmyra, which remain a unique Palmyrene phenomenon in the ancient world still to be studied as a complete corpus. The Ingholt et al. 1955 publication was a good attempt at compiling as comprehensive a corpus as possible. However, in regard to the rich iconography of the corpus it leaves much open.

12. There is one representation stemming from the funerary sphere of a man represented in a banqueting relief (Musée du Louvre, inv. AO 2000) depicted together with his wife, who is termed a priest (PAT 0862). He is, however, not represented in priestly garments and also not with a priestly hat.

13. Status: July 2018.

14. Raja 2017a. In this article, however, only 24 representations divided on 23 objects were included, since that was the corpus status then. This article, however, remains the standard work on the so-called former priests, since the addition of the further five representations has not changed anything regarding the interpretation of these representations nor has it changed anything statistically significantly.

15. Raja 2017a. It should be noted that two representations do not stem from the funerary sphere (catalogue nos. 11 and 12).

liefs can be divided into the following sub-categories within the loculus group of 88 priestly representations. There are 82 single loculus reliefs. There are five multiple loculus reliefs. Four double loculus reliefs show priests together with other individuals (catalogue nos. 42-46, figs. 25-26).[16] These include one relief depicting two priests together; two reliefs depicting a priest and a child; one relief depicting a priest and a woman (mourning mother?). Furthermore, one triple relief depicting a priest, a male and a female also exists. In the loculus relief group, priests were overall almost exclusively shown alone, also to a higher degree than was the rule overall in the loculus relief group.

Banqueting reliefs were also used in the tomb as forms of commemoration of the dead.[17] These reliefs showed reclining family fathers together with either servants or family members. Priests are also included in this type of representation. Three banqueting reliefs of the smaller size exist (catalogue nos. 47-49, fig. 27). They respectively depict one reclining priest alone, one reclining priest together with a servant and the last one shows two reclining priests together with a servant. Two large-scale banqueting reliefs also exist (catalogue nos. 50-51, fig. 28). One is well-preserved and depicts a reclining priest and his wife. The other example is heavily fragmented, but would have included at least one priest. It is not possible to say anything about the original complete state.

While the categories of the loculus reliefs and the banqueting reliefs are fairly uninformative due to the restrictions which their forms impose, the sarcophagi and the sarcophagi reliefs represent a different matter. Loculus reliefs as shown above almost exclusively show priests on their own and the small and larger banqueting relief show the priests in constellations, which are fairly pre-set in their iconography depicting the priest together with a servant or a family member. In the second century CE, locally produced limestone sarcophagi were introduced into the Palmyrene grave sphere and from then on, they were used widely in the graves as lavish monuments showing banqueting scenes including up to eight individuals on a lid and a total of 17 individuals on a box (catalogue nos. 32-33, 52-53, fig. 23).[18] Evidence for more than 300 Palmyrene sarcophagi have been collected within the Palmyra Portrait Project until now.[19] This is a number, which just like the in total more than 3,600 funerary portraits, is far beyond what was expected for the site. In the banqueting scenes displayed on the sarcophagi lids, scenes including Palmyrene priests are also frequently found. In these scenes, they can be both reclining and standing.

The priestly representations found in the context of the Palmyrene sarcophagi present a fascinating group of material. However, it is not uncomplicated to assess these, since most of the material is fragmented to some degree. In total, evidence of 50 different sarcophagi upon which one or more Palmyrene priests were represented exist (catalogue nos. 54-103, figs. 29-47). In the case of the almost complete sarcophagi, it is clear that more than one priest often was depicted.[20] Furthermore, the sar-

16. Raja 2016b. In this publication, I treated the significance of the loculus reliefs depicting priests together with family member. However, only four of the five reliefs where known then. The additional fifth included here is the one showing a priest together with a child from a private collection.
17. See Audley-Miller 2016 for a recent contribution on the banqueting scene in Palmyra, which, however, completely omits the work published within the framework of the Palmyra Portrait Project. See the recent contribution by Krag and Raja 2017 for further references on banqueting reliefs and sarcophagus scenes in general.

18. Max. number of individuals shown on sarcophagus lid: eight (PM329); max. number of individuals shown on sarcophagus box: 17 (PM604); max. number of individuals shown on sarcophagus lid relief: seven (PM539); max. number of individuals shown on box relief: six (PM539, InSitu136).
19. Raja (forthcoming). The rough numbers are at present the following: complete sarcophagi: 29; boxes: 53; lids: 56; complete sarcophagus reliefs: 15; box reliefs: 12; lid reliefs: 26; further fragments stemming from sarcophagi in total: 231.
20. Catalogue nos. 56-58 might originally very well have incorporated more than one priest. Since the heads , as so often is the case, are largely missing, it is impossible to conclude this firmly, but the dress and the other more complete sarcophagi indicate that this might very well have been the case.

cophagi scenes also reveals that the combination of one or more priests shown together with further family members, including the sitting wife at the end of the banqueting couch, as well as additional reclining or standing male figures clad in either chiton/himation or the so-called Parthian inspired banqueting clothes, as well as standing females were common motives in these scenes. The banqueting lid scenes go together with their respective boxes. Not many of these have been handed down to us, but 12 examples are for sure known (catalogue nos. 54-66, figs. 29-33). When held together, the lids and boxes clearly show that priests could and were displayed on both lids and boxes and there are four examples (catalogue nos. 62-65, figs. 31-33) where a total of five Palmyrene priests on each sarcophagus are shown, divided on lid and box. On the one hand an accumulation of priestly representations on some sarcophagi can be observed, and on the other hand the priests are embedded into much larger family constellations. However, what can be underlined is that a Palmyrene priest is rarely seen without a fellow priest in these scenes. This supports conclusions made in earlier publications that the priesthoods of Palmyra were extended within the families and larger families, bestowed or passed on by fathers and uncles.[21] And not least that being a Palmyrene priest was an absolute status symbol and signifier of the Palmyrene elite.

The meaning of the family and the social status of the Palmyrene priests

Palmyrene priests were most often either shown as stated above completely alone on loculus reliefs or they were shown in constellations, very often in the company of other priests on sarcophagi banqueting scenes. These are the two dominant modes of representations of the Palmyrene priests in the funerary sphere. While both men, women and children in some loculus reliefs were shown together with other family members, there are only five examples of priests being shown with family members in the loculus reliefs. These five examples show no consequent pattern, but display a variety of constellations displaying Palmyrene priests with their children, mothers, wives and fathers.[22] In small scale banqueting reliefs, priests are depicted in three examples with their hats next to them and in three examples with their hats on. No family members are included in these small scale banqueting reliefs. However, in the few large scale banqueting reliefs, the priests wearing hats are displayed together with a family member: their wife.[23] Whether this choice holds any significance cannot be concluded for certain, but one hypothesis is that the context of the depicted banqueting scenes could have been different and that the large scale banqueting scenes required family members to be depicted together with the deceased and not solely a servant. Interestingly, other headgear could be worn in the small scale banqueting reliefs, while the priestly hat was displayed on a pedestal beside the male individual (catalogue no. 24, fig. 19).[24] As I have concluded earlier, the phenomenon of displaying the priestly hat next to the priest was a fashion phenomenon and not an indicator of a priest who did not hold a priesthood anymore. The hat placed on a pedestal next to the priest would allow for the display of fashionable hairdos and other sorts of headgear, while still also representing that the individual held a priesthood.

Overall, the representations of Palmyrene priests make up a significant and distinguishable group within the corpus of the Palmyrene funerary sculpture. In an earlier publication, I have concluded that priesthoods in Palmyra should be seen much more as status markers than as professions as such.[25] Being depicted as a Palmyrene priest was an underlining of the important societal status of the individual and therefore also of his family and family connections.

21. Raja 2017d.

22. In Raja 2016b. Only four examples are published since the last one only came to my attention later. All five are included in a short catalogue at the end of this article.

23. There is, however, too little evidence to show any patterns in this form of representation.

24. Raja 2017a.

25. Raja 2017d.

In summary, a clear pattern emerges from this brief analysis of the types of representations of priests in the funerary sphere. On the loculus reliefs Palmyrene priests would most often be shown alone. This was a general pattern in the loculus reliefs across men - priests or not - as well as women. However, the degree to which priests were depicted alone on loculus reliefs exceeds what we observe in the other groups. In the sarcophagi banqueting scenes, there, however, was an emphasis on showing Palmyrene priests together with other Palmyrene priests, which would have belonged to their family. While the single loculus reliefs were expressions of the importance, which the representation of a Palmyrene priest held to the extent that it could stand alone as a status symbol, we must not forget that the single loculus reliefs were meant to be seen surrounded by other representations of family members in the grave. No individual representation in the Palmyrene graves stood completely alone and the surrounding family members would have added to the importance of the individual, underlining how family structure and history stood at the centre of Palmyrene societal structure. However, the clear pattern emerging in the sarcophagi scenes shows explicitly that Palmyrene priests, indeed, were deeply anchored at the centre of Palmyrene societal structure, namely the family, and were carriers of importance and status, which would have reflected on the rest of the family as well.

Conclusion

While Palmyrene funerary portraiture in general has been said to be de-individualised and repetitive in its iconography and the priestly representations have been said to be disappointing in terms of what they tell us about religious life, it is now clear in the light of the corpus collected by the Palmyra Portrait Project that such views of the Palmyrene funerary portraiture must be reconsidered. The sheer amount of portraits, held together with the possibilities for comparing these across groups and a tight chronological framework, now gives completely different ways of enquiring into the meaning behind these portraits and the ways in which they were used in the tombs and the societal meaning, which they would have held across centuries within the upper levels of Palmyrene society. In this article, it has been shown that the portraits of the Palmyrene priests make up a significant group within the funerary portraiture and that looking at the portraiture in details and in the constellations within which it was deliberately set, adds important insights and knowledge about the structure of religious life in Palmyra as well as the central role in Palmyrene societal structure, which the priests held.

Fig. 1: Loculus relief with bust of priest wearing the priestly hat. National Museum of Damascus, Damascus, inv. Dam21 / I.N. 33 / C.26, 50-100 CE (© Palmyra Portrait Project, Ingholt Archive at Ny Carlsberg Glyptotek, PS 141).

Fig. 2: Loculus relief with bust of priest wearing the priestly hat. Ny Carlsberg Glyptotek, Copenhagen, inv. IN 1032, 100-120 CE (Courtesy of Ny Carlsberg Glyptotek, photo by Palmyra Portrait Project).

Catalogue:

Catalogue number: 1 (Fig. 1)
Database number: NMD114
Loculus relief with bust of priest
Date: 50-100 CE
Measurements (in cm): Max. H: 55; W: 53
Location: National Museum of Damascus, Damascus, Syria
Inventory Number: Dam21 / I.N. 33 / C.26
PS Number: 141
Context: –
Inscription:
CIS: 4576; *PAT:* 0937, 1756
Inscription reads:
Image of Zabdelah,
son of Bogdan.
References: Ingholt Archive, PS 141; Ingholt 1928, 105, PS 141; Colledge 1976, 248.

Catalogue number: 2 (Fig. 2)
Database number: NCG001
Loculus relief with bust of priest
Date: 100-120 CE
Measurements (in cm): Max. H: 56; W: 49; D: 29.5; D. (Field): 20.5
Location: Ny Carlsberg Glyptotek, Copenhagen, Denmark
Inventory Number: IN 1032
PS Number: 142
Context: –
Inscription:
CIS: 4285; *PAT:* 0642
Inscription reads:
Alas!
[B]ôlḥâ,
[son of] ʿAtênatan,
(son of) [Bô]lhâ,
(son of(?)) ʾAḥitôr.
References: Ingholt Archive, PS 142; Ingholt 1928, 105, PS 142; Colledge 1976, 248; Hvidberg-Hansen and Ploug 1993, 64, cat. 20; Ploug 1995, 84-85, cat. 20; Heyn 2010, appendix 5, cat. 2.

Fig. 3: Loculus relief with bust of priest wearing the priestly hat. National Museum of Damascus, Damascus, 120-140 CE (© Palmyra Portrait Project, Ingholt Archive at Ny Carlsberg Glyptotek, PS 1283).

Catalogue number: 3 (Fig. 3)

Database number: NMD001
Loculus relief with bust of priest
Date: 120-140 CE
Measurements (in cm): Max. H: 52; D: 14.5
Location: National Museum of Damascus, Damascus, Syria
Inventory Number: –
PS Number: 1283
Context: Southeast necropolis. Hypogeum of Taai, south exedra, section B1
Inscription:
PAT: 1794
Inscription reads:
Image of Neboula,
son of Wahballât,
son of Taai,
Alas!
References: Ingholt Archive, PS 1283; Abdul-Hak 1952, 217, 221-222, cat. 1, pl. 1.1; Heyn 2010, appendix 5, cat. 9.

Fig. 4: Loculus relief with bust of priest wearing the priestly hat. Ny Carlsberg Glyptotek, Copenhagen, inv. IN 1031, 130-150 CE (Courtesy of Ny Carlsberg Glyptotek, photo by Palmyra Portrait Project).

Catalogue number: 4 (Fig. 4)

Database number: NCG068
Loculus relief with bust of priest
Date: 130-150 CE
Measurements (in cm): Max. H: 52; W: 45; D: 29.5; D (Field): 19
Location: Ny Carlsberg Glyptotek, Copenhagen, Denmark
Inventory Number: IN 1031
PS Number: 145
Context: –
Inscription:
CIS: 4395; *PAT:* 0754
Inscription reads:
Malê, son of
Moqîmû, (son of (?))
Bagâš (Ṣagaš(?)). Alas!
References: Ingholt Archive, PS 145; Ingholt 1928, 106, PS 145; Bossert 1951, 38, cat. 546, pl. 168; Colledge 1976, 248; Hvidberg-Hansen and Ploug 1993, 65, cat. 21; Ploug 1995, 86-87, cat. 21; Heyn 2010, appendix 5, cat. 23.

Fig. 5: Loculus relief with bust of priest wearing the priestly hat. Museo di Scultura Antica Giovanni Barracco, Rome, MB 250, 150-170 CE (© Palmyra Portrait Project, Ingholt Archive at Ny Carlsberg Glyptotek, PS 149).

Catalogue number: 5 (Fig. 5)

Database number: MGB001
Loculus relief with bust of priest
Date: 150-170 CE
Measurements (in cm): Max. H: 59; W: 40; D: 22
Location: Museo di Scultura Antica Giovanni Barracco, Rome, Italy
Inventory Number: MB 250
PS Number: 149
Context: –
Inscription:
PAT: 1759
Inscription 1 reads:
Son of
Yarhibôl.
Inscription 2 reads:
Alas! Habbûla,
son of Nesâ.
References: Ingholt Archives, PS 149; Ingholt 1928, 106, PS 149; Colledge 1976, 248; Schneider 1996, 297-299, fig. 3; Guzzo 1996, 302-303; Heyn 2010, appendix 5, cat. no. 21; Raja 2017d, 122, 126. fig. 16; Raja 2017f, 334, 336 fig. 8.

Fig. 6: Loculus relief with bust of priest wearing the priestly hat. Palmyra Museum, Palmyra, inv. F 494 (?), 170-200 CE (© Palmyra Portrait Project, Ingholt Archive at Ny Carlsberg Glyptotek, PS 550A).

Catalogue number: 6 (Fig. 6)

Database number: PM561
Loculus relief with bust of priest
Date: 170-200 CE
Measurements (in cm): Max. H: 30; W: 30
Location: Palmyra Museum, Palmyra, Syria
Inventory Number: F 494 (?)
PS Number: 550A
Context: West necropolis. Valley of the Tombs. Temple/house tomb no. 85b, tomb of A'ailamî and Zebidâ ('Tomb Cantineau')
Inscription: –
References: Ingholt Archive, PS 550A; Cantineau 1929, 13, pl. 4.2; Makowski 1983, 187 cat. 14, pl. 53.c.

Catalogue number: 7 (Fig. 7)

Database number: VMF001
Loculus relief with bust of priest
Date: 170-200 CE
Measurements (in cm): Max. H: 53.3; W: 41.9; D: 26
Location: Virginia Museum of Fine Arts, Richmond (VA),

Fig. 7: Loculus relief with bust of priest wearing the priestly hat. Virginia Museum of Fine Arts, Richmond (VA), inv. VMFA 2497, 170-200 CE (© Palmyra Portrait Project, Ingholt Archive at Ny Carlsberg Glyptotek, PS 1115).

United States of America
Inventory Number: VMFA 2497
PS Number: 1115
Context: –
Inscription: –
References: Ingholt Archive, PS 1115; Brown 1973, 126, cat. 144; Rumscheid 2000, 102, 107, 226-227, cat. 282; Heyn 2010, appendix 5, cat. 40; Raja 2017d, 122, 125, fig. 13.

Catalogue number: 8 (Fig. 8)
Database number: MLP010
Loculus relief with bust of priest
Date: 180-240 CE
Measurements (in cm): Max. H: 56.5; W: 48; D: 22
Location: Louvre, Paris, France
Inventory Number: AO 2069
PS Number: 253
Context: –
Inscription:
CIS: 4497; *PAT:* 0858
The inscription reads:

Fig. 8: Loculus relief with bust of priest wearing the priestly hat. Louvre, Paris, inv. AO 2069, 180-240 CE (© Palmyra Portrait Project, Ingholt Archive at Ny Carlsberg Glyptotek, PS 253).

Image of
ʿOgeilû,
son of
ʿAtênûri.
References: Ingholt Archive, PS 253; Chabot 1922, 122, cat. 14; Ingholt 1928, 119, PS 253; Colledge 1976, 250; Dentzer-Feydy and Teixidor 1993, 177, cat. 179; Heyn 2010, appendix 5, cat. 14.

Catalogue number: 9 (Fig. 9)
Database number: NCG020
Loculus relief with bust of priest
Date: 200-220 CE
Measurements (in cm): Max. H: 56; W: 40; D: 23; D (Field): 14.5
Location: Ny Carlsberg Glyptotek, Copenhagen, Denmark
Inventory Number: IN 1033
PS Number: 302
Context: –
Inscription:
CIS: 4298; *PAT:* 0655

Fig. 9: Loculus relief with bust of priest wearing the priestly hat. Ny Carlsberg Glyptotek, Copenhagen, inv. IN 1033, 200-220 CE (Courtesy of Ny Carlsberg Glyptotek, photo by Palmyra Portrait Project).

The inscription reads:
Alas!
Mariôn,
son of
ʾElâhbêl.
References: Ingholt Archive, PS 302; Ingholt 1928, 124-125, PS 302; Colledge 1976, 252; Hvidberg-Hansen and Ploug 1993, 120, cat. 76; Ploug 1995, 186-187, cat. 76; Heyn 2010, appendix 5, cat. 25; Raja 2017c, 280, fig. 17.8; Raja 2017d, 122, 125, fig. 14; Raja 2017e, fig. 2.

Catalogue number: 10 (Fig. 10)
Database number: NCG011
Loculus relief with bust of priest
Date: 220-240 CE
Measurements (in cm): Max. H: 54; W: 43; D: 31.5; D (Field): 20.5
Location: Ny Carlsberg Glyptotek, Copenhagen, Denmark
Inventory Number: IN 1034
PS Number: 305
Context: –

Fig. 10: Loculus relief with bust of priest wearing the priestly hat. Ny Carlsberg Glyptotek, Copenhagen, inv. IN 1034, 220-240 CE (Courtesy of Ny Carlsberg Glyptotek, photo by Palmyra Portrait Project).

Inscription:
CIS: 4364; *PAT:* 0722
The inscription reads:
Alas! Yarḥai,
son of Yerîʿbêl (Yedîʿbêl),
son of Šimʿôn,
ʿArgân.
References: Ingholt Archive, PS 305; Ingholt 1928, 125, PS 305; Colledge 1976, 252; Hvidberg-Hansen and Ploug 1993, 119, cat. 75; Ploug 1995, 184-185, cat. 75; Heyn 2010, appendix 5, cat. 26; Kropp and Raja 2014, 401, fig. 3; Kropp and Raja 2015, 73, fig. 2.a-d; Raja 2015c, 340-341, figs. 8-9; Krag 2017, 43-45, fig. 9.

Catalogue number: 11 (Fig. 11)
Database number: PM962
Religious altar with male figure
Date: 200-250 CE
Measurements (in cm): Max. H: 26; W: 17
Location: Palmyra Museum, Palmyra, Syria
Inventory Number: –

Fig. 11: Religious altar with male figure; a priestly hat is placed to his right. Palmyra Museum, Palmyra, 200-250 CE (© Palmyra Portrait Project, Ingholt Archive at Ny Carlsberg Glyptotek, PS 1410).

PS Number: 1410
Context: –
Inscription:
PAT: 0062
The inscription reads:
Blessed is his name forever,
the good and compassionate,
in gratitude
[...]
References: Ingholt Archive, PS 1410; Ingholt 1936, 92-93, cat. 3, pl. 18.2-3; Starcky 1955, 43, cat. 15.

Catalogue number: 12 (Fig. 12)

Database number: PM840
Statue of male figure
Date: 200-220 CE
Measurements (in cm): Max. H: 160; D: 40

Fig. 12: Statue of male figure, a priestly hat is placed at his left foot. Palmyra Museum, Palmyra, inv. A 23, 200-220 CE (© Palmyra Portrait Project, Ingholt Archive at Ny Carlsberg Glyptotek, PS 1143).

Location: Palmyra Museum, Palmyra, Syria
Inventory Number: A 23
PS Number: 1143
Context: –
Inscription: –
References: Ingholt Archive, PS 1143; Colledge 1976, 91, 105, 125, 134, 146-148, 224, pl. 127.

Catalogue number: 13 (Fig. 13)

Database number: NCG077
Stele with two standing full figures

Fig. 13: Stele with two full standing figures, a priestly hat is placed on a column between them. Ny Carlsberg Glyptotek, Copenhagen, inv. IN 1024, 230-250 CE (Courtesy of Ny Carlsberg Glyptotek, photo by Palmyra Portrait Project).

Fig. 14: Loculus relief with male bust, a priestly hat is placed above his right shoulder. State Hermitage Museum, St. Petersburg, inv. ДВ-4175, 180-240 CE (© Palmyra Portrait Project, Ingholt Archive at Ny Carlsberg Glyptotek, PS 210).

Date: 230-250 CE
Measurements (in cm): Max. H: 56; W: 47; D: 15; D (Field): 8.5
Location: Ny Carlsberg Glyptotek, Copenhagen, Denmark
Inventory Number: IN 1024
PS Number: 303
Context: –
Inscription:
CIS: 4322; *PAT*: 0679
The inscription reads:
Alas!
Yarḥai,
son of Yarḥai,
son of Yarḥai,
Yedîʿbêl
Yaʿût.
References: Ingholt Archives, PS 303; Ingholt 1928, 125, PS 303; Bossert 1951, 38, no. 554, pl. 170; Colledge 1976, 62, 67, 129, 132, 135, 143, 148, 154, 156, 239, 241, pl. 35; Hvidberg-Hansen and Ploug 1993, 156-157, no. 126; Ploug 1995, 255-256, no. 126; Albertson 2000, 164, n.26; Cussini 2005, fig. 2; Raja 2017a, 63, 64, 65, 67, cat. 1, fig. 1.

Catalogue number: 14 (Fig. 14)
Database number: SHM008
Loculus relief with male bust
Date: 180-240 CE
Measurements (in cm): Max. H: 50.5; W: 39.5
Location: State Hermitage Museum, St. Petersburg, Russia
Inventory Number: ДВ-4175
PS Number: 210
Context: –
Inscription:
PAT: 1767
The inscription reads:
Mezabbenâ,
son of Jarhibôlâ,
(son of) Refabôl (son of) Bogdan,
Annâ his 'guardian',
made this for him.
Alas!
References: Ingholt Archive, PS 210; Ingholt 1928, 113, PS 210;; Ingholt 1938, 131-132, pl. 49.1; Gawlikowski 1966, 86, 92, fig. 5; Colledge 1976, 250; Raja 2017a, 63, 64, 65, 69, cat. 6, fig. 3; https://www.hermitagemuseum.org/wps/

Fig. 15: Loculus relief with male bust, a priestly hat is placed above his right shoulder. Palmyra Museum, Palmyra, inv. B 1757/6581, 175-225 CE (© Palmyra Portrait Project, Ingholt Archive at Ny Carlsberg Glyptotek, PS 1303).

Fig. 16: Loculus relief with male bust, a priestly hat is placed above his left shoulder. Last known to be in the private collection of Baron Poche in Aleppo, 180-240 CE (© Palmyra Portrait Project, Ingholt Archive at Ny Carlsberg Glyptotek, PS 230).

portal/hermitage/digital-collection/25.+archaeological+artifacts/87743 (27.11.2018).

Catalogue number: 15 (Fig. 15)

Database number: PM397
Loculus relief with male bust
Date: 175-225 CE
Measurements (in cm): Max. H: 52; W: 45; D: 15
Location: Palmyra Museum, Palmyra, Syria
Inventory Number: B 1757/6581
PS Number: 1303
Context: West necropolis. Valley of the Tombs. Hypogeum of Shalamallat, central exedra
Inscription:
PAT: 1834
The inscription reads:
Alas!
Ma'an, son of,
Wahbaî.
References: Ingholt Archive, PS 1303; Bounni and Saliby 1957, 48, cat. 16, pl. 6.2; Bounni 1961-1962, 160-161, cat. 20; Gawlikowski 1974, 23-24, cat. 43; Tanabe 1986, 324, pl. 293; Sadurska and Bounni 1994, 160-161, cat. 211, fig. 113; al-As'ad and Gawlikowski 1997, 35, cat. 44, fig. 44; Raja 2017a, 63, 64, 65, 70, cat. 9, fig. 5.

Catalogue number: 16 (Fig. 16)

Database number: BaronPoche002
Loculus relief with male bust
Date: 180-240 CE
Measurements (in cm): Max. H: 60; W: 40
Location: Last known location: Aleppo, private collection of Baron Poche.
Inventory Number: –
PS Number: 230
Context: –
Inscription:
CIS: 4468; *PAT:* 0829
The inscription reads:
Ḥaggagu,

Fig. 17: Loculus relief with male bust, a priestly hat is placed above his right shoulder. Ny Carlsberg Glyptotek, Copenhagen, inv. 1043, 180-240 CE (Courtesy of Ny Carlsberg Glyptotek, photo by Palmyra Portrait Project).

Fig. 18: Loculus relief with male bust, a priestly hat is placed above his right shoulder. British Museum, London, inv. BM 125346, 180-240 CE (© Palmyra Portrait Project, Ingholt Archive at Ny Carlsberg Glyptotek, PS 286).

son of ʿOgê,
son of Iedîʿb[êl].
Alas!
References: Ingholt Archive, PS 230; Ingholt 1928, 116-117, PS 230; Colledge 1976, 250; Raja 2017a, 63, 64, 65, 68, cat. 4, fig. 2.

Catalogue number: 17 (Fig. 17)
Database number: NCG010
Loculus relief with male bust
Date: 180-240 CE
Measurements (in cm): Max. H: 55; W: 49; D: 22; D (Field): 15
Location: Ny Carlsberg Glyptotek, Copenhagen, Denmark
Inventory Number: IN 1043
PS Number: 293
Context: –
Inscription:
CIS: 4611; *PAT*: 0972, 1634
The inscription reads:
Alas!
References: Ingholt Archive, PS 293; Ingholt 1928, 123, PS 293; Colledge 1976, 252-253; Hvidberg-Hansen and Ploug 1993, 114-115, cat. 70; Ploug 1995, 174-176, cat. 70; Raja 2015c, 338-340, figs. 6-7; Raja 2017a, 63, 64, 65, 69, cat. 7, fig. 4.

Catalogue number: 18 (Fig. 18)
Database number: BM024
Loculus relief with male bust
Date: 180-240 CE
Measurements (in cm): Max. H: 49.53; W: 35.56; D: 32
Location: British Museum, London, United Kingdom
Inventory Number: BM 125346
PS Number: 286
Context: –
Inscription:
CIS: 4337; *PAT*: 0695
The inscription reads:
Iarḥibôlê,
son of Rabêl,
(son of) Šalmê. Alas!
References: Ingholt Archive, PS 286; Ingholt 1928, 122-123;

Fig. 19: Banqueting relief with two full figures, a priestly hat is placed between them. Yale University Art Gallery, inv. 1931.38, 180-240 CE (© Palmyra Portrait Project, Ingholt Archive at Ny Carlsberg Glyptotek, PS 1347).

Colledge 1976, 62, 69, 103, 118, 124, 138-139, 141-142, 146, 155, 217, 240-241, 246, 253, pl. 81; Raja 2017a, 63, 64, 65, 70-71, cat. 10, fig. 6.

Catalogue number: 19

Database number: UOW002
Loculus relief with male bust
Date: 180-240 CE
Measurements (in cm): Max. H: 60; W: 36
Location: University of Wyoming, American Heritage Center, Laramie (WY), United States of America
Inventory Number: 1090-33
PS Number: –
Context: –
Inscription: –
References: Albertson 2000, 163-165, fig. 2; Raja 2017a, 63, 64, 65, 71, cat. 11.

Catalogue number: 20

Database number: MLP011
Loculus relief with male bust
Date: 200-220 CE
Measurements (in cm): Max. H: 52; W: 44; D: 24
Location: Louvre, Paris, France
Inventory Number: AO 2398
PS Number: 221
Context: –
Inscription:
CIS: 4381; *PAT:* 0740
The inscription reads:
Yarḥai, son of
Elahbêl.
Alas!
References: Ingholt Archives, PS 221; Ingholt 1928, 115, PS 221; Mackay 1949, 162, 173, pl. LII,3; Ghirshman 1962, 77, fig. 89; Colledge 1976, 62, 68-69, 104, 124, 129, 138, 140-143, 146f, 158, 209-210, 216-217, 240, 246, 250, pl. 79; Ingholt 1976, 117; Taha 1982, 128, fig. XIV; Dentzer-Feydy and Teixidor 1993, 190, cat. 191; Seipel 1996, 179, cat. 2; Albertson 2000, 165, n.27; Raja 2017a, 63, 64, 65, 68-69, cat. 5.

Fig. 20: Banqueting relief with two full figures, a priestly hat is placed between them. Palmyra Museum, Palmyra, inv. CD 27, 220-240 CE (© Palmyra Portrait Project, Ingholt Archive at Ny Carlsberg Glyptotek, PS 1495).

Catalogue number: 21

Database number: PM446
Loculus relief with male bust
Date: 200-220 CE
Measurements (in cm): Max. H: 27; W: 42
Location: Palmyra Museum, Palmyra, Syria
Inventory Number: B 8522/2321
PS Number: –
Context: –
Inscription: –
References: Gawlikowski 1987, 291, cat. 9; Charles-Gaffiot et al. 2001, 271, 347, cat. 163; Clauss 2002, 88, no. 101; Raja 2017a, 63, 64, 65, 67, cat. 2.

Catalogue number: 22

Database number: DGAM033
Loculus relief with male bust
Date: 220-240 CE
Measurements (in cm): Max. H: –; W: –
Location: Directorate-General of Antiquities and Museums, Damascus, Syria
Inventory Number: –
PS Number: –
Context: –
Inscription: –
References: Raja 2017a, 63, 64, 65, 67, cat. 3. http://www.dgam.gov.sy/index.php?d=239&id=1206 (20.07.2018)

Catalogue number: 23

Database number: PM086
Loculus relief with male bust
Date: 239-273 CE
Measurements (in cm): Max. H: 46; W: 37; D: 8
Location: Palmyra Museum, Palmyra, Syria
Inventory Number: 1794/6643
PS Number: –
Context: West necropolis. Valley of Tombs. Hypogeum of Bôlbarak.
Inscription: –
References: Sadurska and Bounni 1994, 146, cat. 194, fig. 129; Raja 2017a, 63, 64, 65, 71-72, cat. 12.

Catalogue number: 24 (Fig. 19)

Database number: UAG006
Banqueting relief with two full figures
Date: 180-240 CE
Measurements (in cm): Max. H: 52; W: 56; D: 8; D (Field): 4
Location: Yale University Art Gallery, New Haven (CT), United States of America
Inventory Number: 1931.38
PS Number: 1347
Context: –
Inscription: –
References: Ingholt Archive, PS 1347; Ingholt 1954, no. 11; Vermeule 1964, 107; Gawlikowski 1966, 93, fig. 6; Brody and Hoffman 2011, 377, pl. 75; Raja 2017a, 63, 64, 65, 73, cat. 15, fig. 9.

Catalogue number: 25

Database number: PM092
Banqueting relief with two full figures
Date: 180-240 CE
Measurements (in cm): Max. H: 42; W: 48; D: 5
Location: Palmyra Museum, Palmyra, Syria
Inventory Number: 1793/6642
PS Number: –
Context: West necropolis. Valley of the Tombs. Hypogeum of Bôlbarak, main exedra

Fig. 21: Complete sarcophagus with banqueting scene and portrait busts on the box, a priestly hat is placed behind the reclining male on the lid. Palmyra Museum, Palmyra, inv. B 1795/6644 (lid), B 1796/6645 (box), 239 CE (© Palmyra Portrait Project, Ingholt Archive at Ny Carlsberg Glyptotek, PS 1262/1264).

Inscription: –
References: Tanabe 1986, 43, 464, cat. 437; Sadurska and Bounni 1994, 145-146, cat. 193, fig. 253; Long 2017, 79-80, fig. 10; Raja 2017a, 63, 64, 65, 73, cat. 16.

Catalogue number: 26 (Fig. 20)

Database number: PM276
Banqueting relief with two full figures
Date: 220-240 CE
Measurements (in cm): Max. H: 40; W: 29; D: 14
Location: Palmyra Museum, Palmyra, Syria
Inventory Number: CD 27
PS Number: 1495
Context: Secondary context: Found in the south building in front of the staircase to Temple of the Standards (Temple des Enseignes)
Inscription: –
References: Ingholt Archive, PS 1495; Michałowski 1966, 49-50, cat. 3, fig. 57; Tanabe 1986, 465, fig. 439; Raja 2017a, 63, 64, 65, 72-73, cat. 14, fig. 8.

Catalogue number: 27

Database number: DGAM012
Banqueting relief with two full figures
Date: 220-240 CE
Measurements (in cm): Max. H: –; W: –
Location: Directorate-General of Antiquities and Museums, Damascus, Syria
Inventory Number: –
PS Number: –
Context: –
Inscription: –
References: Raja 2017a, 63, 64, 65, 75, cat. 17. http://www.dgam.gov.sy/index.php?d=239&id=1199 (20.07.2018)

Catalogue number: 28

Database number: Christie's043
Banqueting relief with full male figure
Date: 220-240 CE
Measurements (in cm): Max. H: 31.8; W: 41.3
Location: Last known location: Christie's, New York, New York, United States of America
Inventory Number: –
PS Number: –
Context: –
Inscription: –
References: Christie's 2002, December 12th, New York, lot 303; Raja 2017a, 63, 64, 65, 72, cat. 13, fig. 7; http://www.christies.com/LotFinder/lot_details.aspx?from=salesummary&intObjectID=4026240 (26.11.2018).

Catalogue number: 29

Database number: PM880 (29a) + PM899 (29b)
Banqueting relief with male figure
Date: 200-250 CE
Measurements (in cm): 29a: Max. H: 56; W: 77. 29b: Max H: 25
Location: Palmyra Museum, Palmyra, Syria
Inventory Number: 346/361/83.13.3, II.19
PS Number: –
Context: West necropolis. Valley of the Tombs. Temple tomb no. 36
Inscription: –
References: 29a: Schmidt-Colinet 1992, vol. I, 149, cat. B 7, fig. 60; vol. II, pls. 38.d, 41.a,f. 29b: Schmidt-Colinet 1992, vol. I, 153, cat. K 14, fig. 53.

Catalogue number: 30 (Fig. 21)

Database number: PM274
Complete sarcophagus with banqueting scene and portrait busts
Date: 239 CE
Measurements (in cm): Max. H: 143; W: 199; D: 12 cm
Location: Palmyra Museum, Palmyra, Syria
Inventory Number: B 1795/6644 (lid) and B 1796/6645 (box)
PS Number: 1262/1264
Context: West necropolis. Valley of the Tombs. Hypogeum of Bôlbarak, central exedra, on podium
Inscription:
Inscription 1 reads:
This image (is that) of Bôlbarak, son of Moqîmû Bôlbarak, who made the exedra and the podium in front of it in April year 550 (CE 239).
PAT: 1527
Inscription 2 reads:
Atâ, daughter of Gaddâ, his mother.
PAT: 1530
Inscription 3 reads:
Amatd'ateh, daughter of Bôlbarak, wife of Bôlbarak.
PAT: 1529
Inscription 4 reads:
Shalmat, daughter of Bôrrefâ, wife of Bôlbarak.
PAT: 1528
Inscription 5 reads:
Moqîmû, his son.
PAT: 1535
Inscription 6 reads:
Shalmat, his daughter.
PAT: 1534
Inscription 7 reads:
Amatnannaî, his daughter.
PAT: 1533
Inscription 8 reads:
Bôlbarak, his son.
PAT: 1532
Inscription 9 reads:
Atâ, his daughter.
PAT: 1531
Inscription 10 reads:
Wahballat, his son.
References: Ingholt Archive, PS 1262/1264; Bounni and Teixidor 1975, 10-12, cat. 2-11; Tanabe 1986, 41, pls. 393-395; Sadurska 1988, 16-17, fig. 1; Sadurska 1994, 16, fig. 3; Sadurska and Bounni, 1994, 146-148, cat. 195, fig. 247; Sadurska 1995, 587-588, fig. 11; al-As'ad and Gawlikowski 1997, 46-47, cat. 65, fig. 65; Raja 2017a, 64, 65, 75-76, cat. 20, fig. 11; Raja 2017d, 121, 124, fig. 11; Raja 2017e, 420, fig. 5; Raja 2017f, 327-328, fig. 4. Inscription: Sadurska and Bounni, 1994, 146-148, cat. 195, fig. 247.

Catalogue number: 31 (Fig. 22)

Database number: UNK231
Standing male from a sarcophagus lid
Date: 180-240 CE
Measurements (in cm): Max. H: –; W: –
Location: –
Inventory Number: –
PS Number: 1150
Context: –
Inscription: –
References: Ingholt Archive, PS 1150.

Catalogue number: 32

Database number: PM604
Sarcophagus box with religious scene
Date: 200-220 CE
Measurements (in cm): Max. H: 92; W: 227; D: 94
Location: Palmyra Museum, Palmyra, Syria
Inventory Number: B 2723/9160
PS Number: –
Context: –
Inscription: –
References: Rumscheid 2000, 222-223, cat. 271, pls. 64.2, 65.1-3.; Kaizer 2002, pls. 5-6; Schmidt-Colinet and al-As'ad 2007, 276-78, pl. 90; Wielgosz-Rondolino 2016, 77-79, cat. 17a-c; Raja 2017a, 64, 65, 75, cat. 22.
Object description: The sarcophagus box is rectangular in shape and is rendered as a kline. There are 17 figures

Fig. 22: Standing male from sarcophagus lid holding a priestly hat. Unknown location, 180-240 CE (© Palmyra Portrait Project, Ingholt Archive at Ny Carlsberg Glyptotek, PS 1150).

depicted on all four sides of the box, between the kline legs.

Side A (portrait A-F) depicts a standing male, a standing female, two standing males, a standing female, and a standing male. Between portrait C and D, at the height of their heads, two cylindrical flat-top headdresses, which are divided in three sections by two vertical grooves (Palmyrene priestly hats), are shown on top of a tall, square pillar. Two wreaths with the leaves pointing towards a central oval are depicted at the lower part of each headdress. A folded cloth with the edges falling down the pillar are depicted under each headdress. A square altar with a triangular top with a flame protruding from it, is also depicted between these portraits.

Side B (portrait G-M) depicts seven male figures. Between portrait G and H, a calf is seen depicted frontally. The calf is depicted with crescent-shaped horns over pointy ears. On top of the head and above the eyes, the fur is rendered by thin, incised lines. The eyes are large and the nose is oval. The chest musculature is rendered by v-shaped incisions. The forelegs are thin with the fetlock joints and coffins rendered. Between portrait I and J, a square altar with a triangular top with a flame protruding from it is depicted.
Side C (portrait N and O) depicts two male figures standing on a protruding lower edge.

Side D (portrait P and Q) depicts two female figures standing on a protruding lower edge.

The kline has four turned legs. They are composed of a plinth, above is a reversed bell-shape element, a concave quarter, a thick torus, a reversed concave quarter, a concave quarter, a biconical element, and two elements of opposed concave quarters. All elements are decorated with a tongue pattern.

Side A:
Portrait A: Standing male.
The figure is shown frontally. The arms appear short in relation to the body, indicating foreshortening. The right arm is bent and held to the torso. The left arm is bent and held outwards. The right leg is slightly bent. The legs are set apart and he rests his weight on his left leg.

His hair is arranged in snail-shell curls around the head. The individual locks of hair are indicated by incised lines. His face is oval. The eyebrows are curving, rendered by incised lines starting from the root of the nose. The eyes are close-set, and the eyeballs are blank. Only the earlobes are visible under the hair. The nose is straight and the mouth is small with full lips. The chin is pointed and the neck is wide with two horizontal grooves.

He wears a tunic and an undergarment. The undergarment is visible in a curving line above the knees, where the edge has fringes. The tunic has a wide, round neckline and short, wide sleeves. On either side of the chest, there are two plain bands extending downwards (clavi). The tunic ends at the knees, revealing the part of the undergarment. The folds of the tunic are rendered by curving and oblique grooves. There is an overfold at the waist. He does not wear shoes, and the toes are rendered by incised lines.

The right hand lies on top of the object carried in his left hand. With the upturned palm of his left hand, he holds a rectangular box. It has a rectangular depression on the frontal side. On top of the box lies a large round object, possibly a roughly carved wreath.

Portrait B: Standing female.
The figure is shown frontally. The arms appear short in relation to the body, indicating foreshortening. The head is turned slightly to the left. The right arm is bent and held to the chest. The left arm is bent and held to the waist. The left leg is slightly bent. The legs are set apart and she rests her weight on the right leg.

She wears two headdresses: a turban and a veil. The turban is coiled and is divided in two layers. Curving grooves indicate the coiling of the fabric. The veil is heavy. It falls over her shoulders, is folded around the arms, and covers the body and thighs. One end of the veil crosses the chest diagonally, falls over the left shoulder and extends down her left side. A zigzag-shaped fold falls from under her left hand extending downwards. An edge of the veil falls from her left wrist and extends downwards in a diagonal line to her left side. The lower edge is rendered in a curving line above the knees and it is pulled back alongside her legs. The folds of the veil are rendered by curving and oblique grooves. The headdresses cover parts of the hair: several strands of hair above the ears are pushed back over the edge of the turban and disappears under the veil. Her face is oval. The eyebrows are indicated by curving grooves. The eyes are close-set and round. The eyeballs are blank. Only the earlobes are visible under the hair and she wears dumbbell-shaped earrings (Colledge Classification: H). The chin is pointed with a cleft. The neck is wide with two horizontal grooves. She wears one necklace composed of small, round beads at the base of the neck.

She wears a tunic. The ankle-length tunic has a wide, round neckline. The folds of the tunic are rendered by curving grooves at the chest and oblique grooves between the legs. She wears shoes.

Her right arm is raised to the chest. She holds the diagonal fold of the himation with her hand. Her left hand lies at the lower right side of her waist, slightly pulling the veil.

Portrait C: Standing male.
The figure is shown in three-quarter view, turned slightly to the left. The arms appear short in relation to the body, indicating foreshortening. The right arm is bent and held across the waist. The left arm is bent end held out from the body. The right leg is slightly bent, and the knee is rendered in the drapery. The legs are set apart and he rests his weight on his left leg.

His hair is voluminous and he wears a wreath high on the forehead with the leaves pointing towards a central rosette. His face is oval. The eyebrows are indicated by curving grooves. The eyes are close-set and round with blank eyeballs. Only the earlobes are visible under the hair. The nose is straight. He has a beard that starts from the temples and covers the cheeks and the chin, as well as a moustache that covers the upper lip. The mouth is small. The neck is wide. A v-shaped groove indicates the jugular notch.

He wears a tunic and a toga. The ankle-length tunic has a wide, round neckline and short, wide sleeves. A wide band decorated with vegetal motifs extends downwards on each side of the chest. The folds of the tunic are rendered by curving grooves. Over the tunic, he wears a toga. The toga is folded from his right side and proceeds horizontally across his abdomen (sinus). The fold from his left shoulder is folded under the horizontal one where it proceeds downwards over his thighs and shins (umbo). Another fold falls from under his left wrist and ends in an s-shape at his left ankle. He probably wears boots.

He holds a pitcher in his right hand, directing it towards the altar. The pitcher has a conical foot, a concave body, and a tall neck. His index finger is extended. With the palm of his left hand turned outwards, he holds an oblong object, possibly a book-roll or a schedula, according to Sokolowski's classification.

Portrait D: Standing male.
The figure is shown frontally. The arms and the torso appear short. The right arm is extended away from the body. The left arm is bent and held to the torso. The left leg is slightly bent, and the knee is rendered in the drapery. The legs are set apart and he rests his weight on his right leg.

His hair is arranged in flame-shaped curls around the head. He wears a wreath high on the forehead with the leaves pointing towards a central rosette. His face is oval. The eyebrows are curving, rendered by thin ridges. The eyes are close-set and almond-shaped with thick upper eyelids. The upper eyelids extend beyond the end of the lower ones. The eyeballs are blank. The ears are small with the helix and scapha depicted. The nose is straight. He has a beard that starts from the temples and covers the cheeks and the chin, as well as a moustache that covers the upper lip. The facial hair is rendered by flame-shaped curls arranged in rows. The moustache is rendered with narrow, oblique incised lines: they are centred over the philtrum and curve downwards and to the left and right of the face, reaching the beard. The mouth is small. The neck is wide. A v-shaped groove indicates the sternocleidomastoid muscles.

He wears a tunic and a toga. The ankle-length tunic has a wide, v-shaped neckline and short, wide sleeves. A wide band decorated with a vegetal motif extends downwards on the right side of the chest. The edge of the right sleeve is folded under the toga. The folds of the tunic are rendered by curving grooves. Over the tunic, he wears a toga. The toga covers most of the body: it is wrapped around the left shoulder and arm, leaving only the upper part of the chest free. The toga is folded from his right side and proceeds horizontally across his abdomen (sinus). A fold coming from his left shoulder is folded under the horizontal fold (umbo) where it proceeds downwards over his thighs and shins. Another fold falls from under his left wrist and ends in an s-shape at his left ankle. He wears footwear, either boots or sandals.

With his right hand, he holds a pitcher, directing it towards the altar. The pitcher has an ovoid body and a tall neck. With his left hand, he holds an oblong object to his torso, possibly a book-roll or schedula according to Sokolowski's classification. The index and little finger are extended.

Portrait E: Standing female.
The figure is shown frontally. The left arm appears short in relation to the body, indicating foreshortening. The right arm is held along the body. The left arm is bent and held to the chest. The right leg is bent with the knee rendered in the drapery. The legs are set apart and she rests her weight on her left leg.

She wears three headdresses: a headband, a turban, and a veil. The details of the headband are unclear. The turban is coiled and divided in two layers. Curving grooves indicate the coiling of the fabric. The veil is heavy and covers the whole body: it falls over her head and is wrapped around the right shoulder and arm, leaving only the upper part of the chest and hand free. One end of the veil crosses the chest diagonally and falls over the left shoulder, leaving the lower arm and hand free. It extends downwards at her left side. The folds of the veil are rendered by curving and oblique grooves. She also wears a head-chain. The chain is fastened at the centre of the turban with a larger bezel, and falls to either side of the forehead with strings of round beads. Her face is oval. The eyebrows are curving. The eyes are almond-shaped and slanting. The eyeballs are blank. Only the earlobes are visible under the headdress. She wears dumbbell-shaped earrings (Colledge Classification: H). The chin is pointed. The neck is wide. She wears a necklace composed of small, round beads at the base of the neck.

She wears a tunic. The ankle-length tunic has a wide, v-shaped neckline. The folds of the tunic are rendered by curving grooves at the chest and oblique grooves between the legs. She wears round toe shoes.

Her right hand is placed at her right thigh, slightly pulling an end of the veil. The index and little finger are extended. Her left arm is raised to the chest. She lightly pulls a diagonal fold of the veil with her hand. The index and little finger are extended.

Portrait F: Standing male.
The figure is shown in three-quarter view. The arms appear short in relation to the body, indicating foreshortening. The arms are bent. He stands with the legs set slightly apart.

His hair is arranged in curls around the head. His face is oval. The eyebrows are curving and the eyes are close-set. The eyeballs appear blank. The nose is small and straight. The cheeks are fleshy. The mouth is small with full lips. The chin is round and prominent. The neck is wide.

He wears an undergarment and a tunic. The undergarment is visible from above the left knee and diagonally under the right knee. The edge of the undergarment has fringes. The tunic has a small, v-shaped neckline and wide sleeves that cover his upper arms and elbow. There is an overfold at the waist. The folds of the tunic are rendered by curving and oblique grooves. He does not wear shoes. The toes are indicated by incised lines.

He holds a large bowl in his hands. It is filled with small, round objects, possibly fruits.

Side B:
Portrait G: Standing male.
The figure is shown in three-quarter view. The arms appear short in relation to the body, indicating foreshortening. The right arm is bent and held to the chest. The

left arm is bent and held out from the body. His legs are set apart and he rests his weight on his bent right leg.

He wears a short himation. It is fastened at the left shoulder by a circular brooch with an incised border (Colledge Classification: h). It covers the left side of the chest and the lower body and thighs, leaving the arms and the upper right part of the chest free. An overfold is depicted at the waist. The folds of the himation are rendered by diagonal and curving grooves. He does not wear shoes.

He holds a small dagger in his right hand: it has a round end, a rectangular main body, and a thin ridge indicating the fuller of the blade. He wears an armlet: a plain hoop. With the left hand, he holds the right horn of the calf.

Portrait H: Standing male.
The figure is shown in three-quarter view. The arms appear short in relation to the body, indicating foreshortening. The right arm is bent and held to the torso. The left arm is bent and held out from the body. He stands with his legs set slightly apart with the weight resting on the left leg, while the right leg is slightly bent.

He wears an undergarment, a tunic, and a mantle. The scalloped edge of the undergarment is visible at his legs falling in a diagonal line from above the left knee and over the right. The folds of the garment are rendered by oblique grooves. The tunic has a round neckline and short, wide sleeves and ends at his knees. The folds of the tunic are rendered by curving and oblique grooves. Over the tunic, he wears a mantle. It is folded around his left shoulder and arm leaving most of the torso and the hand free. The folds of the chlamys are rendered by vertical and curving grooves. He wears sandals: they have a single strap between the big toe and index toe and are tied around the ankles.

With his right hand, he holds a pitcher. The pitcher has a ring base, an ovoid body with decoration (details unclear) and a tall neck. With the left hand, he holds a patera with a long handle. There is a tondo decoration on the inside of the patera.

Portrait I: Standing male.
The figure is shown in three-quarter view. The arms are bent. He stands with his legs set slightly apart with the weight resting on the left leg, while the right leg is slightly bent.

He wears an undergarment and a tunic. The scalloped edge of the undergarment is visible at his legs falling in a diagonal line from above the left knee and over the right. Over this garment, he wears a short-sleeved tunic that proceeds to his thighs. There is an overfold of the tunic. The folds of the tunic are rendered by curving and oblique grooves. He wears sandals.

He holds an octagonal chest with a lid in his hands. The lid is decorated with a panel with a row of lanceolate leaves with incised midribs. On top of the lid lies an oblong object, possibly a diadem with a central oval. The lower part of the chest is divided into three panels. The central square panel is decorated with a flower with four serrated leaves. A beaded band frames the panel. The narrow rectangular panels on either side are decorated with lanceolate leaves in an opposite arrangement on the stem.

Portrait J: Standing male.
The figure is shown frontally. The arms appear short in relation to the body, indicating foreshortening. The right arm is bent and held out from the body. The left is bent and held to the torso. He stands with his legs set slightly apart.

He wears a tunic and a toga. The ankle-length tunic has a round neckline. A panel extends downwards from his right shoulder: it is decorated with lanceolate leaves in an opposite arrangement on the stem. The folds of the tunic are rendered by curving grooves. Over the tunic, he wears a toga. It is wrapped around his left shoulder and arm. It falls in a thick fold from his shoulder (umbo) and is looped under another fold of the toga that runs across his waist (sinus). A fold of the toga falls downwards from under his left wrist, proceeds across his lower legs, and falls behind his right leg. The folds of the toga are rendered by curving and oblique grooves. He wears sandals.

With the right hand, he holds a patera with a long handle. With his left hand, he holds a small rectangular object, possibly a book-roll, or a schedula according to Sokolowski's classification.

Portrait K: Standing male.
The figure is shown in three-quarter view. The arms appear short in relation to the body. The arms are bent. He stands with the legs slightly set apart. The left leg is slightly bent, and he is resting on the right leg.

He wears an undergarment, a tunic, and a mantle. The edge of the undergarment is visible at his legs falling in a diagonal line from above the left knee and over the right, and it is decorated with a scalloped border. The tunic has short sleeves and ends above the knees. There is an overfold of the tunic at the waist. The folds of the tunic are rendered by curving and oblique grooves. Over the tunic, he wears a mantle. It is folded around his left shoulder and upper arm. From the elbow, it falls downwards along his right side. The folds of the mantle are rendered by oblique and curving grooves. He wears sandals.

He holds a large bowl in his hands. It is filled with small, round objects, possibly fruits.

Portrait L: Standing male.
The figure is shown in three-quarter view. The arms appear short in relation to the body. The arms are bent and held to the chest. He stands with the legs apart. The left leg is slightly bent, and he is resting on the right leg.

He wears an undergarment and tunic. The edge of the undergarment is visible at his legs falling in a diagonal line from above the left knee and over the right. The short-sleeved tunic has a small, v-shaped neckline and ends above the knees. He wears a band belt at the waist which creates an overfold of the tunic. The folds of the tunic are rendered by curving and oblique grooves. He wears sandals.

He holds an oblong object in his hands, possibly a jug.

Portrait M: Standing male.
The figure is shown in three-quarter view. The arms appear short in relation to the body. The right arm is slightly bent and held out from the body. The left arm is bent and held to the torso. He stands with his legs slightly set apart. The left leg is slightly bent, and he is resting on the right leg.

He wears an undergarment, a tunic, and a mantle. The edge of the undergarment is visible at his legs falling in a diagonal line from above the left knee and over the right. The tunic has a wide round neckline, wide long sleeves and it ends above the knees. There is an overfold of the tunic at the waist. The folds of the tunic are rendered by curving and oblique grooves. Over the tunic, he wears a mantle. It falls in a wide fold from the back and over his left shoulder. A zigzag-shaped fold falls from under his left hand. The folds of the mantle are rendered by vertical grooves. He wears sandals.

With the right hand, he holds a jug. With the left hand, he holds the vertical fold of the mantle. The left index and little finger are extended.

Side C:
Portrait N: Standing male.
The figure is shown frontally. Both arms are bent and held to the torso. He stands with his legs slightly apart. The right leg is slightly bent, and he is resting on the left leg. He wears a 'Parthian-style' tunic and 'Parthian-style' trousers. The tunic has a wide, round neckline decorated with a beaded band and long sleeves. The cuffs of the sleeves have a wide band decorated with flowers. At the middle, the tunic has a wide band extending downwards decorated with running vines with lobed vine leaves. The tunic ends above the knees and has a decorated lower border with four-petal flowers between two lines at the hem. The folds of the tunic are rendered by curving, wide grooves. He wears a plain band belt, knotted at the centre with the ends looped under on either side of the waist. He also wears another band belt that runs diagonally from the right to the left side of the waist. It is knotted at his left side. The trousers are visible from the knees. Each trouser leg has a wide band extending downwards in the middle, decorated with a vegetal pattern. Along his right side, he has an object with a pointed end and a rectangular main body: a sheathed dagger. He wears plain, round toe boots, which covers the lower part of the shins.

He stands with the arms crossed, the right arm under the left.

Portrait O: Standing male.
The figure is shown frontally. Both arms are bent and held to the torso. He stands with his legs slightly apart. The left leg is slightly bent, and he is resting on the right leg. He wears a 'Parthian-style' tunic and 'Parthian-style' trousers. The tunic has a wide, round neckline decorated with a beaded band and long sleeves. The cuffs of the sleeves have a wide band decorated with flowers. At the middle, the tunic has a wide band extending downwards. It is decorated with floral patterns separated by beaded bands. The tunic ends above the knees and has a decorated lower border with leaves running towards a central rosette. The folds of the tunic are rendered by curving,

wide grooves. He wears a plain band belt, knotted at the centre with the ends looped under on either side of the waist. He also wears another band belt that runs diagonally from the right to the left side of the waist. A long sword is depicted at his left side; with a square top and long rectangular main body. The trousers are visible from the knees. Each trouser leg has a wide band decorated with a running vine with lobed vine leaves, extending downwards. He wears plain, round toe boots, which covers the lower part of the shins.

He stands with the arms crossed, the right arm over the left.

Side D:
Portrait P: Standing female.
The figure is shown frontally. Her head is turned to her right. Both arms are bent. She stands with the legs apart. The right leg is bent and she rests the weight on the left leg.

Her hair is curly. It is short at her forehead where it is brushed back. On each side of the face, the hair is brushed to the back, covering her ears and reaching the shoulders. Her face is round. The eyebrows are curving and the eyes are close-set. The eyeballs appear blank. The nose is straight and wide at the base. The cheeks are full and the mouth is small with full lips. The chin is pointed and the neck is wide.

She wears a tunic. It has a round neckline and short, wide sleeves. There is a large overfold at the waist. The tunic ends at the ankles. The folds of the tunic are rendered by oblique and curving grooves. She wears a closed-toe shoe.

She holds a square chest in her hands. With the right hand, she holds the lifted lid of the chest. Two necklaces are depicted hanging in half-circles from the opening of the chest. The upper necklace is composed of round beads with a drop-shaped pendant suspended from the centre. The lower necklace is composed of alternating square and oval pendants joined by beaded elements. With the left hand, she holds the bottom of the chest.

Portrait Q: Standing female.
The figure is shown frontally. The right arm is bent and held away from the torso. The left is bent and held to the torso. She stands with the legs apart.

Fig. 23: Complete sarcophagus with banqueting scene and portrait busts. Palmyra Museum, Palmyra, inv. B 2723/9160, 220-240 CE (© Palmyra Portrait Project, Ingholt Archive at Ny Carlsberg Glyptotek, PS 896).

She wears one necklace. It is composed of round beads on a string, worn at the base of the neck.

She wears a tunic. It has a v-shaped neckline and short, wide sleeves. There is a large overfold at the waist. The tunic ends at the feet. The folds of the tunic are rendered by oblique, vertical, and curving grooves.

With the right hand, she holds a round mirror with a groove along the outer edge. With the left hand, she holds an oblong object with a round upper part, possible a perfume bottle with a stopper. The thumb, index, and little finger are extended.

Catalogue number: 33 (Fig. 23)
Database number: PM329 (33a) + PM327 (33b)
Complete sarcophagus with banqueting scene and portrait busts
Date: 220-240 CE
Measurements (in cm): Max. H: –; W: –
Location: Palmyra Museum, Palmyra, Syria
Inventory Number: B 2723/9160
PS Number: 896
Context: Southeast necropolis, Valley of the Tombs. Temple/house tomb no. 186 ('Tombeau de l'aviation'/'Tomb Duvaux')
Inscription: –
References: 33a: Ingholt Archive, PS 896; Seyrig 1937, 21, fig.

12; Will 1951, 87-88, figs. 7-8; Parlasca 1984, 290-91, fig. 7; Schmidt-Colinet 1992, vol. II, pl. 73a; Wielgosz 1997, 71, pl. IV,1; Raja 2017a, 64, 65, 75, cat. 18, figs. 10. 33b: Parlasca 1984, 290-91, fig. 8; Schmidt-Colinet 1992, vol. II, pl. 69c; Raja 2017a, 64, 65, 75, cat. 18, fig. 10.

Object description:
The sarcophagus is rectangular in shape and the lid depicts a seated female, two standing males, a reclining male and a standing male. The right lateral side of the sarcophagus box depicts three busts rendered in clipei. Beneath these figures is a box in the shape of a kline with two female busts between the kline legs. On top of the kline are two mattresses. The thin mattress at the top, visible under the reclining figure, is decorated with an intersecting lozenge pattern with flowers in the lozenges. The lower mattress has three vertical panels. The seated female sits on two tall cushions. The central panel is decorated with rosettes set in rhombuses. The panels on either side are decorated with a running scroll with rosettes. Vertical, curving grooves indicate the texture of the mattress. Both ends of the kline are decorated with a fulcrum. The fulcrum on the right side is curving up and slightly projecting outwards. The fulcra are decorated with running scrolls with rosettes.

At the right lateral side of the sarcophagus lid, there is a large panel. At the top there is a long, rectangular panel divided in two horizontal sections: the upper section is decorated with a series of oblique grooves that fan out from the centre towards the right and left. A wide frame with alternating narrow, rectangular and square panels is depicted below; the square panels are decorated each with a rosette with four serrated petals, and the rectangular panels are decorated with a rosette with four serrated petals inside a lozenge, and serrated leaves at the corners of the lozenge.

There are three armless busts in clipei at the lower part of the box: two busts of priests and a female bust. The clipei are carved in low relief and are formed by six concentric grooves. There is a six-petal rosette between each bust at the height of their heads with a small, round edge between each petal.

The central stretcher of the kline is decorated. The central part is divided into two sections by a horizontal, thin line. The upper section is decorated with a crisscross pattern and the lower with a tongue pattern. On either side of the central section is a square inlay decorated with an animal. These inlays are followed by rectangular indentations decorated with a wave pattern, and again followed by a square inlay decorated with an animal. One leg of the kline is depicted at the right side. The leg is turned and composed of a plinth, and above this is a concave quarter, a long reversed concave quarter, a reversed bell-shaped element, a ball, and a bell-shaped element. All elements are decorated with a tongue pattern. The sarcophagus box is further decorated with three animal heads. Each of them has a thick ring gripped in their mouth. Three garlands are fastened to the rings. The central garland is composed of lobed leaves pointing towards a central rosette. The garlands on either side are composed of lanceolate leaves pointing towards a central rosette. The lower part of the box is decorated with four circular elements set between the garlands.

Sarcophagus lid:
Portrait A: Seated female.
The figure is shown in three-quarter view. The left arm is bent and raised to the chest. Her legs are bent with the knees rendered under the drapery. Her feet are obscured by the right foot of the reclining figure to her left.

She wears a veil that falls over her shoulders. It falls back at her right upper arm and appears again below her waist where it proceeds in a wide fold over the cushions and the mattress. She wears two necklaces. One composed of a loop-in-loop chain with a central circular pendant, worn high on the chest. One composed of an interwoven loop-in-loop chain with three circular pendants decorated with armless busts. The two upper pendants are placed on either side of the breasts and the central one at the stomach.

She wears a tunic and a himation. The tunic has a small, round neckline and short, wide sleeves. The folds of the tunic are rendered by curving grooves. The ankle-length himation crosses the chest diagonally from the left shoulder, leaving the right side of the chest free. The himation covers her lower body and legs. The folds of the himation are rendered by oblique and curving grooves.

She wears a bracelet on her left wrist, composed of a wide hoop.

Portrait B: Standing male.
The figure is shown frontally. The arms appear short in relation to the body, indicating foreshortening. The right arm is slightly bent and held in front of the body. The left

arm is held along the body. His lower body and legs are obscured by the right leg of the reclining figure.

He wears a tunic with a small, round neckline and long, wide sleeves. An overfold, possibly created by a belt, is visible at the waist. The folds of the tunic are rendered by oblique and curving grooves.

The outline of a round vessel, possibly a bowl, is visible at his right hand. A vessel, possibly a rhyton, with a flat top and a cylindrical body is visible in front of his left arm (details unclear).

Portrait C: Standing male.
The figure is shown frontally. The arms appear short in relation to the body, indicating foreshortening. The right arm is bent and held to the torso. The left arm is bent and held out in front of the body. His legs are obscured by the reclining figure to his left.
He wears a tunic with a small, round neckline and long, wide sleeves. The folds of the tunic are rendered by oblique and curving grooves.

He holds the ends of a wreath with his hands. The wreath has a small loop visible above the right hand. The contour of the leaves are incised.

Portrait D: Reclining male.
The figure is shown in frontal to three-quarter view. The arms appear short in relation to the body, indicating foreshortening. The right arm is slightly bent and resting on his raised right knee. His right leg is bent and his foot is resting on the kline. The left is bent under the right leg.

He wears a 'Parthian-style' tunic, a chlamys, and trousers. The tunic has a small, round neckline and long, wide sleeves. The cuffs of the sleeves are decorated with two panels separated by a thin band. The tunic ends above his knees and have a border decorated with triangles. At the right side, the border is decorated with large arrow. The folds of the tunic are rendered by oblique and curving grooves. Over the tunic, he wears a chlamys that falls over his left shoulder and covers his upper chest. The edge of the chlamys, visible across the chest, has tassels. The chlamys is fastened at the right shoulder with a circular brooch (details unclear). The folds of the chlamys is rendered by narrow, curving grooves. The trousers are visible from the knees. The folds are indicated by oblique and curving grooves.

With his right hand, he holds a round object, possibly a fruit, with three circular depressions at the middle. The outline of a large object, possibly a bowl, is recognizable at his chest.

Portrait E: Standing male.
The figure is shown frontally. The arms appear short in relation to the body, indicating foreshortening. Both arms are slightly bent and held out in front of the body. The right leg is obscured by the reclining figure to his right.

He wears a tunic with a small, round neckline and long, wide sleeves. The tunic covers his legs and the folds are rendered by oblique and curving grooves.

He holds a plain, high, cylindrical, flat-top headdress divided in three sections by two vertical grooves (Palmyrene priestly hat) with his hands. A wreath with the leaves pointing towards a central oval is depicted at the lower part of the headdress. A piece of cloth is attached at the lower edge of the headdress, extending downwards.

Right lateral side of sarcophagus lid:
Portrait F: Armless bust of a priest.
The figure is shown frontally.

He wears a cylindrical, flat-top headdress: Palmyrene priestly hat (the outline is visible). The neck is short and wide.

He wears a tunic and a himation. The tunic has a wide, round neckline. The folds are indicated by curving grooves. The himation falls in a curving fold across the chest. The folds of the himation are indicated by wide, curving grooves.

Portrait G: Armless bust of a priest.
The figure is shown frontally.

He wears a cylindrical, flat-top headdress: Palmyrene priestly hat (the outline is visible). The neck is short and wide.

He wears a tunic and a himation. The tunic has a wide, round neckline. The folds are indicated by curving grooves. The himation falls in a curving fold across the chest. The folds of the himation are indicated by wide, curving grooves.

Portrait H: Armless female bust.
The figure is shown frontally.

The outline of a veil is visible. It has a scalloped edge. It falls over both shoulders and crosses the chest in a curving fold, falling behind the left shoulder. She wears a necklace composed of large, round beads around the base of the neck.

She wears a tunic with a small, v-shaped neckline. The folds of the tunic are indicated by wide, curving grooves.
Sarcophagus box:
Portrait I: Armless female bust.
The figure is shown frontally, rendered in a clipeus.

She wears a veil with a scalloped edge. It falls over her shoulders in two wide folds that are looped under each other at the centre of the chest. At the base of the neck, she wears a necklace composed of round beads.

She wears a tunic. The folds are indicated by curving grooves.

Portrait J: Armless male bust.
The figure is shown frontally, rendered in a clipeus.

He wears a tunic and a himation. The tunic has a wide, v-shaped neckline. The folds of the tunic are rendered by curving grooves. Over the tunic, he wears a himation. It is wrapped around his left shoulder, leaving most of the chest free. The folds of the himation are rendered by oblique and curving grooves.

Portrait K: Armless female bust.
The figure is shown frontally, rendered in a clipeus.

The figure wears a garment, possibly a veil (details unclear).

Catalogue number: 34

Database number: PM906 (34a) + PM959 (34b)
Complete sarcophagus with banqueting scene and religious scene
Date: 220-240 CE
Measurements (in cm): 34a: Max. H: 75; W: 170; D: 42
Location: Palmyra Museum, Palmyra, Syria
Inventory Number: 301, 284/402/403, 83.28.1
PS Number: –
Context: West necropolis. Valley of the Tombs. Temple tomb no. 36
Inscription: –
References: 34a: Schmidt-Colinet 1992, vol. I, 147, cat. S 4, fig. 65; 149 cat. B 6; vol. II, pl. 40.a-b, d. 34b: Schmidt-Colinet 1992, vol. I, 153, cat. K 11, fig. 53; vol. II, pl. 49.g.

Catalogue number: 35

Database number: PM881
Sarcophagus lid with banqueting scene
Date: 220-240 CE
Measurements (in cm): Fragment A: Max H: 31 cm. W: 57 cm. Fragment B: Max H: 42 cm. W: 43 cm. Fragment C: Max H: 10 cm. Fragment D: Max H: 13 cm. Fragment E: Max H: 38 cm. W: 24 cm. Fragment F: Max H: 40 cm
Location: Palmyra Museum, Palmyra, Syria
Inventory Number: 301, 284/402/403, 83.28.1
PS Number: –
Context: West necropolis. Valley of the Tombs. Temple tomb no. 36
Inscription: –
References: Schmidt-Colinet 1992, vol. I, 150-151, cat. B 11, figs. 53-54; vol. II, pl. 42.a-b, f.

Catalogue number: 36 (Fig. 24)

Database number: InSitu066
Complete sarcophagus with banqueting scene and trade scene
Date: 220-240 CE
Measurements (in cm): Max H: –; W: –
Location: In situ, Palmyra, Syria
Inventory Number: –
PS Number: 984
Context: Southwest necropolis. Tomb no. A120, Hypogeum of Atenatan, exedra of Julius Aurelius Maqqai
Inscription:
PAT: 0025
The inscription reads:
Image of Maqqaî, son of Zabdibôl, who built this exedra.
References: Ingholt Archive PS 984; Ingholt 1935, 58-75, pls. 26-27; Seyrig 1937, pl. 4; Starcky 1941, 28, fig. 21; Bossert 1951, 38-39, cat. 555, pl. 170; Seyrig 1951, 39, fig. 4; Ghirshman 1962, 78 fig. 90; Colledge 1976, 60, 63, 77-78, 87, 120, 124-126, 129, 131-132, 134, 136, 145-148, 155, 157-158, 217, 240-241, pl. 102; Parlasca 1989, 549, fig. 204; Makowski 1985a, 102, fig. 13; Parlasca 1989, 549, fig. 204. Schmidt-Colinet 1992, vol. I, 106, vol. II, pl. 69.b; Equini Schneider 1993, 116, fig. 24; Parlasca 1998, 311; Long 2017, 71-72, 78, fig. 3.

Fig. 24: Complete sarcophagus with banqueting scene and trade scene, a priestly hat is placed between two of the male figures on the box (only the box is illustrated). Found in 1924 in the exedra of Julius Aurelius Maqqai in the hypogeum of Atenatan, 220-240 CE (© Palmyra Portrait Project, Ingholt Archive at Ny Carlsberg Glyptotek, PS 984).

Catalogue number: 37

Database number: PM487

Sarcophagus lid with banqueting scene with three full figures

Date: 220-240 CE

Measurements (in cm): Max H: 117; W: 176

Location: Palmyra Museum, Palmyra, Syria

Inventory Number: 607/I.d.2/II.c.5/II.d.7, inv. no. II.b.4

PS Number: –

Context: West necropolis. Valley of the Tombs. Temple tomb no. 36

Inscription: –

References: al-As'ad and Schmidt-Colinet 1985, 33-34, pls. 10c, 11a; Schmidt-Colinet 1987, 241, fig. 20; Schmidt-Colinet 1992, vol. I, 148, cat. B1, figs. 52-53, 57, vol. II, pl. 34; Raja 2017a, 64, 65, 76, cat. 21.

Catalogue number: 38

Database number: PM494

Complete sarcophagus with banqueting scene and religious scenes

Date: 240-273 CE

Measurements (in cm): Max H: 225; W: 250; D: 107

Location: Palmyra Museum, Palmyra, Syria

Inventory Number: 2677B/8983

PS Number: –

Context: Secondary context: Built into temple tomb no. 176 (found September 10, 1990)

Inscription: –

References: Rumscheid 2000, 223-224, cat. 272, pl. 66.1; Kaizer 2002, pl. 4; Schmidt-Colinet 2004, 193-194, figs. 7-10; al-As'ad and Schmidt-Colinet 1995, 40, figs. 48-51; Schmidt-Colinet and al-As'ad 2007, 271-276, pls. 84-89; Raja 2017a, 64, 65, 75, cat. 19.

Catalogue number: 39

Database number: SMB011

Male figure

Date: 240-273 CE

Measurements (in cm): Max H: 15.5; W: 19.5; D: 8

Location: Vorderasiatisches Museum, Berlin, Germany

Inventory Number: VA 2209

PS Number: –

Context: –

Fig. 25: Loculus relief with bust of priest and a standing child behind his right shoulder. British Museum, London, inv. BM 125033, 130-140 CE (© Palmyra Portrait Project, Ingholt Archive at Ny Carlsberg Glyptotek, PS 151).

Inscription: –
References: Wartke 1991, 87, 95, cat. 18, fig. 21; <http://arachne.uni-koeln.de/item/objekt/214771> (01.12.2017).

Catalogue number: 40

Database number: PM916
Palmyrene priestly hat, possibly from sarcophagus relief
Date: 220-240 CE
Measurements (in cm): Max H: 32
Location: Palmyra Museum, Palmyra, Syria
Inventory Number: II.d.10
PS Number: –
Context: West necropolis. Valley of the Tombs. Temple tomb no. 36
Inscription: –
References: Schmidt-Colinet 1992, vol. I, 153, cat. K 10, vol. II, pl. 49.f.

Catalogue number: 41

Database number: PM971
Palmyrene priestly hat
Date: 200-273 CE
Measurements (in cm): Max H: 38.5; W: 22; D: 13
Location: Palmyra Museum, Palmyra, Syria
Inventory Number: B 1873
PS Number: –
Context: Temple of Baalshamin, found inside stoa C1
Inscription: –
References: Dunant and Stucky 2000, 112, cat. 119, pl. 28.

Catalogue number: 42

Database number: LebanonPriv005
Loculus relief with bust of priest and standing child
Date: 120-140 CE
Measurements (in cm): Max H: 59; W: 48; D: 20
Location: Private collection, Lebanon
Inventory Number: –
PS Number: –
Context: Temple of Baalshamin, found inside stoa C1
Inscription:
Abousamra 2015, 237, fig. 17
The inscription is too fragmentary to be translated
References: Abousamra 2015, 236-237, fig. 16.

Catalogue number: 43 (Fig. 25)

Database number: BM034
Loculus relief with bust of priest and standing child
Date: 130-140 CE
Measurements (in cm): Max H: 63; W: 52.5
Location: British Museum, London, United Kingdom
Inventory Number: BM 125033
PS Number: 151
Context: –
Inscription:
CIS: 4118; *PAT*: 0467
The inscription reads:
Moqîmu,
son of Gadîâ,
(son of) ʿAtêʿaqab,
(son of) [Za]bdâ,
the elder.
References: Ingholt Archive, PS 151; Ingholt 1928, 106-107, PS 151; Colledge 1976, 248; Heyn 2010, appendix 5, cat. 4; Raja 2016b, 133-135, fig. 1; Raja 2017b, 127, fig. 8.7; Raja 2017d, 122, 123, fig. 15; http://www.britishmuseum.org/

research/collection_online/collection_object_details.aspx?objectId=282719&partId=1&searchText=palmyra&page=3 (20.07.2018). Inscription: RES 1624.

Catalogue number: 44

Database number: PM500
Loculus relief with two busts of priests
Date: 150-170 CE
Measurements (in cm): Max H: 68; W: 102
Location: Palmyra Museum, Palmyra, Syria
Inventory Number: 2678/8984
PS Number: –
Context: –
Inscription:
al-As'ad et al. 2012, 165, cat. 1
Inscription 1 reads:
...son of Taibbol,
alas.
Inscription 2 reads:
Ragna (?), his son, alas!
References: al-As'ad et al. 2012, 165, cat. 1; Raja 2016b, 136-138, fig. 4; Raja 2017b, 126, fig. 8.6.

Catalogue number: 45 (Fig. 26)

Database number: Sotheby's033
Loculus relief with two busts
Date: 150-170 CE
Measurements (in cm): Max H: –; W: –
Location: Last known location: Sotheby's, New York, New York, United States of America
Inventory Number: –
PS Number: 252
Context: –
Inscription: –
References: Ingholt Archive, PS 252; Ingholt 1928, 119-120, PS 252; Sotheby's 1963, July 1st, cat. 37; Parlasca 1988, 220, pl. 47.d; Krag and Raja 2016, 152-153, 169, cat. 64, fig. 26; Raja 2016b, 135-136, fig. 2; Raja 2017b, 127, fig. 8.5; Raja 2017d, 123, fig. 18; Raja 2017e, 420, fig. 3; Raja 2017f, 334-335, fig. 9.

Catalogue number: 46

Database number: DGAM004
Loculus relief with two busts and a central standing male
Date: 150-170 CE
Measurements (in cm): Max H: –; W: –

Fig. 26: Loculus relief with two busts, one being of a priest. Last seen in Sotheby's auction catalogue, 150-170 CE (© Palmyra Portrait Project, Ingholt Archive at Ny Carlsberg Glyptotek, PS 252).

Location: Directorate-General of Antiquities and Museums, Damascus, Syria
Inventory Number: –
PS Number: –
Context: –
Inscription:
The inscriptions have not been translated
Note: The object is said to be fake
References: Raja 2016b, 138-140, fig. 5; http://dgam.gov.sy/index.php?d=239&id=1160 (26.11.2018).

Catalogue number: 47 (fig. 27)

Database number: NMAK002
Banqueting relief with two full figures
Date: 240-273 CE
Measurements (in cm): Max H: 44.5; W: 65.1; D: 17.78
Location: Nelson-Atkins Museum of Art, Kansas City, United States of America
Inventory Number: 65-2
PS Number: 1278
Context: –

Fig. 27: Banqueting relief with a reclining priest. Nelson-Atkins Museum of Art, Kansas City, inv. 65-2, 240-273 CE (© Palmyra Portrait Project, Ingholt Archive at Ny Carlsberg Glyptotek, PS 1278).

Inscription: –
References: Ingholt Archive, PS 1278; Vermeule 1981, 385, cat. 334; Parlasca 1984, 285-287, fig. 3; <http://art.nelson-atkins.org/objects/9925/priest-of-bel-and-his-attendant?ctx=bdae8901-8959-4b0a-ae06-428b2b929303&idx=2> (28.06.2018).

Catalogue number: 48

Database number: PM904
Banqueting relief with three full figures
Date: 240-273 CE
Measurements (in cm): Max H: –; W: –
Location: Palmyra Museum, Palmyra, Syria
Inventory Number: –
PS Number: –
Context: –
Inscription: –
References: Will 1951, 89, fig. 12.

Catalogue number: 49

Database number: MSR001
Banqueting relief with full figure of priest
Date: 240-273 CE
Measurements (in cm): Max H: 29; W: 49; D: 29
Location: Musée Saint-Raymond, Toulouse, France
Inventory Number: –
PS Number: –
Context: –
Inscription: –
References: Balty 2010, 25-26, fig. 2; <https://saintraymond.toulouse.fr/Relief-funeraire_a681.html> (28.06.2018).

Catalogue number: 50 (Fig. 28)

Database number: NCG004 (50a) + (50b) NCG003
Banqueting relief with two full figures
Date: 146/147 CE (dated by inscription)
Measurements (in cm): 50a: Max H: 80; W: 52; D: 26.5; D (Field): 12. 50b: Max H: 72.5; W: 84; D: 22; D (Field): 18
Location: Ny Carlsberg Glyptotek, Copenhagen, Denmark
Inventory Number: IN 1160 and IN 1159
PS Number: 38 and 8
Context: –
Inscription:
CIS 4458; *PAT* 0819
Inscription 1 reads:
[X daughter of] Shimʿôn son of Ḥairân Firdushî (Paradasî), his wife.
CIS 4458; *PAT* 0818
Inscription 2 reads:
- - - Malkû son of Lishamsh son of Ḥennibel ʾAʿabî, year (4)58.
References: 50a: Ingholt Archive, PS 38; Chabot 1922, 111, 121, cat. 50 pl. 27.10; Ingholt 1928, Ingholt 1928, 63-64, PS 38; Ingholt 1934, 35; Will 1951, 89, n.2; Champdor 1953, 55; Colledge 1976, 63, 73-74, 124-126, 129, 131, 140, 142, 147, 155,

Fig. 28: Banqueting relief with a reclining priest. Ny Carlsberg Glyptotek, Copenhagen, inv. IN 1159 and IN 1160, 146/147 CE (Courtesy of Ny Carlsberg Glyptotek, photo by Palmyra Portrait Project).

212, 217, 240, 246, pl. 98; Makowski 1985b, 122; Hvidberg-Hansen and Ploug 1993, 50-51, cat. 8; Parlasca 1994, 304, fig. 5; Ploug 1995, 56-65, cat. 8; Wielgosz 1997, 71; Krag 2015, 109, fig. 2; Raja 2015c, 343-347, figs. 12-16; Krag 2016, 188-189, fig. 5; Raja 2016a, 352, fig. 5; Raja 2017b, 125, fig. 8.2; Raja 2017d, 121, fig. 10; Raja 2017e, 420, fig. 4; Raja 2017f, 334-335, fig. 7. 50b: Ingholt Archive, PS 8; Chabot 1922, 111, 121, cat. 50, pl. 27.10; Ingholt 1928, 31-33, PS 8, pl. 3.1; pl. 3.1; Ingholt 1934, 35; Ingholt 1935, 68; Will 1951, 89, n.2; Champdor 1953, 55; Colledge 1976, 63, 73-74, 124-126, 129, 131, 140, 142, 147, 155, 212, 217, 240, 246, pl. 98; Makowski 1985b, 122; Hvidberg-Hansen and Ploug 1993, 50-51, cat. 8; Parlasca 1994, 304, fig. 5; Ploug 1995, 56-65, cat. 8; Wielgosz 1997, 71; Krag 2015, 109, fig. 2; Raja 2015c, 343-347, figs. 12-16; Krag 2016, 188-189, fig. 5; Raja 2016a, 352, fig. 5; Raja 2017b, 125, fig. 8.2; Raja 2017d, 121, fig. 10; Raja 2017e, 420, fig. 4; Raja 2017f, 334-335, fig. 7. Inscription: Ingholt 1928, 32f, 64; Ingholt 1930, 193; Chabot 1922, 121, cat. 50.

Catalogue number: 51

Database number: PM473 (51a) + PM466 (51b)
Banqueting relief
Date: 220-240 CE
Measurements (in cm): 51a: Max H: 27. 51b: Max H: 15
Location: Palmyra Museum, Palmyra, Syria
Inventory Number: II.b.1/2, II.a.1
PS Number: –
Context: West necropolis. Valley of the Tombs. Temple tomb no. 36
Inscription: –
References: 51a: Schmidt-Colinet 1992 vol. I, 153, cat. K 4, fig. 52; vol. II, pls. 49.a-b, 51b: Schmidt-Colinet 1992 vol. I, 154-155, cat. K 29, fig. 56; vol. II, 53.c-d.

Catalogue number: 52

Database number: PM539
Complete sarcophagus relief with banqueting scene and portrait busts
Date: 180-240 CE
Measurements (in cm): Max H: –; W: –
Location: Palmyra Museum, Palmyra, Syria
Inventory Number: –
PS Number: –
Context: Northwest necropolis. Hypogeum of Hatrai
Inscription: –
References: al-As'ad 2013, 19 fig. 9.

Object description:
The relief is rectangular in shape and depicts a kline. A seated female, two reclining males, a standing male, two reclining males and a seated female are depicted resting

on a mattress, and six armless busts are depicted between the legs of the kline. The mattress is decorated with four vertical panels (details unclear). Vertical, curving grooves indicate the texture of the fabric. The seated females at the two ends of the kline (Portraits A and G) sit on two round cushions (details unclear). Two of the reclining males (Portraits B and E) rest on a round cushion decorated with wide bands with rosettes (other details unclear). The central stretcher of the kline has a decorated section on the far left side. It is decorated with a wide rectangular panel flanked by two narrower rectangular panels. The legs are turned. They are composed of a plinth, a convex quarter, a long reversed concave quarter, a torus, a ball, a torus, and a concave quarter. All elements are decorated with a tongue pattern.

Sarcophagus lid relief:
Portrait A: Seated female.
The figure is shown frontally. The head is turned slightly to her left. The right arm is bent and she rests the arm on her right thigh. The left arm is bent and raised at the height of the neck. She sits with the legs set apart with the knees visible under the drapery. Her feet rest on the mattress.

She wears three headdresses: a headband, a turban, and a veil. The band is placed high on her forehead (details unclear). The turban is coiled and is divided in two layers with curving grooves indicating the coiling of the fabric. The veil is heavy. It falls over the shoulders and it is wrapped around her left arm and falls over the back of her right shoulder. Part of the hair is covered by the headdress: several strands of hair above the ears are pushed back over the headband and the edge of the turban and disappear under the veil. Her face is oval. The eyebrows are slightly curving. The eyes are close-set and almond-shaped. Only the earlobes are visible under the hair and she wears earrings (details unclear). The nose is large and narrow with the alae carved. The mouth is small with thin lips. The chin is oval and the neck is slender and long.

She wears a tunic and a himation. The tunic has a wide angular neckline and short, loose sleeves. The folds are indicated by curving, wide grooves. The ankle-length himation crosses the chest diagonally from the left shoulder to the right side, covers the left breast, falls over the body and covers her legs. The himation is fastened at the right shoulder with a circular brooch (details unclear). The folds of the himation are indicated by curving and oblique grooves. She wears round shoes.

She holds a fold of the veil in her right hand. A zigzag-shaped fold falls from her hand and along the right leg across the cushions. The index finger is extended. Her left arm is raised next to the shoulder. She holds a fold of the veil with her hand.

Portrait B: Reclining male.
The figure is shown in frontal to three-quarter view. The arms are bent and held to the torso. He rests the arm against a cushion. His lower legs are obscured by the seated female to his right.

His hair is straight and brushed away from the face. The eyebrow is slightly curving and the eye is round (other details unclear). The neck is wide.

He wears a tunic and a himation. The tunic has a wide round neckline. The folds of the tunic are rendered by curving grooves. Over the tunic he wears a himation. It is wrapped around his left shoulder and arm, leaving most of the chest, body, and hand free. It falls across the left side of his body and is folded across his lower abdomen. A wide zigzag-shaped fold falls from under his left hand, across the cushion and the mattress. The edge of the fold is tied into two knots. The folds of the himation are indicated by vertical and curving grooves.

He holds a skyphos in his right hand. It has a conical foot and lower body. The body is decorated with two horizontal grooves. The skyphos has small looped handles. The index and little fingers are extended. With the left hand he holds the wide fold of the himation. The index finger is extended.

Portrait C: Reclining male.
The figure is shown in frontal to three-quarter view. The head is turned to his left. The right arm is obscured by the reclining male to his right. The left arm is bent and held to the chest. He rests the arm against two cushions. His legs are obscured by the male figure at his right.
His hair is arranged in crescent-shaped curls around the head, covering the ears and reaching the neck. The individual locks of hair are indicated by curving incisions. His face is oval. His eyebrows are slightly curving. The eyes are almond-shaped (details unclear). The nose is narrow and large. He has a beard that starts from his temples and covers his cheeks, upper lip and chin (details unclear). The neck is wide.

He wears a 'Parthian-style' tunic and a himation. The tunic has a wide round decorated neckline. The tunic has a wide decorated band (details unclear) extending downwards from the middle of the neckline. The folds of the tunic are indicated by oblique grooves. Over the tunic, he wears a himation. It is wrapped around his left shoulder and arm, leaving most of the chest, body and hand free. It falls along the left side of his body and is folded across his lower abdomen. A wide zigzag-shaped fold falls from under his left hand, across the cushion and mattress. The folds of the himation are indicated by vertical and curving grooves.

With the upturned palm of the left hand he holds a wide bowl with his fingertips.

Portrait D: Standing male.
The figure is shown frontally. The right arm is bent and held to the chest. The left arm is bent and extended towards the reclining figure to his left. The legs are obscured by the reclining figure to his left.

His hair is straight, covering the ears and brushed away from the face. His face is oval. The eyebrows are curving. The eyes are close-set (other details unclear). The nose is narrow and long. The mouth is small and the chin is oval. The neck is wide.

He wears a tunic and a himation. The tunic has a wide round neckline. The folds of the tunic are indicated by oblique grooves. Over the tunic, he wears a himation. The himation covers most of the body: it is wrapped around the right shoulder and arm, leaving only part of the upper chest and the hand free. One fold of the himation crosses the chest diagonally and falls over the left shoulder ('arm-sling' type). The folds of the himation are indicated by diagonal grooves.

With his right hand he holds lightly the fold of the himation. The left hand lies flat on the upper right arm of the reclining figure to his left.

Portrait E: Reclining male.
The figure is shown in frontal to three-quarter view. The head is turned to his left. The right arm is slightly bent and he rests the hand on the raised right knee. The left arm is bend and held to the chest. He rests the arm against a cushion. It is decorated with a wide panel with a running scroll with rosettes. The right leg is bent and he rest the foot on the mattress. The left leg is bent under the right with the knee pointing outwards.

His hair is arranged in one row of round curls around the head. His face is oval. The eyebrows are slightly curving, rendered as thin ridges. The eyes are close-set and almond-shaped. Only the earlobes are visible under the hair. The nose is large and straight with the alae carved. He has a beard that starts from his temples and covers the cheeks, the upper lip, and the chin. The facial hair is rendered by small, snail-shell curls arranged in rows. His mouth is narrow with a full lower lip. The chin is round and the neck is wide.

He wears a 'Parthian-style' tunic, a chlamys, 'Parthian-style' trousers, and shoes. The tunic has a round neckline and long sleeves. The cuffs of the sleeves are decorated with a band (details unclear). The tunic has a wide decorated band (details unclear) extending downwards from the middle of the neckline. The tunic ends above the knees and has a decorated hem (details unclear). The folds of the tunic are indicated by curving and oblique grooves. Over the tunic, he wears a chlamys that falls over both shoulders, and covers most of the chest. It is fastened at the right shoulder with a circular brooch (details unclear). A wide zigzag-shaped fold falls from under the left arm, across the cushion and the mattress. The folds of the chlamys are indicated by narrow, deep grooves. He wears a plain band belt, knotted at the centre, with the ends looped under either side of the waist. He also wears trousers. In the middle, each trouser leg is decorated with a wide band (details unclear) extending downwards. The folds of the trousers are indicated by oblique and curving grooves. He also wears plain round boots.

The right hand lies on the right knee. He holds an oblong object, possibly a pinecone in his hand. With the upturned palm of the left hand he holds a bowl with his fingertips. It is decorated with pattern of hollow lozenges.

Portrait F: Reclining male.
The figure is shown in frontal to three-quarter view. The head and the left hand appears large in relation to the body. The head is turned to his left. The right arm is bent and held to the torso. The left arm is bent and held to the chest. He rests the arm against two cushions. His legs are obscured by the reclining figure to his right.

His hair is straight and brushed away on each side of the face. His face is oval. The eyebrows are curving and the eyes are almond-shaped (other details unclear). Only the earlobes are visible under the hair. The nose is narrow and long with carved alae. He has a beard that starts from his temples and covers the cheeks, the upper lip, and the chin. The chin is round and the neck is wide.

He wears a tunic and a himation. The tunic has a wide round neckline and short sleeves. The folds of the tunic are indicated by curving and oblique grooves. Over the tunic, he wears a himation. It is wrapped around his left shoulder and arm, leaving most of the chest, body and hand free. It falls along the left side of his body and is folded across his lower abdomen. A wide zigzag-shaped fold falls from under his left hand, across the cushion and mattress. The folds of the himation are indicated by vertical and curving grooves.

With the right hand he holds a fold of the himation. With the upturned palm of the left hand he holds a bowl with his fingertips.

Portrait G: Seated female.
The figure is shown in frontal to three-quarter view. The head is turned to the left. The right hand is raised at the height of the neck. The left arm is held to the torso. The right leg is obscured by two cushions to the right of the figure. The left leg is bent with the knee visible under the drapery. She rests her foot on the mattress.

She wears three headdresses: a headband, a turban and a veil. The band is placed low on her forehead. The turban is rendered in two layers by a horizontal groove. The veil is heavy. It falls over the shoulders and it is wrapped around her right arm and falls over the back of her left shoulder. Part of the hair is covered by the headdress: several strands of hair above the ears are pushed back over the headband and the edge of the turban, and disappear under the veil. Her face is oval. The eyes are almond-shaped (other details unclear). The nose is narrow and large. Only the earlobes are visible under the hair and she wears earrings (details unclear). The mouth is small and the chin is oval. The neck is wide.

She wears a tunic and himation. The tunic has a round neckline and short sleeves. The folds of the tunic are indicated by curving grooves. The ankle-length himation crosses the chest diagonally from the left shoulder to the right side, covers the left breast and falls over the body and covers her legs. The upper end of the himation has a pleaded band. The himation is fastened at the right shoulder with a circular brooch (details unclear). The folds of the himation are indicated by curving and oblique grooves. She does not wear shoes.

The right hand is raised to the neck and she holds the edge of the veil in her hand. The left hand is placed on top of two cushions. The cushions are decorated with two wide panels (details unclear). A zigzag-shaped fold of the veil falls from under her left hand.

Sarcophagus box relief:
Portrait H: Armless bust of a male.
The figure is shown frontally.

His hair is straight and combed around the head. His face is oval. The eyebrows are curving and the eyes are close-set and almond-shaped (other details unclear). The ears are large and protruding with the helix rendered. The nose is narrow and long. The mouth is narrow with thin lips. The chin is oval and the neck is wide.

He wears a tunic and a himation. The tunic has a wide round neckline. The folds of the tunic are indicated by curving and oblique grooves. Over the tunic, he wears a himation. It is wrapped around his left shoulder. Another fold comes from his lower right side and falls in a curving fold across the chest and under the left shoulder.

Portrait I: Armless bust of a female.
The figure is shown frontally.

She wears three headdresses: a headband, a turban, and a veil. The band is placed high on her forehead. The details of the band are unclear. The turban is coiled, it is rendered in two twisting layers by horizontal grooves. The veil is heavy. It falls over her shoulder and continues in a curving fold across the chest and falls back over her left shoulder. The edge of the veil crossing the left shoulder is pleated. Part of the hair is covered by the headdress: several strands of hair above the ears are pushed back over the headband and the edge of the turban, and disappear under the veil. Her face is oval. The neck is wide.

She wears a tunic with a round neckline. The folds of the tunic are rendered by curving grooves.

Portrait J: Armless bust of a male.
The figure is shown frontally. The top of the head reaches the central stretcher of the kline.

His hair is straight and combed around the head. His face is oval. The eyebrows are slightly curving and the eyes are close-set and almond-shaped (other details unclear). The nose is narrow and slightly crocked. He has a beard that starts from the temples and covers the cheeks, the upper lip and chin. The mouth is small with a full lower lip. The chin is oval and the neck is wide.

He wears a tunic and a himation. The tunic has a wide angular neckline. The folds of the tunic, are indicated by curving and oblique grooves. Over the tunic, he wears a himation. It is wrapped around his left shoulder and falls in a curving line across the chest and falls back at his right shoulder. The folds of the himation are indicated by oblique grooves.

Portrait K: Armless bust of a male.
The figure is shown frontally.

His hair is straight and combed around the head. His face is oval. The eyebrows are slightly curving and the eyes are close-set and almond-shaped (other details unclear). The nose is narrow and long with carved alae. He has a beard that starts from his temples and covers the cheeks, the upper lip, and the chin. The mouth is small with a full lower lip. The chin is oval and the neck is wide.

He wears a tunic and a himation. The tunic has a wide angular neckline. The folds of the tunic, are indicated by curving and oblique grooves. Over the tunic, he wears a himation. It is wrapped around his left shoulder, and falls in a curving fold across the chest and falls back at his right shoulder. The folds of the himation are indicated by oblique grooves.

Portrait L: Armless bust of a female.
The figure is shown frontally. The top of the head reaches the central stretcher of the kline.

She wears three headdresses: a headband, a turban, and a veil. The band is placed high on her forehead. The details of the band are unclear. The turban is coiled: it is rendered in one layer by horizontal grooves. The veil is heavy. It falls over her shoulder and continues in a curving fold across the chest and falls back over her left shoulder. The edge of the veil crossing the left shoulder is pleated. Part of the hair is covered by the headdress: several strands of hair above the ears are pushed back over the headband and the edge of the turban, and disappear under the veil. Her face is oval. The eyebrows are slightly curving. The neck is wide.

She wears a tunic with a round neckline. The folds of the tunic are rendered by curving grooves.

Portrait M: Armless bust of a male.
The figure is shown frontally.

His hair is arranged in two rows of round curls around the head. His face is oval. The eyebrows are curving and the eyes are close-set and almond-shaped (other details unclear). The ears are large and protruding with the helix and lobe rendered. The nose is narrow and long with the alae carved. The mouth is narrow with thin lips. The chin is oval and the neck is wide.

He wears a tunic and a himation. The tunic has a wide round neckline. The folds of the tunic are indicated by curving and oblique grooves. Over the tunic, he wears a himation. It is wrapped around his left shoulder. Another fold comes from his lower right side and falls in a curving fold across the chest and under the left shoulder.

Catalogue number: 53

Database number: InSitu136
Sarcophagus box relief with six standing figures.
Date: 180-240 CE
Measurements (in cm): Max H: 85; W: 195
Location: In situ, Palmyra, Syria
Inventory Number: –
PS Number: –
Context: West necropolis. Valley of the Tombs. Temple/house tomb no. 85b, Tomb of Aʿailamî and Zebidâ ('Tomb Cantineau')
Inscription: –
References: Cantineau 1929, 12, pls. 2.2, 3.2; Makowski 1983, 187, cat. 6.

Object description:
The sarcophagus box relief is rectangular in shape and depicts six standing figures. The figures are framed by a plain projecting edge on all four sides. According to Cantineau (1929, 12) the object depicts six caryatids, and according to Makowski (1983, 187) it depicts six pages.

Portrait A: Standing figure.
The figure is shown frontally. The right arm falls along the body.
The figure wears a garment that reaches the ankles. Further details are unclear.

Portrait B: Standing figure.
The figure is shown frontally, the head is turned slightly to the left.
The hair is short and voluminous (details unclear).
The figures wears a garment with short sleeves, and that reaches the ankles. The folds of the garment are indicated by oblique grooves on the chest. Further details are unclear.

Portrait C: Standing figure.
The figure is shown frontally. The arms appear bent and held to the torso.
Details are unclear.

Portrait D: Standing figure.
The figure is shown frontally.
The figure wears a garment that reaches the ankles. Further details are unclear.

Portrait E: Standing figure.
The figure is shown frontally. The arms appear bent and held to the waist.
The figure wears a garment that reaches the knees. Oblique grooves on the chest and thighs indicate the folds of the garment.

Portrait F: Standing figure.
The figure is shown frontally.
The figure wears a garment that reaches the knees. Oblique grooves on the chest indicate the folds of the garment.

Catalogue number: 54

Database number: InSitu059
Complete sarcophagus with banqueting scene and portrait busts
Lid: One priest and two male figures
Box: Two male and one female busts
Date: 130-150 CE
Measurements (in cm): Max H: 171; W: 346; D: 50
Location: In situ, Palmyra, Syria
Inventory Number: –
PS Number: –
Context: Southeast necropolis. Hypogeum F, west niche
Inscription: –
References: Higuchi and Saito 2001, 35-36, pls. 3-4, 5.1, 6-7, appendix 12; Miyashita 2016, 132, fig. 3.3.

Catalogue number: 55

Database number: PM228 (55a) + PM272 (55b)
Complete sarcophagus with banqueting scene and portrait busts
Lid: One priest, two male figures and one female figure
Box: Two female busts and two busts of unclear gender
Date: 220-240 CE
Measurements (in cm): 55a: Max H: 121; W: 168; D: 25. 55b: Max H: 98; W: 240; D: 100.
Location: Palmyra Museum, Palmyra, Syria
Inventory Number: 2283/8275, H 38/71
PS Number: 1434/1435
Context: Southeast necropolis. Hypogeum F, west niche
Inscription: –
References: 55a: Ingholt Archive, PS 1434/1435; Sadurska 1977, 95-99, cat. 2, figs. 36-40, pl. 12; Tanabe 1986, 41, pls. 385-388; Sadurska and Bounni 1994, 176, cat. 233, fig. 249; Stauffer 2013, 128-130, fig. 3; Miyashita 2016, 133, 142, figs. 17. 55b: Sadurska 1977, 114, cat. 8, fig. 51, pl. 40.

Catalogue number: 56

Database number: PM491 (56a) + PM886 (56b) + PM471 (56c) + PM864 (56d)
Complete sarcophagus with banqueting scene and caravan scene
Lid: One priest, one female, and one male figure
Box: Two male figures
Date: 220-240 CE
Measurements (in cm): 56a: Max H: 88; W: 134. 56c: Max H: 25.
Location: Palmyra Museum, Palmyra, Syria
Inventory Number: 652-53, I.d.5/II.a.5-7; 16-19; 23/II.d.5, II.d.3-4, II.15-16, 83.12.2, II.a.11
PS Number: –
Context: West necropolis. Valley of the Tombs. Temple tomb no. 36
Inscription: –
References: 56a: Schmidt-Colinet 1992 vol. I, 148, cat. B 2, figs. 54-55, 57, 61; vol. II, pls. 35.d, 36. 56b: Schmidt-Colinet 1992 vol. I, 146f, cat. S 5, figs. 59, 61; vol. II, pls. 32.b, h, 33. 56c: al-As'ad and Schmidt-Colinet 1985, 34, pl. 11.d; Schmidt-Colinet 1992 vol. I, 152, cat. K 1, fig. 52; vol. II, pl. 47.a-b. 56d: Schmidt-Colinet 1992 vol. I, 154, cat. K 26, fig. 53; vol. II, pl. 49.i.

Fig. 29: Complete sarcophagus with banqueting scene with a reclining priest and portrait busts, two being of priests. Palmyra Museum, Palmyra, inv. A 910/10, 188 CE (© Palmyra Portrait Project, Ingholt Archive at Ny Carlsberg Glyptotek, PS 1391).

Catalogue number: 57

Database number: InSitu058
Complete sarcophagus with banqueting scene and portrait busts
Lid: One priest and two male figures
Box: Two male and one female busts
Date: 130-150 CE
Measurements (in cm): Max H: 171; W: 346; D: 50
Location: In situ, Palmyra, Syria
Inventory Number: –
PS Number: –
Context: West necropolis. Valley of the Tombs. Temple tomb no. 36
Inscription: –
References: Higuchi and Saito 2001, 34-35, pls. 3-4, 5.3, 11-12, appendix 10; Miyashita 2016, 132, fig. 3.2.

Catalogue number: 58

Database number: InSitu046
Complete sarcophagus with banqueting scene and portrait busts
Lid: Two priests, two males, one female, and one child
Box: One priest, one male, and two female busts
Date: 130-150 CE
Measurements (in cm):
Measurements: Lid: Max H: 128; W: 235; D: 40; Box relief: Max H: 53; W: 185; D: 185
Location: In situ, Palmyra, Syria
Inventory Number: –
PS Number: –
Context: Southeast necropolis. Hypogeum F, east niche
Inscription: –
References: Colledge 1976, 247-248, 255-256; Higuchi and Saito 2001, 31-35, pls. 3-4, 5.2, 8-10, appendix 11; Stauffer 2012, 90-95, fig. 4; Miyashita 2016, 131-132, figs. 2-3; Wielgosz-Rondolino 2016, 74-75, fig. 12.

Catalogue number: 59 (Fig. 29)

Database number: PM325
Complete sarcophagus with banqueting scene and portrait busts
Lid: One priest, three females, and one male
Box: Two priests, three female busts, and one standing child
Date: 188 CE (dated by inscription)
Measurements (in cm): Max H: 75; W: 203
Location: Palmyra Museum, Palmyra, Syria
Inventory Number: A 910/10
PS Number: 1391

Fig. 30: Complete sarcophagus with banqueting scene with standing priest and portrait busts, one being of a priest (only the lid is illustrated). Palmyra Museum, Palmyra, inv. 2285/8277, 220-240 CE (© Palmyra Portrait Project, Ingholt Archive at Ny Carlsberg Glyptotek, PS 1432).

Context: Southwest Necropolis. Hypogeum of Malkû, south chamber
Inscription:
Yon 2013, 340, cat. 11
Inscription 1 reads:
Nabî, his daughter.
Inscription 2 reads:
Shullaî
Inscription 3 reads:
Ḥabbaî, his daughter.
Inscription 4 reads:
Image of Ba῾laî, son of Dayyôn, son of Malkû, Shullaî his daughter, in the month of March, year 499 (CE 188).
Inscription 5 reads:
Shalman, his servant.
Inscription 6 reads:
Barbarah, daughter of Ḥaîran, wife of Dayyon, his daughter-in-law.
Inscription 7 reads:
Dayyôn, son of Ba῾laî, his son in the month of May year 499 (CE 188).
Inscription 8 reads:
Ba῾laî, son of Dayyôn. Ramî, daughter of Nabî, daughter of his daughter.
Inscription 9 reads:
Amatâ, daughter of Aḥbaî, his daughter.
References: Ingholt Archive, PS 1391; Ingholt 1970-1971, 182-192, pls. 3, 4; Ingholt 1976, 102-115, pls. 1, 2; Tanabe 1986, 41, pls. 400-403; al-As'ad and Gawlikowski 1997, 52-53, cat. 73, figs. 73.a-d; Yon 2013, 340, cat. 11. Inscription: Yon 2013, 340, cat. 11.

Catalogue number: 60

Database number: PM330
Complete sarcophagus with banqueting scene and portrait busts
Lid: Two female and one male figure
Box: Two priests, and one female bust
Date: 220-240 CE
Measurements (in cm): Max H: –; W: –
Location: Palmyra Museum, Palmyra, Syria
Inventory Number: –
PS Number: –
Context: Southeast necropolis, Valley of the Tombs.

Fig. 31: Complete sarcophagus with banqueting scene with standing priest and two reclining priests and portrait busts, two being of priests. National Museum of Damascus, Damascus, 240-273 CE (© Palmyra Portrait Project, Ingholt Archive at Ny Carlsberg Glyptotek, PS 890 and PS 982).

Temple/house tomb no. 186 ('Tombeau de l'aviation'/'Tomb Duvaux')
Inscription:
The inscriptions have not survived
References: Watzinger and Wulzinger 1932, 70, figs. 68, 69; Schmidt-Colinet 1992, vol. I, 107 n.380g,2 n.383b, 108 n.389, 110 n.403 n.404d, 121 n.440g, 125 n.473 n.476, 130 n.479, 135 n.517; vol. II, pls. 72.d, 73.b.

Catalogue number: 61 (Fig. 30)

Database number: PM229 (61a) + PM270 (61b)
Complete sarcophagus with banqueting scene and portrait busts
Lid: Two female and one male figure
Box: Two priests, and one female bust
Date: 220-240 CE
Measurements (in cm): 61a: Max H: 114; W: 225; D: 33. 61b: Max H: 98; W: 245; D: 98
Location: Palmyra Museum, Palmyra, Syria
Inventory Number: 2285/8277
PS Number: 1432
Context: West necropolis. Valley of the Tombs. Hypogeum of 'Alaine, central exedra, on the podium at the centre
Inscription: –
References: 61a: Ingholt Archive, PS 1432; Sadurska 1976, 25-29, figs. 11, 12; Sadurska 1977, 76-95, cat. 1, figs. 18-35, pl. 11; Taha 1982, 121, fig. 4; Parlasca 1984, 290-292, fig. 10; Tanabe 1986, 41, pls. 374-384; Sadurska 1988, 17, fig. 2; Sadurska and Bounni 1994, 174-176, cat. 232, fig. 248; Fortin 1999, 296, cat. 331; Stauffer 2012, 92-94, fig. 3; Stauffer 2013, 128-129, fig. 2; Long 2017, 72-73, fig. 4. 61b: Sadurska 1976, 24-25; Sadurska 1977, 107-111, cat. 6, fig. 48, pl. 11.

Catalogue number: 62

Database number: PM227 (62a) + PM271 (62b)
Complete sarcophagus with banqueting scene and portrait busts
Lid: Two priests
Box: One priest, two male, and two female busts
Date: 220-240 CE
Measurements (in cm): 62a: Max H: 114; W: 164; D: 34. 62b:

Fig. 32: Complete sarcophagus with banqueting scene with two standing priests and a reclining priests and portrait busts, two being of priests (only the lid is illustrated). National Museum of Damascus, Damascus, 240-273 CE (© Palmyra Portrait Project, Ingholt Archive at Ny Carlsberg Glyptotek, PS 891).

Max H: 96; W: 225; D: 98
Location: Palmyra Museum, Palmyra, Syria
Inventory Number: 2285/8277, H 37/71
PS Number: –
Context: West necropolis. Valley of the Tombs. Hypogeum of ʿAlaine, central exedra, on the podium at the centre
Inscription: –
References: 62a: Sadurska 1977, 101-105, cat. 4, figs. 42-45, pl. 14; Tanabe 1986, 41, pls. 389-392; Sadurska and Bounni 1994, 176-177, cat. 234, fig. 250; Charles-Gaffiot et al. 2001, 343-344, cat. 148; Stauffer 2013, 130, fig. 4. 62b: Sadurska 1976, 24-25, pl. 3, fig. 10; Sadurska 1977, 111-114, cat. 7, fig. 50, pl. 14.

Catalogue number: 63 (Fig. 31)
Database number: NMD063
Complete sarcophagus with banqueting scene and portrait busts

Lid: Three priests, one male, one female
Box: Two priests, two female busts
Date: 240-273 CE
Measurements (in cm): Max H: –; W: –
Location: National Museum of Damascus, Damascus, Syria
Inventory Number: –
PS Number: 890/982
Context: West necropolis. Valley of the Tombs. Hypogeum of Yarhai, west exedra
Inscription: –
References: Ingholt Archive, PS 890+PS 892; Amy and Seyrig 1936, 247-248, pl. 46.1-2; Gawlikowski 1970, 112, fig. 63; Colledge 1976a, 60, 133, 155, pl. 60; Browning 1979, 30, 37-38, fig. 4; Makowski 1985a, 95-100, figs. 11a.c; Tanabe 1986, 31, pls. 237-240; Bounni and al-As'ad 1990, 99; Schmidt-Colinet 1996, 369, fig. 208; Parlasca 1998, 311-312; Zanker 2010, 178- 181, figs. 107a-b; Raja 2017d, 121-122, 124, 127, figs. 12, 17; Raja 2017e, 420-421, fig. 6.

Fig. 33: Complete sarcophagus with banqueting scene with two standing priests and a reclining priest and portrait bust, two being of priests (only the box is illustrated). National Museum of Damascus, Damascus, 240-273 CE (© Palmyra Portrait Project, Ingholt Archive at Ny Carlsberg Glyptotek, PS 893).

Catalogue number: 64 (Fig. 32)

Database number: NMD064
Complete sarcophagus with banqueting scene and portrait busts
Lid: Three priests, one female
Box: Two priests, one female bust
Date: 240-273 CE
Measurements (in cm): Max H: –; W: –
Location: National Museum of Damascus, Damascus, Syria
Inventory Number: –
PS Number: 891
Context: West necropolis. Valley of the Tombs. Hypogeum of Yarhai, west exedra
Inscription:
PAT: 2787
The inscription reads:
Image of Neṣâ, daughter of Theophilos,
wife of Bônnê, son of Taîmarṣû, alas!
References: Ingholt Archive, PS 891; Amy and Seyrig 1936, 248-249, pl. 47.1; Cantineau 1938, 157, cat. d; Tanabe 1986, 31, pls. 241-244; Parlasca 1998, 312.

Catalogue number: 65 (Fig. 33)

Database number: NMD065
Complete sarcophagus with banqueting scene and portrait busts
Lid: Three priests, one female
Box: Two priests, one female bust
Date: 240-273 CE
Measurements (in cm): Max H: –; W: –
Location: National Museum of Damascus, Damascus, Syria
Inventory Number: –
PS Number: 893
Context: West necropolis. Valley of the Tombs. Hypogeum of Yarhai, west exedra
Inscription: –
References: Ingholt Archive, PS 893; Tanabe 1986, 31, pls. 245-246; Parlasca 1998, 311-12.

Catalogue number: 66

Database number: NMD031
Sarcophagus lid with banqueting scene with two full figures
Lid: One priest, one female
Date: 170-200 CE
Measurements (in cm): Max H: 130; W: 200

Location: National Museum of Damascus, Damascus, Syria
Inventory Number: –
PS Number: –
Context: Southeast necropolis. Hypogeum of Taai, west exedra

Fig. 34: Bust of priest from sarcophagus box, the bust is placed on the lower left corner of the kline. Louvre, Paris, inv. AO 4450, 170-200 CE (© Palmyra Portrait Project, Ingholt Archive at Ny Carlsberg Glyptotek, PS 862).

Inscription: –
References: Abdul-Hak 1952, 229-230, cat. 19; Makowski 1985a, 85, fig. 7.

Catalogue number: 67

Database number: PM480
Standing priest from sarcophagus lid
Lid: One priest
Date: 220-240 CE
Measurements (in cm): Max H: 101
Location: Palmyra Museum, Palmyra, Syria
Inventory Number: 662/II.c.7
PS Number: –
Context: West necropolis. Valley of the Tombs. Temple tomb no. 36
Inscription: –
References: Schmidt-Colinet 1992, vol. I, 152, cat. B 19, fig. 52; vol. II, pls. 43.d, 44.c-d.

Catalogue number: 68

Database number: DGAM007
Sarcophagus lid with banqueting scene with five full figures
Lid: Two priests, two females, one male
Date: 170-200 CE
Measurements (in cm): Max H: –; W: –
Location: Directorate-General of Antiquities and Museums, Damascus, Syria
Inventory Number: –
PS Number: –
Context: –
Inscription:
The inscriptions have not been translated
References: http://www.dgam.gov.sy/index.php?d=239&id=1176 (26.11.2018).

Catalogue number: 69

Database number: PalmyraUNK021
Sarcophagus box with portrait busts
Box: One priest, one female, and one bust of unclear gender
Date: 50-150 CE
Measurements (in cm): Max H: –; W: –
Location: Unknown location, Palmyra, Syria
Inventory Number: –
PS Number: –
Context: West necropolis. Valley of the tombs. Tower tomb no. 85d
Inscription: –
References: Henning 2013, 233.

Catalogue number: 70 (Fig. 34)

Database number: MLP018
Bust of priest from sarcophagus box
Box: One priest
Date: 170-200 CE

Measurements (in cm): Max H: 30; W: 43; D: 16
Location: Louvre, Paris, France
Inventory Number: AO 4450
PS Number: 862
Context: –
Inscription: –
References: Ingholt Archive, PS 862; Dentzer-Feydy and Teixidor 1993, 202, cat. 200.

Catalogue number: 71 (Fig. 35)
Database number: UNK222
Bust of priest from sarcophagus box
Box: One priest
Date: 180-240 CE
Measurements (in cm): Max H: –; W: –
Location: Unknown location
Inventory Number: –
PS Number: 547
Context: –
Inscription: –
References: Ingholt Archive, PS 547.

Catalogue number: 72 (Fig. 36)
Database number: UNK225
Bust of priest from sarcophagus box
Box: One priest
Date: 180-240 CE
Measurements (in cm): Max H: –; W: –
Location: Unknown location
Inventory Number: –
PS Number: 1145
Context: –
Inscription: –
References: Ingholt Archive, PS 1145.

Catalogue number: 73
Database number: PM538
Sarcophagus box with banqueting scene with three full figures
Box: One priest, one female, one male figure
Date: 200-220 CE
Measurements (in cm): Max H: –; W: –
Location: Palmyra Museum, Palmyra, Syria
Inventory Number: –
PS Number: –
Context: Southwest necropolis. Hypogeum of Hennibel
Inscription:
al-As'ad 2013, 19.

Fig. 35: Bust of priest from sarcophagus box. Unknown location, 180-240 CE (© Palmyra Portrait Project, Ingholt Archive at Ny Carlsberg Glyptotek, PS 547).

The inscription reads:
Malkû, son of Taîmê
Ḥennibel Ḥamṭûsh
and his wife Rabbanâ.
References: al-As'ad 2013, 19, fig. 9.

Catalogue number: 74
Database number: Christie's025
Bust of priest from sarcophagus box
Box: One priest
Date: 200-220 CE
Measurements (in cm): Max H: 47
Location: Last known location: New York, Christie's
Inventory Number: –
PS Number: –
Context: –
Inscription: –
References: Christie's 2008, December 9th, New York, lot

Fig. 36: Bust of priest from sarcophagus box, the bust is placed on the lower left corner of the kline. Unknown location, 180-240 CE (© Palmyra Portrait Project, Ingholt Archive at Ny Carlsberg Glyptotek, PS 1145).

63; http://www.christies.com/LotFinder/lot_details.aspx?from=salesummary&intObjectID=5157891 (19.07.2018).

Catalogue number: 75 (Fig. 37)

Database number: UNK223
Bust of priest from sarcophagus box
Box: One priest
Date: 240-273 CE
Measurements (in cm): Max H: –; W: –
Location: Unknown location
Inventory Number: –
PS Number: 1149
Context: –
Inscription: –
References: Ingholt Archive, PS 1149.

Catalogue number: 76 (Fig. 38)

Database number: MLP019
Bust of priest from sarcophagus box
Box: One priest
Date: 240-273 CE
Measurements (in cm): Max H: 27; W: 23; D: 12; D (Field): 8.5
Location: Louvre, Paris, France
Inventory Number: AO 5000
PS Number: 323
Context: –
Inscription:
CIS 4377; *PAT* 0736
The inscription reads:
Malkâ son of [...].
References: Ingholt Archive, PS 323; Ingholt 1928, 126, PS 323; Colledge 1976, 252; Dentzer-Feydy and Teixidor 1993, 204, cat. 202. Inscription: Chabot 1922, 123, cat. 27; Dentzer-Feydy and Teixidor 1993, 204, cat. 202.

Catalogue number: 77 (Fig. 39)

Database number: PM784
Sarcophagus box with portrait busts

Fig. 37: Bust of priest from sarcophagus box, the bust is placed on the lower left corner of the kline. Unknown location, 240-273 CE (© Palmyra Portrait Project, Ingholt Archive at Ny Carlsberg Glyptotek, PS 1149).

Box: One priest, five busts of unclear gender
Date: 200-273 CE
Measurements (in cm): Max H: –; W: –
Location: Palmyra Museum, Palmyra, Syria
Inventory Number: –
PS Number: 874
Context: North necropolis. Temple tomb no. 174
Inscription: –
References: Ingholt Archive, PS 874; Gawlikowski 1970, 133, fig. 77.

Catalogue number: 78 (Fig. 40)
Database number: UNK166
Sarcophagus box with portrait busts
Box: Two priests, two male busts
Date: 150-170 CE
Measurements (in cm): Max H: –; W: –
Location: Unknown location
Inventory Number: –
PS Number: 611
Context: –
Inscription: –
References: Ingholt Archive, PS 611; Kammerer 1929, 310 n. 2, pl. 119.1.

Catalogue number: 79
Database number: DGAM006
Sarcophagus box with portrait busts
Box: Two priests, two female busts

Fig. 38: Bust of priest from sarcophagus box. Louvre, Paris, inv. AO 5000, 240-273 CE (© Palmyra Portrait Project, Ingholt Archive at Ny Carlsberg Glyptotek, PS 323).

Date: 170-200 CE
Measurements (in cm): Max H: –; W: –
Location: Directorate-General of Antiquities and Museums, Damascus, Syria
Inventory Number: –
PS Number: –
Context: –
Inscription: –
References: http://www.dgam.gov.sy/index.php?d=239&id=1176 (19.07.2018).

Catalogue number: 80
Database number: PM738
Sarcophagus box with portrait busts
Box: Two priests, two female busts
Date: 170-200 CE
Measurements (in cm): Max H: –; W: –
Location: Palmyra Museum, Palmyra, Syria
Inventory Number: –
PS Number: –
Context: Southwest necropolis. Found (1990) near the Tomb of the Three Brothers

Fig. 39: Sarcophagus box with portrait busts, one being of a priest. Palmyra Museum, Palmyra, 200-273 CE (© Palmyra Portrait Project, Ingholt Archive at Ny Carlsberg Glyptotek, PS 874).

Fig. 40: Sarcophagus box with portrait busts, two being of priests. Unknown location, 150-170 CE (© Palmyra Portrait Project, Ingholt Archive at Ny Carlsberg Glyptotek, PS 611).

Inscription:
Yon 2013, 355, cat. 113.
Inscription 1 reads:
ʿAteʾêm, daughter of Ḥagegû son of Barîkaî Amrishâ, wife of Malkû son of Yarḥibôlâ.
Inscription 2 reads:
Ḥagegû, son of Barîkaî Amrishâ.
Inscription 3 reads:
Alas! Moqîmû, son of Ḥagegû, son of Barîkaî Amrishâ.
Inscription 4 reads:
Shalam, daughter of Neshâ - - -, wife of Ḥagegû.
References: Degeorge 2001, 238-239; Degeorge 2002, 198-199.

Catalogue number: 81 (Fig. 41)
Database number: AMI035
Sarcophagus box with portrait busts
Box: Two priests
Date: 200-220 CE
Measurements (in cm): Max H: 44; W: 91
Location: Archaeological Museum, Istanbul, Turkey
Inventory Number: 3787/O.M.246
PS Number: 316
Context: –

Fig. 41: Sarcophagus with two busts of priests. Palmyra Museum, Palmyra, inv. 3787/O.M.246, 220-240 CE (© Palmyra Portrait Project, Ingholt Archive at Ny Carlsberg Glyptotek, PS 316).

Inscription: –
References: Ingholt Archive, PS 316; Ingholt 1928,126, PS 316; Colledge 1976, 252.

Catalogue number: 82 (Fig. 42)

Database number: PM331
Sarcophagus box with portrait busts
Box: Two priests, two female busts
Date: 240-273 CE
Measurements (in cm): Max H: –; W: –
Location: Palmyra Museum, Palmyra, Syria
Inventory Number: –
PS Number: 903
Context: Southeast necropolis, Valley of the Tombs. Temple/house tomb no. 186 ('Tombeau de l'aviation'/'Tomb Duvaux')
Inscription: –
References: Ingholt Archive, PS 903; Schmidt-Colinet 1992, vol. I, 107, 130; vol. II, pl. 74.a-c.

Catalogue number: 83

Database number: PM737
Sarcophagus box with portrait busts
Box: Three priests
Date: 150-170 CE
Measurements (in cm): Max H: 84; W: 235
Location: Palmyra Museum, Palmyra, Syria
Inventory Number: B 2722/9159
PS Number: –
Context:–
Inscription:
Inscription 1 reads:
Neshâ, son of
Ananî.
Inscription 2 reads:
Malkû, son of
Ananî.
Inscription 3 reads:
Malê, son of
Ananî.
References: al-As'ad and Gawlikowski 1997, 75, cat. 117, fig 117.

Catalogue number: 84

Database number: InSitu086 (84a) + InSitu087 (84b)
Complete sarcophagus relief with banqueting scene and portrait busts and belonging loculus relief
Loculus relief: Three male busts
Lid: One priest, two females, one male, one child
Box: Male and female bust

Date: 150-170 CE
Measurements (in cm): 84a: Max H: 60; W: 125; D: 10. 84b: Max H: 197; W: 217; D: 15
Location: In situ, Palmyra, Syria
Inventory Number: –
PS Number: –
Context: Southeast necropolis. Tomb no. 5, Hypogeum of Artaban
Inscription:
InSitu086: PAT 2671
The inscription reads:
Alas! Yarḥaî,
son of Arṭaban,
son of ʿOggâ
PAT 2672
The inscription reads:
Alas!
Artaban, son of
Yarhai, his father.
PAT 2673
The inscription reads:
Alas! ʿOggâ,
son of Yarhai,
(son of) Artaban, his son.
InSitu087: *PAT* 2667
The inscription reads:
Berretâ, daughter of
Yarḥaî Barâ,
his wife.
PAT 2670
The inscription reads:
Arṭaban,
son of ʿOggâ,
his son.
PAT 2669
The inscription reads:
Berretâ,
daughter of
ʿOggâ, his daughter.
PAT 2668
The inscription reads:
Arṭaban,
son of
Yarḥaî Barâ.
PAT 2666
The inscription reads:
[Arṭa]ban, son of
[ʿOggâ], his father.
PAT 2665
The inscription reads:
Martabû, daughter of
Barâ, his mother.
PAT 2664
The inscription reads:
Oggâ, son of Artaban, son of
Oggâ. Alas! (he made) this for this father,
and for his brother, in his lifetime.
References: 84a: Tanabe 1986, 31, pls. 229-232; Parlasca 1987b, 281, fig. 3; Sadurska and Bounni 1994, 37-39, cat. 41, figs. 222-224. 84b: Tanabe 1986, 31, pls. 229-232; Parlasca 1987b, 281, fig. 3; Sadurska 1994, 15, fig. 8; Sadurska and Bounni 1994, 37-39, cat. 41, figs. 222-224; Parlasca 1995, 68-69, fig. 10; Heyn 2010, 640, fig. 8. Inscriptions: Sadurska and Bounni 1994, 37-38.

Catalogue number: 85

Database number: PM113 (85a) + PM114 (85b) + PM116 (85c)
Complete sarcophagus relief with banqueting scene and bust and two full figure children
Lid: One female, two males
Box: One bust of priest, one female bust, two standing children.
Date: 130-150 CE
Measurements (in cm): 85a: Max H: 49; W: 27; D: 16; D (Field): 1.3; 85b: Max H: 47; W: 66; D: 16; D (Field): 1.2; 85c: Max H: 46; W: 89; D: 6; D (Field): 1.5
Location: Palmyra Museum, Palmyra, Syria
Inventory Number: 2152/7614, 2157/7619, 2156/7621
PS Number: –
Context: Southeast necropolis. Hypogeum of Zabd'ateh and Moqîmû, section 35, at the niche of the north exedra
Inscription:
PM113: PAT 1859
The inscription reads:
Antonia, alas!
PM114: PAT 1864
The inscription reads:
Marcus,
alas!
PAT 1864
The inscription reads:
Valens, alas!
PM116: *PAT* 1863
Inscription 1 reads:
ʿAbdʿastôr
his/her son,

alas!
Inscription 2 reads:
Martâ
their mother,
alas!
Inscription 3 reads:
Beʿeshegâ,
his/her daughter,
alas!
References: 85a: al-As'ad and Taha 1965, 44, cat. 16, pls. 4-5; Gawlikowski 1974, 295, cat. 67; Makowski 1985b, 120f; Tanabe 1986, 34, 43, pls. 276, 428; Sadurska and Bounni, 1994, 134-135, cat. 181, figs. 217-219; Charles-Gaffiot et al. 2001, 355, cat. 191; Clauss 2002, 90, cat. 103. 85b: Gawlikowski 1974, 296, cat. 71; Tanabe 1986, 43, pl. 428; Sadurska and Bounni 1994, 134-135, cat. 181, figs. 217-219. 85c: al-As'ad and Taha 1965, 45, cat. 20, pls. 4-5; Gawlikowski 1974, 34, cat. 71, pl. 3; Tanabe 1986, 43, pl. 428; Sadurska and Bounni 1994, 134-145, cat. 181, figs. 217-219. Inscriptions: Gawlikowski 1974, 295, cat. 67; 296-297, cat. 72; 296, cat. 71; Sadurska and Bounni 1994, 134-135.

Catalogue number: 86

Database number: InSitu112
Complete sarcophagus relief with banqueting scene and portrait busts
Lid: One priest, one female, one child
Box: One male, two female busts
Date: 170-200 CE
Measurements (in cm): Max H: –; W: –
Location: In situ, Palmyra, Syria
Inventory Number: –
PS Number: –
Context: Southeast necropolis. Tomb no. H, Hypogeum of Taibol.
Inscription: –
References: Saito 2007, 83-94, fig. 16; Miyashita 2016, 132, figs. 11-12; http://www.dgam.gov.sy/?d=314&id=1511 (19.07.2018).

Catalogue number: 87

Database number: PM395
Complete sarcophagus relief with banqueting scene and portrait busts
Lid: One priest, one female, one male figure, one child
Box: One male, two female busts
Date: 200-220 CE
Measurements (in cm): Max H: 187; W: 172; D: 27
Location: Palmyra Museum, Palmyra, Syria
Inventory Number: 1785/6608 and 1786/6609
PS Number: –
Context: West necropolis. Valley of the Tombs. Hypogeum of Shalamallat, vestibule, south wall
Inscription: –
References: Bounni and Saliby 1957, 34-36, cat. 38, figs. 11-12; Tanabe 1986, 41, pls. 396-399; Sadurska and Bounni 1994, 170-171, cat. 231, fig. 237; Albertson 2000, 166; Miyashita 2016, 133, fig. 16.

Catalogue number: 88

Database number: InSitu075
Complete sarcophagus relief with banqueting scene and portrait busts
Lid: One priest, one female, three male figures
Box: One priest, one male, two female busts
Date: 200-220 CE
Measurements (in cm): Max H: 170; W: 182; D: 18; D (Field): 2.1
Location: In situ, Palmyra, Syria
Inventory Number: –
PS Number: –
Context: Southeast necropolis. Tomb no. 7, Hypogeum of Bôlḥâ, north exedra, last niche
Inscription:
PAT: 1893
Image of ʿAttâ, daughter of Nebôdʿa,
son of Maqqaî, wife of Malkû.
Inscription 2 reads:
Image of
Nebôdʿa,
son of Malkû, son of
Ogeîlû.
Inscription 3 reads:
Image of ʿOgeîlû,
son of Malkû, son of
Ogeîlû.
Inscription 4 reads:
This image (is that) of Malkû, son of ʿOgeîlû, son of Zabdibôl, son of Bôlḥâ Nebôshûr.
Inscription 5 reads:
Image of ʿOgeilû, son of Zabdibôl, son of
Bôlḥâ Nebôšhûr, alas!
Inscription 6 reads:
Corbulo,
son of Malkû,
son of ʿOgeîlû.

Fig. 42: Sarcophagus box with portrait busts, two being of priests. Palmyra Museum, Palmyra, 240-273 CE (© Palmyra Portrait Project, Ingholt Archive at Ny Carlsberg Glyptotek, PS 903).

Inscription 7 reads:
Image of Baʿdâ,
daughter of Malkû, son of
Ogeîlû.
Inscription 8 reads:
Image of Tammê,
daughter of Ḥûrâ, son of
Bôlḥâ, alas!
References: al-As'ad and Taha 1968, 101-106, cat. 28; Tanabe 1986, 29, pls. 188-191; Sadurska 1994, 15, fig. 9; Sadurska and Bounni 1994, 86-88, cat. 120, figs. 231-232. Inscription: Gawlikowski 1974, 307-308, cat. 101; Sadurska and Bounni 1994, 87-88.

Catalogue number: 89

Database number: InSitu074
Complete sarcophagus relief with banqueting scene and portrait busts
Lid: One priest, two female, two male figures
Box: One priest, one male, two female busts
Date: 200-220 CE
Measurements (in cm): Max H: 190; W: 204; D: 25; D (Field): 2
Location: In situ, Palmyra, Syria
Inventory Number: –
PS Number: 1374
Context: Southeast necropolis. Tomb no. 7, Hypogeum of Bôlḥâ, the podium at the end of the exedra
Inscription:
PAT: 1895
Inscription 1 reads:
Image of Aqmê daughter of Barʿateh
Inscription 2 reads:
Image of Nebôshûr son of ʿOgeîlû son of ʿOgeîlû.
Inscription 3 reads:
Image of ʿOgeîlû son of ʿOgeîlû son of ʿOgeilû, which has been made for him by Nebôshûr his son, after his death at the age of 60.
Inscription 4 reads:
Image of Aqmê daughter of ʿOggâ Aqqamal, mother of Nebôshûr.
Inscription 5 reads:
Image of Haggâ daughter of ʿOgeîlû
References: Ingholt Archive, PS 1374; al-As'ad and Taha 1968, 106-108, cat. 30; Tanabe 1986, 30, pls. 209-212; Sadurska and Bounni 1994, 89-90, cat. 121, fig. 246. Inscription: Gawlikowski 1974, 47-48, cat. 103; Sadurska and Bounni 1994, 89-90, cat. 121.

Catalogue number: 90

Database number: NMD111 (90a) + NMD112 (90b)
Complete sarcophagus relief with banqueting scene and portrait busts

Fig. 43: Sarcophagus lid relief with banqueting scene with a reclining priest. National Museum of Damascus, Damascus, inv. C 19, 130-150 CE (© Palmyra Portrait Project, Ingholt Archive at Ny Carlsberg Glyptotek, PS 62).

Lid: One priest, one female, two male figures
Box: One priest, one male, one female busts
Date: 220-240 CE
Measurements (in cm): 90a: Max H: 155; W: 126; D: 28
Location: National Museum of Damascus, Damascus, Syria
Inventory Number: B 7405, B 7406
PS Number: –
Context: –
Inscription:
Yon 2013, 343, cat. 34.
Inscription 1 reads:
Martî, wife of
Taîbbôl.
Inscription 2 reads:
Taîbbôl, son of
Yaddîʿaî Taîbbôl
Qirdâ.
References: 90a: al-As'ad 1993, 298-299, cat. 238; Kaizer 2010, 26, fig. 3. 90b: al-As'ad 1993, 298-299, cat. 238.

Catalogue number: 91 (Fig. 43)

Database number: NMD046
Sarcophagus lid relief with banqueting scene with two full figures
Lid: One priest, one female figure
Date: 130-150 CE
Measurements (in cm): Max H: 55; W: 94
Location: National Museum of Damascus, Damascus, Syria
Inventory Number: 19
PS Number: 62
Context: –
Inscription:
The inscriptions are falsified
References: Ingholt Archive, PS 62; Ingholt 1928, 94, PS 62; Ingholt 1935, 68, pl. 28.1; Abdul-Hak and Abdul-Hak 1951, 30, cat. 4, pl. 10.2; Parlasca 1982, 197-199, cat. 177; Parlasca 1985, 397-398, cat. 189. Inscription: Ingholt 1928, 94.

Catalogue number: 92 (Fig. 44)

Database number: PM546
Sarcophagus lid relief with banqueting scene with five full figures
Lid: One priest, one female, three male figures
Date: 140-160 CE
Measurements (in cm): Max H: 90; W: 175; D: 18
Location: Palmyra Museum, Palmyra, Syria
Inventory Number: A 218/218
PS Number: 61
Context: –
Inscription:
CIS: 4231; *PAT*: 0587
Inscription 1 reads:
ʿAtemâ, (daughter of)
Moqîmû
Gaddibôl,
his mother.
Inscription 2 reads:
Nebôgaddaî, son of

Fig. 44: Sarcophagus lid relief with banqueting scene with a reclining priest. Palmyra Museum, Palmyra, inv. A 218/218, 140-160 CE (© Palmyra Portrait Project, Ingholt Archive at Ny Carlsberg Glyptotek, PS 61).

Barnebû, his brother.
Inscription 3 reads:
Barnebû, son of Barnebû,
his brother.
Inscription 4 reads:
Barʿateh, son of
Barnebû, his brother.
Inscription 5 reads:
Image of Barʿateh,
son of Barnebû, son of
Barnebû.
References: Ingholt Archive, PS 61; Chabot 1922, 111-112, pl. 27.13; Ingholt 1928, 94, PS 61; Kammerer 1929, 310 n.2, pl. 120.1; Seyrig 1934, 174, pl. 24.2; Gawlikowski 1966, 85, fig. 4; Ingholt 1974, 40-43, pl. 1.3; al-As'ad and Gawlikowski 1997, 68, cat. 104, fig. 104; Savignac 2001, 167; Heyn 2008, 170-173, 178, fig. 6.2; <http://www.gerty.ncl.ac.uk/photo_details.php?photo_id=540> (28.06.2018); <http://www.gerty.ncl.ac.uk/photo_details.php?photo_id=312> (28.06.2018). Inscription: Chabot 1922, 112; Ingholt 1974, 41-43; al-As'ad and Gawlikowski 1997, 68, cat. 104, fig. 104.

Catalogue number: 93

Database number: PM544
Sarcophagus lid relief with banqueting scene with two full figures
Lid: One priest, one female figure
Date: 150-170 CE
Measurements (in cm): Max H: 115; W: 182
Location: Palmyra Museum, Palmyra, Syria
Inventory Number: –
PS Number: –
Context: Southwest necropolis. Hypogeum of Aqraban
Inscription: –
References: al-Hariri 2013, 150-151, fig. 10.

Catalogue number: 94

Database number: RoMou004
Sarcophagus lid relief with banqueting scene
Lid: One priest, one female figure
Date: 240-273 CE
Measurements (in cm): Max H: –; W: –
Location: Robert Mouawad Private Museum, Beirut, Lebanon
Inventory Number: –
PS Number: –
Context: –
Inscription: –
References: Parlasca 1987a, 108f, 113, appendix no. 3; http://rmpm.info/antiquities.html#prettyPhoto[gallery1]/32/ (28.06.2018).

Catalogue number: 95

Database number: PM545
Sarcophagus lid relief with banqueting scene with four full figures

Lid: One priest, one female figure
Date: 150-170 CE
Measurements (in cm): Max H: 115; W: 182
Location: Palmyra Museum, Palmyra, Syria
Inventory Number: –
PS Number: –
Context: Southwest necropolis. Hypogeum of Aqraban
Inscription: –
References: al-Hariri 2013, 150-151, fig. 11.

Catalogue number: 96

Database number: NMD058
Sarcophagus lid relief with banqueting scene with five full figures
Lid: Three priests, two female figures
Date: 220-240 CE
Measurements (in cm): Max H: 105; W: 208
Location: National Museum of Damascus, Damascus, Syria
Inventory Number: C4946
PS Number: –
Context: Southwest necropolis. Hypogeum of Malkû
Inscription: –
References: Abdul-Hak and Abdul-Hak 1951, 42, cat. 37, pl. 19.1; Tanabe 1986, 42, pls. 410-415; Parlasca 1987a, 114, cat. 5; Finlayson 2004, 60, 65, figs. 1-2.

Catalogue number: 97

Database number: PM885
Sarcophagus box
Box: One priest, five figures of unclear gender, one bust
Date: 220-240 CE
Measurements (in cm): Max H: 87.5; W: 208; D: 83
Location: Palmyra Museum, Palmyra, Syria
Inventory Number: C
PS Number: –
Context: West necropolis. Valley of the Tombs. Temple tomb no. 36
Inscription: –
References: Schmidt-Colinet 1992, vol. I, 146, cat. S 1; vol. II, pl. 31.c-d.

Catalogue number: 98

Database number: PM951
Sarcophagus box relief with banqueting scene
Box: One priest, one female, one male figure
Date: 180-240 CE
Measurements (in cm): Max H: –; W: –
Location: Palmyra Museum, Palmyra, Syria
Inventory Number: –
PS Number: –
Context: West necropolis. Valley of the Tombs. Near Temple/house tomb no. 85b, tomb of Aʿailamî and Zebidâ ('Tomb Cantineau')
Inscription: –
References: Will 1951, 87, fig. 9.

Catalogue number: 99

Database number: PM332
Sarcophagus box relief with portrait busts
Box: Two priests, one female figure
Date: 130-150 CE
Measurements (in cm): Max H: 57; W: 96; D: 9
Location: Palmyra Museum, Palmyra, Syria
Inventory Number: 1776/6602
PS Number: –
Context: West necropolis. Valley of the Tombs. Hypogeum of Shalamallat, vestibule, north wall
Inscription: –
References: Bounni and Saliby 1957, 36-37; Tanabe 1986, 45, pl. 473; Sadurska and Bounni 1994, 169, cat. 227, fig. 225.

Catalogue number: 100 (Fig. 45)

Database number: PM382
Sarcophagus box relief with portrait busts
Box: Two priests, one female figure
Date: 130-150 CE
Measurements (in cm): Max H: 55; W: 93; D: 11
Location: Palmyra Museum, Palmyra, Syria
Inventory Number: 1780/6603
PS Number: 1281
Context: West necropolis. Valley of the Tombs. Hypogeum of Shalamallat, vestibule, north wall
Inscription: –
References: Ingholt Archive, PS 1281; Bounni and Saliby 1957, 37, fig. 10; Tanabe 1986, 45, pl. 472; Sadurska and Bounni 1994, 169, cat. 228, fig. 226.

Catalogue number: 101 (Fig. 46)

Database number: PM913
Sarcophagus box relief with banqueting scene
Box: Two priests, two female figures
Date: 180-240 CE
Measurements (in cm): Max H: 83; W: 205
Location: Palmyra Museum, Palmyra, Syria

Fig. 45: Sarcophagus box relief with portrait busts, two being of priests. Palmyra Museum, Palmyra, inv. 1780/6603, 130-150 CE (© Palmyra Portrait Project, Ingholt Archive at Ny Carlsberg Glyptotek, PS 1281).

Fig. 46: Sarcophagus box relief with banqueting scene with two reclining priests. Palmyra Museum, Palmyra, 180-240 (© Palmyra Portrait Project, Ingholt Archive at Ny Carlsberg Glyptotek, PS 531A/882).

Inventory Number: –
PS Number: 531A/882
Context: West necropolis. Valley of the Tombs. Temple/house tomb no. 85b, Tomb of A'ailamî and Zebidâ ('Tomb Cantineau)
Inscription: –
References: Ingholt Archive, PS 531A; Cantineau 1929, 12, pls. 2.2, 6.4; Will 1951, 88f, fig. 9; Makowski 1983, 187, cat. 4, pl. 52.a.

Catalogue number: 102

Database number: PM319
Sarcophagus box relief with portrait busts
Box: Two priests, one female figure
Date: 180-240 CE
Measurements (in cm): Max H: 46; W: 86
Location: Palmyra Museum, Palmyra, Syria
Inventory Number: –
PS Number: –
Context: Southeast necropolis. Hypogeum of Zabd'ateh and Moqîmû.
Inscription: –
References: Tanabe 1986, 42-43, pl. 427.

Catalogue number: 103 (Fig. 47)

Database number: AUB011
Figure of priest
Date: 130-150 CE
Measurements (in cm): Max H: –; W: –
Location: American University Museum, Beirut, Lebanon

Inventory Number: 19
PS Number: 152
Context: –
Inscription: –
References: Ingholt Archive, PS 152; Ingholt 1928, 107, PS 152; Colledge 1976, 248.

Catalogue number: 104

Database number: PM895 (104a) + PM476 (104b)
Head of priest and male head
Date: 200-250 CE
Measurements (in cm): 104a: Max H: 13.
Location: Palmyra Museum, Palmyra, Syria
Inventory Number: II.b.3, III.b.7
PS Number: –
Context: West necropolis. Valley of the Tombs. Temple tomb no. 36
Inscription: –
References: 104a: Schmidt-Colinet 1992, vol. I, 153 cat. K 7; vol. II, pl. 49.c. 104b: Schmidt-Colinet 1992, vol. I, 154, cat. K 27; vol. II, pl. 49.h.

Abbreviations

CIS J.-B. Chabot (ed.) 1926, *Corpus Inscriptionum Semiticarum, Pars secunda, Tomus III: Inscriptiones palmyrenae*, Paris.

PAT D. R. Hillers and E. Cussini 1996, *Palmyrene Aramaic Texts*, Baltimore.

Fig. 47: Figure of priest. American University Museum, Beirut, inv. 19, 130-150 CE (© Palmyra Portrait Project, Ingholt Archive at Ny Carlsberg Glyptotek, PS 152).

Bibliography

Abdul-Hak, S. 1952, L'hypogée de Taai à Palmyre, *AAS* 2, 193-251.

Abdul-Hak, S. and A. Abdul-Hak 1951, *Catalogue illustré du Département des antiquités gréco-romaines au Musée de Damas*, Damascus.

Abousamra, G. 2015, Palmyrene Inscriptions on Seven Reliefs, *Semitica* 57, 217-242.

Albertson, F. C. 2000, Three Palmyrene reliefs in the Colket collection, University of Wyoming, *Syria* 77, 159-168.

Amy, R. and H. Seyrig 1936, Recherches dans la nécropole de Palmyre, *Syria* 17, 3, 229-266.

al-As'ad, K. 2013, Some tombs recently excavated at Palmyra, *Studia Palmyreńskie* 12, 15-24.

al-As'ad, K. 1993, Palmyre, in S. Cluzan, E. Delpont and J. Mouliérac (eds.), *Syrie: Mémoire et Civilisation*, Paris, 276-179, 294-310.

al-As'ad, K. and M. Gawlikowski 1997, *The inscriptions in the Museum of Palmyra: a catalogue*. Warsaw.

al-As'ad, K., M. Gawlikowski and J.-B. Yon 2012, Aramaic inscriptions in the Palmyra Museum: new acquisitions, *Syria* 89, 163-184.

al-As'ad K. and A. Schmidt-Colinet 1995, Zur Einführung, in A. Schmidt-Colinet (ed.), *Palmyra: Kulturbegegnung im Grenzbereich*, Mainz am Rhein, 28-53.

al-As'ad, K. and A. Schmidt-Colinet 1985, Das Tempelgrab Nr. 36 in der Westnekropole von Palmyra. Ein Vorbericht, *DM* 2, 17-35.

al-As'ad, K. and O. Taha 1968, Madfan Zabd-ʿAtah al-Tudmurî (The Tomb of Zabdʿateh), *AAS* 18, 83-108.

al-As'ad, K. and O. Taha 1965, The Tomb of Zabdʿateh (in Arabic), *AAS* 15, 29-46.

Audley-Miller, L. 2016, The Banquet in Palmyrene Funerary Contexts, in C. M. Draycott and M. Stamatopoulou (eds.), *Dining and Death: Interdiciplinary Perspectives on the 'Funerary Banquet' in Ancient Art, Burial and Belief*, Leuven, Paris and Bristol, 553-590.

Balty, J.-C. 2010, Deux reliefs palmyréniens du Musée Saint-Raymond, Musée des Antiques de Toulouse, in B. Bastl, V. Gassner and U. Muss (eds.), *Zeitreisen: Syrien, Palmyra, Rom, Festschrift für Andreas Schmidt-Colinet zum 65. Geburtstag*, Wien, 23–28.

Bossert, H. T. 1951, *Altsyrien: Kunst und Handwerk in Cypern, Syrien, Palästina, Transjordanien und Arabien von den Anfängen bis zum völligen Aufgehen in der griechisch-römischen Kultur*, Tübingen.

Bounni, A. 1961–1962. Inscriptions palmyreniennes inedites, *AAS* 11–12, 145–162.

Bounni, A. and K. al-As'ad 1990, *Palmyra: Geschichte, Denmäler, Museum, Damascus.*

Bounni, A. and N. Saliby 1957, Madfan šalam allât (The Tomb of Shallamallat), *AAS* 7, 25–52.

Bounni, A. and J. Teixidor 1975, *Inventaire des inscriptions de Palmyre: Vallée des tombeaux et textes funéraires divers,* vol. 12, Damascus.

British Museum, 2018, *Bust*, http://www.britishmuseum.org/research/collection_online/collection_object_details.aspx?objectId=282719&partId=1&searchText=125033&page=1 (accessed 20.07.2018).

Brody, L. R. and G. L. Hoffman 2011, *Dura-Europos: Crossroads of Antiquity,* Chestnut Hill.

Brown, J. M. 1973, *Ancient Art in the Virginia Museum*. Richmond.

Browning, I. 1979, *Palmyra*, London.

Cantineau, J. 1938, Tadmorea, *Syria* 19, 2, 153–171.

Cantineau, J. 1929, Fouilles a Palmyra. *Mélanges de l'Institut Francais de Damas* 1, 3–15.

Chabot, J. B. 1922, *Choix d'inscriptions de Palmyre,* Paris.

Champdor, A. 1953, *Les ruines de Palmyre,* Paris.

Charles-Gaffiot, J., H. Lavagne and J.-M. Hofman 2001. *Moi, Zénobie: Reine de Palmyra*, Paris, Rome, and Milan.

Christie's New York, 9 December 2008, *A Palmyrene limestone bust of a priest*, lot 63, http://www.christies.com/LotFinder/lot_details.aspx?from=salesummary&intObjectID=5157891 (accessed 16.07.2018).

Christie's New York, 12 December 2002, *A Palmyrene limestone funerary relief*, lot 303, https://www.christies.com/LotFinder/lot_details.aspx?from=salesummary&intObjectID=4026240 (accessed 16.07.2018).

Clauss, P. 2002, Morire ai tempi di Zenobia, in A. Gabucci (ed.), *Zenobia: Il sogno di una regina d'Oriente*: Milan, 75–99.

Colledge, M.A.R. 1976, *The Art of Palmyra*, London.

Cussini, E. (ed) 2005, *A Journey to Palmyra: Collected Essays to Remember Delbert R. Hillers,* Leiden and Boston.

Degeorge, G. 2002, *Palmyra*, Munich.

Degeorge, G. 2001, *Palmyre: Métropole Caravanière*, Paris.

Dentzer-Feydy, J. and J. Teixidor 1993, *Les antiquités de Palmyre au Musée du Louvre*, Paris.

Directorate-General of Antiquities & Museums, 2014, ةرداصم ةيرثأ ليثامت ةعست ديعتست رمدت راثآ ةيريدم, http://www.dgam.gov.sy/index.php?d=239&id=1199 (accessed 16.07.2018).

Directorate-General of Antiquities & Museums, 2014, ةرداصم ةيرثأ ليثامت ةعست ديعتست رمدت راثآ ةيريدم, http://www.dgam.gov.sy/index.php?d=239&id=1206 (accessed 16.07.2018).

Directorate-General of Antiquities and Museums, 2014, ةرداص, ةيرثأ ليثامت ةعست ديعتست رمدت راثآ ةيريدم, http://www.dgam.gov.sy/index.php?d=239&id=1176 (accessed 16.07.2018).

Directorate-General of Antiquities and Museums, 2014, ةرداصم ةيرثأ ليثامت ةعست ديعتست رمدت راثآ ةيريدم, http://www.dgam.gov.sy/?d=314&id=1511 (accessed 16.07.2018).

Directorate-General of Antiquities and Museums, 2014, ةرداصم ةيرثأ ليثامت ةعست ديعتست رمدت راثآ ةيريدم, http://dgam.gov.sy/index.php?antiquid=239&id=1160 (accessed 16.07.2018).

Dirven, L. 1999. *The Palmyrenes of Dura-Europos: a Study of Religious Interaction in Roman Syria*, Leiden, Boston and Cologne.

Drijvers, H. J. W. 1976, *The religion of Palmyra,* Iconography of religions XV.15, Leiden.

Dunant, C. and R. A. Stucky 2000, *Le Sanctuaire de Baalshamîn à Palmyre: The Sculptures, Bibliotheca Helvetica Romana. Le Sanctuaire de Baalshamîn à Palmyre, Mission archéologique Suisse en Syrie, 1954–1966, vol. IV*, Rome.

Equini-Schneider, E. 1993, *Septimia Zenobia Sebaste*, Rome.

Finlayson, C. 2004, Textile Exchange and Cultural and Gendered Cross-Dressing at Palmyra, Syria (100 BC-AD 272), in *Textile Society of America Symposium Proceedings*, Los Angeles, 60–70.

Fortin, M. 1999, *Syrien: Wege der Kultur*, Mainz am Rhein.

Gawlikowski, M. 2015, Bel of Palmyra, in M. Blömer, A. Lichtenberger and R. Raja (eds.), *Religious Identities in the Levant from Alexander to Muhammad: Continuity and Change, Contextualising the Sacred,* Turnhout, 247–254.

Gawlikowski, M. 2005, The City of the Dead, in E. Cussini (ed.), *A Journey to Palmyra: Collected Essays to Remember Delbert R. Hillers*. Leiden and Boston, 44–73.

Gawlikowski, M. 2003, Palmyra: from a Tribal Federation

to a City, in K. S. H. Freyberger, A. Henning and H. von Hesberg (eds.), *Kulturkonflikte im Vorderen Orient an der Wende vom Hellenismus zur römischen Kaiserzeit*, Rahden, 7-10.

Gawlikowski, M. 1990, Les dieux de Palmyre, *ANRW* 2, 18, 4, 2605-2658.

Gawlikowski, M. 1987. Objektbeschreibungen, nr. 1-76, in: E. M. Ruprechtsberger ed. 1987. *Palmyra: Gesichte, Kunst und Kultur der syrischen Oasenstadt*, Linz and Paris, 287-339.

Gawlikowski, M. 1979-1980, Aus dem syrischen Götterhimmel: Zur Ikonographie der palmyrenischen Götter, *Trierer Winckelmannsprogramme* 1-2, 17-26.

Gawlikowski, M. 1974, *Recueil D'Inscriptions Palmyréniennes: Provenant de Fouilles Syriennes et Polonaises Récentes à Palmyre,* Mémoires présentés par divers savants à l'Académie des Inscriptions et Belles-Lettres de l'Institut de France 16, Paris.

Gawlikowski, M. 1970, *Monuments Funéraires de Palmyre*, Warsaw.

Gawlikowski, M. 1966, Problemy ikonogra i kapłanów palmyreńskich: Les prêtes de Palmyre problems d'iconographie, *Studia Palmyreńskie* 1, 74-95.

Gertrude Bell Archive, 2014, *Photographs A_309*, http://www.gerty.ncl.ac.uk/photo_details.php?photo_id=312 (accessed 16.07.2018).

Gertrude Bell Archive, 2014, *Photographs A_536*, <http://www.gerty.ncl.ac.uk/photo_details.php?photo_id=540 (accessed 16.07.2018).

Ghirshman, R. 1962, *Persian Art: The Parthian and Sassanian Dynasties, 249 B.C.-A.D. 651*, New York.

Guzzo, M. G. A. 1996, Le iscrizioni palmirene del Museo Barracco, in M. G. Picozzi and F. Carinci (eds.), *Vicino Oriente, Egeo, Grecia, Roma e mondo romano: Tradizione dell'antico e collezionismo di antichità: Studi in Memoria di Lucia Guerrini, Studi Miscellanei* 30. Rome, 301-303.

al-Hariri, K. 2013, The tomb of 'Aqraban, *Studia Palmyreńskie* 12, 149-157.

Henning, A. 2013, *Die Turmgräber von Palmyra: Eine lokale Bauform im kaiserzeitlichen Syrien als Ausdruck kultureller Identität*, Rahden.

Heyn, M. K. 2010, Gesture and Identity in the Funerary Art of Palmyra, *AJA* 114, 4, 631-661.

Heyn, M. K. 2008, Sacerdotal Activities and Parthian Dress in Roman Palmyra, in C. S. H. Colburn and M. Heyn, *Reading a Dynamic Canvas: Adornment in the Ancient Mediterranean World*, Newcastle, 170-193.

Higuchi, T. and K. Saito 2001, *Tomb F-Tomb of BWLH and BWRP: Southeast Necropolis, Palmyra, Syria*, Nara.

Hvidberg-Hansen, F. O. and G. Ploug 1993, *Katalog: Palmyra samlingen, Ny Carlsberg Glyptotek*, Copenhagen.

Ingholt, H. 1976, Varia Tadmorea, in E. Frézouls (ed.), *Palmyre, Bilan et perspectives: Colloque de Strasbourg 18-20 Octobre 1973*, Strasbourg, 101-137.

Ingholt, H. 1974, Two unpublished tombs from the southwest necropolis of Palmyra, Syria, in D. K. Kouymjian (ed.), *Near Eastern numismatics, iconography, epigraphy and history: studies in honor of George C. Miles*, Beyrouth, 37-54.

Ingholt, H. 1970-1971, The sarcophagus of Be'elai and other sculptures from the tomb of Malkû, Palmyra, *MelBeyrouth* 46, 171-200.

Ingholt, H. 1954, *Palmyrene and Gandharan sculpture*, New Haven.

Ingholt, H. 1938, Inscriptions and sculptures from Palmyra, *Berytus* 5, 93-140.

Ingholt, H. 1936. Inscriptions and sculptures from Palmyra, *Berytus* 3, 93-140.

Ingholt, H. 1935, Five dated tombs from Palmyra, *Berytus* 2, 58-120.

Ingholt, H. 1934, Palmyrene sculptures in Beirut, *Berytus* 1, 32-43.

Ingholt, H. 1930, The oldest known grave-relief from Palmyra, *ActaArch* 1, 191-195.

Ingholt, H. 1928, *Studier over Palmyrensk Skulptur*, Copenhagen.

Ingholt, H., H. Seyrig and J. Starcky 1955, *Recueil des tessères de Palmyre*, Paris.

Kaizer T. 2010, Funerary Cults at Palmyra, in O. Hekster (ed.), *Cultural messages in the Graeco-Roman world: Acta of the BABESCH 80th Anniversary Workshop Radboud University Nijmegen, September 8th 2006*, Leuven, 23-31.

Kaizer, T. 2002, *The Religious Life of Palmyra: A Study of the Social Patterns of Worship in the Roman Period*, Stuttgart.

Kammerer, A. 1929, *Pétra et la nabatène*, Paris.

Krag, S. 2017, Changing Identities, Changing Positions: Jewellery in Palmyrene Female Portraits, in T. Long and A. H. Sørensen (eds.), *Positions and Professions in Palmyra*, Palmyrene Studies 2, Copenhagen, 36-51.

Krag, S. 2016, Females in Group Portraits in Palmyra, in A. Kropp and R. Raja (eds.), *The World of Palmyra*, Palmyrene Studies 1, Copenhagen, 180-193.

Krag, S. 2015, The Secrets of the Funerary Buildings in Palmyra During the Roman Period, in E. Mortensen and S. Grove Saxkjær (eds.), *Revealing and Concealing in Antiquity: Textual and Archaeological Approaches to Secrecy*, Aarhus, 105-118.

Krag, S. and R. Raja 2017, Representations of Women

and Children in Palmyrene Banqueting Reliefs and Sarcophagus Scenes, *Zeitschrift für Orientarchäologie* 10, 196–227.

Kropp, A. and R. Raja 2016, *The World of Palmyra*, Palmyrene Studies 1, Copenhagen.

Kropp, A. and R. Raja (eds.) 2015. The Palmyra Portrait Project, in J. M. Álvarez Martínez, T. Nogales Bassarate and I. Rodà de Llanza (eds.), *Proceedings of the XVIIIth International Congress of Classical Archaeology II: Centre and Periphery in the Ancient World*, Merida, 1223-1226.

Kropp, A. and R. Raja 2014, The Palmyra Project. *Syria* 91, 393–407.

Long, T. 2017, The Use of Parthian Costume in Funerary Portraiture in Palmyra, in A. H. Sørensen and T. Long (eds.), *Positions and Professions in Palmyra*, Palmyrene Studies 2, Copenhagen, 68–83.

Mackay, D. 149, The jewellery of Palmyra and its significance, *Iraq* 2, 2, 160-187.

Makowski, K. C. 1985a, La sculpture funéraire palmyrénienne et sa function dans l'architecture sépulcrale, *Studia Palmyreńskie* 8, 69–117.

Makowski, K. C. 1985b, Recherces sur le banquet miniaturisé dans l'art funéraire de Palmyre, *Studia Palmyreńskie* 8, 119–130.

Makowski, K. C. 1983, Recherches sur le tombeau de A'ailamî e Zebîdâ, *DM* 1, 175–187.

Michalowski, M. 1966, *Palmyre: Fouilles Polonaises 1963 et 1964*, Warsaw.

Miyashita, S. 2016, The Vessels in Palmyrene Banquet Scenes: Tomb BWLH and BWRP amd Tomb TYBL, in J. C. Meyer, E. H. Seland and N. Anfinset (eds.), *Palmyrena: City, Hinterland and Caravan Trade between Orient and Occident,* Oxford, 131–146.

Morehart, M. 1956–1957, Early Sculpture at Palmyra, *Berytus* 12, 53–83.

The Nelson Atkins Museum of Art, 2018, *Priest of Bel and His Attendant*, http://art.nelson-atkins.org/objects/9925/priest-of-bel-and-his-attendant?ctx=bdae8901-8959-4b0a-ae06-428b2b929303&idx=2 (Accessed 16.07.2018).

Parlasca, K. 1998. Palmyrenische Sarkophage mit Totenmahlreliefs - Forschungsstand und ikonographische Probleme, *SarkSt* 1, pp. 311-320.

Parlasca, K. 1995, Some problems of palmyrene plastic art, *ARAM* 7, 59–71.

Parlasca, K. 1994, Eine palmyrenische Tierkopffibel in Privatbesitz: Ein Beitrag zur Kulturgeschichte Palmyras, *AKorrBl* 24, 299–310.

Parlasca, K. 1989, La sculpture grecque et la sculpture d'époque romaine Impériale en Syrie, in J.-M. Dentzer and W. Orthmann (eds.), *Archéologie et histoire de la Syrie* 2, Saarbrücken, 537-556.

Parlasca, K. 1988, Ikonographische Probleme palmyrenischer Grabreliefs, *DM* 3, 215–221.

Geshichte, Kunst und Kultur der syrischen Oasenstadt, Linz. 276–282

Parlasca, K. 1987a, Ein antoninischer Frauenkopf aus Palmyra in Malibu, in J. Frel (ed.), *Ancient Portraits in the J. Paul Getty Museum*, vol. 1, Los Angeles, 107–114

Parlasca, K. 1987b, Aspekte der palmyrenischen Skulpturen, in E. M. Ruprechtsberger (ed.), *Palmyra: Geschichte, Kunst und Kultur der syrischen Oasenstadt,* Linz, 276–282.

Parlasca, K. 1985, Roman Art in Syria, in H. Weiss (ed.), *Ebla to Damascus. Art and Archaeology of Ancient Syria*, Washington D.C., 386–440.

Parlasca, K. 1984, Probleme der palmyrenischen Sarkophage, *Marburger Winckelmann-programm 1984. Symposium über die Antiken Sarkophage, Pisa 5.-12. September 1982*, 283–296.

Parlasca, K. 1982, Römische Kunst in Syrien, in K. Kohlmeyer and E. Strommenger (eds.), *Land des Baal: Syrien, Forum der Völker und Kulturen*, Mainz am Rhein, 186–226.

Piersimoni P. 1995a, Compiling a Palmyrene prosopography: methodological problems, *ARAM* 7, 252–260.

Piersimoni, P. 1995b, *The Palmyrene Prosopography*, 2 vols., unpublished PhD Thesis, University College London.

Ploug, G. 1995, *Catalogue of the Palmyrene Sculptures, Ny Carlsberg Glyptotek*, Copenhagen.

Raja, R. 2017a, Representations of the so-called "former priests" in palmyrene funerary art: A methodological contribution and commentary, *Topoi* 21, 1, 51-81.

Raja, R. 2017b, Networking beyond death: Priests and their family networks in Palmyra explored through the funerary sculpture, in H. F. Teigen and E. H. Seland (eds.), *Sinews of Empire: Networks in the Roman Near East and Beyond*, Oxford, 121–136.

Raja, R. 2017c, Going Individual: Roman Period Portraiture in Classical Archaeology, in A. Lichtenberger and R. Raja (eds.), *The Diversity of Classical Archaeology*, Turnhout, 271–286.

Raja, R. 2017d, To be or not to be depicted as a priest in Palmyra: A matter of representational spheres and societal values, in T. Long and A. H. Sørensen (eds.), *Positions and Professions*, Palmyrenske Studier 2, Copenhagen, 115–130.

Raja, R. 2017e. 'You can leave your hat on'. Priestly representations from Palmyra: Between visual genre, religious importance and social status, in R. L. Gordon, G. Petridou and J. Rüpke (eds.), *Beyond Priesthood, Religious Entrepreneurs and Innovators in the Imperial Era*, Berlin, 417-442.

Raja, R. 2017f, Powerful images of the deceased: Palmyrene funerary portrait culture between Local, Greek and Roman representations, in D. Boschung and F. Queyrel (eds.), *Bilder der Macht: Das griechische Porträt und seine Verwendung in der antiken Welt*, Paderborn, 319-348.

Raja, R. 2016a, In and Out of Contexts: Explaining Religious Complexity through the Banqueting Tesserae from Palmyra, *Religion in the Roman Empire* 2, 3, 340-371.

Raja, R. 2016b, Representations of Priests in the Funerary Sculpture from the Palmyra: Methodological Considerations on the Meaning of the Representation of Priesthood in Roman Period Palmyra, *Religion in the Roman Empire* 2, 1, 125-146.

Raja, R. 2015a, Staging "private" religion in Roman "public" Palmyra. The role of the religious dining tickets, in J. Rüpke and C. Ando (eds.), *Public and private in Ancient Mediterranean Law and Religion,* Historical and Comparative Studies, Berlin, 165-186.

Raja, R. 2015b, Cultic dining and religious patterns in Palmyra: The case of the Palmyrene banqueting tesserae, in S. Faust, M. Seifert and L. Ziemer (eds.), *Antike, Architektur, Geschichte: Festschrift für Inge Nielsen zum 65. Geburtstag*, Aachen, 181-200.

Raja, R. 2015c. Palmyrene Funerary Portraits in Context: Portrait Habit between Local Traditions and Imperial Trends, in J. Fejfer, M. Moltesen and A. Rathje (eds.), *Tradition: Transmission of Culture in the Ancient World*, Copenhagen, 329-362.

Raja, R. (forthcoming), *Palmyrene Sarcophagi. Sarkophag Studien*, Berlin.

Robert Mouawad Private Museum, 2018, http://rmpm.info/antiquities.html#prettyPhoto[gallery1]/32/ (accessed 16.07.2018).

Rumscheid, J. 2000, *Kranz und Krone: Zu Insignien, Siegespreisen und Ehrenzeichen der römischen Kaiserzeit*, Tübingen.

Ruprechtsberger, E. M. 1987, Antikes Palmyra - Topographie und Denkmäler, in E. M. Ruprechtsberger (ed.), *Palmyra: Gesichte, Kunst und Kultur der syrischen Oasenstadt*, Linz, 44-114.

Sadurska, A. 1995, La famille et son image dans l'art de Palmyre, in F. E. Koenig and S. Rebetez (eds), *Arculiana: Ioanni Boegli anno sexagesimo Quinto feliciter peracto amici discipuli college socii dona dederunt A. D. XIIII Kalendas Decembris MDCCCCLXXXXV*, Avenches, 583-589.

Sadurska, A. 1994, L'art et la société: Recherches iconologiques sur l'art funéraire de Palmyre, *Archeologia-War* 45, 11-23.

Sadurska, A. 1988. Die palmyrenische Grabskulptur, *Altertum* 34, 14-23.

Sadurska, A. 1977, *Palmyre: Le tombeau de famille de 'Alaine*, vol VII, Warsaw.

Sadurska, A. 1976, Nouvelles recherches dans la nécropole ouest de Palmyre, in E. Frézouls (ed.), *Palmyre: Bilan et perspectives: Colloque de Strasbourg 18-20 Octobre 1973*, Strasbourg, 1-32.

Sadurska, A. and A. Bounni 1994, *Les sculptures funéraires de Palmyre*, Rome.

Saito, K. 2007, Sheep bones accompanies the dead from an underground tomb in Palmyra: especially on metacarpal bones (in Japanese), *Rāfidān* 28, 83-94.

Savignac, M. R. 2001, Mission épigraphique à Palmyre (juillet 1914), in J. Charles-Gaffiot, H. Lavagne and J.-M. Hofman (eds.), *Moi, Zénobie: Reine de Palmyre*, Paris, Rome, and Milan, 163-170.

Schmidt-Colinet, A. 2004, Palmyrenische Grabkunst als Ausdruck lokaler Identität(en): Fallbeispiele, in A. Schmidt-Colinet (ed.), *Lokale Identitäten in Randgebeiten des Römischem Reiches, Akten des Internationalen Symposiums in Wiener Neustadt 2003*, Wien, 189-198.

Schmidt-Colinet, A. 1996, Antike Denkmäler in Syrien. Die Stichvorlagen von Louis-Francois Cassas (1756-1827) im Wallraf-Richartz-Museum in Köln, *KölnJb* 29, 343-548.

Schmidt-Colinet, A. 1992, *Das Tempelgrab Nr. 36 in Palmyra: Studie zur Palmyrenischen Grabarchitektur und ihrer Ausstattung*, 2 vols., Mainz am Rhein.

Schmidt-Colinet, A. 1987, Das Tempelgrab einer Aristokratenfamilie (Neue deutsche Ausgrabungen in Palmyra), in E. M. Ruprechtsberger (ed.), *Palmyra: Geschichte, Kunst und Kultur der syrischen Oasenstadt*, Linz, 228-243.

Schmidt-Colinet, A. and K. al-As'ad 2007, Zwei Neufunde Palmyrenischer Sarkophage, in G. Koch (ed.), *Akten des Symposiums des Sarkophag-Corpus, Marburg 2.-7. Juli 2001*, Mainz am Rhein, 271-278.

Schneider, E. E. 1996, Ritratti funerari palmireni del Museo Barracco, in M. G. Picozzi, and F. Carinci, *Vicino Oriente, Egeo, Grecia, Roma e mondo romano: Tradizione dell'antico e collezionismo di antichità: Studi in Memoria di Lucia Guerrini, Studi Miscellanei 30*, Rome, 293-300.

Seipel, W. 1996, *Weihrauch und Seide: Alte Kulturen an der Seidenstrasse*, Milan.
Seyrig, H. 1951, Le repas des morts et le "Banquet Funèbre" a Palmyre, *AAS* 1, 1-11.
Seyrig, H. 1937, Antiquités syriennes, *Syria* 18, 1, 1-53.
Seyrig, H. 1934, Antiquités Syriennes: 17. Bas-reliefs monumentaux du temple de Bêl à Palmyre, *Syria* 15, 2, 155-186.
Sotheby's auction catalogue, July 1st 1963.
Starcky, J. 1955, Inscriptions Palmyréniennes conserves au Museée de Beyrouth, *BMusBeyr* 12, 29-44.
Starcky, J. 1941, Palmyre: Guide archéologique, *MélBeyrouth* 24, 5-68.
The State Hermitage Museum, 2018, *Palmyrene Funerary Relief of Mezzabena*, https://www.hermitagemuseum.org/wps/portal/hermitage/digital-collection/25.+Archaeological+Artifacts/87743/?lng=da> (accessed 16.072018).
Stauffer, A. 2013, Kleidung und Tracht in Palmyra, in M. Tellenbach, R. Schulz and A. Wieczorek (eds.), *Die Macht der Toga: DressCode im Römischen Weltreich*, Regensburg, 127-131.
Stauffer, A. 2010, Kleidung in Palmyra: Neue Fragen und alte Funde, in B. Bastl, V. Gassner and U. Muss (eds.), *Zeitreisen: Syrien - Palmyra - Rom, Festschrift für Andreas Schmidt-Colinet zum 65. Geburtstag*, Wien, 209-218.
Stucky, R. A. 1973, Prêtres syriens I: Palmyre, *Syria* 50, 163-180.
Taha, A. 1982, Men's costume in Palmyra, *AAS* 32, 117-132.
Tanabe, K. 1986, *Sculptures of Palmyra I*, Tokyo.
Vermeule, C. C. 1981, *Greek and Roman sculpture in America: masterpieces in public collections in the United States and Canada*, Berkeley.
Vermeule, C. C. 1964, Greek and Roman portraits in North American collections open to the public: A Survey of Important Monumental Likeness in Marble and Bronze which have not been published extensively, *PAPS* 108, 99-134.
de Vogüe, M. 1868, *Syrie Centrale: Inscriptions Sémitiques*, Paris.
Wartke, R.-B. 1991, Palmyrenische Plastik im Vorderasiatischen Museum, *FuB* 31, 67-100.
Watzinger, C. and K. Wulzinger 1932, Die Nekropolen, in T. Wiegand (ed.), *Palmyra: Ergebnisse der Expeditionen von 1902 und 1917*, Berlin, 44-76.
Wielgosz, D. 1997, Funeralia Palmyrena, *Studia Palmyreńskie* 10, 69-75.
Wielgosz-Rondolino, D. 2016, Orient et Occident unis par enchantement dans la pierre sculptée: La sculpture figurative de Palmyre, in M. al-Maqdissi and E. Ishag (eds.), *La Syrie et le désastre archéologique du Proche-Orient: "Palmyre cité martyre"*, Beirut, 66-82.
Will, E. 1951, Le relief de la tour de Khitôt et le banquet funéraire à Palmyre, *Syria* 28, 1-2, 70-100.
Will, E. 1949, La tour funéraire de Palmyre, *Syria* 26, 1-2, 87-116.
Yon, J.-B. 2013, L'epigraphie palmyrénienne depuis PAT, 1996-2011, *Studia Palmyreńskie* 12, 333-379.
Zanker, P. tr. H. Heitmann-Gordon 2010, *Roman art*, Los Angeles.

CHAPTER 6

The participation of Palmyrene women in the religious life of the city

Sanne Klaver

Introduction

The remains of the ancient city Tadmor, also known as Palmyra, are situated in the Syrian desert, about halfway between Damascus and Deir ez Zor at the Euphrates.[1] After the 'rediscovery' of Palmyra in the seventeenth century, Palmyra has received a lot of scholarly attention. However, at first little interest was given to the women of Palmyra. In recent years, Palmyrene women have been studied in more detail, with a focus on female participation in the funerary and public spheres.[2] Based on the epigraphic material, Jean-Baptiste Yon argues that the public life of Palmyra was predominantly male orientated, since women are underrepresented in the inscriptions, and when women were honoured with inscriptions and statues it was always in relation to their family.[3] According to Yon, Palmyrene women gained prestige through traditional roles as mothers, wives and daughters of important men.[4]

From her studies of the epigraphic material from the funerary realm, Eleonora Cussini concludes that Palmyrene women were entitled to own, buy and sell funerary property, at least from the second century CE onwards.[5] She bases her findings on inscriptions containing abstracts of legal documents, the so-called cession texts, found in the tombs of Palmyra. Seventeen out of sixty-three cession texts mention women as buyers or sellers of funerary property.[6] Other scholars have focused on the funerary portraiture. Maura Heyn argues that in general the status of a Palmyrene woman is connected to the status of her family and her domestic virtues, which is attested by attributes found in the funerary portraiture, e.g. the spindle, the distaff and keys.[7] However, Cussini states that the modesty of women portrayed in the funerary portraits is misleading, since some Palmyrene women managed their own funerary property and were active in the civic life of Palmyra.[8] The ability of women to buy and sell funerary property indeed points to a greater independence for some Palmyrene women than generally assumed from the portraits in the funerary sphere.[9] Signe Krag and Rubina

---

1. This paper is a result of research conducted for my PhD thesis with the title 'Women in Roman Syria: the cases of Dura-Europos, Palmyra, and Seleucia on the Euphrates' financed by the University of Amsterdam. I am grateful to Signe Krag and Sara Ringsborg for inviting me to speak at the workshop Representations of women and children in Roman period Palmyra: The religious life of women, children and the family hosted by Aarhus University on 6 February 2017. I am also thankful for the comments made by various scholars present at the workshop. I am especially appreciative to Nathanael Andrade for improving my Palmyrene translations, any faults remaining are my own. See Drijvers 1976, 1-5; Dirven 1999, 19-32; Sommer 2014, 848-872, for an overview of the history of Palmyra.
2. In recent years, Palmyrene women have been studied by several scholars, for example, see Cussini 1995, 233-250; 2005, 26-43; 2012, 161-171; Yon 2002, 166-186; Finlayson 2008, 99-138; 2013, Heyn 2010, 631-661; 2012, 439-441; Krag 2016, 180-193; 2017, 36-51; Krag and Raja 2016, 134-178.
3. Yon 2002, 170.
4. Yon 2002, 166-186; Heyn 2010, 631-661; 2012, 439-441.
5. Cussini 1995, 233-250; 2005, 26-43; 2012, 161-171.
6. Cussini 2005, table 1.
7. Heyn 2010, 631-661; 2012, 439-441.
8. Cussini 2005, 38.
9. Heyn 2010, 635-636. The shift in focus from the spindle and distaff to jewellery from 150 CE onwards, has also been viewed

Raja, both from the Palmyra Portrait Project, have studied the funerary representations of women and their children.[10] They conclude that women are more often portrayed together with their young and adult child or children than men, stressing aspects of motherhood.[11] Similar to what can be observed in the inscriptions from the Palmyrene public life, family was an important signifier of social identity in the funerary sphere.

This present study addresses the participation of Palmyrene women in the religious life of Palmyra, a topic that has so far received little scholarly attention. There is no clear evidence in the epigraphic or pictorial material to suggest that Palmyrene women acted as priestesses.[12] However, five reliefs show women as participants in religious processions and engaging in sacrificial events and based on these reliefs, I shall argue that Palmyrene women were active participants in religious rites. In addition, several limestone dedicatory altars for libations and burning incense were erected by or on behalf of women. According to Aleksandra Kubiak, these women mostly belonged to the middle class of Palmyra, indicating that not only elite women participated in the religious life of the city.[13] Finally, information on the role of Palmyrene women in the religious sphere can be retrieved from a handful of so-called religious benefactions. From this evidence, I will demonstrate that in the funerary life of the city, as in the public and funerary spheres, Palmyrene women acted as representatives for their families.[14]

Religious benefactions

Euergetism in Palmyra mainly focused on erecting religious buildings or parts of religious buildings.[15] Yon points out that some Palmyrene inscriptions are ambiguous in character: they may be honorary inscriptions, but they also provide us with insights into the religious realm.[16] One of the most interesting inscriptions mentions Thomallachis, daughter of Addoudanos (Haddûdan), for whom the tribe of Benê Khônites erected a statue in the temple of Bel.

> Θομαλλαχις Αδδουδανου τοῦ Ιαριβωλεου[ς]
> τοῦ Αδδουδανου τοῦ Φιρμωνος οἱ
> ἀπὸ φυλῆς Χωνειτῶν Τειμῆς ἕνε-
> κεν φειλοτειμησαμένην
> δηνάρια δισχείλια πεντα-
> κόσια εἰς οἰκοδομὴν βα-
> λανείου ᾽Αγιλβωλου (*sic*) καί
> Μαλαχιβηλου θεῶν
> ἔτους γ(ϙ)υ´ Λώου

Thomallachis (daughter of) Haddûdan, (son of) Yarḥibôlê, (son of) Haddûdan, (son of) Firmôn, those of the tribe of the Khônites in her honour, she having presented 2500 denarii towards the building of the bath of the gods ᾽Aglibôl and Malakbel. Year 493 August (= 182 AD)[17]

Thomallachis had donated 2500 denarii towards the building of the baths of the gods Aglibôl and Malakbel and she received her statue in honour of this gift.[18]

by some scholars as a sign of a growing (financial) independence of Palmyrene women, for example, see Sadurska 1996, 285-288.

10. Krag and Raja 2016, 134-178.

11. Krag and Raja 2016, 137, 158-159.

12. Contra Anna Sadurska and Adnan Bounni who identify one woman as a priestess on a funerary relief because she holds a bowl and appears to be stirring (Sadurska and Bounni 1994, 27-28, 185).

13. Kubiak 2016, 330.

14. In my forthcoming dissertation on women in Roman Syria, this topic will be discussed in detail, here a selection of the material is presented.

15. Yon 2002, 150-164. The most important benefactions were made in the temple of Bel, for which the benefactors in turn received inscriptions and statues erected by the boule and the demos. Yon mentions for example CIS 3914 (PAT 0260) in which two cousins are rewarded with an inscription by the boule and the demos for their donation of a set of bronze doors (Yon 2002, 151).

16. Yon 2002, 170.

17. Text after and translation from Ingholt 1936, no. 11.

18. According to Harald Ingholt, one denarius had a value of sixteen asses in the second century CE (Ingholt 1936, 110-111). Compared with benefactions from the Latin West the sum of

Thomallachis was related to Addoudanos Firmôn, who was part of the Benê Komarê, a tribe associated with the gods Aglibôl and Malakbel, making her donations both signs of euergetism and devoutness.[19] The woman was in all likelihood the heir to her family's wealth; in another inscription she is mentioned as 'daughter of Firmôn' (bat-firmon), which may be a Palmyrene phrase used when a family only had a female heir.[20] Thus, it seems, Thomallachis had the responsibility to preserve the presence of her family in the public and religious realm.

Thomallachis was not the only woman to finance parts of religious buildings. A dedicatory inscription from 23 CE mentions several benefactresses: Attaî and Shebhaî, daughters of Shahra, and Attâ, daughter of Perdesh, offered two columns in the temple of Baalshamîn for the life of themselves and their sons and brothers.

byrḥ knwn šnt 3.100+20+10+5
qrbw ʾty wšbḥy bnt šḥrʾ
wʿtʾ brt prdš ʿmwdyʾ ʿln
tryhwn lbʿlšmyn ʾlhʾ ṭbʾ
ʿl ḥyyhn wḥyy bnyhn wʾḥyhn

In the month of Kanun, the year 335 (23 CE), Attaî and Shebhaî, daughters of Shahra, and Attâ, daughter of Perdesh have offered these two columns to Baalshamîn, the Good god, for the life of themselves and for the life of their sons and their brothers[21]

A woman named Amtallât, daughter of Baraâ and wife of Taima also offered a column to Baalshamîn for the life of herself, for the life of her son and her brother. In all likelihood, the inscription mentions her husband's name and his tribe to legitimise her social position and presence in the temple of Baalshamîn of which the tribe of Benê Mîtâ were the guardians.[22]

byrḥ ṭbt šnt 3.100+60+3
ʿmwdʾ dnh qrbt ʾmtlt b[r]t
brʿʾ br ʿtntn dy mn bnt mytʾ
ʾtt tymʾ br blḥzy br zbdbl dy
mn pḥd bny mʿzyn lbʿlšmn ʾlhʾ
ṭbʾ wškrʾ ʿl ḥyyh wḥyy bnyh
wʾḥyh

In the month of Tebet, the year 363 (=52 CE), Amtallât, daughter of Baraâ, son of Aténatan, of Bené Mîtâ, wife of Taima, son of Bêlhazai, son of Zabdibêl, of the tribe Benê Mazîn, offered this column to Baalshamîn, the Good and Bountiful god, for the life of herself and for the life of her sons and her brother(s)[23]

Furthermore, a fragmentary inscription on a door lintel informs us that a woman named Shegel offered parts of a building in the memory of her husband. Finally, a bas relief was offered by Babatâ for her husband, whose name is now lost.[24]

As mentioned above, it is not always clear whether these dedications from the religious sphere were civic benefactions or votive gifts, but they indicate that some women actively participated in the religious life by donating their funds to the gods and temples. This may have been the reason for setting up two additional statues. A statue base of a woman named Attéemm was found near the Efqa spring, and it was erected by the gods Aglibôl and Malakbel and the tribe Benê Komarê in the year 17 BCE.[25] It is the earliest honorary statue of a woman and the only known example of a female statue erected by the gods.[26]

2500 denarii was rather small. See Hemelrijk 2015, table 3.1, for female benefactions in the Latin West, where some women donated sums of 100,000 sestertii or even more to religious buildings.

19. Yon 2002, 152.

20. Milik 1972, 35, 258-259; Dijkstra 1995, 128; Yon 2002, 168, especially n.23.

21. Text after PAT 0167, translation by author.

22. Yon 2002, 170; Smith 2013, 92.

23. Text after PAT 0168, translation by author with minor corrections by Nathanael Andrade.

24. PAT 0334, 1644.

25. The statue base with the inscription was found at the Efqa spring, it is unknown whether the statue was originally placed there.

26. Yon 2002, 170. Cussini argues that the statue was set up by two men, perhaps sons, named ʿAglibôl and Malakbêl

ṣlmtʾ dh dy ʿtʾm b[rt...]
ʾwšy ʾtt bwlḥʾ [br...]
dy ʾ qym lh ʿglbwl w?[mlkbl]
wbny kmrʾ byrḥ ʾ dr š[nt 2.100]
80+10+4

This statue is that of Attéemm d[aughter of ..., son of] Aušai, wife of Bôlhâ, [son of ...] which was erected for her by Aglibôl and [Malakbel] and Benê Komarê, in the month of Adar, year [2] 94 (17 BCE)[27]

A second woman named Beththeis, daughter of Moukianos and wife of Soados, was honoured with a statue along the Great Colonnade by the tribe of Mathabôl.

Βεθθεὶν Μουκιανοῦ Μαλί-
χου τοῦ ʾΑνανίδου γυναῖκα Σο-
άδου Ελαβήλου Βάρθη Μαθ-
θαββωλίων φυλὴ τειμῆς χά-
ριν μηνὶ Πανήμῳ ἔτους
θιφʹ

For Beththeis (daughter of) Moukianos (son of) Malichos (son of) Ananidos, wife of Soados (son of) Elabelos Barthe, by the tribe of the Matthabolios (Mathabôl), to her honour, in the month of Panemos, year 519 (208 CE)[28]
Although the benefactions that inspired these statues are not recorded in the inscriptions, from the inscription of Thomallachis we may suggest that these women donated funds to sanctuaries connected with the tribes. This hypothesis is supported by other inscriptions set up by gods and tribes to honour benefactors of sanctuaries.[29]

(Cussini 2005, 28). This seems unlikely because the tribe Benê Komarê was in charge of the sanctuary of ʿAglibôl and Malakbêl, making it more likely that the gods erected the statue, which was not uncommon in Palmyra.
27. Text after PAT 0315, translation by author with minor corrections by Nathanael Andrade.
28. Text after Yon 2012, no. 84, translation by author.
29. Yon 2002, 170.

Religious sculpture

In addition to benefactions, the participation of Palmyrene women in religious life is also attested in religious sculpture. Five reliefs show women as participants in religious processions and engaging in sacrificial events. From these reliefs, it can be deduced that Palmyrene women were active participants in religious rites.[30] Three reliefs depict women in sacrificial settings. A small relief from the temple of Bel, dated to the first century CE, depicts a sacrifice by a man and a woman.[31] On the left side of the relief, stands a man dressed in a long-sleeved tunic and a mantle before a now poorly-visible altar. The man probably offers incense with his right hand and holds an object, possibly a jug, in his left.[32] It is not clear whether the man was a priest since he does not wear the priestly headgear known to us from the funerary sphere, although we know of priests without headgear.[33] Behind him stands a woman in profile wearing similar garments: an ankle-length long-sleeved tunic and a mantle draped over the top of her head and over her left arm. The woman holds a pointed container, which probably contains sacrifices.

A second sacrificial relief from the temple of Bel resembles the first; a woman dressed in a tunic and a mantle raises her right hand in an act of worship and she carries an unidentified object in her left hand.[34] On the left side of the relief, two men stand around an altar. The man on the left is poorly preserved, but the second man is in a better state of preservation and has

30. Finlayson 2013, 61-85.
31. Sacrificial relief from the temple of Bel with a man and a woman, first century CE, 39x15 cm, National Museum of Damascus (Colledge 1976, no. 19).
32. Sabeh 1953, 17-18.
33. Seyrig 1941, 32; Colledge 1976, 140.
34. Sacrificial relief from the temple of Bel, two men and a woman in a sacrificial scene, early first century CE, 33x39 cm, National Museum of Damascus (Seyrig 1941, fig. 2). For similar gestures of worship see 'The sacrifice of Konon' in the temple of Bel from Dura-Europos (Klaver 2016, 375-391). On 'The sacrifice of Konon' also see the contribution by Kaizer in this volume.

Fig. 1: Relief fragment of sacrificial scene, after Colledge 1976, fig. 26 (drawing by author).

been identified as a priest due to the libation jug in his left hand.[35] A third relief was found in a secondary context in the agora and it depicts a sacrificial scene with two men performing sacrifices on the left and two female worshippers holding offerings in their upraised right arms: the first an incense burner and the second a cup with two handles (fig. 1).

In addition to these reliefs, a well-known relief on the crossbeam of the peristyle from the temple of Bel from 180 CE shows a religious procession which centres around a donkey, a camel driver and a camel carrying a tent (fig. 2).[36] This was probably a so-called *qubba*, a shrine originally used by Arabs to transport sacred objects.[37] Above the donkey, stand four men or gods with their right arms raised. On the top left side and the lower right side of the relief, completely veiled women are represented. At least four women are depicted on the right side of the relief; they wear ankle-length tunics and their slightly bent heads and faces are wrapped in their mantles which were originally brightly coloured.[38] Their right arms are raised to their heads. The women on the upper left side of the relief show great similarity with these women apart from their smaller size. Lucinda Dirven identifies the scene as the arrival of the goddess Allat to Palmyra, but to this day there is discussion on the identification of the relief.[39] A comparable relief from the temple of Allat pictures a group of completely veiled women also following a camel, which suggests that these women are likewise participating in a religious procession.[40] This relief from the temple of Allat is made of soft limestone and belongs to the group of so-called 'archaic' sculptures dated to before 50 CE.[41] Due to the similarities, the relief in the temple of Bel may be a later copy, although small differences are noticeable.[42]

35. Seyrig 1941, 32.
36. The crossbeam was in all likelihood destroyed by Daesh in 2015 with the destruction of the temple of Bel.
37. Dirven 1999, 84.
38. Dirven 1999, 82.

39. Dirven 1999, 81-86. Dagmara Wielgosz-Rondolino mentions that there is discussion on the meaning of the relief: it may be the arrival of Allat, the foundation of the city, or something else (Wielgosz-Rondolino 2016, 67). Since a very similar relief is found in the temple of Allat, I am inclined to follow Dirven's assessment.
40. Relief from the temple of Allat, veiled women and a camel, before 50 CE (Tanabe 1986, no. 156).
41. For the so-called 'archaic' sculptures, see Seyrig 1940, 277-328; 1941, 31-48; Morehart 1956-57, 53-83. For a general overview of the Palmyrene sculptures, see Wielgosz-Rondolino 2016, 66-82.
42. Suggested to me by Lucinda Dirven. According to Wielgosz-Rondolino, the reliefs found in the temple of Bel have a

Fig. 2: Religious procession on crossbeam of the peristyle from the temple of Bel (Wikimedia, photo: Gianfranco Gazzetti / GAR, CC BY-SA 4.0) https://commons.wikimedia.org/w/index.php?curid=504650464995 (28.11.2018)).

To my knowledge, these reliefs are the only images of completely veiled women from the religious sphere in the Graeco-Roman world. Although the evidence is too sparse to draw conclusions on their choice of dress, I suggest that they are either wearing a type of ceremonial dress or that they are protecting themselves against the harsh conditions of the desert.[43] If the scenes indeed represent the arrival of the goddess Allat to Palmyra, it might be that this procession started outside of Palmyra and one can imagine that the participants protected themselves against the desert winds. The men in the relief also wear typical garments worn by men and gods from the desert: a semi long-sleeved tunic with a cloak.[44]

Whether these images represent actual religious processions is still a subject of discussion among scholars, but what we can conclude from these images is that the Palmyrenes were familiar with processions, and if we do interpret them as religious processions, it implies that women actively participated in them.[45] From this early sculptural material, we can conclude that Palmyrene women participated in the religious life of the city through their active roles in religious processions and sacrificial settings. Unfortunately, all the reliefs are dated relatively early and pictorial evidence for female participation in the second or third centuries CE is rare. Apart from an altar depicting a mother and her son in an act of worship and a fragment of an altar showing the heads of two women and a man, I know of no examples of women engaging in religious ceremonies.[46] However, the active role of Palmyrene women in these centuries is attested by the small altars dedicated to the so-called Anonymous God and it is to these altars that we now turn our attention.

different composition compared to the 'archaic' sculptures and the reliefs from the temple of Bel are 'les oeuvres majeures de l'art religieux de Palmyre' (Wielgosz-Rondolino 2016, 67).

43. Ernest Will argues that these women may have been members of the public who participated in the procession, and stresses that the image is unique in the ancient world. He adduces from the dress of the men that the women may be nomads. He raises interesting questions on whether all Palmyrene women were completely veiled or only women from a certain ethnic group, or perhaps women only covered their faces in the temples (Will 1992: 109-111). Sadurska argues that the faces of the women are covered by a veil because they have entered a sanctuary (Sadurska 1994, 18).

44. [...] 'tunique demi-longue à manches, manteau jeté en arrière et étoffe roulée autour des hanches en boudin et couvrant les jambes, dont deux bords frangés forment entre les jambes un pli vertical, très caractéristique' (Wielgosz-Rondolino 2016, 67).

45. Krag 2018, chapter 6.

46. Hvidberg-Hansen 1998, no. 129.

Dedicatory altars to He whose name is blessed forever

The limestone dedicatory altars for sacrifices are found scattered throughout the city, unfortunately only two were found in situ in a temple.[47] The corpus consists of more than 200 altars, most of which are dedicated to a deity evoked by the phrase 'He whose name is blessed forever' (*bryk šmh l ʿlm ʿ*), also known as the so-called Anonymous God, others are dedicated jointly to 'He whose name is blessed forever' and Baalshamin and the remaining number to a variety of gods.[48] The altars are dedicated by a variety of Palmyrenes: women, men, freedwomen and freedmen and from individuals to families.[49] Over thirty altars are dedicated by or 'for the life of' women.[50]

The identity and nature has been the subject of discussion.[51] Javier Teixidor argues that the Anonymous God can be identified as Yarhibôl, an identification which he bases on the fact that many altars were found around the Efqa spring of which Yarhibôl was the ancestral deity.[52] This identification is problematic since only a few altars were found in situ and we have no knowledge of how the other altars were scattered throughout the city. Han J. W. Drijvers suggests that the Anonymous God: '[...] is a certain aspect of Baʿalshamēn, a development in a more spiritual direction'.[53] He draws this conclusion on the basis of iconographic features shared by the two gods, but stresses that the altars dedicated to the Anonymous God by individuals for help indicate a more intimate relationship between the worshippers and the deity.[54] Michał Gawlikowski also sees the Anonymous God as '[...] une forme évoluée de celui de Baʿalšamîn [...]' and he also argues that the Anonymous God belongs to the private realm of the religious sphere.[55] According to him, the deity listens to 'the voice' of his worshippers.[56] The intimate bond between the worshippers and the god is underlined by phrases that imply a direct and personal relationship, for example 'because he called upon Him and He has answered him', or through verbs as 'to call for help' (*qry*), 'answered him/her' (*dʿnh* or *wʿnh*), and 'heard his/her voice' (*wšm ʿbqlh*).[57]

The phrases also imply that the Palmyrenes erected the altars as *ex-voto* inscriptions to remember their invocation to the deities.[58] According to Klaas Dijkstra, the fact that the dedicators only cite themselves and family members as beneficiaries confirms that there was a personal relationship between the god and his worshippers.[59] Dedications with the phrase 'for the life of' (*ʿl ḥyy*) may have been the equivalent of Greek dedications for 'salvation' (*sôtêria*).[60] These Greek dedications were often set up for the salvation of family and expressed thanksgiving for salvation either obtained or anticipated, which assured the personal relationship between the dedicator and the god.[61] This becomes explicit in several inscriptions: for example, we know that Moqîmû dedicated an altar to He whose name is blessed

47. Kubiak 2016, 328; PAT 0180, 1710.
48. See Dijkstra 1995 and PAT.
49. Kubiak 2016, 327-338.
50. PAT 0065, 0334, 0347, 0352, 0356, 0360, 0363-0366, 0370, 0373, 0388, 0394, 0402, 0404, 0413, 0415, 0420, 0426-0427, 0429, 0433, 1430, 1451, 1001-1002, 1434, 1619, 1911, 1915-1916, 2636; Seyrig 1940, no. 20.
51. We have no archaeological evidence that the god had his own temple and it appears that the god was worshipped at different locations throughout the city (Dijkstra 1995, 154). Dijkstra also mentions that the altars are found in clusters at the Efqa spring, at the so-called Diocletian's Camp and the temple of Bel, but most altars were found throughout the city. Aleksandra Kubiak recently completed her dissertation 'Celui dont le nom est béni pour l'éternité. Une étude comparative des dédicaces votives sans théonymes de Palmyre' under the supervision of professor Michał Gawlikowski on the subject of He whose name is blessed forever. Unfortunately, the dissertation is not published yet.
52. He comes to this conclusion, although he rightfully mentions the fact that many altars were found elsewhere in the city (Teixidor 1977, 122-130).
53. Drijvers 1976, 15.
54. Drijvers 1976, 15.
55. Gawlikowski 1990, 2632-2634.
56. Gawlikowski 1990, 2634.
57. Also suggested by Dijkstra 1995, 153; Cussini 2012, 165.
58. Cussini 2012, 165.
59. Dijkstra 1995, 152-154.
60. Moralee 2004, 3.
61. Moralee 2004, 3-4.

forever for his daughter Shegel, who had been sick.[62] The concept of personal salvation may also explain why Palmyrene women could relate to the cult; women dedicated altars for the life of themselves, but also for the life of their children, fathers and siblings.

So what can we deduce from these inscriptions with regards to female participation in the religious life? Over a dozen altars have female dedicators.[63] The inscriptions are dated between the early second century to 262 CE although most are undated.[64] Most women erect altars for the life of themselves and their children.[65]

lb .yk šmh lʿlmʾ
ṭbʾ w.ḥmnʾ ʿltʾ
dnh ʿbdt mky b.t
ʿgʾ ʾtt mlʾ b.
mlkw lḥyh wlḥyʾ
b.th by.ḥ ṭbt
šnt 5.100+10+5+3

To He whose name is blessed forever, the Good and the Merciful, this altar was made (by) Makkai, daughter of ʿOgâ, wife of Malê, son of Malikû, for the life of herself, and for the life of her daughter(s). In the month of Tèbet, year 518 (= 207 CE)[66]

However, women also offered altars for the life of other family members. For example, a daughter of Malikû and wife of a man also named Malikû offered an altar for the life of herself, her son and her brother.

[ʿl]tʾ dh lbʿlšmn rbʾ wrḥmnʾ ʿbdt ʿt[..
brt]
[m]lkw br whblt br ʿrgn ʾ tt mlkw br ʿgʾ
ʾʿ [by]
[ʿ]l ḥyyh wḥyy bnyh wʾ -ḥyh byrḥ šbṭ šnt
4.100+[...]

This altar was made to Baalshamin, the Great and Merciful, by At[..., daughter of Ma]likû, son of Wahballat, son of Argan, wife of Malikû, son of Ogâ [son of bai?] for the life of herself, the life of her sons, and the life of her brother. In the month of Sebat, the year 4[...][67]

What is of interest here is that her husband is mentioned in the inscription as a sign of her family affiliations, but she does not erect the altar for his well-being, perhaps because he was already deceased.

Furthermore, it seems that even in marriage, when a woman became part of the family of her husband, the bond with the birth family remained important in Palmyrene society. A testimony of this bond is also found in other inscriptions, for example, Mazbê, daughter of Mezabbenâ offered an altar for her father and brother. Since no husband and children are mentioned, we may assume that she was unmarried or a (childless) widow at the time of the dedication.

mzbʾ brt mzbnʾ
mwd[yʾ] <l>bryk šmh lʿlmʾ
dʿnh
[w]ʾbwh wʾḥh

Mazbê daughter of Mezabbenâ offered in thanksgiving to He whose name is blessed forever, He answered her, her father and her brother[68]

In addition, we have over a dozen altars, dated between 161 CE and 251 CE, which mention women as recipients.[69] Most of these altars are offered to He whose name is blessed forever and they are erected for the life

62. PAT 0404.
63. PAT 0065, 0334, 0352, 0356, 0360, 0366, 0373, 0388, 0394, 0413, 0420, 0426-0427, 0429, 0433, 1001, 1434, 1451, 1915.
64. The earliest attested mention of the phrase ‘*bryk šmh lʿlm*’’ is PAT 0339 dated to 111 CE (Kubiak 2016, n.9).
65. For example, see PAT 0356, 0360, 0420, 0427, 0433, 1451, 1915.
66. Text after PAT 0360, translation by author with minor corrections by Nathanael Andrade.
67. Text after PAT 0334, translation by author with minor corrections by Nathanael Andrade.
68. Text after PAT 0413, translation by author with minor corrections by Nathanael Andrade.
69. PAT 0347, 0363-0365, 0370, 0402, 0404, 0415, 1002, 1430, 1619, 1911, 1916, 2636; Seyrig 1940, no. 20.

of the dedicator and his family members. In 175 CE, Yarḥai, son of Ḥalaphathâ, dedicated an altar for the life of himself, his wife Šullâ, his son, and his brother.

bryk šmh lʿlmʾ ṭb
wrḥm[n]ʾ ʿbd ʿlwtʾ ʾln
[y]rḥy br ḥlptʾ br yrḥy
br ḥlptʾ ʿl ḥywhy wḥyʾ
šlʾ brt ḥṭry ʾ tt!h
wḥy bnwhy wʾḥwhy
byrḥ nysn šnt 4.100
+80+5+1

He whose name is blessed forever, the Good and the Merciful, this altar was made (by) Yarḥai son of Ḥalaphathâ son of Yarḥai son of Ḥalaphathâ, for the life of himself and the life of Šullâ daughter of Ḥatrai, his wife, and for the life of his sons and the life of his brother(s). In the month of Nisan, year 486 (175 CE).[70]

Other altars are similar: a man erects an altar for the life of himself and his family members, ranging from his son and brother, to his daughter, sister and wife.[71] No'arai, son of Moqîmû not only mentions his wife and children, but also his entire household.[72] Others name their mothers as the recipients.[73] For example, Shimeʿôn offered an altar for the life of himself, his father, mother and brother(s).

bryk šmh lʿlmʾ
ṭbʾ wrḥmnʾ ʿbd
wmwdʾ šmʿwn br
[ʾw]šy ʿl ḥywhy wḥyʾ
[ʾ]byhy wʾmh wʾḥwh
y byrḥ nysn šnt 5.100
+20+4

He whose name is blessed forever, the Good and the Merciful, (This) has been made in order to express thanksgiving (by) Shimeʿôn son of [ʾAw]sai, for the life of himself and the life of his father and mother and brother(s). In the month of Nisan, the year 524 (213 CE)[74]

Since the status of Palmyrene women within public life and the funerary realm is connected to their family, it comes as no surprise that Palmyrene women functioned as dedicators on behalf of their families. In two inscriptions, a husband is mentioned but the altars are not erected by or for them. Their names were probably inscribed for the purpose of portraying family affiliations. Most other altars dedicated by women do not mention a husband or father, which suggests that some Palmyrene women were responsible for the salvation of their families, including their birth family.

Conclusion

The active participation of women within the religious sphere implies that it was socially accepted for them to partake in the religious life. As it turns out, at least until the middle of the first century CE, women participated in religious processions and sacrifices, which is attested by the reliefs. It must be stressed that the degree of participation of women was not the same as that of men. There is no evidence that Palmyrene women acted as priestesses, and the visual material indeed suggests a secondary role in religious ceremonies: women participated or witnessed the processions and carried the sacrifices, but the actual sacrifice was performed by men. However, the religious benefactions and the altars illustrate that Palmyrene women still engaged in religious life as benefactors and recipients in the second and third centuries CE. The fact that most dedicators of the small altars belonged to the middle class suggest that a relatively

70. Text after PAT 1619, translation by author with minor corrections by Nathanael Andrade.
71. For example, see PAT 0363, 0415, 1429, 1911.
72. PAT 1911.
73. PAT 0364-0365, 0370, 0402, 1002.
74. Text after PAT 1002, translation by author with minor corrections by Nathanael Andrade.

large section of Palmyrene women had access to the religious life of Palmyra. Similar to the public and funerary realm, Palmyrene women participated in the religious life as a member of her family unit. In the end, family was still the most important social unit for women in Palmyra.

Abbreviations

PAT D. R. Hillers and E. Cussini 1996, *Palmyrene Aramaic Texts*, Baltimore.

Bibliography

Colledge, M. A. R. 1976, *The Art of Palmyra*, London.

Cussini, E. 2012, What Women Say and Do (in Aramaic Documents), in G. B. Lanfranchi, D. Morandi Bonacossi, C. Pappi, and S. Ponchia (eds.), *Leggo! Studies presented to Prof. Frederick Mario Fales on the occasion of his 65th Birthday,* Wiesbaden, 161–172.

Cussini, E. 2005, Beyond the Spindle: Investigating the Role of Palmyrene Women, in E. Cussini (ed.), *A Journey to Palmyra; Collected Essays to Remember Delbert R. Hillers,* Leiden and Boston, 26–43.

Cussini, E. 1995, Transfer of Property at Palmyra, *ARAM periodicals* 7, 233–250.

Dijkstra, K. 1995, *Life and Loyalty. A Study in the Socio-Religious Culture of Syria and Mesopotamia in the Graeco-Roman Period based on Epigraphical Evidence*, Leiden, New York and Cologne.

Dirven, L. A. 1999, *Palmyrenes in Dura-Europos: A Study of Religious Interaction in Roman Syria,* Leiden, Boston and Cologne.

Drijvers, H. J. W. 1976, *The religion of Palmyra,* Iconography of religions XV.15, Leiden.

Finlayson, C. S. 2013, New perspectives on the ritual and cultic importance of women at Palmyra and Dura Europos: processions and temples, *Studia Palmyreńskie* 12, 61–85.

Finlayson, C. S. 2008, *Mut'a* Marriage in the Roman Near East: The Evidence from Palmyra, Syria, in B. A. Nakhai (ed.), *The World of Women in the Ancient and Classical Near East*, Newcastle upon Tyne, 99–138.

Gawlikowski, M. 1990, Les dieux de Palmyre, *ANRW* 2, 18, 4, 2605–2658.

Hemelrijk, E. A. 2015, *Hidden Lives, Public Personae: Women and Civic Life in the Roman West*, Oxford.

Heyn, M. K. 2012, Female Portraiture in Palmyra, in S. L. James and S. Dillon (eds.), *A Companion to Women in the Ancient World*, Oxford, 439–441.

Heyn, M. K. 2010, Gesture and Identity in the Funerary Art of Palmyra, *AJA* 114, 4, 631–661.

Hvidberg-Hansen, F. O. 1998, *The Palmyrene inscriptions, Ny Carlsberg Glyptotek*, Copenhagen.

Ingholt, H. 1936, Inscriptions and sculptures from Palmyra, I, *Berytus* 3, 83–128.

Klaver, S. 2016, Dress and Identity in the Syrian-Mesopotamian Region: The Case of the Women of Dura-Europos, *ARAM periodicals* 28, 1–2, 375–391.

Krag, S. 2016, Females in Group Portraits in Palmyra, in A. Kropp and R. Raja (eds.), *The World of Palmyra*, Palmyrene Studies 1, Copenhagen, 180–193.

Krag, S. 2018, *Funerary Representations of Palmyrene Women: From the First Century BC to the Third Century AD*, Studies in Classical Archaeology, Turnhout.

Krag, S. 2017, Changing Identities, Changing Positions: Jewellery in Palmyrene Female Portraits, in T. Long and A. H. Sørensen (eds.), *Positions and Professions in Palmyra*, Palmyrene Studies, 2, Copenhagen.

Krag, S. and R. Raja 2016, Representations of Women and Children in Palmyrene Funerary *Loculus* Reliefs, *Loculus Stelae* and Wall Paintings, *Zeitschrift für Orient-Archäologie* 9, 134–178.

Kubiak, A. 2016, The gods without names? Hatra, Palmyra, Edessa, *ARAM periodicals* 28, 1–2, 327–338.

Milik, J. T. 1972, *Dedicaces faites par des dieux (Palmyre, Hatra, Tyr) et des thiases sémitiques à l'époque romaine*, Paris.

Moralee, J. 2004, *'For Salvation's Sake: Provincial. Provincial Loyalty, Personal Religion, and Epigraphic Production in the Roman and Late Antique Near East*, New York and London.

Morehart, M. 1956–57, Early sculptures at Palmyra, *Berytus* 12, 53–83.

Sabeh, J. 1953, Sculptures palmyréniennes inédites de musée de Damas, *AAS* 3, 3–26.

Sadurska, A. 1996, L'art et la société: recherches iconologiques sur la sculpture funéraire de Palmyra, in *AAS* 42, 285–288.

Sadurska, A. 1994, L'art et la société: recherches iconologiques sur l'art funéraire de Palmyre, *Archeologia-War* 45, 11–23.

Sadurska, A. and A. Bounni 1994, *Les sculptures funéraires de Palmyre*, Rome.

Seyrig, H. 1941, Antiquités syriennes, *Syria* 22, 31–48.

Seyrig, H. 1940, Ornamenta palmyrena antiquiora, *Syria* 21, 277–328.

Smith, A.M. 2013, *Roman Palmyra: Identity, Community, and State Formation*, New York.

Sommer, M. 2014, Palmyra, *Reallexikon für Antike und Christentum* 26, 848–872.

Tanabe, K. (ed.) 1986, *Sculptures of Palmyra I*, Tokyo.

Teixidor, J. 1977, *The Pagan God: Popular Religion in the Greco-Roman Near East*, Princeton.

Wielgosz-Rondolino, D. 2016, Orient et Occident unis par enchantement dans la pierre sculptée: La sculpture figurative de Palmyre, in M. al-Maqdissi and E. Ishaq (eds.), *La Syrie et le désastre archéologique du Proche-Orient: 'Palmyre', cite martyre*, Beirut, 66–82.

Will, E. 1992, *Les palmyréniens: La Venise des sables*, Paris.

Yon, J.-B. 2002, *Les notables de Palmyre,* Beirut.

Yon, J.-B. 2012, *Inscriptions grecques et latines de la Syrie. Palmyre,* Beirut.

CHAPTER 7

Burying Odainath: Zenobia and women in the funerary life of Palmyra*

Nathanael J. Andrade

Introduction

In recent years, excavations and research initiatives have amplified what we can know about the status and practices of women and children at Roman Palmyra. The Palmyra Portrait Project and scholarship that it has inspired deserve special mention in this regard.[1] However, the inscriptions, funerary portraits and material remains from Palmyra are limited in a key respect. They reflect traces of past individuals whose lives, personalities and subjectivities are otherwise lost. Even the dynast Zenobia is only known through a few such textual and material traces, and despite her immense fame, we only know marginally more about her than most other Palmyrene women. This begs an obvious question. Is it possible to narrate any of her lived experiences based on the fragmented or dispersed nature of the evidence?

To explore the possibilities, my contribution to this volume focuses on an event in which Zenobia, I believe, played a vital role: the funeral and burial of her husband Odainath. No source provides any information on Odainath's funeral or any contribution that Zenobia made to it. The discussion to follow suggests that recent work on inscriptions, funerary portraiture and burial and their implications for the social activity of women enable us to create a narrative for how Zenobia experienced her husband's death in various aspects. It thus reflects on what Zenobia's social obligations to her husband were, and how she would have proceeded to fulfil them. So, the goal is not so much to communicate new insights regarding Palmyra but to explore how recent insights can enable us to narrate individual experiences, especially for people who have some documentation, however little it may be.

Writing about Zenobia

One specific challenge, already mentioned, must be repeated. So few sources provide empirical information on Zenobia. The fourth-century *Historia Augusta*'s treatment of her is largely unreliable. It provides us with a likeness of Zenobia's character, and it even imparts a physical description of her.[2] But by doing so, it raises many of the issues that pertain to the images of Zenobia on coins. These same issues are also relevant to the vital and important funerary portraits of Palmyrene women that survive, or really, any representation, whether written or visual. All such representations make their subjects accessible in some ways while concealing them in others. The likeness from the *Historia Augusta* in particular, it seems, conceals Zenobia much more than it communicates about her.[3]

*I would like to express my deep gratitude to the conference organizers and participants for insightful feedback on the earlier version of this article that I presented to them. I also offer sincere thanks to Stefan Vranka and Oxford University Press for permitting me to use some material from Andrade 2018, esp. 152-61.

1. Kropp and Raja 2014; Krag 2015; 2016; Raja 2015a; 2015b; Krag and Raja 2016; Long 2016.

2. HA Tyr. Trig. 30, with 15-16 for physical features.

3. HA Tyr. Trig. 30 is devoted to Zenobia. Otherwise, she makes appearances in HA Gall., other biographies of HA Tyr. Trig., HA Claud., and HA Aurel. Beyond HA, Zosimus

Otherwise, we know some explicit information about her from inscriptions and coins. But the inscriptions are not many,[4] the coins only repeat certain themes in abundance,[5] and in the end, they are only representations too.[6] Remarkably, in spite of her fame, it could be surmised that Zenobia is only somewhat better documented than most Palmyrene women. It is thus a daunting task to create a narrative of Zenobia's life experiences, which I aim to do in my current book.[7]

Before I get to the details, I want to make a couple of statements about what I think it means to write a history of Zenobia. One statement refers to methodology and conceptualization. The other pertains to contemporary politics and political ideologies. At a certain level, Zenobia is unknowable to us and her interiority inaccessible. The sources for her life are either too fragmented or unreliable, and again, they are representations. The best that we can do, in my view, is create a likeness for her that enables us to glimpse, however obliquely, fleetingly or imperfectly, the person who lived. In this respect, my take on Zenobia is consistent with that of ancient biographers. They sometimes likened writing about an historical figure to the creation of a likeness in words in ways that were analogous to how Roman and Palmyrene sculptors, for example, created likenesses in stone.[8] Creating a likeness for an ancient person is undoubtedly an interpretative enterprise, and what constitutes an appropriate likeness for Zenobia in words is something that will probably be endlessly debated. One of the goals of my current work on Zenobia is to communicate the likeness that I have been creating for her based on my own interpretative engagement with the ancient evidence for Palmyrene women and Palmyra's social context. If the image crafted by the author of the *Historia Augusta* is a curtain, I hope to create one that is more a window.

My second point pertains to a need to create likenesses for Zenobia that are controlled by the Palmyrene evidence and the exciting new insights that have been made possible by scholarly initiatives like the Palmyra Portrait Project. This need is ever present due to what could be defined as the political agendas that have in past and present governed the creation of Zenobia's likenesses; agendas noted by Judith Weingarten and by recent work of Annie and Maurice Sartre.[9] In recent years, we have witnessed the exploitation of Palmyra by the Islamic State and the Assad regime, along with their respective allies, amid the catastrophic human suffering that they have been inflicting in Syria.[10] But the site of Palmyra has a longer

provides sporadic treatment of her, and she receives brief mention in various later Roman fragments and Byzantine chronicles. For some modern treatments, see Stoneman 1992; Schneider 1993; Hartmann 2001; Southern 2008; Sartre and Sartre 2014.

4. Of the inscriptions, only PAT 0317, IGLS 17.1.57, and IGR 3.1065=OGIS 647 provide any serious information, however meager, on Zenobia herself. The few other surviving inscriptions add nothing substantive. These include OGIS 650 (=IGR 3.1029), with 649, as well as a tesserae piece (Schneider 1993, 98, fig. 18).

5. Bland 2011; Schwentzel 2011.

6. This statement pertains to the specific series of coins at Alexandria that are sometimes deemed to bear 'realistic' images of her physical features. Schneider 1993, 95–96; Sartre and Sartre 2014, 75–76. For example, see BNF 3646–3647: http://gallica.bnf.fr/ark:/12148/btv1b8485689n.r=zenobie?rk=150215;2 (27.11.2018); http://gallica.bnf.fr/ark:/12148/btv1b84856909.r=zenobie?rk=21459;2 (27.11.2018).

7. Andrade 2018.

8. Plut., Alex. 1.1–3, Cim. 2.3, and Per. 1.3–4; more comically, Lucian, Alex., esp. 3 and Peregr., esp. 5–7. Hägg 2012, 4–5, 268–276; Andrade and Rush 2016, 172–174.

9. Judith Weingarten, 'Queen Zenobia in History, A.D. 267–2016', Metropolitan Museum, NY, May 23, 2016 (public lecture), which is now Weingarten 2018. Sartre and Sartre 2014, esp. 252–257 and Sartre and Sartre 2016, esp. 162–168.

10. Kaizer 2016; Sartre and Sartre 2016, 206–218.For some relevant reports of the Syrian Heritage Initiative: http://www.asor-syrianheritage.org/wp-content/uploads/2015/09/Palmyra_UpdateReport_FINAL4reduced.pdf; http://www.asor-syrianheritage.org/wp-content/uploads/2015/03/NEW2_PalmyraSpecialReport3-FINAL.pdf; http://www.asor-syrianheritage.org/wp-content/uploads/2015/03/ASOR-CHI-Palmyra-Military-Base-Report-r.pdf; http://www.asor-syrianheritage.org/wp-content/uploads/2016/05/ASOR_CHI_Weekly_Report_85%E2%80%9386r.pdf;

history of being the focus of vested political interests, for it is arguably an artefact of western imperialism(s) in many respects. For example, after western travellers largely absconded with its portable antiquities and disturbed its material contexts in the late 19th and early 20th centuries, authorities of the French mandate relocated Bedouins who lived on the site to the immediate north, created the new town of Tadmor and made Palmyra's ancient remains accessible to organized excavation.[11] This was on the heels of the Great Syrian Revolt (1925-1927), which witnessed the aerial and artillery bombing of Damascus by the French military.[12]

Yet, the political exploitation of Palmyra finds an analogy in the likenesses that have been created for Zenobia. For example, the images of Zenobia that circulate in the works of European authors from the 18th and 19th centuries sometimes depict her Syrian subjects as incapable of autonomous governance; despite her remarkable qualities, she cannot prevent them from being governed by the more vigorous Romans.[13] More recently, for certain members of the Assad regime, Zenobia was a Baathist heroine who resisted the forces of western imperialism. Mustafa Tlass, a close associate of Hafez and Bashar al-Assad, wrote a book arguing as much.[14] Zenobia's likeness, modelled on that of her coins, has appeared on the regime's currency.[15] On Syrian television, a dramatic series portrayed Zenobia's struggle against the Romans in 1997.[16] The Assad regime even organized parades for a brass image of Zenobia after ceding her Palmyra to the Islamic State for the first time in 2015.[17] In this respect, the regime has exploited its own Baathist likeness of Zenobia for what has been in practice a violent, self-interested and, arguably, a non-Baathist autocracy. By contrast, for the Islamic State, in all its iconoclasm and unrestrained violence, the ideal Zenobia is arguably characterized by the absence of an image, an erasure of Palmyra's pre-Islamic past through the staged destruction or the illicit sale of its antiquities including its portraits. Its likeness of Zenobia is in a sense a non-existent one. My brief description of how Zenobia's image has been used to communicate political messages is by no means exhaustive.[18] But my main point is that certain authors, past and present, have engaged in the overt politicizing of Zenobia's likeness. This phenomenon is not unusual for famous figures of antiquity, and I am not implying that my likeness of Zenobia is any less political. But I believe that historians have an obligation to define their likeness, however political, within the limits of empirical evidence and what is known of ancient contexts. There is now a greater need for such likenesses of Zenobia than ever before.

Nevertheless, creating a likeness of Zenobia is not easy. Different people are bound to interpret the ancient evidence in different ways. Let us take Zenobia's

---

http://www.asor-syrianheritage.org/wp-content/uploads/2016/05/ASOR_CHI_Weekly_Report_87%E2%80%9388r.pdf;
http://www.asor-syrianheritage.org/wp-content/uploads/2016/07/ASOR_CHI_Weekly_Report_99%E2%80%93100r.pdf;
http://www.asor-syrianheritage.org/new-damage-in-palmyra-uncovered-by-asor-chi/;
http://www.asor-syrianheritage.org/update-palmyra-new-photographs-detail-damage-to-the-unesco-world-heritage-site-of-palmyra/.

11. Starcky and Gawlikowski 1985, 25; Degeorge 2001, 282-283; Neep 2012, 142-143, with Lt. Frisch 1936, 9. William Wright (1895) generally provides a good indication of how visitors treated Palmyra's remains at the time, despite the notable discoveries of the Palmyrene Tax Law (see Gawlikowski 2013) and the more scientific expeditions of the World War I period represented by Theodor Wiegand (1932) and the rigorous work of Harald Ingholt (on which see n.45; Raja and Sørensen 2015; Raja and Yon (forthcoming)).

12. Neep 2012, esp. 37-38 and 50-57; McHugo 2015, 85-88.

13. Gibbon 1776, 1.319; Wright 1895, 154.

14. Tlass 1985 in Arabic, 1986 in French, 2000 in English. Sartre and Sartre 2014, 253-255; 2016, 21-32, 219-221, 229-230.

15. Stoneman 1992, fig. 25d.

16. Southern 2008, 1. At the time of this article's composition, the series al-Ababid or al-Ababeed (Anarchy) could be found on Youtube fairly easily.

17. As announced by http://sana.sy/en/?p=53820 (27.11.2018), the regime's state-sponsored media. I owe this observation to Judith Weingarten, 'Queen Zenobia in History, A.D. 267-2016', Metropolitan Museum, NY, May 23, 2016 (public lecture), which is now Weingarten 2018.

18. See Sartre and Sartre 2014, 191-262; Woltering 2014; Sartre 2016, for treatments of Zenobia in European and Arab literature after antiquity and until the present.

smile as an example. In a recent study, archaeologists have demonstrated that high fluoride levels in Palmyra's water often induced discoloured teeth among Palmyrenes.[19] On the basis of the *Historia Augusta*, which compares Zenobia's teeth to pearls, they suggest that Zenobia had uniquely white teeth despite Palmyra's water content.[20] But I believe that the likeness provided by the *Historia Augusta* is more a curtain than a window. My image of Zenobia is more in line with the archaeology and Palmyra's material context; she probably had discoloured teeth.

The scarcity and unreliability of the literary testimony is one reason why our knowledge of Palmyra's material context and, by extension, its social practices are so important. It was this context that shaped the terms of Zenobia's existence and within which she crafted individual subjectivity during the various stages of her life, until she was forcibly removed by the emperor Aurelian. This context enables us to define some of Zenobia's practices and experiences at key moments of her life even without explicit documentation in ancient sources. We can take Zenobia's funeral for Odainath as one example. In what follows, I am going to argue that Zenobia was almost certainly responsible for ensuring that Odainath was buried with proper funerary rites. From there, I will try to create a narrative for her experience of burying Odainath based on the insights made by recent scholarship on Palmyra's funerary life and portraiture.

Issues and challenges

Odainath and his eldest son Herodian Hairan were assassinated in late 267 or early 268 CE.[21] Much about their murders remains mysterious and unresolved.[22] When Odainath died, he was the recognized governor of the Roman East. Zenobia succeeded him, on behalf of their common son Wahballath.

19. Yoshimura et al. 2016.
20. HA Tyr. Trig. 30.15-16.
21. Hartmann 2001, 230-241 (esp. 238); Southern 2008, 76-78.
22. Hartmann 2001, 218-230; Kaizer 2005.

Amid the political turbulence, Odainath had to be buried with proper funerary rites, and I think that Zenobia was responsible for ensuring that these were completed.

Before discussing what Zenobia's funeral for Odainath was or could have been like, we do have to confront certain difficulties. There are several reasons that one could doubt that Zenobia organized a funeral for Odainath at all. The first is that Odainath was apparently murdered while absent from Palmyra. He was either at nearby Emesa or, more remotely, Pontus (north Turkey).[23] Would the Palmyrenes have repatriated his corpse? I surmise that this is the case. Recent scholarship on the repatriation of mortal remains indicates that this practice was not too unusual in the Roman empire generally.[24] We also can cite an inscription indicating that a Syrian who had died in Zenobia's invasion of Egypt in 270 was apparently repatriated to the Hauran.[25] Surely Odainath's body was repatriated for patriotic purposes too. However, we also know from an inscription of Odainath that he had intended for his remains to be at Palmyra, and he may even have left a will to this effect.[26]

The second difficulty is that it is not immediately clear when or whether wives, as opposed to other relatives or intimates, were under social expectation to arrange or organize the burials of their husbands in Palmyrene society, in addition to the prominent roles that women surely played in their husbands' funerary and mourning rituals. In the Roman empire, it was not unusual for wives to arrange funerary monuments; they are also known to have organized funerals.[27] From Palmyra's epigraphy, we know of mothers, wives, foster-mothers and sisters who commissioned funerary monuments.[28] This implies that they made funerary arrangements for loved ones, but we cannot

23. Zosimus 1.39; Syncellus, 717 (Mosshammer 467).
24. Tybout 2016.
25. Seyrig 1954, 214-217; Tybout 2016, 431.
26. IGLS 17.1.545.
27. For an example of a will in which a husband expects his wife to ensure proper treatment of his body, P. Oxy. 38.2857; Keenan et al. 2014, 213-214.
28. Cussini 2005, 27.

Fig. 1: Funerary portrait of woman and her two children, made by her husband. Archaeological Museum, Istanbul, inv. 3751 (© Palmyra Portrait Project, Ingholt Archive at Ny Carlsberg Glyptotek, PS 363).

be sure. An obvious problem is that different people could make funerary portraits for the same person.[29] Those who made memorials may not have organized the actual funerals. Moreover, most inscribed funerary portraits do not specify who made them. The relatively few that do describe a variety of relationships between living and dead: parents and children, children and parents, siblings and spouses. I cannot find any coherent pattern; much was presumably contingent on household dynamics, affective bonds, who happened to be alive to honour the dead and whether the deceased had made funerary arrangements in advance. Still, most people who take credit for making funerary portraits or posthumous honorific statues are men; only a tiny number made explicitly by women is known.[30]

It thus seems that adult women fulfilled the obligation of arranging and organizing funerals when male relatives could not do so for some reason. One woman honoured her father and brother with honorific statues after their deaths.[31] Likewise, a man who made a funerary portrait for his wife and two of their children claimed to do so to 'honour' her for having 'honoured' his brother and his children (fig. 1).[32] He seems to be referring to how she made funerary portraits for his dead brother and his sons. Foster-mothers made portraits for children whose natal parents were deceased or absent.[33] Significantly, we have evidence that women could assume legal authority over households when their husbands had died, and without the intervention of male guardians prescribed by Roman law for children.[34] In such cases, they could find themselves organizing and managing funerals for deceased children or husbands in ways that may have been somewhat unusual. Women surely participated in funerary and mourning rituals in many significant capacities and played visible roles in them. As tomb owners, they could control access to funerary spaces.[35] However, it was perhaps less frequent for them to find themselves under social expectation to assume responsibility for the overall management of funerary

29. Colledge 1976, 62, n.185; Dentzer-Feydy and Teixidor 1993, n.175-80; Heyn 2010, 640; Kropp and Raja 2014, 404, fig. 4; Raja 2015a, 352, figs. 17, 24; Albertson 2016, 158-159.

30. Eleonora Cussini (2005, 27) notes four examples of funerary portrait made explicitly by women: PAT 0840, 0877, 0901, and 0915. I do not claim comprehensiveness, but excluding non-funerary images and likenesses on sarcophagi, I have encountered at least 20 examples of funerary reliefs or portraits that were explicitly commissioned by men in PAT and Yon 2013. See n.32 for one of them.

31. IGLS 17.1.257.

32. PAT 0879 (Istanbul Inv. 3751): Alas, Aqme, daughter of Malku, son of Dionysios, which Bonnouri, her husband, made for her in her honor (*lyqrh*) because she honored (*'wqrt*) Malku, his brother, and his sons.

33. Cussini 2005, 27; PAT 0840.

34. See in particular PAT 0095 and 1791; Cussini 2005, 35; 2012, 163-164; 2016, 49.

35. Key articles are Cussini 1995 (on tomb ownership and transfer) and 2005 (on women at Palmyra).

arrangements and portraits (including financial costs) for others. Even so, there were situations in which they did.

It seems that Odainath had no surviving adult male relatives at the time of his death. The sources do not mention any brothers. His eldest son Herodian Hairan, who was probably of age, was dead and could not bury him.[36] His surviving household thus consisted of Zenobia, his under-aged son Wahballath and a debatable number of children who were still quite young.[37] As the only mature person in the household and Odainath's widow, Zenobia exercised legal and practical authority over it. Zenobia would have undoubtedly played a prominent role in Odainath's funerary and mourning rituals under any circumstance. But in the absence of other adult heirs, the social obligation for arranging his funeral and for any funerary monuments that Odainath had not already commissioned, as understood by the Palmyrene community, surely fell on Zenobia herself. In the chaotic moments of her transition to power, Zenobia certainly had many concerns on her mind. But burying Odainath was one of them. Therefore, the section that follows communicates a narrative of how Zenobia had Odainath laid to rest.

Odainath's funeral

Now Odainath perhaps never envisioned how he would die. Nevertheless, he knew that he had to die someday, and so he had a tomb built. He also had an inscription identify him as its owner.

Greek:

Septimius Odainath, the most illustrious senator, the son of Hairan, the son of Wahballath, the son of Nasor, founded at his own expense this burial monument for himself, his children, and his grandchildren, to honor them forever.

Palmyrenean:

Odainath the senator, son of Hairan, son of Wahballath, son of Nasor, built this tomb for himself, his children, and the children of his children, forever.[38]

Odainath's tomb inscription is very formulaic, but in its banality, it reminds us of an element of Zenobia's life that is often overlooked. In the tumult of 268, she had to bury her fallen husband.

At this moment in Zenobia's career, most standard narratives shift to her consolidation of power. It was certainly a pressing concern. But Zenobia was apparently the only surviving adult member of Odainath's household. Therefore, she had assumed legal authority over it. Now as the guardian of Odainath's children and heirs, she had to conduct appropriate rites for her husband too. She presumably held Odainath's funeral only after she had firmly grasped control. But she surely arranged for his body to be repatriated to Palmyra and prepared in the meantime. Unfortunately, no sources specify how Zenobia treated her husband's corpse. So let us explore how the Palmyrenes dealt with death and burial. In this way, we can understand what it meant for Zenobia to lay Odainath to rest.

In his funerary inscription, Odainath bears the status of *vir clarissimus*. This in theory dates the tomb's construction to the late 240s or early 250s. But we do not know where Odainath was actually buried. When

36. Hairan and Herodian both appear as the names of Odainath's son in inscriptions; these almost certainly refer to a single person. See Gawlikowski 1985; 2007a; 2010; 2016. Hairan Herodian appears in an inscription as early as 252 CE. IGLS 17.1.58.

37. This paper does not address the difficulties of identifying the children of Odainath and Zenobia. But see Hartmann 2001, 108-128; Sartre and Sartre 2014, 183-185. Andrade 2018, 119-123 explores the issue.

38. IGLS 17.1.545: Τὸ μνημῖον τοῦ ταφεῶνος ἔκτισεν ἐξ ἰδίων Σεπτίμιος Ὀδαιναθος ὁ λαμπρότατος συνκλητ[ικὸς] Αιρανου Ουαβαλλαθου τοῦ Νασωρου αὐτῷ τε καὶ υἱοῖς αὐτοῦ καὶ υἱωνοῖς εἰς τὸ παντελὲς αἰώνιον τειμήν; *qbr' dnh bn' 'dynt sqlṭyq' br ḥyrn whblt nṣwr lh wlbnwh wlbn' bnwhy l'lm'*.

Odainath commissioned the inscription, he was not yet at the peak of his career. He and Zenobia were probably not yet married either.[39] However unique the act may have been at Palmyra, Odainath may have 'upgraded' to a more elaborate resting place closer to the end of his life, after becoming 'King of kings' (*mlk mlk'*).[40] He may even have transferred or sold spaces in his former tomb to clients, friends or buyers.[41] Moreover, the inscription was found outside its original context. It had become building material for the Ayyubid bastion at the temple of Bel.[42] We do not know from which tomb it originates.

We will return to Odainath's tomb shortly. But for now, we can think about his corpse. We have little secure knowledge for how Palmyrenes conceived of the afterlife, despite varied interpretations based on funerary materials and art.[43] However, we know more about how Palmyrenes dressed and buried their dead. At Palmyra, known cremations are very rare.[44] Palmyrenes instead practiced inhumation. Some corpses were deposited in simple graves marked by tombstones. But many were interred in tombs, where they occupied burial niches (loculi) or even sarcophagi.[45] Among the wealthy, corpses could be mummified. Certainly, the evidence for the practice comes from earlier tower tombs.[46] But it possibly continued into the third century.

If Zenobia opted to mummify Odainath's corpse, she followed a distinctive procedure. After Odainath's body was washed, Zenobia had it wrapped in strips of linen and other textiles so that it could dehydrate.[47] Once the body was dressed in the first white layer, a paste made of imported myrrh and bitumen was applied.[48] A layer of coarser cloth followed. The third and final was made of finer, dyed textiles embroidered with impressive and intricate patterns.[49] Otherwise, if Zenobia chose not to mummify her husband's remains, she probably arranged for simple and unadorned dress, like a tunic.[50]

Zenobia then had Odainath's body laid in state in their townhouse. In mourning, Zenobia probably avoided public appearances. Her attire surely was somber. She would not have displayed any elegant clothes and jewellery that Odainath had gifted her.[51] She would have worn no cosmetics. Meanwhile, Odainath's friends and clients came to pay their condolences. After the mourning period, Odainath was then given the public display and burial that Zenobia had arranged. The funeral involved processions, prayers, wailing and solemn rituals. These enabled Zenobia to communicate the current transition of power to the Palmyrene public in a very visible way.[52] Their details mostly elude us. Nevertheless, we can be certain that Zenobia had Odainath's body laid to rest in a tomb. Inside it, only Odainath's loved ones and

39. Wahballath was still in his minority when Zenobia took power in 268. This suggests that she and Odainath were married in the late 250s. Schneider 1993, 32; Southern 2008, 4; Sartre and Sartre 2014, 127-128.

40. For title, PAT 0292, also perhaps IGLS 17.1.120. Herodian Hairan had the title too (IGLS 17.1.61), as Wahballath would later (PAT 0317).

41. For property transfer and cession inscriptions in tombs, see Cussini 1995.

42. See Sartre and Sartre 2014, 127-128 and IGLS 17.1.545 (commentary) on tomb and date.

43. Piacentini 2005; Kaizer 2010.

44. al-Hariri 2013; de Jong 2017, 295.

45. Michał Gawlikowski (2005) provides overview of tombs and funerary life. De Jong 2017 provides recent illumination of burial practices in Palmyra and Syria throughout (with 286-301 providing exclusive treatment of the site). Various sarcophagi and reliefs are published by Ingholt 1928; 1934; 1935; 1936; 1938; 1962; 1966; 1970; Tanabe 1986; Sadurska and Bounni 1994; Finlayson 1998; Krag 2016.

46. De Jong 2017, 111, 295.

47. Schmidt-Colinet and Stauffer 2000, esp. 55-56; al-As'ad et al. 2005; Piacentini 2005, 249 for what follows.

48. For bitumen sources, Diod. 2.48 and 19.98-100; Strabo, 16.2.42-4; Plin., HN 2.235 and 5.72; Amm. 23.6.15-19. Finlayson 1998, 1.6, n.4; Healy 1999, 254-255.

49. Schmidt-Colinet and Stauffer 2000, esp. 55-56; Stauffer 2012, 89.

50. Stauffer 2012, 89.

51. In the funerary portraiture, mourning women usually wear no jewellery, a contrast with the many portraits of bejeweled women at Palmyra, see Krag 2017, 42-43.

52. See Hope 2009, 71-77; Stol 2016, 375-379 (on wailing); Mirto 2012, 65-70.

heirs would conduct intimately emotional funerary rituals where he lay.[53]

Odainath surely had his own tomb. In this respect, Odainath and Zenobia had several options. Numerous tombs speckled Palmyra's immediate hinterland. The tower tombs and underground hypogea provide us with some of Palmyra's best funerary remains.[54] But it was probably in the more obscure funerary temple or temple tomb that Zenobia laid Odainath to rest. Their peak of popularity was after the mid-second century.[55] Resembling temples, these were square structures on podiums that bore Corinthian pilasters, Greek entablatures and, for the larger ones, porches with Corinthian columns. Their interiors sometimes had open-air courtyards surrounded by roofed columns and galleries lined with burial niches. Unfortunately, their internal outlays are usually not well preserved. But one in particular (tomb 36) has been meticulously excavated.[56] The largest of them all, it had over 300 burial niches. Its floor plan was widely used among the housing complexes, palaces and religious sanctuaries of the Roman and Parthian Near East; at its centre was a peristyle courtyard open to the air.[57] Its architectural decorations suggest connections to coastal Syria and its Greek and Roman influences, but they were locally made. These included images of Dionysos, of Nereids and Erotes (winged babies) on dolphins, of winged Victories and Medusas and of tragic masks. This temple in particular may have belonged to Odainath's deputy Worod or an older relative of the same name.[58]

Fig. 2: Tomb 86, Located at the western end of Palmyra's Great Colonnade (photo by the author).

Because of its prominent location, some have noted the possibility that a prominent temple tomb (tomb 86; fig. 2) at the western end of Palmyra's colonnaded street is Odainath's resting place.[59] Even if the tomb's foundation inscription is gone, it is a tempting theory. Partially reconstructed by archaeologists, the tomb is uniquely placed.[60] The Palmyrenes normally buried their dead outside the city, presumably due to beliefs in pollution.[61] But this tomb was among the few that are known to have been enmeshed in Palmyra's civic terrain. Its occupant must have been notable. He also must have disregarded the principles of equity that Palmyrene elites valued. If this is Odainath's tomb, it may have given his enemies at Palmyra another among the many reasons to kill him.[62] Still, one notes other Palmyrene tombs in the vicinity too (and perhaps some yet undiscovered), and we cannot be certain how transgressive Pal-

53. Krag 2015, esp. 113–115 provides key formulation.
54. Notable examples of preserved tombs are in Higuchi and Izumi 1994; Sadurska and Bounni 1994; Higuchi and Saito 2001. See Henning 2013 for a study of the tower tombs.
55. Gawlikowski (1970, 44–51 and 2005, 56) and Schmidt-Colinet (1992, 42–66) discuss chronology and features. Also, Henning 2013, 16; de Jong 2017, 290–291.
56. Schmidt-Colinet 1992 is the main publication.
57. Schmidt-Colinet 1992, 35–39. For houses at Dura-Europos, Palmyra, and the Near East, see Butcher 2003, 302–307; Gawlikowski 2007b; Baird 2014;. For religious architecture, Downey 1988; Freyberger 1998; Gawlikowski 1989; Butcher 2003, 351-370; Ball 2016, 372–407.
58. Schmidt-Colinet 1992; Schmidt-Colinet et al. 2013, 299–302. For small finds and skeletons, Schmidt-Colinet 1992, 141–145. Tomb inscription is IGLS 17.1.440.
59. Sartre and Sartre 2014, 127–128, cite the hypothesis. For treatment of the particular tomb, Watzinger and Wulzinger 1932, 71–76, pls. 38–44; Gawlikowksi 2005, 55, 57–58.
60. Gawlikowski 2005, 55.
61. On this, de Jong 2017, 34 and 148.
62. See Hartmann 2001, 218–230; Kaizer 2005; 2014, 304–305; Yon 2010 on these issues.

Fig. 3: Sarcophagus with banquet scene on lid and sacrificial scene on front. Palmyra Museum, Palmyra, B 2677/8983 (photo by the author).

Fig. 4: Banquet relief portraying household on lid. National Museum of Damascus, Damascus, C4947, Hypogeum of Malkû, south-west (© Palmyra Portrait Project, Ingholt Archive at Ny Carlsberg Glyptotek, PS 1094).

myrenes would have deemed such a tomb to be.[63] The tomb is certainly not the most elaborate temple tomb at Palmyra either; tomb 36 (mentioned above) is much grander. At present we ultimately do not know where exactly Odainath was buried.

We can infer the décor of Odainath's tomb from some relatively well preserved or reconstructed ones at Palmyra. Galleries were lined with burial niches. The ceilings were coffered in geometric shapes coloured with stucco. The coffering may have included portrait busts too.[64] On a stone bench in a prominent niche, Odainath's sarcophagus would have featured a banquet scene (fig. 3 is a Palmyrene sarcophagus; fig. 4 is a largely intact banquet scene).[65] If Odainath had not commissioned it, then Zenobia did. On the lid, an image of Odainath reclined as though dining on a *kline* (dining couch). His face was bearded. He may have worn an oak crown, but he did not have any of the royal headgear that he or Herodian Hairan bear on known tesserae and perhaps a marble head from the agora.[66] He probably wore the trousers, embroidered tunic and mantle that he donned in wartime or while traveling in the dry Syrian heat. He held a drinking cup, and a dagger may even have dangled from his belt (fig. 3 contains such an image).[67] The lid of Odainath's sarcophagus featured images of his household, like Hairan, Wahballath and of course Zenobia.[68]

63. Krag 2015, 110–111. For other tombs at the edge of urban Palmyra, see Watzinger and Wulzinger 1932, 62–69, pl. 27; the maps of Palmyra's urban center in Schnädelbach 2010 and Henning 2013. One also notes the apparent continued use of the early underground tomb at the temple precinct for Baal-Shamin, see Fellman 1970, esp. 111–119. I thank Rubina Raja for pointing out the possibility of undiscovered tombs underground.
64. Colledge 1976, 83–84; Tanabe 1986, no. 183; Henning 2013, pls. 13–14, 18–19, 50–51.
65. Colledge 1976, 60.
66. Gawlikowski (2016) discusses surviving images of Odainath and his household, as well as oak crowns on men in third-century Palmyrene funerary portraits.
67. Schmidt-Colinet 1997, 161–165; 2004, 193–198; 2009, with corresponding images, discusses my fig. 3. Maura Heyn (2010, 643–644, 656–658) treats portraits of 'men of the desert'. A dagger is admittedly rare on sarcophagus portraits, but they become more frequent in the third century. I thank Signe Krag for this observation.
68. See n.45 for some standard publications on sarcophagi. For tombs and households, Hauser 2016, 564–565.

If Odainath had commissioned his sarcophagus before his death, his first wife probably made a prominent appearance too. One thinks of the sarcophagus of Bolbarak, on which inscriptions identify a seated woman and a standing one as 'the wife of Bolbarak' each.[69] However, even if two wives of the same man were being depicted in this instance (and this is not certain, if likely), sarcophagi exhibit an overwhelming tendency to portray only one wife for a deceased man. Zenobia now held sway, and she probably would have opted to have herself (and not the former wife) represented as the revered matron of Odainath's household. Therefore, she appeared seated beside him as he reclined (for a seated women, see fig. 4). Portraits representing other family members probably adorned the sarcophagus' various sides. The banquet scene may reflect beliefs about the afterlife or maybe it was simply commemorative. We cannot be sure.[70] On one of the sides, an image of Odainath may have depicted him in a Roman toga as he made an incense sacrifice to his gods (for such a man in toga, see fig. 3). On the walls near the sarcophagus, there were perhaps frescos made with red, blue, black, green and yellow dies (some quite rare) and maybe even coloured stucco. These would have portrayed Greek mythic scenes or they would have showed Odainath and members of his household as they stood and faced their viewers or reclined on couches while attended by servants.[71] Otherwise, walls and ceilings would have sported floral patterns and maybe busts of people circumscribed by medallions.

One also wonders what the funerary portraits of Zenobia were like. She was alive but her likeness certainly inhabited Odainath's tomb. On Odainath's sarcophagus, she appeared seated at his feet, a position of eminence and spousal harmony (for a seated woman, fig. 4).[72] But this was probably not her only portrait. Her likeness also may have decorated a loculus intended for her. Her portraits would have been consistent with those of third-century Palmyrene women (for portraits of women, figs. 1 and 5).[73] She wore a mantle over her tunic. A headscarf and a turban adorned her head. Her mantle veiled her hair. She also wore many articles of jewellery. These displayed the wealth of her household and her husband's admiration. Among modern Bedouin, the women often wear the jewellery gifted to them by their husbands. The jewellery of women can embody a vast portion of a household's wealth, and their display communicates household harmony and trust.[74] In a gesture of modesty, Zenobia may have even raised a hand to her shoulder or veil.[75] In such ways, her portrait would have commemorated Odainath's generosity as her husband. It would have displayed her value as his household's matron. But reliefs from funerary contexts sometimes feature reclining women, often as part of domestic scenes. So Zenobia perhaps had a relief portray her as reclining, just as Odainath did on his sarcophagus lid.[76] She maybe even had herself represented as banqueting. Scenes of banqueting women were admittedly rare at Palmyra. Yet, one would have befitted an acting head of household and an imperial ruler.

Zenobia expected to be buried in Odainath's tomb. Married matrons often rested with their husbands, maidens with their fathers or brothers.[77] Such expectations are even attested in burials at modern Tadmur too.[78] But departed Palmyrene women could also rest with natal households. Many different factors in fact governed where women could be en-

69. Sadurska and Bounni 1994, cat. no. 195.

70. Finlayson 1998, 1.12-13; Piacentini 2005, 253-255; Kaizer 2010, 25.

71. Sørensen 2016, 104-116 provides key treatment of tomb paintings, with Colledge 1976, 84-87; al-As'ad 2013, 18, Fig. 7; Buisson et al. 2015.

72. Finlayson 2008, 112; 2014, 247.

73. Key works are Ingholt 1928; College 1976; Heyn 2016, with Krag 2016 and Krag and Raja 2016. Also, Sartre and Sartre 2014, 76.

74. Lancaster 1997, 66.

75. Heyn (2010, 635-636) describes the pose.

76. See Krag 2016, 190-191; Schmidt-Colinet 1992, pls. 45a, 72a, c, e, 73b; Tanabe 1986, no. 424, with PAT 1802.

77. Kiyohide Saito (2013) makes this argument; but see Krag and Raja 2016, 143-144.

78. Saito 2013, 291.

Fig. 5: 'The Beauty of Palmyra', funerary portrait of a woman in elaborate jewellery. Ny Carlsberg Glyptotek, Copenhagen, IN 2795 (Courtesy of Ny Carlsberg Glyptotek, photo by Palmyra Portrait Project).

Fig. 6: Altar with figures raising their arms in prayer. Ny Carlsberg Glyptotek, Copenhagen, IN 1080 (Courtesy of Ny Carlsberg Glyptotek, photo by Ana Cecilia Gonzales).

tombed.[79] Funerary inscriptions hint at this. Some specify that only male descendants were to be buried in tombs or funerary niches.[80] These are unusual. Most leave open the possibility for daughters and granddaughters to be buried with their natal male kin. One man explicitly built a tomb for his daughters' burials.[81] Altogether, Palmyrene women could expect to be buried with either their marital or natal household depending on their particular situation. In Zenobia's case, we can surmise that she planned to be buried with her husband for dynastic purposes. So Zenobia expected to lie with Odainath. This would not happen.

In Odainath's tomb, intimate rites were performed beyond the gazes of the public. Zenobia and her children would replicate them until they were whisked from Palmyra in 272. Lit oil lamps created light in the tomb's darkness. These were left at his sarcophagus. Incense was burned on an altar; libations of perfumed oil and wine were poured. A banquet may even have

79. See Krag's contribution to this volume. I thank the author for sharing her research with me.

80. IGLS 17.1.445, 473, 475, 477, 518, and 530 for example; Cussini 2005, 30.

81. Such as in PAT 0002.

been held. At a certain point, Zenobia, Wahballath and those with them raised their arms and prayed (for Palmyrenes in prayer, fig. 6).[82] Grave goods were not often left with Palmyrene men.[83] But women were accompanied beyond death by their accessories. If Zenobia had died at Palmyra, her loved ones and heirs would have buried her there with rings, earrings, necklaces, bracelets, pendants, containers made of glass, metal, or leather or maybe even a mirror.[84] But this was not to be. Before departing Odainath's tomb, Zenobia perhaps had a lamp left in his sarcophagus to light his way.[85] Her funerary obligations fulfilled, at least for the moment, she left Odainath to govern her empire.

Such were Zenobia's acts of piety toward her dead husband. She presumably conducted them for her stepson Hairan Herodian too, whatever their living relationship had been like. Now in her late 20s or early 30s, she was a grieving widow but she also had a real fight on her hands. She had to confront a hostile imperial court and its Palmyrene collaborators. She had to protect her children. How she did so is one of the topics of my current book about her.[86] I invite you to fix your gaze on its likeness of queen Zenobia, 'mother of the king'.

82. See Dentzer-Feydy and Teixidor 1993, nos. 149, 157; Ploug 1995, no. 129; Hvidberg Hansen 1998, no. 129: most probably a woman and her daughter.

83. We can infer funerary activities from finds of glass containers, earthenware vessels, bowls and pots, as well as lamps and incense burners in tombs and basins and wells at their entrances. See Gawlikowski 1970, esp. 177–181; Saliby 1992, 286–288; Saito 2005; 2013; Piacentini 2005, 256; Kaizer 2010; Krag 2015, 113–114; de Jong 2017, 292–293. For male grave goods, see Khalil al-Hariri (2013) on the tomb of Atenatan. See also see Higuchi and Izumi 1994, esp. 71–106; Higuchi and Saito 2001, esp. 118–145.

84. Women's grave goods are discussed by Saito 2005; 2013. See also Higuchi and Izumi 1994, 71–106; al-As'ad 2013, 15–24. For tombs and grave goods, see prior note.

85. For lamps and other finds in tombs, see previous footnotes.

86. Andrade 2018.

Ancient Sources and Abbreviations

*Standard *OCT* and *Teubner* editions for ancient authors cited in the text are not listed here

BNF Bibliothèque nationale de France

IGLS L. Jalabert and R. Mouterde 1929–[1986], *Inscriptions grecques et latines de la Syrie,* Paris.

IGLS XVII.1 J.-B, Yon 2012, *Inscriptions grecques et latines de la Syrie, Palmyre, Tome 17, Fascicule 1: Palmyre,* Beirut.

IGRR R. Cagnat et al. (eds.) 1901–1927, *Inscriptiones graecae ad romanas pertinentes,* Paris.

OGIS W. Dittenberger (ed.) 1903–1905, *Orientis graeci inscriptiones selectae,* 2 vols., Hildesheim.

P. Oxy. *The Oxyrhynchus Papyri* 1898, London.

PAT D. R. Hillers and E. Cussini, 1996 *Palmyrene Aramaic Texts,* Baltimore.

Historia Augusta F. Paschoud 2011, *Histoire Auguste, Vies des trente tyrans et de Claude,* vol. 3.4, Paris.

Strabo S. Radt 2002–2011, *Strabons Geographika,* 10 vols., Göttingen.

Syncellus A. A. Mosshammer 1984, *Ecloga chronographica,* Berlin.

Zosimus F. Paschoud 1971–1989 *Historie Nouvelle,* Paris.

Bibliography

Albertson, F. 2016, Typology, Attribution, and Identity in Palmyran Funerary Portraiture, in A. Kropp and R. Raja (eds.), *The World of Palmyra*, Palmyrene Studies 1, Copenhagen, 150–165.

Andrade, N. J. 2018, *Zenobia: Shooting Star of Palmyra*, New York.

Andrade, N. J. and E. Rush 2016, Introduction: Lucian, a Protean *Pepaideumenos*, *Illinois Classical Studies* 41, 1, 151–184.

al-As'ad, K., J. Chehade and A. Schmidt-Colinet 2005, Die Textilien aus Palmyra: ein internationales und interdisziplinäres Project, in A. Schmidt-Colinet (ed.), *Palmyra: Kulturbegegnung im Grenzbereich*, Mainz am Rhein, 64-66.

al-As'ad, W. 2013, Some Tombs Recently Excavated in Palmyra, *Studia Palmyreńskie* 12, 15–24.

Asor Cultural Heritage Initiatives, 2018, *New Damage in Palmyra Uncovered by ASOR CHI*, http://www.asor-syrian-heritage.org/new-damage-in-palmyra-uncovered-by-asor-chi/ (accessed 20.07.2018).

Asor Cultural Heritage Initiatives, 2018, *Update Palmyra: New photographs detail damage to the UNESCO World Heritage site of Palmyra*, http://www.asor-syrianheritage.org/update-palmyra-new-photographs-detail-damage-to-the-unesco-world-heritage-site-of-palmyra/ (accessed 20.07.2018).

Baird, J. 2014, *The Inner Lives of Ancient Houses: An Archaeology of Dura-Europos*, Oxford.

Ball, W. 2016, *Rome in the East: The Transformation of an Empire*, second edition, London.

Bland, R. 2011, The Coinage of Vabalathus and Zenobia from Antioch and Alexandria, *NC* 171, 133–186.

BnF, Gallica, 2013, *Monnaie: Bronze, Alexandrie, Égypte, Zénobie*, 3646, http://gallica.bnf.fr/ark:/12148/btv1b8485689n.r=zenobie?rk=150215;2 (accessed 20.07.2018).

BnF, Gallica, 2013, *Monnaie: Bronze, Alexandrie, Égypte, Zénobie*, 3647, http://gallica.bnf.fr/ark:/12148/btv1b84856909.r=zenobie?rk=21459;2 (accessed 20.07.2018).

Buisson, N., D. Burlot, H. Eristov, M. Eveno and N. Sarkis 2015, The Tomb of the Three Brothers at Palmyra: The Use of Mimetite, a Rare Yellow Pigment, in a Rich Decoration, *Archeometry* 57, 1025–1044.

Butcher, K. 2003, *Roman Syria and the Near East*, London.

Colledge, M. A. R. 1976, *The Art of Palmyra*, London.

Cuneo, C., S. Penacho, M. Danti and M. Gabriel 2016, Update from Palmyra: DigitalGlobe satellite imagery shows the construction of a military base within the protected zone of the UNESCO World Heritage Site, (pdf) *Asor Cultural Heritage Initiatives*, http://www.asor-syrianheritage.org/wp-content/uploads/2015/03/ASOR-CHI-Palmyra-Military-Base-Report-r.pdf (accessed 20.07.2018).

Cuneo, C., S. Penacho and L. B. Gordon 2015, Update on the Situation in Palmyra, (pdf) *Asor Cultural Heritage Site*, http://www.asor-syrianheritage.org/wp-content/uploads/2015/09/Palmyra_UpdateReport_FINAL-4reduced.pdf; http://www.asor-syrianheritage.org/wp-content/uploads/2015/03/NEW2_PalmyraSpecialReport3-FINAL.pdf (accessed 20.07.2018).

Cussini, E. 2016, Reconstructing Palmyrene Legal Language, in A. Kropp and R. Raja (eds.), *The World of Palmyra*, Palmyrene Studies 1, Copenhagen, 42–52.

Cussini, E. 2012, What Women Say and Do (in Aramaic Documents), in G. B. Lanfranchi, D. M. Bonacossi, C. Pappi and S. Ponchia (eds.), *Leggo! Studies Presented to Prof. Frederick Mario Fales on the Occasion of his 65th Birthday*, Wiesbaden, 161–172.

Cussini, E. 2005, Beyond the Spindle: Investigating the Role of Palmyrene Women, in E. Cussini (ed.), *A Journey to Palmyra: Collected Essays to Remember Delbert Hillers*, Leiden and Boston, 26–43.

Cussini, E. 1995, Transfer of Property at Palmyra, *ARAM periodicals* 7, 233–250.

Danti, M. D., A. Al-Azm, A. Cuneo, S. Penacho, B. Rouhani, M. Gabriel, K. Kaercher and J. O'Connell 2016, Planning for Safeguarding Heritage Sites in Syria and Iraq, (pdf) *Asor Cultural Heritage Site*, http://www.asor-syrianheritage.org/wp-content/uploads/2016/05/ASOR_CHI_Weekly_Report_85%E2%80%9386r.pdf (accessed 20.07.2018).

Danti, M. D., A. Al-Azm, A. Cuneo, S. Penacho, B. Rouhani, M. Gabriel, K. Kaercher and J. O'Connell 2016, Planning for Safeguarding Heritage Sites in Syria and Iraq, (pdf) *Asor Cultural Heritage Site*, http://www.asor-syrianheritage.org/wp-content/uploads/2016/05/ASOR_CHI_Weekly_Report_87%E2%80%9388r.pdf (accessed 20.07.2018).

Danti, M. D., A. Al-Azm, A. Cuneo, S. Penacho, B. Rouhani, M. Gabriel, K. Kaercher and J. O'Connell 2016, Planning for Safeguarding Heritage Sites in Syria and Iraq, (pdf) *Asor Cultural Heritage Site*, http://www.asor-syrianheritage.org/wp-content/uploads/2016/07/ASOR_CHI_Weekly_Report_99%E2%80%93100r.pdf (accessed 20.07.2018).

Degeorge, G. 2001, *Palmyre: métropole caravanière*, Paris.

De Jong, L. 2017, *The Archaeology of Death in Roman Syria: Burial, Commemoration, and Empire*, Cambridge.

Dentzer-Feydy, J. and J. Teixidor 1993, *Les antiquités de Palmyre au Musée de Louvre*, Paris.

Downey, S. 1988, *Mesopotamian Religious Architecture: Alexander through the Parthians*, Princeton.

Fellman, R. 1970, *Le sanctuaire de Baalshamîn à Palmyre: Die Grabanlage*, vol. V, Rome.

Finlayson, C. S. 2014, Review of Andrew Smith II, 'Roman Palmyra', *BASOR* 376, 246–249.

Finlayson, C. S. 2008, *Mut'a* Marriage in the Roman Near East. The Evidence from Palmyra, Syria, in B. A. Nakhai (ed.), *The World of Women in the Ancient and Classical Near East*, Newcastle-upon-Tyne, 99–138.

Finlayson, C. S. 1998, *Veil, Turban, and Headpiece: Funerary Portraits and Female Status at Palmyra, Syria*, unpublished PhD Thesis, University of Iowa.

Freyberger, K. 1998, *Die frühkaiserzeitlichen Heiligtümer der Karawanenstationen im hellenisierten Osten: Zeugnisse eines kulturellen Konflikts im Spannungsfeld zweier politischer Formationen*, Mainz am Rhein.

Frisch, Lt. 1936, Palmyre et sa garnison au début de 1936, *Revue des troupes de Levant* 7, 7–32.

Gawlikowski, M. 2016, The Portraits of Palmyrene Royalty, in A. Kropp and R. Raja (eds.), *The World of Palmyra*, Palmyrene Studies 1, Copenhagen, 126-134.

Gawlikowski, M. 2013, In the Footsteps of Prince Abamelek in Palmyra, *Studia Palmyreńskie* 12, 87-96.

Gawlikowski, M. 2010, The Royalty from Palmyra Once Again, in B. Bastl, V. Gassner and U. Muss (eds), *Zeitreisen: Syrien - Palmyra - Rom: Festschrift für Andreas Schmidt-Colinet zum 65. Geburtstag*, Vienna, 67-72.

Gawlikowski, M. 2007a, Odainat et Hérodian, rois des rois, *MélBeyrouth* 60, 289-313.

Gawlikowski, M. 2007b, Beyond the Colonnades: Domestic Architecture in Palmyra, in K. Galor and T. Waliszewski (eds.), *From Antioch to Alexandria: Recent Studies in Domestic Architecture*, Warsaw, 79-94.

Gawlikowski, M. 2005, The City of the Dead, in E. Cussini (ed.), *A Journey to Palmyra: Collected Essays to Remember Delbert Hillers*, Leiden and Boston, 44-73.

Gawlikowski, M. 1989, Les temples dans la Syrie à l'époque hellénistique et romaine, in J.-M. Dentzer and W. Orthmann (eds.), *Archéologie et histoire de la Syrie: La Syrie de l'époque achéménide a l'avenement de l'Islam*, vol. II, Saarbrücken, 323-346

Gawlikowski, M. 1985, Les princes de Palmyre, *Syria* 62, 251-261.

Gawlikowski, M. 1970, *Monuments funéraires de Palmyre*, Warsaw.

Gibbon, E. 1776, *The History of the Decline and Fall of the Roman Empire,* vol. 1, ed. D. Wormsley 1994, London.

Hägg, T. 2012, *The Art of Biography in Antiquity*, Cambridge.

al-Hariri, K. 2013, The Tomb of ʿAqraban, *Studia Palmyreńskie* 12, 149-158.

Hartmann, U. 2001, *Das palmyrenische Teilreich*, Stuttgart.

Hauser, S. 2016, Social Space and Territory at Palmyra, *ARAM periodicals* 28, 1-2: 555-567

Healy, J. 1999, *Pliny the Elder on Science and Technology*, Oxford.

Henning, A. 2013, *Die Turmgräber von Palmyra: Eine lokale Bauform im kaiserzeitlichen Syrien als Ausdruck kultureller Identität*, Rahden/Westf.

Heyn, M. 2016, Status and Stasis: Looking at Women in the Palmyrene Tomb, in A. Kropp and R. Raja (eds.), *The World of Palmyra*, Palmyrene Studies 1, Copenhagen, 194-206.

Heyn, M. 2010, Gesture and Identity in the Funerary Art of Palmyra, *AJA* 114, 631-661.

Higuchi, T. and T. Izumi (eds.) 1994, *Tombs A and C: Southeast Necropolis, Palmyra Syria: Surveyed in 1990-92*, Nara.

Higuchi, T and K. Saito 2001, *Tomb F - Tomb of BWLH and BWRP: Southeast Necropolis, Palmyra, Syria*, Nara.

Hope, V. M. 2009, *Roman Death: The Dying and the Dead in Ancient Rome*, London.

Hvidberg-Hansen, F. O. 1998, *The Palmyrene inscriptions, Ny Carlsberg Glyptotek*, Copenhagen.

Ingholt, H. 1970, The Sarcophagus of Beʿelai and other Sculptures from the Tomb of Malkû, Palmyra, *MélBeyrouth* 45, 173-200.

Ingholt, H. 1966, Some Sculptures from the Tomb of Malkû at Palmyra, in M.-L. Bernhard (ed.), *Mélanges offerts à Kazimierz Michałowski*, Warsaw, 457-476.

Ingholt, H. 1962, Palmyrene Inscription from the Tomb of Malkû, *MélBeyrouth* 38, 101-119.

Ingholt, H. 1938, Inscriptions and sculptures from Palmyra, II, *Berytus* 5, 93-140.

Ingholt, H. 1936, Inscriptions and sculptures from Palmyra, I, *Berytus* 3, 83-128.

Ingholt, H. 1935, Five dated tombs from Palmyra, *Berytus* 2, 57-120.

Ingholt, H. 1934, Palmyrene sculptures in Beirut, *Berytus* 1, 32-43.

Ingholt, H. 1928, *Studier over Palmyrensk Skulptur*, Copenhagen.

Kaizer, T. 2016, The Future of Palmyrene Studies, *JRA* 29, 924-931.

Kaizer, T. 2014, Euhemerism and Religious Life in the Roman Near East, in T. Gnoli and F. Muccioli (eds.), *Divinizzazione, culto del sovrano e apoteosi: tra antichità e medioevo*, Bologna, 295-306.

Kaizer, T. 2010, Funerary Cults at Palmyra, in O. Hekster and S. T. A. M. Mols (eds), *Cultural Messages in the Graeco-Roman World: Acta of the BABESCH 80th Anniversary Workshop Radboud University Nijmegen, September 8th 2006*, Leuven, 23-31.

Kaizer, T. 2005, Odaenathus von Palmyra: Römischer Orient, 267/68, in M. Sommer (ed.), *Politische Morder: Vom Altertum bis zur Gegenwart*, Darmstadt, 73-79.

Keenan, J., J. G. Manning and U. Yiftach-Firanko 2014, *Law and Legal Practice in Egypt from Alexander to the Arab Conquest: A Selection of Papyrological Sources in Translations, with Introductions and Commentary*, Cambridge.

Krag, S. 2017. Changing Identities, Changing Positions: Jewellery in Palmyrene Female Portraits, in T. Long and A. H. Sørensen (eds.), *Positions and Professions in Palmyra*, Palmyrene Studies 2, Copenhagen, 36-51.

Krag, S. 2016, Females in Group Portraits in Palmyra, in A. Kropp and R. Raja (eds.), *The World of Palmyra*, Palmyrene Studies 1, Copenhagen, 180-193.

Krag, S. 2015, The Secrets of the Funerary Buildings in Palmyra during the Roman Period, in E. Mortensen and S. G. Saxkjær (eds.), *Revealing and Concealing in Antiquity: Textual and Archaeological Approaches to Secrecy*, Aarhus, 105-118.

Krag, S. and R. Raja 2016, Representations of Women and Children in Palmyrene Funerary *Loculus* Reliefs, *Loculus Stelae*, and Wall Paintings, *Zeitschrift für Orient-Archäologie* 9, 134-178.

Kropp, A. and R. Raja. 2014, The Palmyra Portrait Project, *Syria* 91, 393-408.

Lancaster, 1997, *The Rwala Bedouin Today*, second edition, Prospect Heights.

Long, T. 2016, Facing the Evidence: How to Approach the Portraits, in A. Kropp and R. Raja (eds.), *The World of Palmyra*, Palmyrene Studies 1, Copenhagen, 135-149.

McHugo, J. 2015, *Syria: A History of the Last Hundred Years*, New York.

Mirto, M. S. 2012, *Death in the Greek World: From Homer to the Classical Age*, Norman.

Neep, D. 2012, *Occupying Syria under the French Mandate: Insurgency, Space, and State Formation*, Cambridge.

Piacentini, D. 2005, The Palmyrene Attitudes toward Death, *ARAM periodicals* 17, 245-258.

Ploug, G. 1995, *Catalogue of the Palmyrene Sculptures, Ny Carlsberg Glyptotek*, Copenhagen.

Raja, R. 2015a, Palmyrene Funerary Portrait in Context: Portrait Habit between Local Traditions and Imperial Trends, in J. Fejfer, M. Moltesen and A. Rathje (eds.), *Tradition: Transmission of Culture in the Ancient World*, Copenhagen, 329-361.

Raja, R. 2015b, Staging 'Private' Religion in 'Public' Palmyra: The Role of the Religious Dining Tickets (Banqueting *Tesserae*), in J. Rüpke and C. Ando (eds.), *Public and Private in Ancient Mediterranean Law and Religion*, Berlin, 165-186.

Raja, R., and A. H. Sørensen 2015, *Harald Ingholt and Palmyra*, Aarhus.

Raja. R. and J.-B. Yon (eds.) (forthcoming), *The Excavation Diaries of Harald Ingholt: The Palmyra Expeditions of 1924, 1925, and 1928*, Copenhagen.

Sadurska, A. and A. Bounni 1994, *Les sculptures funéraires de Palmyre*, Rome.

Saito, K. 2013, Female Burial Practices in Palmyra: Some Observations from the Underground Tombs, *Studia Palmyreńskie* 12, 287-298.

Saito, K. 2005, Palmyrene Burial Practices from Funerary Goods, in E. Cussini (ed.), *A Journey to Palmyra. Collected Essays to Remember Delbert Hillers*, Leiden and Boston, 150-165.

Saliby, N. 1992, L'hypogeé de Sassan fils de Malê à Palmyre (with a bibliography appendix by Klaus Parlasca), *DM* 6, 267-292.

SANA: Syrian Arab News Agency, 2018, *Statue of Palmyra queen Zenobia in Damascus for four days*, http://sana.sy/en/?p=53820 (accessed 20.07.2018).

Sartre, A. and M. Sartre, 2016, *Palmyre: vérités et légendes*, Paris.

Sartre, A. and M. Sartre. 2014, *Zénobie: de Palmyre à Rome*, Paris.

Sartre, M. 2016, Zénobie dans l'imaginaire occidental, in A. Kropp and R. Raja (eds.), *The World of Palmyra*, Palmyrene Studies 1, Copenhagen, 207-221.

Schmidt-Colinet, A. 2009, Nochmal zur Ikonographie zweier palmyrenischer Sarkophage, in M. Blömer, M. Facella and E. Winter (eds.), *Lokale Identität im römischen Nahen Osten: Kontexte und Perspektiven*, Stuttgart, 223-234.

Schmidt-Colinet, A. 2004, Palmyrenische Grabkunst als Ausdruck lokaler Identität(en): Fallbeispiele, in A. Schmidt-Colinet (ed.), *Lokale Identitäten in Randgebieten des römischen Reiches: Akten des Internationalen Symposiums in Weiner Neustadt 2003*, Vienna, 189-198.

Schmidt-Colinet, A. 1997, Aspects of 'Romanization': The Tomb Architecture at Palmyra and Its Decoration, in S. E. Alcock (ed.), *The Early Roman Empire in the East*, Oxford, 157-178.

Schmidt-Colinet, A. 1992, *Das Tempelgrab Nr. 36 in Palmyra: Studien zur palmyrenischen Grabarchitektur und ihrer Ausstattung*, 2 vols., Mainz am Rhein.

Schmidt-Colinet, A., K. al-As'ad and W. al-As'ad 2013, Thirty years of Syro-German/Austrian Archaeological Research at Palmyra, *Studia Palmyreńskie* 12, 299-318.

Schmidt-Colinet, A. and A. Stauffer 2000, *Die Textilien aus Palmyra. Neue und alte Funde*, Mainz am Rhein.

Schnädelbach, K. 2010, *Topographia Palmyrena I: Topography*, Bonn.

Schneider, E. E. 1993, *Septima Zenobia Sebaste*, Rome.

Schwentzel, C.-G. 2011, La propaganda de Vaballath et Zénobie d'après le témoignage des monnaies et tessères, *RIN* 111, 157-172.

Seyrig, H. 1954, Antiquités syriennes, *Syria* 31, 3-4, 212-224.

Southern, P. 2008, *Empress Zenobia: Palmyra's Rebel Queen*, London and New York.

Sørensen, A. H. 2016, Palmyrene Tomb Paintings in Context, in A. Kropp and R. Raja (eds.), *The World of Palmyra*, Palmyrene Studies 1, Copenhagen, 103-117.

Starcky, J. and M. Gawlikowski 1985, *Palmyre*, Paris.

Stauffer, A. 2012, Dressing the Dead in Palmyra in the Second and Third centuries AD, in M. Carroll and J. Wild (eds.), *Dressing the Dead in Classical Antiquity*, Stroud, 89-98.

Stol, M. 2016, *Women in the Ancient Near East*, Berlin.

Stoneman, R. 1992, *Palmyra and its Empire: Zenobia's Revolt against Rome*, Ann Arbor.

Tanabe, K. 1986, *Sculptures of Palmyra I*, Tokyo.

Tlass, M. 2000, *Zenobia: The Queen of Palmyra*, Damascus.

Tlass, M. 1986, *Zénobie, reine de Palmyre*, Damascus.

Tlass, M. 1985, *Zanūbiyā malikat Tadmur*, Damascus.

Tybout, R. 2016, Dead Men Walking: The Repatriation of Mortal Remains, in L. de Ligt and L. Tacoma (eds.), *Migration and Mobility in the Early Roman Empire*, Leiden, 390–437.

Watzinger, C. and K. Wulzinger 1932, Die Nekropolen, in T. Wiegand (ed.), *Palmyra. Ergebnisse der Expeditionen von 1902 und 1917*, 2 vols. Berlin, 44–76.

Weingarten, J. 2018, Zenobia in History and Legend, in J Aruz (ed.), *Palmyra: Mirage in the Desert*, New York, 130-147.

Wiegand, T. (ed.) 1932, *Palmyra: Ergebnisse der Expeditionen von 1902 und 1917*, 2 vols. Berlin.

Woltering, R. A. F. L. 2014, Zenobia or al-Zabbā': The Modern Arab Literary Reception of the Palmyran Protagonist, *Middle Eastern Literatures* 17, 1, 25–42.

Wright, W. 1895, *An Account of Palmyra and Zenobia, with Travels and Adventures in Bashan and the Desert*, London.

Yon, J.-B. 2013, L'épigraphie palmyrénienne depuis *PAT*, 1996–2011, *Studia Palmyreńskie* 12, 333–379.

Yon, J.-B. 2010, Kings and Princes at Palmyra, in T. Kaizer and M. Facella (eds.), *Kingdoms and Principalities in the Roman Near East*, Stuttgart, 229–240.

Yoshimura, K. S. Wu, T. Nakahashi and S. Saito 2016, Inorganic Impurities in Teeth of the Ancient Inhabitants of Palmyra, in J. C. Meyer, E. H. Seland, and N. Anfinset (eds.), *Palmyrena: City, Hinterland and Caravan Trade between Orient and Occident*, Oxford, 161–170.

CHAPTER 8

Model families in Imperial Rome and Palmyra

Mary T. Boatwright

Introduction

This paper responds to the desideratum, expressed recently by Rubina Raja, to analyse Palmyrene funerary portraits in the context not only of local conventions and values, but also of imperial trends and styles.[1] Our knowledge of the local context has been greatly advanced by the Palmyra Portrait Project that now includes more than 3000 portraits. This rich and varied resource underscores the importance of family portraiture at Palmyra. Its working conclusions include that 'group portraits constitute close to 40% of the funerary sculpture of the first century BCE to the third century CE, women appear in approximately 40% of the sculptures and children are featured in around 7%', numbers supplemented by depictions of women and adult children alongside husbands and fathers in banquet reliefs and sarcophagi.[2] The 'Representations of Women and Children in Roman period Palmyra' conference added nuance for Palmyra. For example, Agnes Henning's tantalizing information from the tower tombs suggests the significance of extended family units, and Eleonora Cussini's analysis of epigraphic and other texts implies women and men were identified by familial relations rather than an occupational identifier or another individual descriptor. My own research on the imperial family has prompted me to look at the wider Roman context. My aims are to illuminate variations in the presentation of the imperial family over time, particularly through the Severan period, and to consider if and how that imagery was disseminated from Rome. I hope thus to contribute to the analysis of Palmyrene portraits by identifying important and shifting representations of family that added to the 'knowledge culture' Raja has stressed in Palmyra.[3]

The Palmyra Portrait Project's findings raise broad questions, especially if the loculus reliefs and other portraits are compared to the rare, dissimilar earlier funerary portraiture from when the oasis city of Tadmôr/Palmyra first became involved with Rome in the mid first century BCE.[4] The later phenomenon of Palmyra's numerous and distinctive loculus and other portraits might somehow be tied to Rome's arrival in this far eastern region through diplomacy, armed engagements and economic contacts. Funerary portraiture in other borderlands developed after Rome's military intrusion brought soldiers and veterans who were commemorated in 'Roman'-style funerary portraits and inscriptions at their deaths where they had served.[5] For Palmyra, this hypothesis is complicated both by the city's distance from Rome, since the fastest journey from Rome to Palmyra would have taken 28.1 days to cover 3284 kilometres, and by the uncertainties attending Rome's presence in Palmyra.[6] Despite Rome's continuing interest in Palmyra from the late Republic through the late third century

1. Raja 2015, 356.
2. See also Krag and Raja 2016, 136 and passim.

3. Raja 2015, 333.
4. Earlier portraits, on free-standing funerary stelae with rounded tops, recall Hellenistic types, see e.g. Seyrig 1936; Parlasca 1976; Raja 2015, 335; Heyn 2010, 632. Dates in this paper are CE unless otherwise noted.
5. On Roman Britain, for example, see Hope 1997, 245.
6. Although this is about the same 'real' distance of Rome to Aquincum, Pannonia (Inferior), 28.8 days to cover 1216 km (figures derived from Orbis: http://orbis.stanford.edu/, accessed 27.09.2016), Rome was more closely tied politically and militarily to Aquincum, the capital of Pannonia Inferior.

CE, it never dominated the city as it did so many other places within and at the edges of its empire.

There is ample evidence for Rome's military and economic involvement here, however, such as the city's attack by Mark Antony's forces in 41 BCE, Tiberius' and Germanicus' interactions with Palmyrenes in 18/19 CE, a visit from Hadrian in 129/130 that included renaming the city Hadriana Palmyra, the reworking of Palmyra's tax law in 137 with Roman input, Palmyra's designation as a Roman *colonia* with the *ius Italicum* under Septimius Severus or Caracalla and its re-conquest by the emperor Aurelian in 273 after its break from Rome under Septimius Odainath, Zenobia and Wahballath.[7] Palmyra participated in Roman communications and trade. It was incorporated in the Roman road system in the Flavian period, and it engaged in the importation and use of Roman marbles and other precious stone from the Mediterranean, for example.[8]

Although the date of Palmyra's integration into the Roman province of Syria is debated, Roman influence on Palmyra's public institutions and structures, from the first through the third centuries CE, has been reasserted convincingly by Andrew M. Smith.[9] At the same time, however, he underscores that Palmyra's civic organization and public spaces also reveal elements from Parthian, Greek and Persian cultures, and enduring local traditions such as the use of Palmyrene Aramaic.[10] In any case, Palmyra did not see a permanent Roman military presence before 167.[11]

This is more than halfway through the dated funerary portraiture and in the second of the three chronological phases of Palmyrene portraits Harald Ingholt proposed: 50-150 CE, 150-200 CE and 200-273 CE.[12] The Palmyra Portrait Project exposes the lack of secure provenance and dating for most of Palmyra's portraits. With such uncertainties, the search for direct Roman influence may be illusory. Yet Palmyrene portraits, distinctive for their almost rigidly frontal pose, large eyes, gestures, clothing and other diagnostics, share compositional elements with other funerary portraiture in Rome and some Roman provinces, including a focus on the family.[13] Their rich content, particularities, and similarities raise the question of local and external elements in their composition: that is, the choices available to commemorators and workshops in Palmyra.

My paper examines the creation and variations of representations for Rome's imperial family as possible external elements for Palmyra's funerary portraits. This family was a central institution of the principate, and its prominence was cemented in 2 BCE by Augustus' assumption of the title *Pater Patriae* that thereafter featured significantly in all media.[14] Despite literary sources' no-

7. Mark Anthony, App. B Civ. 5.9, for which see Hekster and Kaizer 2004; Tiberius and Germanicus, see Smith 2013, 24; Hadrian's visit, see Smith 2013, 25; the Palmyrene Tax Law, see Shifman 2014 and Matthews 1984 (I have consulted this law as translated and presented in Matthews); Palmyra as a Roman *colonia* with the *ius Italicum*, Dig. 50.15.1. Further for this history, for example, see Sartre 2005, 351; Millar 1993, 164-173, 326-327. Archaeology does not corroborate the literary sources' account that Aurelian destroyed the city (Zos. 1.61.1; Hist. Aug., Aurel. 31.5-10); rather, Palmyra's subsequent decline seems due to economic circumstances (for example, see Southern 2008, 149-155).

8. For the Roman road system, see Smith 2013, 146; for the marble trade, particularly notable in the later Hadrianic and early Antonine periods, see Wielgosz 2010.

9. For example Maurice Sartre (2005, 69-70, 350) and Fergus Millar (1993, 34-35) date the incorporation to 18/19 CE or before, in part because of Germanicus' presumed visit then. Smith (2013, 146) more cautiously dates it to the Flavian period, when Roman roads were constructed through the region (see also Matthews 1984, 161-162). Anthony R. Birley (1997, 230) suggests it was still 'technically outside the empire' in 129/130.

10. Smith 2013, esp. Chapter 5, concurring with, for example, Millar 1993, 327.

11. For example, see Edwell 2008, 36-37, 50.

12. Ingholt 1928. These phases are still generally accepted, for example, see Raja 2015, 329, 337; Heyn 2010, 632.

13. For Palmyrene portraits, see e.g. Ingholt 1928; Colledge 1976; Raja 2015; Krag and Raja 2016 (especially for depictions of women and children). Jason Mander (2013, 113-115) remarks that on the tombstones he analyses from Rome, Italy and the western provinces most 'recipients... stare outwards to meet the eyes of the viewer, their portraits posed with rigidity', in contrast to classical Greek monuments on which '[a]t least superficially the representations are more naturalistic'. Tonio Hölscher (2004) underlines the complexity of 'Roman art'.

14. Alföldi 1971; Severy 2003; Milnor 2005. I am interested in the imperial family, not the emperor himself.

torious depiction of some imperial women, that is women born or married into the imperial family writ large, imperial women are portrayed visually and in documents primarily within family settings and with family members. Such 'family' depictions are positive, but they are not static: as we see below, the official imagery of the imperial family changes over time in occurrence and in composition. That family, however, was but one in the wider Roman world and itself must be set into context.

Approaching family in the Roman world

Assessing conceptions of 'the family' in the Roman world and along its borders is difficult, and the various approaches and interpretations undertaken in the last forty years have ultimately emphasized the importance of local traditions even while stressing the paramount value of this social unit, as we see below. The inquiry must first acknowledge that most individuals and families were unreported and are thus totally unknown. Although families and family members appear more frequently on funerary material than in other sources, women and children are underrepresented, as indicated also by the numbers from the Palmyra Portrait Project cited at the opening of this paper. Whatever the source, visual, legal, literary, even documentary, ancient evidence tells us more about normative behaviour and cultural expectations than about realities of ancient life, although some connection with lived experience was always present. Each source and area reveals interplay between individual agency and larger social and cultural determinants, including the example of the Roman imperial family.

Most funerary inscriptions and reliefs, however, centre not on the emperor and court but on less privileged individuals. Although, especially in the aggregate, such tombstones may seem to reveal a great deal of demographic and other types of information; the material is culturally influenced.[15] Richard P. Saller's and Brent D. Shaw's seminal analysis in the early 1980s of some 12–13,000 funerary epitaphs from a larger sample of 25,000, which generally concluded that the 'nuclear family', or mother-father-children triad, was foundational for the western Roman empire, was challenged almost immediately on grounds of its conclusion that 'familial duty and feelings of affection' impelled funerary commemoration.[16] Others pointed out that the conclusions did not seem valid outside of the Latin West.[17] Studies for parts of Italy, moreover, have highlighted the 'male commemorative dominance' that is the tendency to commemorate more males than females.[18] This seems echoed in the ratios of men, women and children depicted on the funerary material analysed by the Palmyra Portrait Project. In Roman Spain, however, women have 'striking prominence' as commemorators of the dead.[19] Clearly, local cultures and choices individually influenced funerary commemoration in the Roman world.[20] But imperial models of the family were shared throughout that world as well.

'The family' is even harder to discern outside of funerary material. Ancient authors are generally indifferent and uninformative about women and children, especially below the most elite circles.[21] Rome's legal sources

15. Maureen Carroll (2006, 180–208) for example provides an overview of 'family and household' on Roman funerary commemoration in the Latin West.

16. Saller and Shaw 1984, esp. 145. Elizabeth A. Meyer (1990, esp. 76, 95–96) argues that funerary commemoration relates to Roman rules of inheritance and (Roman citizen) legal heirs' primary responsibility of commemoration, which was not necessarily the nuclear family.

17. Dale B. Martin (1996, 57–58) sees greater diversity of household patterns in commemorations from Asia Minor and suggests that degrees of intimacy influenced commemoration. Jonathan Edmondson (2005, esp. 187–188) surveys the work of Saller and Shaw and the resulting controversy.

18. Gallivan and Wilkins 1997, 242–244 (term on p. 243). Italian epitaphs commemorating families with boys outnumber those with girls with an overall ratio of roughly 7:3 (cf. Churchin 2000–2001, 539; Edmondson 2005, 204–205). Roughly comparable numbers of females and males are born and die (Bagnall and Frier 1994, 94–95).

19. Edmondson 2005, 188, 202.

20. See also Hope 2001.

21. For example, see Fantham 2006, 17–19. Even senatorial women are poorly attested despite Marie-Thérèse Raepsaet-Charlier's optimistic conclusion from her prosographical research that some 20% are at least named and that records exist for 100% of the imperial women (1987, x, n.35).

are concerned with what constituted a family and its members, but their interest lies in inheritance and the orderly transmission of property, not so much with affection, familial groupings and the like.[22] Further, Roman law does not simply represent social reality, even though it helped shape norms in its response to social abnormalities.[23] Papyri, and especially census returns, furnish rich demographic information for Roman Egypt that exhibits idiosyncrasies and common traits alike. Roger S. Bagnall and Bruce W. Frier note that the census returns, which were official documents, have peculiar biases: for example, metropolitan declarants may have failed to report girls, especially ones younger than five years old.[24] Yet, these scholars also venture, as they conclude their analysis of this material and modern *comparanda*, that the basic demographic attributes of Roman Egypt 'are, at the least, thoroughly at home in the Mediterranean'.[25] This quick overview of the evidence reveals the interplay of empire-wide commonalities and local features in Roman family formations.

I examine the public, official representation of the imperial family through official inscriptions, public portraiture and coins, perforce sometimes supplemented with literary and other material.[26] Official documents were to be exhibited 'in the most visited place of the most populous city of each province and ... in the winter quarters of each legion', as the *Senatus Consultum de Pisone patre* of 20 CE puts it; similarly, the inscription recording the tax law of Palmyra of 137 made clear that both the new regulations and those they replaced were to be inscribed and displayed on a stone column in a public place.[27] Such inscriptions, even if not particularly legible after initial installation accompanied by a public reading, conveyed messages both within and on the edges of Rome's empire.[28] Public portraits and their accompanying inscriptions presented official messages to the Roman empire and its neighbours, as did central coinage, that is coins struck in Rome. Carlos F. Noreña has recently used such evidence to argue persuasively for dissemination, acceptance and modification of Rome's 'imperial virtues' in local communities in the Latin West, and Sonja Nadolny turns primarily to such official material in her recent investigation of the Severan imperial women.[29] When assessing possible transmission of Roman images and concepts to Palmyra below, I touch on coinage and portraiture alike, even when imperial statues are now attested only by inscriptions.

The imperial example

A common way to assess imperial influence on private portraiture and relief has involved the notion of the *Zeitgesicht*, or 'period face'. This holds that the official depiction of the emperor was so dominant, even charismatic, that private individuals in Rome, Italy and the empire chose to have themselves represented in ways reminiscent of imperial portraits.[30] Ascertaining the influence of *Zeitgesicht* particularly focuses on diagnostic elements such as the arrangement of hair, including facial hair for men, but also encompasses facial features. The concept, first articulated by Paul Zanker in 1982, has become commonplace and is often used to help date reliefs and statues lacking external dating elements.[31] Various scholars have offered important refinements. It has now been convincingly argued, for example, that the assimilation of private individuals to the emperor was loose enough that imperial images remained distinctively those of the emperor; further, there were probably at least a few 'pe-

22. See Treggiari 1991, 379-393.
23. For example, see Bradley 2005.
24. Bagnall and Frier 1994, 42. They also note that the surviving returns significantly underrepresent villages (1994, 48).
25. Bagnall and Frier 1994, 173.
26. Roman authors are generally hostile to imperial women, and frequently at odds with the official portrayal of an individual. Thus, I do not often refer stories in literary works that denigrate an imperial woman's familial sentiment and roles (for example, see Ginsburg 2006; Nadolny 2016).
27. The SCPP, Eck et al. 1996, 50-51, 266-270 (lines 170-172); Palmyrene Tax Law, Matthews 1984, 175 (section 1(a)).
28. Callie Williamson (1987, 164-165) concludes that although bronze tablets were probably little legible, they had important symbolism as reflecting the permanency of Roman law and might.
29. Noreña 2011; Nadolny 2016.
30. See Zanker 1982; D'Ambra 2013, 518; Fejfer 2008, 270-279.
31. Zanker 1982.

riod faces' in any era, so that an individual patron and/or sculptor had some choice of models.[32] Analogously, Raja has pointed out that examples of imperial modelling among portraits from Palmyra are scarce, usually for 'non-indigenous' individuals.[33] It is clear that the imperial example provided a choice but not a mandate for commissioners of funerary portraits.

The notion of the *Zeitgesicht*, however, is buttressed by the ubiquity and authority of the emperor's image. Large-scale images of the emperor and of his designated heirs embellished and centred many public and religious spaces. In Palmyra, for example, statues were raised, probably in 18/19 CE, to Tiberius, Drusus the Younger, and Germanicus in Palmyra's Temple of Bel by Minucius Rufus, the *legatus* of the Legio X Fretensis; images of Septimius Severus, his sons and his sister-in-law Julia Maesa (and perhaps his wife, Julia Domna?) were later installed by Palmyrenes at an entrance into the agora.[34] Smaller *imagines* were displayed in military camps, carried in processions and graced governors' halls.[35] The emperor's visage, and the framing hair that was much more distinguishable at a distance, were constantly found in settings associated with command, status and religion: public venues in cities and camps more frequented by men than by women. Although not as public, even a small-scale portrait of an emperor on a coin or a ring had 'power', to judge from the story that carrying such an object into a latrine or brothel could be a capital crime under Tiberius.[36] The spread of coins bearing imperial portraits, although the depictions are very small scale and almost always in profile, contributed to the functioning of *Zeitgesicht*. Although it is hard to see how a coin could serve as a model for an almost life-sized bust, the same local sculptural workshops probably produced both larger-scale imperial and private portraits.[37]

The notion of *Zeitgesicht* is not as persuasive for understanding female portraiture in the Roman empire, however. The imaging of imperial women was much less distinctive than that of emperors, though women's official portraits were commissioned by the imperial administration.[38] Some portraits make imperial women themselves resemble their imperial husbands or sons in the features of their faces, thus enhancing the image of a close-knit and harmonious imperial family.[39] Further, as Eve D'Ambra has recently argued for portraits of Julia Titi (Titus' daughter) and Domitia Longina (Domitian's wife), images of some imperial women share obvious characteristics with those of non-imperial women. The toupet, the crescent of hair presumably characteristic of female Flavian imperial portraits that rises prominently from a woman's forehead to crown her face, is found from the late Julio-Claudian period into the second century on portraits of imperial and of private women.[40] Imperial women also did not have as many images made and circulated as the emperors, either in statuary, including relief, or on coins.[41] Most of the statues and reliefs known of imperial women, moreover, clearly reference the emperor and other members of the imperial family.[42] Even numis-

32. Jane Fejfer (2008, 278–281), noting abandonment of the very top-heavy model presumed by Zanker.

33. Raja 2015, 335, 338.

34. With Rufus' inscription in Latin, see Inv. IX.2 = Yon 2012, 14–15 no. 3. Statues raised to Tiberius, Drusus the Younger and Germanicus, for example, see Edwell 2008, 36–37; Kaizer 2002, 37, n.12. Portraits of Septimius Severus and the imperial family, see Smith 2013, 28, with n.117; Delplace and Dentzer-Feydy 2005, 162–163 (IV.03 and IV.04) and 334, referring to Inv. X.64 and X.67 = Yon 2012, 187–189 nos. 191, 192 (in Greek).

35. For example, see Plin. Ep. 10.96. Publicly, Palmyrene notables were also represented by metal statues, and bronze statues are referred to in the Tax Law (Matthews 1984, 173, 180).

36. Suet. Tib. 58.3. See also Rowan 2010.

37. See Fejfer 2008, 279, referring to CIL XI 7126.

38. Fittschen 1996; Fejfer 2008, 410, 418–419. Analogously, Mander (2013, 3) points out that the portraits of Nero and others marked out for imperial succession while still a child are not standardized.

39. Susan Wood (1999, 14–15) discusses this with Livia's changing portraits from the Augustan to the Tiberian period. See also Fittschen 1996. The ears of Agrippina the Younger are very similar to those of Claudius on the coin shown in fig. 2.

40. D'Ambra 2013. She thus suggests that imperial women may have been influenced by 'private' women in their behaviour and fashions, thus changing the direction of influence. See also Fittschen 1996, 48; Alexandridis 2010, 193.

41. For statuary, see Alexandridis 2004, and for coins, see Duncan-Jones 2006.

42. For instance, more than half of the twenty-six inscriptions

Fig. 1: Zenobia, on a tetradrachm minted in Alexandria, 271-272. On the obverse, Zenobia is depicted with a stephane, or crown-like hairpiece, often worn by Roman imperial women on second century CE or later coins; the Greek legend identifies her as SEPTIM(ia) ZENOBIA SEB(asta). On the reverse, is Homonoia (= Concordia), raising her right hand and holding a double cornucopia with her left. British Museum, no. 1860,0327.273 (© Trustees of the British Museum).

matic portraits of imperial women, despite usually featuring a single woman in profile on the obverse or reverse, often had a 'familial' context, since that portrait was backed by an image of the woman's imperial consort, Pietas, Vesta, Ceres or some other abstraction or deity associated with family and familial duties or prestige.[43]

The significance of such public, official depictions of imperial women is hard to gauge for Palmyrene women and families. Distinctive numismatic images of Rome's imperial women had some attraction, to judge from two tesserae that are apparently modelled on coins of Hadrian's wife Sabina.[44] Yet it has long been maintained that, other than Zenobia (fig. 1), women in Palmyra had very little public presence, especially as individuals: here scholars adduce both the general absence of evidence for women in public settings, including as priestesses, and the few but well-known depictions of massed and heavily veiled women in religious processions.[45] Recent work, however, has suggested that Palmyrene women had a more active presence than hitherto thought: Eleonora Cussini, for example, has highlighted Palmyrene women's financial agency as recorded on inscriptions, and Dagmara Wielgosz has discussed three marble statues of

attesting statues of Livia make clear her relationship to Augustus, either by designating her as his wife (*gynaika*) or by using the genitive form of his name (Bartman 1999, 72-73).

43. For example, see Keltanen 2002, focusing on the Antonine period.

44. One is in the Damascus National Museum (RTP 1 Nr. 1, Pl. 1.1), and the other in a private collection. Dieter Salzmann (1989, with photos and references), connects them with Hadrian's visit in 129/130.

45. See Yon 2002-2003, 216; Raja 2015, 351-352. The illustrated coin of Zenobia is BMC Greek (Alexandria) 2400, 311; Roger Bland (2011, 157 and passim) provides a recent study of the coinage of Zenobia and Wahballath. Veiled women in processions, for example, see Charles-Gaffiot et al. 2001, 346, no. 159 and cf. his frontispiece.

women from public sites in the city.[46] On the other hand, scholars have noted that funerary portraits of Palmyrene woman rarely suggest imitation of imperial women's hairstyles, other than perhaps some twenty depictions of bare-headed women with coiffures reminiscent of those of Faustina the Elder or Faustina the Younger.[47]

In any case, the emperor's family symbolized imperial stability and the promise of the future. Although the 'imperial family' was essential to the principate from the beginning, its image was not constant. A more precise idea of how the imperial family was construed publicly should help us understand representations of families elsewhere in the Roman world, including Palmyra. I group the following discussion according to Ingholt's phasing of Palmyrene portraiture, giving more attention to the earlier, perhaps foundational periods. Ingholt's three chronological phases do not map precisely on the evidence from Rome, and it probably took some time for changes at Rome to be perceived in the provinces and along Rome's edges.

The imperial family 50–150 CE

By the mid-first century CE, when Ingholt starts his first phase of Palmyrene funerary portraiture, the 'imperial family' was already established as an ideological and visual focus. The apparent reluctance of Augustus and Tiberius to have coins issued with identified portraits of Livia or another imperial women was in the past, although it was not before the Flavian period that imperial coins fairly regularly depicted female members of the house.[48] From the time of Gaius Caligula, central coinage, followed and amplified by provincial coinage especially in the East, depicted and named living and deceased female members of the imperial family.[49] Some women were 'in the guise of' goddesses, such as Agrippina, Drusilla and Julia, the three sisters of Caligula, who in 37/38 were portrayed standing together with the attributes of *Securitas*, *Concordia* and *Fortuna*.[50]

In most cases, the woman portrayed on one side of the coin was 'fronted' by a portrait of the ruling emperor.[51] That was usually her son or her husband. The deceased Agrippina the Elder was shown on the reverse of an aureus with a portrait of Caligula in 37–38. Agrippina the Younger, the first imperial woman to be depicted and identified on coins during her lifetime, appears on the reverse of an aureus portraying Claudius in 50–54 (fig. 2).[52] In various cities, groups of statues, sometimes assembled over an extended period of time, showed male and female family members together, identifying them with inscriptions that often spelled out the family relationships.[53] The imperial family itself was so important that it was designated the *domus Augusta* or *domus divina* by the middle of Tiberius' reign.[54] The consecration of deceased members, notably of emperors, preceded by Julius Caesar but after 38 including imperial women as well, just as the growing honours of imperial women after Livia's designation as 'Iulia Augusta' and

46. Cussini 2005; Wielgosz 2010, 77.

47. Jean-Baptiste Yon (2002–2003, 216) stresses the low number of images apparently influenced by imperial women's hairstyles, but Eleonora Cussini (2000, 281, n.19, 282, n.27) and Klaus Parlasca (1976, 40–41) adduce a dozen or so examples of portraits with 'melon' or 'Faustina the Elder' hairstyles, or with the hairstyle of Faustina the Younger around 149–154. Dagmara Wielgosz (2010, 77) discusses a Palmyrene public statue of a woman who has both a hairstyle resembling that of Faustina the Younger (138 onwards), and facial similarities to Faustina the Younger after 150.

48. Alexandridis 2010, 196. Annetta Alexandridis notes that sculptures in the round are more frequent for Julio-Claudian women (2010, 193). For the earlier group, see Rose 1997.

49. I do not here discuss "portraits" modern scholars have identified with imperial women, such as the SALVS AVG-VSTA image often claimed to be Livia (Julia Augusta) on issues of 22 CE (RIC I^2, Tiberius no. 47 (dupondius)).

50. For example, the rare sestertius RIC I^2, Gaius/Caligula no. 33.

51. Alexandridis 2010, 198.

52. Agrippina the Elder, see RIC I^2, Gaius/Caligula nos. 7–8, pl. 13, fig. 7; Agrippina the Younger, see RIC I^2, Claudius no. 80, see also fig. 2.

53. This contrasts the Ara Pacis of 9 BCE, on which women and children are so indistinguishable as still to occasion scholarly controversy over identification (cf. Rose 1997, 103–104).

54. Domus Augusta, from 13 CE; *domus divina*, from c. 31/32 CE: Fishwick 1991, II.1, 423.

Fig. 2: Claudius and Agrippina the Younger, on an aureus minted in Rome, 50-54. The legend on the obverse identifies Claudius, depicted facing right. The reverse shows a bust of Agrippina, draped and with a diadem, facing right, and the legend (in the dative) AGRIPPINAE AVGVSTAE. British Museum, no. R.6496 (© Trustees of the British Museum).

adoption into the Julian gens at Augustus' death, heightened the charisma of the imperial family.[55] As women began to receive lasting imperial cult with Livia's official consecration under Claudius in 42, their remembrance and familial roles became incorporated into recurring rituals in Rome and the provinces. The appointment of local women as their priestesses furthered the memory of Julia Augusta and of other imperial women who were deified, such as Plotina, Marciana and Matidia the Elder. Their images now accompanied those of deified emperors in temples and processions of the imperial cult.[56]

Historical happenstance, however, helped to ensure that the first-century imperial family was composed primarily of adult males. Only a handful of children were born into the imperial house during the first century.[57] Most brought into public prominence were males, such as the twins of Tiberius' son Drusus the Younger celebrated on coins as emerging from twin cornucopiae facing one another.[58] Two children 'born to the purple', Claudia the daughter of Nero and Poppaea, and 'Divus Caesar' the son of Domitian and Domitia, died early and were divinized.[59] Their honours were ephemeral, now known only from a few coins and a stray literary reference or two.[60] The adult and male cast of the impe-

55. The meaning and specific import of the clearly honorific 'Augusta' is debated, see, in brief, Temporini 1978, 27-35; Kuhoff 1993.
56. Hemelrijk 2015, 69-82.

57. I speak primarily about the post-Augustan period.
58. Sestertius of 22-23 CE, RIC I^2, Tiberius no. 42.
59. See McIntyre 2013, specifying the coins (Claudia appears only on provincial coinage). The one-year old daughter of Caligula, Julia Drusilla, was killed with her mother Milonia Caesonia right after his assassination (Jos. AJ 19.11.190-400; for other references, see FOS no. 438).
60. This is true also for Drusilla, the sister of Caligula.

rial family was strengthened considerably with the Flavians, for Vespasian's consolidation of power in 70 came when his two sons were already mature. Titus was 31, and Domitian 19. Vespasian's wife and daughter, both named Flavia Domitilla, were deceased.[61] The brotherly bonds of Titus and Domitian, and their unity of dynastic purpose with their father, were celebrated in the coinage and on public monuments such as the Arch of Titus despite rumours of their tension in the literary sources.[62] The importance of women was minimized, again perhaps by historical circumstance. Domitian's wife Domitia has the greatest presence on the Flavian coinage, but 'her' coins still constitute a small overall percentage of about 5%.[63]

In short, in the first century CE the concept of the imperial family as a cornerstone of social and political life develops significantly and is presented publicly in official documents; for example the *Senatus Consultum de Pisone patre*, coinage and monuments.[64] The members of that family most singled out, however, are adult males; women and children appear less frequently in both absolute and relative numbers.

Although she was divinized after her death in 38, there is no record of her worship after his assassination in 41 (Wood 1995, 465).

61. Titus' daughter, (Flavia) Iulia who is often called Julia Titi, was a child in 70. We know almost nothing about her before her engagements and marriage (FOS no. 371). For Flavia Domitilla (the daughter of Vespasian and the homonymous Flavia Domitilla), see FOS no. 368; for Flavia Domitilla mater, see FOS no. 367; for Titus' wife or wives see FOS nos. 93 and 525. See also Alexandridis 2010.

62. For example, Tac. Hist. 4.51-52; Suet. Dom. 2.

63. Domitia Longina, see FOS no. 327. For the coinage, see Alexandridis 2010, noting on 200-201 the different politics of Flavian rulers for women on coins.

64. Though focusing on Tiberius, Germanicus, Piso and his family, and senatorial deliberations after Germanicus' death in which Piso pater was implicated, the SCPP includes information on the relationship between Tiberius and his mother (lines 109-120, on which see Eck et al. 1996, esp. 88, 109-120), and on Germanicus' wife, mother, and sister, Agrippina the Elder, Antonia, and Livilla (lines 136-144). The unity of purpose and shared self-restraint of Tiberius and Julia Augusta (and Germanicus' brother Drusus) are also stressed (lines 132-133, 148-150).

Publicity for imperial women becomes more prevalent with Trajan and Hadrian, and women's numismatic depiction notably more frequent after 128. Trajan came to imperial power as a 45-year old adult; he and his wife Plotina, presumably some 10-15 years younger than him, had no children.[65] His wife Plotina, sister Marciana and niece Matidia the Elder all had significant visibility in public settings, from Plotina's and Marciana's entrance into the imperial palace in 98 through the women's accompaniment of Trajan on his voyages.[66] Although Hadrian's wife Sabina, who was the younger daughter of Matidia the Elder and the sister of Matidia the Younger, is relatively poorly attested, she too travelled with her imperial consort, accompanying Hadrian to the Greek East in 128-133.[67] Reportedly, Hadrian found Sabina so morose and sharp that he said he would have divorced her had he been a private citizen; this very comment, which follows a report of his concern for the propriety of the imperial house, underscores the importance of women to the image of the imperial family.[68]

The persona of Trajanic-Hadrianic women is 'domestic' and private, with the women praised for modesty and reluctance to ask for favours or otherwise use their familial influence. That image, however, had impressive public visibility. At Matidia the Elder's death in 119, Hadrian extolled her for her affection for him and others of the imperial family, and for her humble virtues: his lengthy speech praising his mother-in-law has been partially preserved in a now lost inscription from Tibur, modern Tivoli.[69] A similarly public record was made of his favourable response to Plotina's reserved petition concerning the Epicureans in Athens; in Plotina's accompanying letter to the Epicureans, she praises Hadrian as the emperor, and calls him 'to me very dear

65. For Pompeia Plotina, see FOS no. 631; Temporini 1978, 10-23.

66. Public settings, for example, see Plin. Pan. 83-84, where they are not named but identified only as *uxor* and *soror*; Cass. Dio 68.5.5; voyages of Trajan, for example, see Hist. Aug., Hadr. 5.9, Plotina and Matidia the Elder travelled to the East with Trajan 113-117 (Boatwright 1991, 532; Temporini 1978, 171).

67. Halfmann 1986, 91; Syme 1988, 162-168.

68. Hist. Aug., Hadr. 11.3.

69. See Jones 2004, for a new reading of CIL XIV 3579 = I.Ital. IV, 1. 77.

Fig. 3: Faustina the Elder and Concordia, on a denarius minted in Rome, 141-161. This 'empress coin' depicts the deceased Faustina the Elder, DIVA AVG(usta) FAVSTINA (Deified Augusta Faustina). On the reverse are a togate man and a veiled and draped woman (Antoninus Pius and Faustina the Elder?), with the legend CONCORDIAE (for marital harmony). The man holds a roll in his left hand and clasps his right hand with the woman's, who holds a vertical sceptre in her left. The British Museum, no. R.13132 (© Trustees of the British Museum).

in every way as both an outstanding guardian and a loyal son'.[70] The bestowal of the imperial women's names on newly founded, or re-founded, cities, like the *colonia Marciana Traiana Thamugadi* in Numidia in 100 CE and Plotinopolis and Marcianopolis in Thrace in the early 100s, associated the women with community building.[71] Public buildings, most of which were temples, in Rome and the provinces bore these women's names and associated them with the divine.[72]

Perhaps more importantly for dissemination of female family virtues is the noticeable rise in 128 of coin issues bearing images of imperial women, especially on the obverse, which Richard P. Duncan-Jones has called 'empress coin'. These numismatic portraits were often paired with depictions of Roman abstractions and goddesses associated with the family, such as Pietas, Venus, Demeter and Vesta. The 'Empress coin' in precious and base metal continued throughout the second century, apparently peaking at about a sixth of all lower-denomination coins produced in Rome in the Severan period.[73] Faustina the Elder, for example, was honoured by an unprecedented number of issues, the more extraordinary given their emission for 20 years after she died within the first three years of her husband's rule as An-

70. See Birley 1997, 109; Bremen 2005.

71. For the cities, for example, see Hildegard Temporini (1978, 88-90), who argues these names do not commemorate the presence of the women at the sites (as was true for the earlier *colonia Claudia ara Agrippinensium* and the later Faustinopolis). These women, and Sabina as well, were also linked with neighbourhoods in Hadrian's Antinoopolis, see Boatwright 2000, 194 and n.124.

72. See Boatwright 1991, 534-535.

73. Duncan-Jones 2006; Rowan 2011.

toninus Pius (fig. 3).[74] No literary source now mentions the phenomenon of 'empress coin,' but Palmyra's 'Sabina' tesserae, mentioned above, and coins' repurposing for jewellery even in antiquity suggest the impact of this change.[75]

In sum, during Ingholt's first phase of Palmyrene funerary portraiture from 50 to 150, the image of Rome's imperial family shifted from being dominated by adult males, particularly the *Pater Patriae* (and *paterfamilias*), to include women. At first, the women were the wife, mother or daughter of the emperor, and their representation was rare. The women were significant, however: Agrippina the Elder, Agrippina the Younger, Julia Titi and Domitia the wife of Domitian were obvious dynastic links.[76] With Trajan, however, the 'imperial family' included the emperor's sister and niece, Marciana and Matidia the Elder; with Hadrian, an emperor's adoptive mother and mother-in-law, Plotina and Matidia the Elder. The more inclusive concept of the imperial 'family' widened further in the next generation, when Matidia the Younger was celebrated epigraphically as the *matertera* or maternal aunt of Antoninus Pius.[77] Can we trace in the Palmyrene funerary portraits a similarly broadening representation of family?

The imperial family 150-200 CE

This period, coinciding roughly with the 'high Antonine' era and reigns of Antoninus Pius through Commodus, assassinated on December 31, 191, and extending into the Severan period, sees remarkable public focus on the imperial family, now frequently called the *domus divina*.[78] Three changes are especially notable: greater attention to special bonds between husband and wife, the inclusion of young children, and the further elevation of imperial women's public visibility through honorific 'maternal' titles such as *Mater Castrorum* and *Mater Senatus* (Mother of the Camps, Mother of the Senate). Although at first sight these titles may seem analogous to *Pater Patriae*, they differ by clearly associating their honourees with 'public' realms traditionally barred to women.[79] Of these three changes, only the third continues at Rome into the third century, and in Palmyra into Ingholt's final phase of portrait sculpture.

In the second half of the second century, the emperor's wife, together with her husband, symbolizes the virtue *Concordia* that is especially associated with harmonious marriages. At the death of Faustina the Elder in 140, an over-life size statue group was installed in Rome, perhaps at the Temple of Venus and Roma, and depicted Faustina and her husband Antoninus Pius exchanging the *dextrarum iunctio*; young men and women about to get married were to sacrifice at its altar (fig. 3). Coins apparently show the statuary group, sometimes with a sacrificing couple before it, and the shrine seems to have been duplicated in Ostia, perhaps on a smaller scale.[80] After the death of Faustina the Younger in 175, a similar shrine was raised at the Temple of Venus and Roma, this time with silver statues of this deceased Augusta and her husband Marcus Aurelius.[81] Peter Weiss has traced the effects of this imperial promotion of marriage both visually, on sarcophagi of the late second century and afterwards in Rome and Italy, and in changes in privileges granted to auxiliary soldiers upon their discharge.[82] In other words, the model of the imperial family was voluntarily followed by some patrons of funerary monu-

74. Beckmann 2012, 2. For identification of the coin illustrated in fig. 3, see n.80 below.
75. See Rowan 2010, 4, although she does not specifically discuss images of women on coins reused for jewellery.
76. The unusual depiction of Caligula's three sisters on coins of 37/38 was complemented by other issues commemorating his family members including his (deceased) brothers, his mother Agrippina the Elder, his father Germanicus and Augustus (Wood 1995).
77. Celebrated as maternal aunt of Antoninus Pius, e.g. CIL X 4745. See also Chausson 2008.
78. This term, usually in the formula *'in honorem domus divinae'* or in h. d. d., recurs in military inscriptions from the late second and third century (Raepsaet-Charlier 1975).
79. Boatwright 2003.
80. The coin illustrated here as fig. 3 is RIC III, Antoninus Pius no. 381b. For the Ostia shrine, see CIL XIV 5326.
81. Cass. Dio 72.31.1. See Weiss 2008, 1-8; Beckmann 2012, 35-37.
82. Weiss 2008.

Fig. 4: Faustina the Younger and children, on a sestertius minted in Rome, 161-176. This 'empress' coin depicts and identifies Faustina the Younger (FAVSTINA AVGVSTA) on the obverse. On the reverse stands a woman (Faustina?) holding a child on each arm and with four children standing near, two right and two left; the legend reads TEMPOR(um) FELIC(itas) (Happiness of the Times, a term often associated with successful births) and S C (by degree of the senate). British Museum, no. R.14328 (© Trustees of the British Museum).

ments, and was perhaps perpetrated institutionally through the army.[83]

Further, the remarkable fertility of Faustina the Younger, Antoninus Pius' daughter and Marcus Aurelius' wife, who bore at least twelve and perhaps as many as fifteen children between 147 and 170, was commemorated in numerous ways. Klaus Fittschen has argued that her differing portrait types can be keyed to the births of children.[84] On coins with her portrait, and on others of the time, reverses show infants and toddlers with a standing or seated female with the legend TEMPORVM FELICITAS (Happiness of the Times), or a similar personification, perhaps suggesting Faustina herself (fig. 4).[85] The depiction of seated or standing maternal figures holding an infant or two and being tugged at by a child extends even to childless imperial women, such as Lucilla the daughter of Faustina the Younger and Marcus Aurelius: rare aurei from 164-167 pair her with FECVNDITAS.[86] The focus is on a maternal female figure with a small child or children; men are not included in the field. Thus, children are shown as important to the imperial family.

The third change in the representation of imperial women and the family in this period is the appearance of honorific maternal titles for the wife and mother of the emperor. This begins with Faustina the Younger, who re-

83. In 167 CE, the first garrison of Roman auxiliary soldiers came to Palmyra, but there is no evidence of their intermarriage with individuals commemorated by Palmyrene portrait sculpture.

84. Fittschen 1982.

85. For example, RIC III, Marcus Aurelius no. 1673, see also fig. 4.

86. RIC III, Marcus Aurelius no. 764: Fecundity.

Fig. 5: Julia Domna, on an aureus minted in Rome, 211-217. The obverse of this 'empress' coin depicts a bust of Julia Domna, with the legend IVLIA PIA FELIX AVG(usta), a frequent appellation starting in 211. On the reverse is a draped and seated woman, Julia Domna (or Pax?), holding a branch in her right hand and a sceptre in her left, with the legend MAT AVGG MAT SEN M PATR (Mother of the Emperors, Mother of the Senate, Mother of the Fatherland). British Museum, no. 1844,1015.224 (© Trustees of the British Museum).

ceived the title *Mater Castrorum* in 174 while accompanying Marcus Aurelius in the Marcomannic War.[87] The epithet is shown on coins as well.[88] In 195, the title was granted to Julia Domna, the wife of Septimius Severus. The maternal titles of Julia Domna, the mother of Caracalla and Geta, begin to proliferate thereafter: she is called *Mater Caesaris* in 196, *Mater Augusti et Caesaris* perhaps in 197, *Mater Augustorum* in 209(?), *Mater Castrorum et Senatus et Patriae*, from early 211(?), and often some combination of these.[89] In some cases, as on the aureus minted under her son Caracalla and illustrated here (fig. 5), it is only the titles that convey a 'maternal' aspect to the woman celebrated on the coin.[90] But with this note we pass to the last of Ingholt's three phases of Palmyrene funerary portraiture.

87. Cass. Dio 71.10.5.

88. On coins, for example, see RIC III, Marcus Aurelius nos. 1659-1664; Boatwright 2003.

89. See Kienast 1996, 167-168; FOS no. 436.

90. For the coin, see RIC IV, Caracalla no. 381.

The imperial family 200-273

Nadolny's recent monograph on the Severan imperial women, Julia Domna, Julia Soaemias, Julia Maesa and Julia Mamaea, argues persuasively that coinage struck densely in Rome (over 3000 different types), together with provincial coinage and inscriptions ensured that these women were very much in the public eye.[91] Further, these women were presented with their husbands and sons; daughters are out of the picture, again thanks to historical circumstance. Although Julia Maesa was also honoured as *Avia Augusti* (grandmother of the emperor) for her grandson Severus Alexander, the more regular image of the imperial family in this period was the nuclear one of a child or children with a parent or

91. Nadolny 2016. Other imperial women, such as Caracalla's wife Plautilla or the wives of Elagabalus, were so briefly associated with the imperial family that they have left little trace.

parents.[92] This image was especially prominent with Julia Domna and Septimius Severus.[93] The significance of the mother to the imperial dynasty was clearly implied in the frequent title *Mater Augusti*, which was used for Elagabalus' mother Julia Soaemias, after 218, and for Severus Alexander's mother Julia Mamaea, after 222.[94] But some coins for these powerful women, such as the aureus with Julia Domna that was struck under Caracalla after 211 (fig. 5), depict them without family members. Such depictions have correspondences with to the coinage of Zenobia later struck in Alexandria and Antioch (fig. 1).[95]

The chaotic political and military history of Rome after the Severans through to the reign of Aurelian means that no imperial family was in power long enough to leave a lasting public impression, so I end my survey with the assassination of Severus Alexander and Julia Mamaea in 235.

Conclusions

The Palmyra Portrait Project has greatly illuminated how individuals and families were depicted during three centuries of funerary portraits from this glorious city, bringing together images whose records and materials were scattered throughout the modern world until this initiative. Further study of the growing Palmyrene corpus may refine dates and original physical contexts for individual pieces, helping to identify continuities, developments and variances in the portraits. My article has attempted to identify analogous trends in the official presentation of Rome's imperial family from about 50 CE into the third century. My contribution may help us interpret outcomes from the Project, such as the group of loculus images showing women with small children on their left arms that Signe Krag and Rubina Raja have identified. Of these 28 compelling references to the women's identities as mothers, eighteen roughly date to the period 150–200, eight to Ingholt's final phase 200–273, and only two before 150.[96] In other words, the striking Palmyrene image seems coincident with the inclusion of small children in imperial imagery of the Antonine period that I noted above. But this is only a suggestion. We can never know how Rome impacted the private lives and self-images of Palmyrene individuals and families, just as we cannot know if the women and children who increasingly represented 'the imperial family', especially in the second century, welcomed their roles. Nevertheless, the more nuanced understanding of the imperial family, which was presented so publicly and exemplarily in the Roman world, provides an important background in which to analyse Palmyrene portraits of the family.[97]

Abbreviations

BMC Greek (Alexandria) R. S. Pool 1892, *A Catalog of the Greek Coins in the British Museum, Alexandria,* London.

FOS M. T. Raepsaet-Charlier 1892, *Prosopographie des femmes de l'ordre senatorial (I-II siècles),* Louvain. References to FOS are by entry number.

Inv. I-12 J. Cantineau et al. 1930–1975, *Inventaire des inscriptions de Palmyre*, vol. I-XII, Beirut and Damascus.

RIC H. Mattingly et al. 1923–, *The Roman Imperial Coinage,* London.

RTP H. Ingholt et al. 1955, *Recueil des tessères de Palmyre,* Paris.

Bibliography

Alexandridis, A. 2010, The Other Side of the Coin: The Women of the Flavian Imperial Family, in N. Kramer and C. Reitz (eds.), *Tradition und Erneuerung. Mediale Strategien in der Zeit der Flavier*, Berlin and New York, 191–237.

92. For Julia Maesa's title, see Kienast 1996, 181.
93. Nadolny 2016, 61–62.
94. Julia Soaemias, see Kienast 1996, 175; Julia Mamaea, see Kienast 1996, 180.
95. See Bland 2011.
96. Krag and Raja 2016, 145–149, and cat. nos. 31–58.
97. I thank Signe Krag and Sara Ringsborg for inviting me to the stimulating conference on 'Representations of Women and Children in Roman period Palmyra', as well as the other members of the conference, including Rubina Raja, for their illuminating papers and responses. I am also grateful to the editors of this volume for their helpful suggestions.

Alexandridis, A. 2004, *Die Frauen des römischen Kaiserhauses. Eine Untersuchung ihrer bildlichen Darstellung von Livia bis Iulia Domna*, Mainz am Rhein.

Alföldi, A. 1971, *Der Vater des Vaterlandes im römischen Denken*, Darmstadt.

Bagnall, R. S. and B. W. Frier 1994, *The Demography of Roman Egypt,* Cambridge and New York.

Bartman, E. 1999, *Portraits of Livia: Imaging the Imperial Woman in Augustan Rome*, Cambridge and New York.

Beckmann, M. 2012, *Diva Faustina: Coinage and Cult in Rome and the Provinces*, New York.

Birley, A. R. 1997, *Hadrian: The Restless Emperor*, London and New York.

Bland, R. 2011, The Coinage of Vabalathus and Zenobia from Antioch and Alexandria, *NC* 171, 133–186.

Boatwright, M. T. 2003, Faustina the Younger, *Mater Castrorum*, in R. Frei-Stolba, A. Bielman, and O. Bianchi (eds.), *Les femmes antiques entre sphère privée et sphère publique*, Bern, 249–268.

Boatwright, M. T. 2000, *Hadrian and the Cities of the Roman Empire*, Princeton, New Jersey.

Boatwright, M. T. 1991, Imperial Women of the Early Second Century A.C., *AJP* 112, 513–540.

Bradley, K. R. 2005, Review: Roman Family Law, *CR* 55, 280–282.

Bremen, R. van 2005, 'Plotina to all her friends': The Letter(s) of the Empress Plotina to the Epicureans in Athens, *Chiron* 35, 499–532.

Carroll, M. 2006, *Spirits of the Dead: Roman Funerary Commemoration in Western Europe,* Oxford.

Charles-Gaffiot, J., H. Lavagne and J.-M. Hofman (eds.) 2001, *Moi, Zénobie: reine de Palmyre*, Paris, Rome, and Milan.

Chausson, F. 2008, Une dédicace monumentale provenant du théâtre de *Suessa Aurunca*, due à Matidie la Jeune, belle-soeur de l'empereur Hadrian, *JSav* 2, 233–259.

Churchin, L. A. 2000–2001, The Roman Family: Recent Interpretations, *Zephyrus: Revista de prehistoria y arquelogia* 53–54, 535–550.

Colledge, M. A. R. 1976, *The Art of Palmyra*, London.

Cussini, E. 2005. Beyond the Spindle: Investigating the Role of Palmyrene Women, in E. Cussini (ed.), *A Journey to Palmyra. Collected Essays to Remember Delbert R. Hillers*, Leiden and Boston, 26–43.

Cussini, E. 2000. Palmyrene Eunuchs? Two Cases of Mistaken Identity, in E. Rova (ed.), *Patavina orientalia selecta*, Padova, 279–290.

D'Ambra, E. 2013, Mode and Model in the Flavian Female Portrait, *AJA* 117, 511–525.

Delplace, C. and J. Dentzer-Feydy (eds.) 2005, *L'Agora de Palmyre*, Bordeaux and Beirut.

Duncan-Jones, R. P. 2006, Crispina and the Coinage of the Empresses, *NC* 166, 223–228.

Eck, W., A. Caballos and F. Fernández 1996, *Das senatus consultum de Cn. Pisone patre*, Munich.

Edmondson, J. 2005, Family Relations in Roman Lusitania: Social Change in a Roman Province?, in M. George (ed.), *The Roman Family in the Empire: Rome, Italy, and Beyond*, Oxford and New York, 183–229.

Edwell, P. M. 2008, *Between Rome and Persia: The Middle Euphrates, Mesopotamia and Palmyra under Roman Control*, London and New York.

Fantham, E. 2006, *Julia Augusti: The Emperor's Daughter*, London and New York.

Fejfer, J. 2008, *Roman Portraits in Context*, Berlin and New York.

Fishwick, D. 1987–2005, *The Imperial Cult in the Latin West: Studies in the Ruler Cult of the Western Provinces of the Roman Empire*, vols. 1–3, Leiden and New York.

Fittschen, K. 1996, Courtly Portraits of Women in the Era of the Adoptive Emperors (AD 98–180) and their Reception in Roman Society, in D. E. E. Kleiner and S. B. Matheson (eds.), *I Claudia: Women in Ancient Rome*, New Haven and Austin, 42–52.

Fittschen, K. 1982, *Die Bildnistypen der Faustina Minor und die Fecunditas Augustae*, Göttingen.

Gallivan, P. and P. Wilkins 1997, Familial Structures in Roman Italy: A Regional Approach, in B. Rawson and P. Weaver (eds.), *The Roman Family in Italy: Status, Sentiment, Space*, Canberra and Oxford, 239–279.

Ginsburg, J. 2006, *Representing Agrippina: Constructions of Female Power in the Early Roman Empire*, Oxford and New York.

Halfmann, H. 1986, *Itinera Principum: Geschichte und Typologie der Kaiserreisen im römischen Reich*, Stuttgart.

Hekster, O. and T. Kaizer 2004, Mark Antony and the Raid on Palmyra: Reflections on Appian, "Bella Civilia" V, 9, *Latomus* 63, 70–80.

Hemelrijk, E. A. 2015, *Hidden Lives, Public Personae: Women and Civic Life in the Roman West*, New York.

Heyn, M. K. 2010, Gesture and Identity in the Funerary Art of Palmyra, *AJA* 114, 631–661.

Hölscher, T., tr. A. Snodgrass and A. Kunzl-Snodgrass 2004, *The Language of Images in Roman Art*, Cambridge and New York.

Hope, V. M. 2001, *Constructing Identity: The Roman Funerary Monuments of Aquileia, Mainz and Nîmes*, Oxford.

Hope, V. M. 1997, Words and Pictures: The Interpretation of Romano-British Tombstones, *Britannia* 28, 245–258.

Ingholt, H. 1928, *Studier over Palmyrensk Skulptur*, Copenhagen.

Jones, C. P. 2004, A Speech of the Emperor Hadrian, *CQ* 54, 266–273.

Kaizer, T. 2002, *The Religious Life of Palmyra: A Study of the Social Patterns of Worship in the Roman Period*, Stuttgart.

Keltanen, M. 2002, The Public Image of the Four Empresses - Ideal Wives, Mothers and Regents?, in R. Berg, R. Hälikkä, P. Raitis and V. Vuolanto (eds.), *Women, Wealth and Power in the Roman Empire*, Rome, 105–146.

Kienast, D. 1996, *Römische Kaisertabelle: Grundzüge einer römischen Kaiserchronologie*, second edition, Darmstadt.

Krag, S. and R. Raja 2016, Representations of Women and Children in Palmyrene Funerary *Loculus* Reliefs, *Loculus Stelae* and Wall Paintings, *Zeitschrift für Orient-Archäologie* 9, 134–178.

Kuhoff, W. 1993, Zur Titulatur der römischen Kaiserinnen während der Prinzipatszeit, *Klio* 75, 244–256.

Mander, J. 2013, *Portraits of Children on Roman Funerary Monuments*, Cambridge and New York.

Martin, D. B. 1996, The Construction of the Ancient Family: Methodological Considerations, *JRS* 86, 40–60.

Matthews, J. F. 1984, The Tax Law of Palmyra: Evidence for Economic History in a City of the Roman East, *JRS* 74, 157–180.

McIntyre, G. 2013, Deification as Consolation: The Divine Children of the Roman Imperial Family, *Historia* 62, 222–240.

Meyer, E. A. 1990, Explaining the Epigraphic Habit in the Roman Empire: The Evidence of Epitaphs, *JRS* 80, 74–96.

Millar, F. 1993, *The Roman Near East, 31 BC - AD 337*, Cambridge, Massachusetts and London.

Milnor, K. 2005, *Gender, Domesticity, and the Age of Augustus: Inventing Private Life*, Oxford and New York.

Nadolny, S. 2016, *Die severischen Kaiserfrauen*, Stuttgart.

Noreña, C. F. 2011, *Imperial Ideals in the Roman West: Representation, Circulation, Power*, Cambridge and New York.

Orbis, 2012, *The Stanford Geospatial Network Model of the Roman World*, http://orbis.stanford.edu/ (accessed 09.27.16).

Parlasca, K. 1976. Probleme palmyrenischer Grabreliefs. Chronologie und Interpretation, in E. Frézouls (ed.), *Palmyre: Bilan et perspectives. Colloque de Strasbourg 18–20 Octobre 1973*, Strasbourg, 33–43.

Raepsaet-Charlier, M.-T. 1987, *Prosopographie des femmes de l'ordre sénatorial (Ier–IIe siècles)*, Louvain.

Raepsaet-Charlier, M.-T. 1975, La datation des inscriptions latines dans les provinces occidentales de l'Empire romain d'après les formules '*in h(onorem) d(omus) d(ivinae)*' et '*deo deae,*' *ANRW* 2, 3, 232–282.

Raja, R. 2015, Palmyrene Funerary Portraits in Context: Portrait Habit between Local Traditions and Imperial Trends, in J. Fejfer, M. Moltesen and A. Rathje (eds.), *Tradition: Transmission of Culture in the Ancient World*, Copenhagen, 329–361.

Rose, C. B. 1997, *Dynastic Commemoration and Imperial Portraiture in the Julio-Claudian Period*, Cambridge and New York.

Rowan, C. 2011, The Public Image of the Severan Women, *PBSR* 79, 241–273.

Rowan, C. 2010, Slipping out of circulation: the after-life of coins in the Roman World, *Journal of Numismatic Association of Australia* 20, 3–14.

Saller, R. P. and B. D. Shaw 1984, Tombstones and Roman Family Relations in the Principate: Civilians, Soldiers and Slaves, *JRS* 74, 124–156.

Salzmann, D. 1989, Sabina in Palmyra, in H.-U. Cain, H. Gabelmann and D. Salzmann (eds.), *Festschrift für Nikolaus Himmelmann: Beiträge zur Ikonographie und Hermeneutik*, Mainz am Rhein, 361–368.

Sartre, M., tr. C. Porter and E. Rawlings, with J. Routier-Pucci 2005, *The Middle East under Rome*, Cambridge, Massachusetts.

Severy, B. 2003, *Augustus and the Family at the Birth of the Roman Empire*, New York.

Seyrig, H. 1936, Note sur les plus anciennes sculptures palmyréniennes, *Berytus* 3, 137–140.

Shifman, I. S., tr. S. Khobnya, J. F. Healey (ed.) 2017, *The Palmyrene Tax Tariff*, Oxford.

Smith, A. M. 2013, *Roman Palmyra: Identity, Community, and State Formation*, New York.

Southern, P. 2008, *Empress Zenobia: Palmyra's Rebel Queen*, London and New York.

Syme, R. 1988, Journeys of Hadrian, *ZPE* 73, 159–170.

Temporini, H. 1978, *Die Frauen am Hofe Trajans*, Berlin and New York.

Treggiari, S. 1991, *Roman Marriage: Iusti Coniuges from the Time of Cicero to the Time of Ulpian*, Oxford.

Weiss, P. 2008, Die vorbildliche Kaiserehe: Zwei Senatsbeschlüsse beim Tod der älteren und der jüngeren Faustina, neue Paradigmen und die Herausbildung des 'antoninischen' Prinzipats, *Chiron* 38, 1–45.

Wielgosz, D. 2010, La sculpture en marbre à Palmyre, *Studia Palmyreńskie* 11, 75–106.

Williamson, C. 1987, Monuments of Bronze: Roman Legal Documents on Bronze Tablets, *ClAnt* 6, 160–183.

Wood, S. 1999, *Imperial Women: A Study in Public Images, 40 B.C. - A.D. 68*, Leiden and Boston.

Wood, S. 1995, Diva Drusilla Panthea and the Sisters of Caligula, *AJA* 99, 457–482.

Yon, J.-B. 2012, *Inscriptions grecques et latines de la Syrie, Tome 17, Fascicule 1: Palmyre*, Beirut.

Yon, J.-B. 2002–2003, Zenobie et les femmes de Palmyre, *AAS* 45–46, 215–220.

Zanker, P. 1982, Herrscherbild und Zeitgesicht, *Wissenschaftliche Zeitschrift der Humboldt-Universität zu Berlin, Reihe Gesellschaftswissenschaften* 31, 307–312.

CHAPTER 9

Children and religious participation in Roman Palmyra*

Ville Vuolanto

Introduction

In the pre-modern world, religion was ubiquitous. It was in many ways inextricably woven into the structures and practices of everyday life, both in private, in households and in public civic life. Consequently, religious practices were one of the major ways in which social practices and identities were transmitted, and their influence on the maturing mind is hard to overestimate. Through religious life, children were socialized to their cultural world and integrated into communal life.[1] For the understanding of the roles and involvement of boys and girls both in the civic sphere and in activities inside the households, the study of religious practices offers a very fruitful point of view.

In what follows, I will contextualize what can be known about the children of Palmyra, compared with the significance of children's participation in the religious life in the better-documented regions in the rest of the Roman world during the first three centuries CE. What kind of roles did children have in the contexts of religion in Palmyra – were these roles mainly passive, imposed by the parents, or can we see any signs of a more active religious participation by children? How were children being socialized and how were they socializing themselves with the dominant cultural background? The picture that thus forms is necessarily quite patchy, because of the limited evidence we have for the religious life of Palmyra[2] and especially with regard to the Palmyrene children. Indeed, the latter issue is a field untouched by previous scholarship.

Nor is the religious participation of children in the Roman world a topic much studied in its own right, even despite the recent rise of studies of childhood in the ancient world. Even less attention has been paid to the inevitable regional and cultural variations.[3] Methodologically, therefore, the present article will be of interest also as a case study for pondering the

* I am deeply grateful to Signe Krag and Sara Ringsborg for their indispensable help and critical comments during the process of writing this paper, to the Palmyra Portrait Project as a whole for initially inviting me to Aarhus to give a lecture on which this article is based, and to Brian McNeil for proofreading my English.

1. Katajala-Peltomaa and Vuolanto 2011, esp. 79–80, with further scholarship.

2. For example, Rubina Raja writes that: '[...] we do not, in fact, know very much about the rituals and practices undertaken as part of the religious life of Palmyra' (2015, 347). Nevertheless, some important work has been done on the religious life in Palmyra, see recently especially the work by Ted Kaizer (Kaizer 2002; 2008 (with references to further studies)). For a comparative view of the local religious landscape, see Kaizer (ed.) 2016.

3. Mantle (2002) has a groundbreaking treatment of the subject matter, although she dealt especially with (the city of) Rome itself. Other relevant research on children and (polytheistic) religion in the Roman world include Johnston 2001 (the use of children in divination); Prescendi 2010; Vuolanto 2010 (culturally a more inclusive but also more general perspective); Katajala-Peltomaa and Vuolanto 2011; Tulloch 2012; and now especially Mackey 2017. See also Rawson 2003, esp. 269–271, although she pays surprisingly little attention to the religious activities of children in her work in general. Among scholars of the Greek and Hellenistic world, the theme has aroused more interest, see e.g. Dillon 2002; Neils 2003; Garland 2013 – and in the still relevant classic treatment of the issue in Golden 2015 (1st ed. 1990), esp. 35–43, 55–67. On the status quo for research on children in the Roman world, see Vuolanto 2014.

Fig. 1: Stele depicting ʿAgabâ, daughter of Taimai, holding a bird and a bunch of grapes. National Museum of Damascus, Damascus, inv. C13, 150–200 CE (© Palmyra Portrait Project, Ingholt Archive at Ny Carlsberg Glyptotek, PS 522).

potential fruitfulness of the regional perspective on studying childhood history in the Roman world.

Who are the children we deal with from Palmyra? First, they are from the upper echelons of society – even if not necessarily from the local aristocracy, but certainly from a wealthy family background. Our information on the children from Palmyra comes almost exclusively from the visual sources and in particular from funerary contexts. To be able to invest in a grave marker, one needed wealth, and even a lower-quality relief or monument would have been out of reach for the majority of the population. A second aspect is the age of the children. We are here interested in the individuals, who are portrayed as non-adults by the contemporary culture. Therefore, no exact ages can be given a priori. Indeed, one of the relevant questions for the study of Palmyrene children and childhood is in which contexts a person would in fact be depicted as a child. However, it is possible to point out that at least in one loculus relief, an individual is recorded to have been sixteen years old at death, while being clearly depicted as an adult.[4] And childhood was connected to some visual topoi: being underage seems to have been pointed out by placing birds (especially doves)[5] and, in a less systematic way, bunches of grapes, in the hands of the individuals – and girls would not have their head covered (see, as an example, fig. 1).[6]

Divine protection of childhood: amulets

In the Roman world in general, a child was presented immediately after its birth both to the relatives and to the gods: purification rites with sacrifices and rituals connected to name-giving would ensure that this took place in a proper manner.[7] In these activities, naturally, children could not have any personal agency of

4. National Museum of Damascus, Damascus, inv. 15020.
5. Some editors of the visual material (for example, see Sadurska and Bounni 1994, 82–83, commenting on cat. no. 113, fig. 191) claim that the children of the aristocracy would have been depicted with falcons – I have not been able to ascertain this, since the reproduction of the pictures does not make it possible to make such a distinction clear.
6. For attributes, see e.g. Tanabe 1986, 249, pl. 216, 206, pl. 173, 292–295, pls. 261–264, 388, pl. 357, 456, pl. 428. For girls, see Sadurska and Bounni 1994, cat. no. 96, fig. 2 and cat. no. 94, fig. 17. Also see Tanabe 1986, 302, pl. 271. Unfortunately, we do not know if the covered hair was a symbol of being of age, or rather of being married (or if there was any difference between these categories in the Palmyrene society), or even of being respectably married within an elite household. Also, branches of a tree (laurel or olive) appear frequently, but this cannot be understood a specific attribute connected to childhood, since these regularly appear also in other contexts with possibly an apotropaic function (see Heyn 2010, 637).
7. Hänninen 2005, 55–58; Rawson 2003, 108–111.

Fig. 2a-b: Two details from the Ara Pacis Augustae (Rome): an elite boy with a *bulla* and an elite girl with a *lunula* (probably Gnaeus Domitius Ahenobarbus and Domitia), Museo dell'Ara Pacis Augustae, Rome, 13-9 BCE (© Roma, Sovrintendenza Capitolina ai Beni Culturali, photo by Ville Vuolanto).

their own. Nor was children's agency significant in their early childhood, when their parents tried with many different rituals and practices to gain protection for them against the evil spirits and illnesses - which were not two different things, but were understood to be linked together. In particular, amulets and charms were understood to be powerful in the everyday protection of children, and it was customary for children across the Roman world to carry various apotropaic necklaces and other items. The mark of the Roman freeborn underage child, the *bulla*, was only one of the practices connected to this phenomenon. Many girls seem to have worn a *lunula*, a crescent moon shaped amulet, around their neck, although adult women also used them. *Fascina*, the phallus-formed pendants and rings, were used to ward off evil especially from infants (see fig. 2a-b).[8]

For Palmyra, we have no information about the rites surrounding the birth of a child, but it would be surprising if the newborn would not have been immediately introduced to the gods, including prayers for divine protection. Moreover, the funerary reliefs show that the protective amulets were used by a number of the Palmyrene children. In many reliefs, amulets were carved hanging around the necks of some children who were already older, but still underage. In some cases, such amulets on Palmyrene children (on boys and at least once even on a girl) very closely resemble the Roman habit of underage children wearing the *bullae* (see fig. 3).[9] There is a nice example of

8. Dasen 2003.

9. See esp. Tanabe 1986, 405-415, pls. 374-383; Sadurska and Bounni 1994, 174-176, cat. no. 323, fig. 248. For other cases, see Tanabe 1986, 390, pl. 359 (a child with an amulet and a bird at his hand), 270-272, pls. 237-240, 313, pl. 282 (a young male person, holding a bird and having an amulet around his neck - the editor calls him 'young man', but the comparative evidence and the attributes here presented would point to an age below majority). See also Tanabe 1986, 308, pl. 277,

Fig. 3: A funerary bust of Zerbâ, son of ʻAteʻaqab, wearing a necklace with an amulet, and holding a bird in his hand. Palmyra Museum, Palmyra, inv. A 898, 200–273 CE (© Palmyra Portrait Project, Ingholt Archive at Ny Carlsberg Glyptotek, PS 1078).

this type of amulet/medallion also in one relief that unquestionably depicts an underage girl (without a veil, but with a dove and a branch of an olive tree in her hands).[10]

It has been claimed that the *bullae* that appear in some Palmyrene contexts indicate that the children in question would have had Roman citizenship.[11] However, we cannot make such an assumption; even if the funerary reliefs seem to have been a Roman medium, and therefore this iconography would probably have borrowed from the culture of the dominating power some of its forms of expression, the local priorities, as well as the local cultural connotations of the particular visual signs, might have been quite different. The identity expressed by means of specific attributes need not have had anything to do with any 'original' meaning these symbols would have had in Roman - or in other Mediterranean - contexts *per se*.[12] It is indeed true that the use and shape of the pendants, appearing often with Roman-style clothing, would point towards a Roman cultural influence and seemingly be connected with the relatively high social status of those (young) people who wear these amulets; many of the children depicted with an amulet (but not all) seem to be connected with priestly families. Moreover, in the context of the Roman culture, the implication would have been that the children who had *bullae* would surely have been freeborn, and therefore also having the citizenship. However, especially as we have no independent (literary) sources about how this issue was understood in Palmyra, we cannot make the conceptual leap to claim the *bullae* would necessarily indicate citizenship of Rome, instead of having, for example, a connotation with only the local Palmyrene citizenship. After all, it was a commonplace all over the Mediterranean cultures in the Roman world for children to have protective amulets. Nevertheless, the visual similarities between the Palmyrene medallions worn by children and the Roman *bulla* are indeed striking. It seems reasonable to assume that those families who had adopted this feature in their reliefs wanted by this usage to point out their, and especially their children's, belonging to the

404–406, pls. 435–437, although the picture in these cases is not clear enough here to make firm conclusion about what (if anything) is actually hanging around the neck.

10. Tanabe 1986, 302, pl. 271; Sadurska and Bounni 1994, cat. no. 94, fig. 17. It must be pointed out that in Palmyra, some older females also seem to have carried a *bulla*-like medallion (e.g. Hvidberg-Hansen and Ploug 1993, no. 84, 87–88; Tanabe 1986, 382, pl. 351, 390, pl. 359), although the *lunula*-shaped pendants seem to have been more usual.

11. See Sadurska and Bounni 1994, 175 - as their reasoning does not necessarily hold true, their proposed date for the relief scene in question, which is derived from this reasoning with a terminus post quem set on 212 CE, is untenable.

12. See also Maura K. Heyn on the interpretation of gestures in these reliefs: the cultural connections of the (iconography of the) reliefs with Rome can be of help in unraveling their visual rhetoric, but 'it is not at all clear that the identity expressed with the hand gestures had anything to do with being Roman per se' (2010, 635). On the Hellenistic and local contexts and the Roman influences on Palmyrene funerary portraits, see Raja 2017b, esp. 322–325, 342–343.

Fig. 4: Loculus relief depicting Ḥertâ, daughter of ʿAqîbâ, wearing a necklace with a crescent shaped amulet. Ny Carlsberg Glyptotek, Copenhagen, inv. IN 1058, 200-273 CE (Courtesy of Ny Carlsberg Glyptotek, photo by Palmyra Portrait Project).

empire-wide cultural elites - after all, as observed above, a striking number of the males with *bulla*-shaped pendants belong to priestly families.

In the visual evidence from Palmyra, there appears no unambiguous case of a *lunula* with an underage girl, although it seems that in many reliefs adult women appear (or, women who wear a veil, which would signify a married status) with pendants which clearly resemble the *lunulae* we see in sources from other places in the Roman world (see fig. 2b and fig. 4). In some cases, ring-shaped pendants also appear, which could depict those kinds of *lunulae*, again quite common across the Roman world, in which the horns of the crescent moon turn very near to or even touch each other. It would be tempting to claim that these kinds of *lunula*-shaped amulets, with the association to the moon, would have been used to mark an association with lunar goddesses and the menarche and thus with adulthood.[13] This conclusion, however, is bound to remain speculative.

Shrines and votive gifts

It is clear that families in the Roman world invested much of their time and resources in protecting children. In case of illness, families would visit shrines of the local healing deities with their sick children in seek of a cure. Children's health was often a reason for votive gifts, and children appear along with their parents both as votive dedicators themselves and as worshippers of divinities. Pausanias, for example, notes in passing that little children are cured in the temple by the springs of the river Pamisos in the Peloponnese.[14] It is curious, however, that while we see research into these phenomena both from Classical Greek and from Late Antique Christian contexts, this practice has not been systematically studied in connection to the Roman Empire.[15] In any case, however, we may plausibly assume that children frequented shrines with their parents and other relatives all around the Roman world.

I have not been able to find any examples of religious euergetism in Palmyra with underage individuals being active themselves. However, a reference to children is included as a standard feature in the euergetic inscriptions. In some bilingual texts, the Greek word used is *tekna*: children. While the Aramaic word

13. For *lunulae*, see Dasen 2003, pl. 4; 2015, 304-305 with figs. 8 and 9. For ring/*lunula*-shaped pendants in Palmyrene material worn by (adult) women, see e.g. Sadurska and Bounni 1994, figs. 158-161, 180, 185, 187-188, 200-204; Tanabe 1986, 387, 392-393 pls. 356, 361-362. See also Tanabe 1986, 424-426, pls. 393-395, with a ring/*lunula*-shaped pendant around the neck of both a mother and her adult daughter in a banquet relief dated to 238/9 CE.

14. See Pausanias 4.31.4. On the Hellenistic temple there, see Luraghi 2008, 120-121.

15. For shrines, votive gifts and healing, see e.g. Lawton 2007; Holman 2009. For votive gifts for children's health, see e.g. Aldhouse-Green 1999; Hughes 2017, 109-11, 153, 166, 180-181. For dedications with children included, see e.g. Schultz 2006, 52; Vuolanto 2002.

Fig. 5: An altar with a woman and her child. Ny Carlsberg Glyptotek, Copenhagen, inv. IN 1080, 230–250 CE (Courtesy of Ny Carlsberg Glyptotek, photo by Ana Cecilia Gonzales).

used here, *bny*, would refer more particularly to sons, it was also used simply to refer to children of both sexes in general. These children might, of course, be already adults at the time of making the donation in question. Sometimes, however, we can identify the child in question as very probably a minor. There is a Palmyrene altar now in Ny Carlsberg Glyptotek, with a relief of a woman and a child, with the text stating that a mother had donated it 'for the life of her son', either to urge the gods to heal the child, or, more probably, as an ex-voto gift after this had happened (see fig. 5).[16] Thus, at least some children would have been included in the protective sphere of this kind of donations and inscriptions, linking them intimately with the deities in question.

Naturally, there was also another motivation at play here, as can be seen in foundation inscriptions belonging to the funerary monuments in the city, which record that the buildings were explicitly meant for the use of one's own offspring. The donations celebrated by inscriptions 'would immortalize the donators and whomever they wished to include, and to make their links with the deities in question public and remembered'. Whether the children mentioned were minors or already adults, to mention them would not only ensure one's own memory, but also boast the continuity of the lineage as far as possible. This kind of thinking seems to have been shared in many places in the Roman world.[17] Moreover, a vow fulfilled was also a matter to be proclaimed openly for the whole community to see: a votive gift made publicly visible was a striking proclamation of closeness to the divine realm, and as such, a continuing source of social capital also for the next generations.

16. Ny Carlsberg Glyptotek, Copenhagen, inv. IN 1080, with an inscription: '*lbryk šmh l'lm' 'bd[t] / [r]mlh' whrmz 'l ḥy' brh*' ('For He whose name is blessed in eternity made by [R]mallhâ and Hurmuz (this altar) for the life of her son'), see Hvidberg-Hansen and Ploug 1993, 160, no. 129; Hillers and Cussini 1996, PAT 0420. See also an altar in Palmyra Museum, Palmyra, inv. A 1121: '*'bd wmwd' / lgd' dy gn / y' wl'rṣw / wrḥm / yrḥbwl' br / '[.]b' bn' / wb'lw / brh*' ('Offered in this thanksgiving, to the god of the garden, and to Arsû, and Rahîm, Yarḥibolâ son of, [...]bâ Bana, and Ba'lo, his son'), see Tanabe 1986, 265, pl. 132; Hillers and Cussini 1996, PAT 1621. For further examples, see Smith 2013, 64, 90, 171; Dirven 1999, 202–203. For Palmyrene epigraphy in general, and the use of the concept *bny*, see Yon 2002, especially ch. 5, par. 63.

17. Quoted from Kaizer 2011, 451. See also Krag 2015. For a similar habit of including one's family in the donations, often anonymously, see Vuolanto 2002, on the Jewish and slightly later Christian usages (drawing their origin, in fact, from the Syro-Palestinian area).

Family festivals and rites of passage

In the Greco-Roman world, children would have had a participatory and assisting role in the family cult, especially in the habitual sacrifices to the various family gods and in the sacrifices related to eating together. Children could also take a more active part in these occasions, as with the Roman harvest celebrations, or with their own birthdays. Moreover, children's presence in various religious family gatherings, as in marriage ceremonies and in funerals, was taken for granted, and they would have had ritual tasks on these occasions. The family as such was a religious unit. It was important that proper religious practices and family traditions with a certain family identity were transmitted from one generation to the next.[18]

Children's own agency was most pronounced in the various rituals, processions and sacrifices dealing with their coming of age, all according to the local practices. For girls, marriage itself often marked this stage, and no separate rituals for reaching the adulthood were celebrated; for boys, the local conventions and rituals varied more. Often, however, these took place when the boys had passed their fourteenth or sixteenth birthday, depending on the cultural background, even if often the actual physiological reaching of puberty seems to have been more significant than any specific age in years. Both marriage and these male rituals for reaching adulthood often had both a public and a more private component.[19]

Unfortunately, we have no specific information about children's roles in domestic religious settings or during family gatherings in Palmyra. Nor do we have any information about any rites of passage children might have gone through to reach adulthood. Nevertheless, it is worth noting that the striking difference in the ways in which 'girls' on the one hand and 'married women' on the other hand were represented in the Palmyrene sculpture might reflect some specific rituals of passage during the wedding ceremonies, or linked to them.[20] The continuity of the family cult was wholly dependent on the next generation's learning them early enough by heart, a need accentuated by the high mortality rate. Family groups, each with its own set of deities and cults, would have needed to teach children the proper cultic action effectively, through practice and participation, while they were still young.[21]

Children in civic religion

In Greco-Roman public life in the local communities, children regularly took part in religious processions and public festivals in honour of various deities as participants and spectators with their families. Moreover, children often had assisting roles in these rituals. In the Greek and Hellenistic world, girls had a special role in many festival processions as *kanephoroi* ('basket-bearers') and as tray-bearers in more ordinary sacrifices. Similarly, boys had assisting roles, especially in animal sacrifices. There were also some special tasks for children in various festivities, which would take them to the fore, like those of 'a child of the hearth' of the Eleusinian mysteries - and some children could become initiates there too.[22] In the Roman world, children were active especially in special events in connection with the state cult, such as the Secular Games, Troy Games and triumphs.[23] Even more generally, in the Roman cultural sphere, the presence of *camilli* and *camillae*, young prepubescent assistants, was a visible part of any sacrificial ritual. They carried vessels and utensils at sacrifices, processions and weddings.[24] Moreover, in the Greek and the Roman world, older children also had important roles in public religious practices as members of the choirs.[25]

Likewise, in Palmyrene iconographical sources at-

18. Mantle 2002, 99-102; Rawson 2003, 212-215, 336-339; Vuolanto 2010, 138-139.
19. Parkin 2010, 102-104; Harlow and Laurence 2002, 13-19, 67.
20. For (unveiled) women and adolescent representation in Palmyrene visual sources, see Cussini 2000.
21. Palmyra is a case in point in this sense: see e.g. Kaizer 2011, 451; with Dirven 1999, 43-47, 62-63, 77, 169-170.
22. Golden 2015, 35-43; Dillon 2002, 92-93.
23. Rawson 2003, 311- 328.
24. Mantle 2002, 91-99.
25. For choirs, see Mackey 2017; Mantle 2002, 86-91.

Fig. 6: Sarcophagus depicting a reclining priest, a seated woman and two smaller priests standing behind the reclining male. National Museum of Damascus, Damascus, hypogeum of Yarḥaî, 237–255 CE (© Palmyra Portrait Project, Ingholt Archive at Ny Carlsberg Glyptotek, PS 891).

tendants appear, assisting in solemn sacrifice scenes in the same manner as in other parts of the Roman Empire. Some earlier scholars have identified these as 'servants',[26] but this designation alone fails to do full justice to their presence: the fact that these attendants are included in this kind of depictions, which certainly do not aim at a realistic portrayal of the situation as such, points to their importance, even if they were subordinated hierarchically to the main characters, namely, the gods and the devotees who offered the sacrifice. These small figures are sometimes named and, indeed, in one of the Palmyrene frescoes from Dura Europos, one of these characters is identified as a son of the main person offering the sacrifice.[27] It is indeed true that hierarchical scaling sometimes makes it hard to spot whether the small figures in visual representations actually denote (underage) children. Even adult children are often depicted as significantly smaller than their parents; younger children are depicted much smaller than their older brothers and sisters, regardless of their actual age and age difference; and servants and slaves are depicted in many contexts as smaller that their masters. One needs extra clues to identify someone as an underage child, such as texts, proportions of various body parts, clothes, toys or gestures.[28] Here, however, in the context of sacrificing, even if these attendants did not need to be of elite status, nor even always free, it is indeed most probable that they were underage children.

Moreover, in some Palmyrene funerary reliefs, children are prominently depicted with references to assisting (religious) roles, with boys often depicted as having small jugs (used in sacrifices) in their hands. This may have been a visual allusion to their tasks in the Palmyrene religious life in general, but this could also have something to do with their specific tasks within the funeral rituals more specifically.[29] In any

26. See e.g. Dirven 1999, 315–318.

27. For Iabsumsos, the councillor, with his son Abdaates, see Dirven 1999, 296–302, fig. XII and SEG II 778. See also Dirven 1999, 292–293, fig. XI (TEAD VI 147–151) (where 'a beardless youth (boy) wearing a dark green chiton that reaches to his knees is standing. In his outstretched hand he holds a bowl of wine, in his left he carries a ladle') and 315–318, fig. XIV (TEAD V 153–156): '[…] left of a sacrificant a boy holding a palm branch in his right, and a box in his left hand advances to the right […]'.

28. See e.g. Mander 2013, 19–27 on identifying children and assigning them ages.

29. See esp. a funerary banquet scene in Sadurska and Bounni 1994, cat. no. 232, fig. 248, and fig. 6 above. See also Tanabe

case, this is a clear reference to the religious sphere and cultic life, even if the reference could be to more private religious practices here, rather than to the civic religion in the strict sense. Likewise, in some Palmyrene reliefs, youngsters are depicted as if garlanding the deceased, it is, however, hard to say if the laurel garlands are used as symbols of fruitfulness and honour (along with grapes), or if they also refer to some real-life rituals linked, perhaps, with funerals or commemoration.[30]

In several Roman cults, too, children had a special visibility, since underage girls and boys who had not yet reached their puberty were directly charged with different priestly functions. This regularly happened with the Vestal virgins, who had to be recruited at the age between six and ten, and with the selected boy attendants who were present at the meetings of the priesthood of the Arval brothers in Rome. There is also, for example, evidence of a priestess of Diana from Tusculum who was under the age of seven. Moreover, in many local cults, the highest elite used the priesthoods to promote the early civic careers of their sons, like a certain Thrason from Stratonikeia in Western Anatolia, who claims among his other civic and religious duties to have served as a 'high priest' at the age of ten.[31] It was, indeed, common, above all among the local elites, that the children would follow their parents both in continuing the family cult and in continuing the official public religious roles their parents had had.

In the Roman world as a whole, religious contexts were a central way for children to appear in public. Children participated in religious life as full members of the community, in many cases having a mediating role for divination and insight between our world and the world of the gods, a role that was open for both girls and boys, acting on behalf of a certain social group, whether a family, a neighborhood or a polis.[32]

In the case of Palmyra, inscriptions very seldom give any specific information about an individual career or public duties, and therefore we have very little information about priestly offices.[33] For the Palmyrene children, we have nothing written down on these matters. We have no information about underage persons who held priesthoods, but there are some indications that priesthood could have run in the family. In one relief, for example, which depicts a man, his son and a third person who seems to have been a grandson of the first-mentioned, they all wear the Palmyrene priestly hat.[34] This does not mean that priesthood as such would be hereditary, but it could imply a kind of apprenticeship, in which the younger generation would learn the necessary ritual skills from the previous one.

In one of the funerary banquet reliefs, moreover, we may encounter an underage priest.[35] The deceased reclines on a *triclinium*, and wears a Palmyrene priestly hat, with a woman (his spouse) sitting on a chair near his feet, and three smaller figures standing behind the

1986, 462–463, pls. 435–436, and Sadurska and Bounni 1994, cat. no. 193, fig. 253 with a youth offering a priestly hat to a reclining man with a bowl, with jugs as ritual utensils in Palmyra in Raja 2015, 341. Indeed, jugs (or bowls) on their own do not seem to refer to a priestly status of the individuals depicted (see e.g. Tanabe 1986, 221–226, pls. 188–193; Sadurska and Bounni 1994, cat. no. 231, fig. 237, cat. nos. 13–14, 121, 195, 232–234, figs. 246–252. In this connection, it is maybe necessary to comment on the issue of Palmyrene 'sacred banquets' with texts referring to 'the sons of X'. I agree with Ted Kaizer (2008, 187–188) that, most probably, these texts do not refer to the inclusion of the relatives of the person who paid for the banquet, since it was common to use kinship terms to refer to the members of the cult group or a professional community all around the Greco-Roman world. Thus, we have no evidence that children would have been included in the dining companies or *marzeah* confraternities.

30. See e.g. Tanabe 1985, 262, 264, pls. 229, 231 (with a son (?) of the deceased about to garland his father), 206, pl. 173 (a youngster about to garland his father).

31. Thrason I Stratonikeia 667, with Laes 2011, 179. For other cases of imperial and local elite children, see Laes 2011, 169, 181. See Rawson (2003, 324, 327) for the priestess from Tusculum, and for the boy attendants of the Arvals. For Vestals, see Mustakallio 2007.

32. Further, see Vuolanto 2010, 147–151.

33. Raja 2015, 340.

34. Tanabe 1986, 206, pl. 173. See also Raja 2017a on priestly families.

35. Tanabe 1986, 441–446, pls. 410–415.

reclining figure, who are presumably the children of the deceased person. Of these, the one on the extreme right, a man with a priestly hat, appears without any further attributes; the male figure in the middle wears a standard priestly hat and is holding an animal on his palm, seemingly a bird.[36] The third of the standing figures, on the left, is clearly in the hierarchically lowest position of the scene, at the feet of the deceased, and somewhat behind the female figure, who is presumably her mother. She is depicted as an adolescent girl, with a medallion pendant of the ring/*bulla* type around her neck, and as if drawing the folds of her tunica so that special attention is paid to the pendant.[37] As we seem to have here in the middle an individual with both a priestly hat and the attribute for children, a bird, one could make a strong case that it would have been possible to become a priest even before majority. However, it is also possible that the scene represents more the hopes for the future than the actual situation, symbolizing the potential of the next generation in an elite family: the girl as a future bride under protection of the gods, and the boy as a future priest in the manner of his brother and father.[38] In any case, however, this funerary banquet scene would introduce a family strongly linked with the elite aspirations and priestly activities in Palmyra through a number of family members in at least two generations. The scene directs the viewers' gaze to the future of the household, and toward the hope that the next generation gives to the family.

Before proceeding to conclusions, we need to point out one special feature or, rather, a striking absence in the Palmyrene evidence. Not one single girl, or even adult woman for that matter, with any official connection to religious practices can be traced in the material: no priestesses, no girls helping with the sacrifices, nothing to do with female religious professionals.[39] Naturally, with evidence like this, any argument from silence certainly cannot be taken as conclusive. We have, for example, no information about choirs, and almost nothing about rituals connected with festivals – and it is hard to believe that such features of religious life, which elsewhere included female visibility, would have been unknown in Palmyra.

Conclusions

In the Roman world in general, religion embraced all aspects of family and communal life: it became a key feature in the growing-up processes of a child and in the children's integration into the life of the local community. Religious socialization took place in family settings in the context of the more or less private rituals, and in the more public sphere in the various festivals, sacrifices and feasts. During the life of an individual child, various rituals marking the transitions from one life stage to another would have been the most significant events. In connection with the public rituals, the tasks reserved for children were limited to the well-born, but participation in public festivals, domestic cults and prayer, together with the ubiquity of shrines and temples, ensured the religious framework for everyday experience for all children. Religion created the sense of belonging through participation: religious practices lay at the heart of the sense of identity and adherence to certain family tradition. Through them, children were socialized into the duties and the roles proper to one's social status and gender.

In general, children's religious activities can be categorized into three groups: first, cultic practices in which children themselves played the major role.

36. A bird would be a logical alternative, but the animal in the pictures looks a bit like a miniature ram (see Tanabe 1986, 445, pl. 414); one would have to see the original relief to clarify this issue.

37. See Tanabe 1986, 446, pl. 415. On other 'adolescent' unveiled females with different hairstyles, see also Cussini 2000 and Krag 2016.

38. I owe this (latter) remark to Signe Krag.

39. What we do have, is information about adult women dedicating altars and participating in sacrifices (but without actively sacrificing). Finlayson (2013) highlights the women's active participation in the religious sphere in Palmyra (see also Cussini 2005) – but if seen in the wider Syrian (or Roman) context, the information we have about women's religious activities in Palmyra is indeed quite limited in scale, as Yon (2016) stresses.

These mostly concerned their own transition from one life stage to another. There are few traces of these in Palmyra, although it might have been possible that some boys had priestly functions to perform. Second, we have those instances in which children had special religious tasks, like an assisting role in sacrifice, or acting as a tool for some sort of divine revelation. For this latter type of activities, there are no clear indications from Palmyra. However, this does not mean that no such activities took place. It seems, in any case, that the presence of boys or young men, helping at the altar with the offering, occurred in Palmyra in a way similar to that in many other places around the Roman Empire. Third, those religious practices in which children had no specified active role themselves, but were present as members of a certain group of devotees or spectators. For these, we have, again, little information from Palmyra, but we need not assume that they would have been excluded from the public religious life of the community. In addition, the Palmyrene children were also included in the religious networks and the world of gods through prayers, protective amulets and votive offerings.

Unfortunately, we can say only a little about the role of children in the religious life of Palmyra, and about the role of religion in the socialization process of children there. Much is beyond our knowledge; or at least, we have no explicit evidence. There is basically no information about rituals at birth or during infancy, or passages to adulthood, there seem to be no named children among the religious donations and nothing can be said about possible changes over the course of time. But, perhaps with the exception of the lack of information about female religious duties (especially with regard to girls, although there is very little on women of any age group),[40] there is nothing to suggest that Palmyra would have been a special case when we search for the religious life of children. Children were included in the protective sphere of the gods both in an abstract and in a concrete sense; they seem to have been integrated early on into the religious roles their family and the community expected from them; and they had some, even if very restricted roles in cult life, at least as assistants in sacrifices and probably also in religious rituals in the households. We may assume that children were included as ordinary participants and spectators in major civic religious festivals in a similar manner to adult citizens. As far as we can say, the Palmyrene children were integrated into the religious life of the community in a manner similar to children of other local communities in the Roman Empire.

40. Even here, there are some comparative examples from the ancient world, like the Jewish practices, which are geographically not very far away.

Bibliography

Aldhouse-Green, M. 1999, *Pilgrims in Stone. Stone images from the Gallo-Roman sanctuary of Fontes Sequanae*, Oxford.

Cussini, E. 2005, Beyond the Spindle: Investigating the Role of Palmyrene Women, in E. Cussini (ed.), *A Journey to Palmyra: Collected Essays to Remember Delbert R. Hillers*, Leiden and Boston, 26-43.

Cussini, E. 2000, Palmyrene Eunuchs? Two Cases of Mistaken Identity, in E. Rova (ed.), *Patavina orientalia selecta*, 279-290.

Dasen, V. 2015, *Le Sourire d'Omphale: Maternité et petite enfance dans l'Antiquité*, Rennes.

Dasen, V. 2003, Les amulettes d'enfants dans le monde gréco-romain, *Latomus* 62, 275-289.

Dillon, M. 2002, *Girls and Women in Classical Greek Religion*, New York.

Dirven, L. 1999, *The Palmyrenes of Dura-Europos: A Study of Religious Interaction in Roman Syria*, Leiden, Boston and Cologne.

Finlayson, G. 2013, New perspectives on the ritual and cultic importance of women at Palmyra and Dura Europos: processions and temples, *Studia Palmyreńskie* 12, 61-85.

Garland, R. 2013, Children in Athenian Religion, in J. Evans Grubbs, T. Parkin and R. Bell (eds.), *The Oxford Handbook of Childhood and Education in the Classical World*, Oxford and New York, 207-226.

Golden, M. 2015, *Children and Childhood in Classical Athens*, second edition, Baltimore.

Hänninen, M.-L. 2005, From Womb to Family: Rituals and Social Conventions Connected to Roman Birth, in K. Mustakallio, J. Hanska, M.-L. Sainio and V. Vuolanto (eds.), *Hoping for Continuity: Childhood, Education and Death in Antiquity and the Middle Ages*, Rome, 49-60.

Harlow, M. and R. Laurence 2002, *Growing up and growing old in ancient Rome: A life course approach*, London and New York.

Heyn, M. K. 2010, Gesture and Identity in the Funerary Art of Palmyra, *AJA* 114, 4, 631-661.

Hillers, D. R. and E. Cussini 1996, *Palmyrene Aramaic Texts*, Baltimore.

Holman, S. R. 2009, Sick Children and Healing Saints: Medical Treatment of the Child in Christian Antiquity, in C. B. Horn and R. R. Phenix (eds.), *Children in Late Ancient Christianity*, Tübingen, 143-170.

Hughes, J. 2017, *Votive Body Parts in Greek and Roman Religion*, Cambridge.

Hvidberg-Hansen, F. O. and G. Ploug 1993, *Katalog: Palmyra samlingen, Ny Carlsberg Glyptotek*, Copenhagen.

Johnston, S. I. 2001, Charming Children: The Use of the Child in Ancient Divination, *Arethusa* 34, 1, 97-117.

Kaizer, T. (ed.), 2016, *Religion, Society and Culture at Dura-Europos*, Cambridge and New York.

Kaizer, T. 2011, Religion in the Roman East, in J. Rüpke (ed.), *A Companion to Roman Religion*, Oxford, 446-456.

Kaizer, T. 2008, Man and god at Palmyra: Sacrifice, *Lectisternia* and Banquets, in T. Kaizer (ed.), *The Variety of Local Religious Life in the Near East: In the Hellenistic and Roman Periods*, Leiden and Boston, 179-191.

Kaizer, T. 2002, *The Religious Life of Palmyra: A Study of the Social Patterns of Worship in the Roman Period*, Stuttgart.

Katajala-Peltomaa, S. and V. Vuolanto 2011, Children and Agency: Religion as Socialisation in Late Antiquity and the Late Medieval West, *Childhood in the Past* 4, 1, 79-99.

Krag, S. 2016, Females in Group Portraits in Palmyra, in A. Kropp and R. Raja (eds.), *The World of Palmyra*, Palmyrene Studies 1, Copenhagen, 180-193.

Krag, S. 2015, The Secrets of the Funerary Buildings in Palmyra during the Roman Period, in E. Mortensen and S. G. Saxkjær (eds.), *Revealing and Concealing in Antiquity: Textual and Archaeological Approaches to Secrecy*, Aarhus, 105-118.

Laes, C. 2011, *Children in the Roman Empire: Outsiders Within*, Cambridge.

Lawton, C. L. 2007, Children in Classical Attic Votive Reliefs, in J. Neils and J. H. Oakley (eds.), *Coming of Age in Ancient Greece: Images of Childhood from the Classical Past*, New Haven and London, 41-60.

Luraghi, N. 2008, *The Ancient Messenians: Constructions of Ethnicity and Memory*, Cambridge.

Mackey, J. L. 2017, Roman Children as Religious Agents: The Cognitive Foundations of Cult, in C. Laes and V. Vuolanto (eds.), *Children and Everyday Life in the Roman and Late Antique World*, London and New York, 179-197.

Mander, J. 2013, *Portraits of Children on Roman Funerary Monuments*, Cambridge and New York.

Mantle, I. C. 2002, The Roles of Children in Roman Religion, *GaR* 49, 1, 85-106.

Mustakallio, K. 2007, The Changing Role of the Vestal Virgins, in L. L. Lovén and A. Strömberg (eds.), *Public Roles and Personal Status: Men and Women in Antiquity, Proceedings of the Third Nordic Symposium on Gender and Women's History*, Sävedalen, 185-203.

Neils, J. 2003, Children and Greek religion, in J. Neils and J. H. Oakley (eds.), *Coming of Age in Ancient Greece: Images of Childhood from the Classical Past*, New Haven and London, 7-12.

Parkin, T. 2010, Life Cycle, in M. Harlow and R. Laurence (eds.), *A Cultural History of Childhood and the Family, vol. 1: Antiquity*, Oxford, 97-114, 199-201.

Prescendi, F. 2010, Children and the Transmission of Religious Knowledge, in V. Dasen and T. Späth (eds.), *Children, Memory, and Family Identity in Roman Culture*, Oxford and New York, 73-93.

Raja, R. 2017a, Networking beyond death: Priests and their family networks in Palmyra explored through the funerary sculpture, in H. F. Teigen and E. H. Seland (eds.), *Sinews of Empire: Networks in the Roman Near East and Beyond*, Oxford, 121-135.

Raja, R. 2017b, Powerful images of the Deceased: Palmyrene funerary portrait culture between Local, Greek and Roman Representations, in D. Boschung and F. Queyrel (eds.), *Bilder der Macht. Das griechische Porträt und seine Verwendung in der antiken Welt*, Paderborn, 319-348.

Raja, R. 2015, Palmyrene Funerary Portrait in Context: Portrait Habit Between Local Traditions and Imperial Trends, in J. Fejfer, M. Moltesen and A. Rathje (eds.), *Tradition: Transmisson of Culture in the Ancient World*, Copenhagen, 329-361.

Rawson, B. 2003, *Children and Childhood in Roman Italy*, Oxford.

Sadurska, A. and A. Bounni 1994, *Les sculptures funéraires de Palmyre*, Rome.

Schultz, C. E. 2006, *Women's Religious Activity in the Roman Republic*, Chapel Hill.

Smith, A. M. 2013, *Roman Palmyra: Identity, Community and State Formation*, Oxford.

Tanabe, K. 1986, *Sculptures of Palmyra I*, Tokyo.

Tulloch, J. H. 2012, Visual Representations of Children and

Ritual in the Early Roman Empire, *Studies in Religion/Sciences Religieuses* 41, 3, 408–438.

Vuolanto, V. 2014, Children in the Roman World: Cultural and Social Perspectives, A Review Article, *Arctos* 48, 435–450.

Vuolanto, V. 2010, Faith and Religion, in M. Harlow and R. Laurence (eds.), *A Cultural History of Childhood and the Family in Antiquity*, vol. I, Oxford, 133–151, 203–206.

Vuolanto, V. 2002, Male and Female Euergetism in Late Antiquity: A Study on Italian and Adriatic Church Floor Mosaics, in P. Setälä, R. Berg, R. Hälikkä, J. Pölönen and V. Vuolanto (eds.), *Women, Wealth and Power in the Roman Empire*, Rome, 245–302.

Yon, J.-B. 2016, Women and the Religious Life of Dura-Europos, in T. Kaizer (ed.), *Religion, Society and Culture at Dura-Europos*, Cambridge and New York, 99–113.

Yon, J.-B. 2002, *Les notables de Palmyre,* Beirut.

List of contributors

Nathanael J. Andrade
Binghamton University (SUNY)
Binghamton, NY 13902 USA
nandrade@binghamton.edu

Mary T. Boatwright
Department of Classical Studies
Duke University
Box 90103
Durham, NC 27705 USA
tboat@duke.edu

Eleonora Cussini
Department of Studies on Asian and Mediterranean Africa (DSAAM)
Università Ca' Foscari
30123 Venezia Italy
cussini@unive.it

Agnes Henning
Winckelmann-Institut
Humboldt-Universität zu Berlin
Unter den Linden 6
10099 Berlin Germany
Agnes.Henning@hu-berlin.de

Ted Kaizer
Department of Classics and Ancient History
Durham University
DH1 3LE Durham, England
ted.kaizer@durham.ac.uk

Sanne Klaver
Bushuis/Oost-Indisch Huis
Kloveniersburgwal 48
1012 CX Amsterdam Netherlands
s.f.klaver@uva.nl
sfklaver@hotmail.com

Signe Krag
Department of Classical Studies
Aarhus University
Jens Chr. Skous Vej 5, Building 1461, Office 318
8000 Aarhus C Denmark
signekrag@yahoo.dk

Rubina Raja
Department of Classical Studies
Aarhus University
Jens Chr. Skous Vej 5, Building 1461, Office 326
8000 Aarhus C Denmark
rubina.raja@cas.au.dk

Ville Vuolanto
History / Faculty of Social Sciences
University of Tampere
33014 Tampere Finland
ville.vuolanto@uta.fi

Abbreviations

Standard abbreviations according to American Journal of Archaeology along with other abbreviations below.

AA
: Archäologischer Anzeiger

AAS
: Les annales archéologiques de Syrie (1951–1965)

ActaArch
: Acta archaeologica (Copenhagen)

AJA
: American Journal of Archaeology

AJP
: American Journal of Philology

AKorrBl
: Archäologisches Korrespondenzblatt: Urgeschichte, Römerzeit, Frühmittelalter

ANRW
: Aufstieg und Niedergang der römischen Welt

ARAM periodicals
: ARAM Society for Syro-Mesopotamian Studies, Periodicals

ArcheologiaWar
: Archeologia: Rocznik Instytutu historii kultury materialnej Polskiej akademii nauk (Warsaw)

Arctos
: Arctos: Acta Philologica Fennica

BASOR
: Bulletin of the American Schools of Oriental Research

Berytus
: Berytus: Archaeological Studies

BMC Greek (Alexandria)
: R. S. Pool, *A Catalog of the Greek Coins in the British Museum, Alexandria* (London 1892)

BMusBeyr
: Bulletin du Musée de Beyrouth

BNF
: Bibliothèque nationale de France

Britannia
: Britannia: A Journal of Romano-British and Kindred Studies

Chiron
: Chiron: Mitteilungen der Kommission für alte Geschichte und Epigraphik des Deutschen Archäologischen Instituts

ClAnt
: Classical Antiquity

CIS
: J.-B. Chabot (ed.), *Corpus Inscriptionum Semiticarum. Pars secunda. Tomus III. Inscriptiones palmyrenae* (Paris 1926)

CR
: Classical Review

CRAI
: Comptes rendus des séances de l'Académie des inscriptions et belles-lettres (Paris)

CQ
: Classical Quarterly

DM
: Damaszener Mitteilungen

ÉtTrav
: Études et travaux: Studia i prace. Travaux du Centre d'archéologie méditerranéenne de l'Académie des sciences polonaise

FOS
: M. T. Raepsaet-Charlier, *Prosopographie des femmes de l'ordre senatorial (I–II siècles): Stemmata* (Louvain 1987)

FuB
: Forschungen und Berichte: Staatliche Museen zu Berlin

GaR
: Greece and Rome

Historia
: Historia: Zeitschrift für alte Geschichte

Historia Augusta
F. Paschoud, *Histoire Auguste, vol. 4.3: Vies des trente tyrans et de Claude* (Paris 2011)

IGLS XVII.1
J.-B, Yon, *Inscriptions grecques et latines de la Syrie, Tome 17, Fascicule 1: Palmyre* (Beirut 2012)

IGLSyr
L. Jalabert and R. Mouterde, *Inscriptions grecques et latines de la Syrie* (Paris 1929-[1986])

IGRR
R. Cagnat et al. (eds.) *Inscriptiones graecae ad romanas pertinentes* (Paris 1901–1927)

Inv. 1–12
J. Cantineau et al., *Inventaire des inscriptions de Palmyre*, vol. 1-12 (Beirut and Damascus 1930–1975)

Iraq
Iraq. Iraq, published by the British School of Archaeology in Iraq

JAOS
Journal of the American Oriental Society

JdI
Jahrbuch des Deutschen Archäologischen Instituts

JRA
Journal of Roman Archaeology

JRS
Journal of Roman Studies

JSav
Journal des savants

JSS
Journal of Semitic Studies

Klio
Klio: Beiträge zur alten Geschichte

KölnJb
Kölner Jahrbuch für Vor- und Frühgeschichte

Latomus
Latomus: Revue d'études latines

MélBeyrouth
Mélanges de l'Université Saint Joseph, Beyrouth

NC
Numismatic Chronicle

OGIS
W. Dittenberger (ed.), *Orientis graeci inscriptiones selectee*, 2 vols. (Hildesheim 1903–1905)

P. Oxy.
The Oxyrhynchus Papyri (London 1898-)

PAPS
Proceedings of the American Philosophical Society

PAT
D. R. Hillers and E. Cussini, *Palmyrene Aramaic Texts* (Baltimore 1996)

PBSR
Papers of the British School at Rome

Phoenix
Phoenix: The Classical Association of Canada

RALouvain
Revue des archéologues et historiens d'art de Louvain

RIC
H. Mattingly et al., *The Roman Imperial Coinage* (London 1923-)

RIN
Rivista italiana di numismatica e scienze affini

RM
Mitteilungen des Deutschen Archäologischen Instituts, Römische Abteilung

RTP
H. Ingholt et al., *Recueil des tessères de Palmyre* (Paris 1955)

Semitica
Semitica. Revue publiée par l'Institut d'études sémitiques du Collège de France

Strabo
S. Radt, *Strabons Geographika,* 10 vols. (Göttingen 2002-2011)

Syncellus
A. A. Mosshammer, *Ecloga chronographica* (Berlin 1984)

Syria
Syria: Revue d'art oriental et d'archéologie.

Zosimus
F. Paschoud, *Historie Nouvelle* (Paris 1971-1989)

ZPE
Zeitschrift für Papyrologie und Epigraphik

Subject index

Altar 13, 14, 68, 69, 72, 78, 82, 83, 88, 89, 90, 91, 105, 114, 115, 116, 158, 160, 162, 163-165, 178, 194, 206, 210, 211
Attribute:
bird 29, 202, 203, 204, 210
bup with two handles 161
dagger 117, 118, 176
drinking cup 72, 176
grapes 29, 202, 209
incense burner 161, 179
laurel garland 209
laurel wreath 88
libation jug 161
oak crown 176
priestly hat 97, 99, 101-151, 209-210
skyphos 13, 128
twig 13
Avia Augusti 196
Bani Komara, tribe of, *see* Benê Komarê, tribe of
Banot Mita 92
Banot 89, 92
Banquet 9, 21, 68, 86-87, 97, 178-179
Banquet, religious 13, 95, 97, 209
Banqueting couch, *see also* kline 99
Banqueting relief 21, 22, 31, 34, 35, 50, 52, 53, 71, 82, 97, 98, 99, 110-113, 125-127, 131, 184, 205, 209-210
Banqueting scenes 9, 11, 22, 28, 45, 48-49, 52, 61, 74-76, 84-87, 97, 98, 99, 100, 176-177, 208, 210
Banqueting tesserae, *see* tesserae
Belshuri family 41-42, 50, 54, 89
Benê Khônites, tribe of 158
Benê Komarê, tribe of 78, 159-160
Bene Mattabol 89
Benê Mazîn / Maziyan / Ma'ziyan tribe of89, 92, 159
Benê Mîtâ, tribe of 159
Bene Nurbel 89
Bene Taimarsu 88
Bny, *see also* tekna 26, 31, 90-92, 159, 160, 164, 205-206
Bulla 15, 203-205, 210
Burial practices 11, 14-15, 21-22, 23, 28-29, 34-36, 48-54, 68, 69, 73, 78-79, 80, 97-99, 171-178
Camel driver 161
Camel 87, 161
Camillus/a 207
Catuvellauni, tribe of 68
Census returns 187
Child of the hearth 207
Children:
as benefactors 205
imperial 191-192, 194-197
in civic sphere 12-15
in religious sphere 12-15, 83-84, 91-92, 164-165, 201-211
in scholarship 7, 8
in the funerary sphere 8-12, 28-29, 39-63, 69-74, 82-83, 95, 98, 172-173, 177-78, 186-187
representations 11-12, 29, 69, 71-74, 76-78, 82, 83, 95, 98, 124, 133-134, 143, 144, 145, 158, 172, 184, 186, 188, 191, 194-197, 202-206, 207-211
roles in society 12-13, 15, 25, 168, 186-187, 207-211
Chomarenoi, tribe of, *see* Benê Komarê, tribe of
Cloak, *see* clothes: mantle
Clothes:
Chiton 99, 208
Himation 69, 99, 115, 117, 120, 121, 122, 128, 129, 130, 131
Mantle 32, 88, 97, 117, 118, 160, 161, 162, 176, 177
Parthian-style 99, 118, 121, 129
Priestly attire 28, 84, 97
Toga 115, 116, 117, 177, 193
Trousers 118, 119, 121, 129, 176
Tunic/tunica 69, 97, 114, 115-116, 117, 118, 119, 120, 121, 122, 128, 129, 130, 131, 160, 161, 162, 174, 176, 177, 210
Veil 69, 73, 87-88, 115, 116, 120, 122, 128, 130, 131, 161-162, 177, 189-190, 193, 204, 205
Coinage:
minted in Rome 187, 190, 192, 196
of Zenobia 69, 189, 197
provincial 190, 191, 196
Colonia 185, 193
Confraternity 83
Cremation 174
Dedication, *see* religious reliefs
Dextrarum iunctio 36, 194
diis patriis, *see* to the Good gods
Donation 161, 162, 209, 214
Donkey 87, 161
Dorsalium, *see* hanging curtain
Double relief 74, 76

Dura Europos:
- House of the Banquet 84-86
- Sacrifice of Konōn 84
- Temple of Bel 84
- Temple of the Palmyrene Gods, *see* Dura Europos: Temple of Bel

Elahbel family 29-36, 89
Eleusinian Mysteries 207
Empress coin 193-196
Epicureans 192
Epigraphy:
- civic 7, 8, 12-13, 15, 88, 157-158, 173, 187, 189, 190-194
- funerary 7, 8-11, 12, 15, 24-29, 31, 38, 39-54, 55-63, 67-80, 82, 97, 101-105, 107-110, 113, 122, 124-126, 134, 137, 139-140, 142-148, 157-158, 168, 171-172, 173-174, 175, 178, 184, 186, 189
- military 194
- religious 7, 8, 12-14, 15, 82-84, 88-92, 106, 158-160, 163-165, 205-206, 209
- *see also* inscription, inscriptions

Epitaph 67-80, 186
Ethnonym 69
Euergetism 158-160, 208
Family:
- burial patterns 11, 34-35, 36, 48-54
- in civic sphere 8, 12-14, 160-169,
- in funerary sphere 7, 8-12, 24-36, 40-54, 67-80, 82, 95-100, 171-182
- imperial 190-200
- in religious sphere 8, 12-14, 82-92, 157-166, 205-211
- in Roman world 186-187
- in scholarship 7-8
- representations 7, 8-9, 11-12, 13, 21, 23, 26-36, 40-63, 67-68, 71, 74-80, 82-86, 88, 95-96, 98-100, 113-131, 176-177, 184, 185-186, 188-189, 206
- role in society 8, 15, 19, 89, 92, 99-100, 157-158, 165-166, 209-211
- wealthy 202

Fascina 203
Filiation, *see* lineage
Formula ʿlʾyy, *see* Inscriptions 'for the life of'
Freedman 45, 48-49, 59
Funeral 15, 78, 168, 171-179, 207, 208-209
Funerary buildings:
- cession 8, 11, 38, 39, 69, 71, 73, 78, 157, 174
- chronology 9
- foundation inscription 9-10, 23-29, 31, 38, 39, 45, 47, 71, 73, 78, 79, 96, 175, 206
- sale 13, 38, 69, 73, 79
- types 9, 19, 38-39, 175

Funerary:
- epigraphy 12, 14
- ritual 13, 77, 171-175, 208-209
- sculpture 7-8, 9-12, 13, 15, 19, 38-63, 67-68, 69-70, 71-72, 73-77, 79-80, 95-151, 157-158, 168, 171-173, 175, 209-211

Grandchildren 42, 45, 47-48, 71, 173
Grave goods 179
Hairstyles:
- imitation of imperial 190
- imperial 190
- uncovered 8, 205, 207, 210

Hanging curtain 71, 72, 73, 74
Haumal, clan 70
Headcloth, *see* headgear
Headdress, *see* headgear
Headgear 8, 84, 99, 114, 116, 128, 130, 131, 160, 176
Heiress 71
Household 86, 90, 92, 165, 172-173, 176-179, 186, 201, 202, 210, 211
In honorem domus divinae 194
Incense 84, 88, 158, 160-161, 177, 178, 179
Inhumation 174
Inscription:
- bilingual 23, 24-25, 28, 41, 63, 67, 68, 72, 78, 83, 86, 88-89, 91-92, 173-174
- Greek 69, 84, 85, 86, 90-92, 163, 188, 189
- Latin 89-90, 188
- Palmyrene Aramaic 23, 24-25, 31, 32, 54-63, 68-79, 82-85, 88-92, 101-110, 113, 122, 124-126, 134, 137, 139-140, 142-148, 159-160, 163-165, 173, 205-206

Inscriptions 'for the life of' 83-84, 90-92, 159, 163-165, 206
Inscriptions to the Good gods 89-90
Inscriptions, honorific, *see* civic
Ius italicum 185
Jewellery: 8, 11, 12, 72, 84, 157-158, 174, 177, 178, 194
- bracelet 69, 120, 179
- brooch 11, 69, 117, 121, 128, 129, 130
- earrings 115, 116, 128, 130, 179
- head-chain 116
- necklace 15, 69, 115, 116, 119, 120, 122, 179, 203, 204, 205
- pendant 8, 119, 120, 179, 203, 204, 205, 210
- ring 11, 36, 69, 179, 188, 203

Kanephoroi 207
King of kings / mlk mlk' 69, 78, 174
Kline 68, 71, 74, 75, 113-114, 120, 121, 127-128, 131, 140, 141, 176
Legatus 188
Legio X Fretensis 188

Libation 158, 161, 178
Lineage 13, 15, 24-32, 34, 38, 39-40, 48, 49, 54, 89, 206
Loculus: 22, 34, 48, 180
 bust relief 9, 12, 40, 41, 42, 45, 47, 49, 50, 51, 54-63, 101-105, 107-111, 124-125, 143, 205
 relief 23, 29, 34, 35, 36, 97-98, 99, 100, 177, 184, 197, 202
 shaft 22, 34
 slab 23, 74
 stelae 9, 12, 40, 41-42, 45, 47, 55, 58, 59, 61
Lunula 203, 204, 205
Marcomannic War 196
Marriage: 9, 11, 25, 29, 32, 36, 38, 40-41, 48-50, 54, 76-80, 92, 164-165, 192, 194-195, 207
 ceremony 194, 207
 customs 11
 Intermarriage 32, 36, 50, 54, 195
 remarriage: 50, 78, 80
 representation9-10, 19, 24-36, 48-52
marzeaḥ 79, 88, 209
Mater:
 Augusti et Caesaris 196
 Augusti 197
 Augustorum 196
 Caesaris 196
 Castrorum et Senatus et Patriae 196
 Castrorum 194, 196
 Senatus 194
Matertera 194
Mathabôl / Maththabôl / Matthabôl, tribe of 28, 160
Matrimony, *see* marriage 163
Matthabolios, tribe of, *see* Matthabôl, tribe of
Mother of the King 69, 78, 179
Motherhood, *see also* women as mothers8, 158
Mummification 174
Nuclear family 186, 196-197
Palmyra:
 and Rome, circulation of ideas 8, 15
 baths of the gods Aglibôl and Malakbel 158-159
 Efqa spring 159, 163
 funerary building, hypogeum 9, 10, 11, 19, 23, 28, 36, 38, 96, 139, 175, 211
 funerary building, temple tomb 9, 10, 19, 38, 39, 175-176
 funerary building, tower tomb 9, 10, 19-36, 38, 39, 73, 78, 96, 174, 175, 184
 Great Colonnade 160, 175
 hypogeum and Tower tomb of Yadi`bel 78
 hypogeum C 36
 hypogeum F 132, 133
 hypogeum of 'Alaine 135, 136
 hypogeum of Aqraban 148, 149
 hypogeum of Artaban 39, 46-48, 50, 61-63, 144
 hypogeum of Aštôr 28
 hypogeum of Atenatan 122, 179
 hypogeum of Bôlbarak 111, 113
 hypogeum of Bôlḥâ / Bolaha 39, 44-45, 48, 50, 52-53, 58-61, 73, 80, 145, 146
 hypogeum of Hatrai 127
 hypogeum of Hennibel 139
 hypogeum of Malkû 134, 149, 176
 hypogeum of Sasan/Sassan and Maṯṯtaî families 39, 40-44, 48, 49, 50, 54-58, 74
 hypogeum of Shalamallat 48, 70, 74, 108, 145, 149
 hypogeum of Ta'ai/ Taai 70, 82, 102, 137
 hypogeum of Taibol 145
 hypogeum of the Three Brothers 141
 hypogeum of Yarhai/Yarḥaî 136, 137, 208
 hypogeum of Zabd'ateh and Moqîmû 74, 144, 150
 middle class 14, 158, 165-166
 necropoleis 19, 23, 38, 82
 sack of 96
 temple 'of Nebu' 88, 89
 temple of Allat 82-83, 88, 89, 161
 temple of Baalshamin / Baal-Shamin / Baalshamîn 89, 124, 159, 176
 temple of Bel 84, 87, 158, 160, 161, 162, 163, 174, 188
 temple of Rabaseire 88
 temple tomb no. 174 141
 temple tomb no. 176 123
 temple tomb no. 186, "de l'aviation" 119, 135, 143
 temple tomb no. 36 113, 122, 123, 124, 127, 132, 133, 138, 149, 151, 175-176
 temple tomb no. 85b, tomb of A'ailamî and Zebidâ 103, 131, 149, 150
 temple tomb no. 86 175-176
 tower tomb no. 85d 138
 tower tomb of Nebuzabad 28
 tower tomb with hypogeum 78
 upper class 14, 79, 204
Papyri 187
Parapetasma, *see* hanging curtain
Pater familias 84, 194
Pater patriae 185, 194
Priest 11, 13, 28, 29, 57, 60, 62, 63, 68, 84, 86, 88, 95-100, 101-151, 160-161, 204, 209, 210
Priestess 13, 158, 165, 189, 191, 209, 210
Priesthood 13, 88-89, 95-99, 209
Priestly function 209, 211

Procession:
funerary 174
religious 14, 87-88, 95, 158, 160, 161-162, 165, 188, 189, 191, 207
Prostitutes 68, 71-72, 79
qubba 161
Religious:
reliefs 12-13, 14, 15, 74, 82-84, 87-88, 91, 92, 158, 159, 160-162, 165, 209
ritual 82-83, 191, 201, 202-203, 207, 209, 210, 211
Repatriation of remains 171
Roman Empire 8, 15, 89, 171-172, 186, 187, 188, 205, 208, 211
Rome:
Ara Pacis Augustae 203
Arch of Titus 192
Temple of Venus and Roma 194
Sacrifice 83, 84, 160-161, 163, 165, 177, 194, 202, 207-208, 210, 211
Sarcophagus of Bolbarak 177
Sculpture, process 32
Secular Games 207
Senator 88-89, 173
Senatus Consultum de Pisone patre 187, 192
Statue 9, 13, 14, 69, 70, 72, 73, 75, 79, 83-84, 88-89, 90, 92, 106, 157, 158, 159, 160, 172, 187, 188-190, 194
Stratègos 82
Tariff, *see* tax law
Tax law 68, 71-72, 170, 185, 187, 188
Tékna, *see also* children 205-206
Tessera 13, 68, 69, 79, 86, 97, 169, 176, 189, 194
Textiles 8, 174
Tray-bearers 207
Triumph 207
Troy Games 207
Vestal Virgin 209
Vidua, *see* widow
Vir clarissimus, *see* senator
Wall painting 9, 12, 13, 19, 21-22, 82, 84-87
Widow 73, 77, 91, 164, 173, 179
Women:
as cousins 32, 71
as daughters 12, 26, 27, 35, 36, 40-41, 49, 50, 54- 63, 67, 68, 69, 70, 71, 72, 73, 74, 76, 77, 78, 78, 80, 82, 84, 89, 91, 92, 96, 113, 126, 134, 137, 142, 144-147,157, 158-159, 160, 164, 165178, 194
as daughters-in-law 71, 134
as dedicators 73, 158-160, 163-165
as foster-mothers 77, 92, 171-172
as granddaughters 12, 71, 79
as mothers 12, 15, 52, 60-61, 69, 71, 74, 75, 76-78, 80, 91, 113, 144-147, 157, 194, 195, 197
as nieces 71, 79
as sisters 49, 71, 73, 79, 171
as tomb founders 9-10, 25, 171
as wives 25, 26, 27-29, 34, 35-36, 45, 49, 50, 52, 54-55, 58-59, 61, 63, 67, 68, 70-71, 72, 73, 74, 75, 76, 78, 79, 80, 91, 92, 96, 113, 126, 134, 137, 139, 142, 144-145, 147, 159, 160, 164, 177, 194
professions 12, 68-69
Zeitgesicht 187-188
πατρῷοις θεοῖς, *see* to the Good gods
Χήρα, *see* widow

Index of geographical places

Agrippinensium 193
Ana 82
Antinoopolis 193
Asia Minor 186
Athens 192
Bazuriyye 73
Beirut 67, 68, 69, 83
Dacia 89
Damascus 91, 157, 170
Deir ez Zor 157
Dura Europos 13, 69, 82, 84, 85, 157, 160, 175, 208
Egypt / Egyptian 69, 171, 187
Emesa 171
Euphrates 19, 85, 157
Faustinopolis 193
Gamla 82
Greece / Greek 69
Hadriana Palmyra, *see* Palmyra
Hatra 90
Hauran 171
Hierapolis 84
Italy 185, 186, 187, 194
Khirbet Semrine 82
Marciana Traiana Thamugadi 193
Nabatea / Nabataean 69, 90
Nazala 91
Numidia 193
Palmyra / Palmyrene(s) 7, 8, 9, 10, 11, 12, 13, 14, 15, 19, 22, 23, 31, 32, 36, 38, 41, 47, 48, 50, 54, 67, 68, 69, 79, 82, 83, 84, 85, 86, 88, 89, 90, 91, 92, 95, 96, 97, 98, 99, 100, 157, 158, 160, 161, 162, 163, 165, 166, 168, 169, 170, 171, 173, 174, 175, 176, 177, 178, 179, 184, 185, 187, 188, 189, 190, 194, 195, 197, 201, 202, 203, 204, 205, 207, 209, 210, 211
Palmyrena 82
Pamisos 205
Peloponnese 205
Pontus 171
Rome 15, 36, 83, 84, 91, 92, 184, 185, 186, 189, 190, 191, 193, 194, 195, 196, 197, 201, 203, 204, 209
Ruha / Ruhaean 69
Sarmizegetusa 89
Spain 186
Stratonikeia 209
Syria /Syrian 7, 83, 157, 158, 169, 171, 174, 175, 185
Tadmor / Tadmôr / Tadmorean 25, 27, 74, 75, 82, 91, 157, 170, 184
Thrace 193
Tibur 192
Tusculum 209
Western Anatolia 209

Index of personal names

Abdaates 208
'Abd'astôr 144
'Abd'ateh 78
Abday Zabdibol 82
'Abdelâ 62
Abdu 91
Abibiôn Nasraios, *see* Ḥabîbîôn Naṣraî
Addoudanos, *see* Haddûdan
'Agabâ 202
Aggodomos, *see* Aggudum
Aggudum 78
Agrippina 188, 190, 191, 192, 194
Ahiba 62
'Aḥitôr 101
Aieda'an 78
Akamat 77, 78
Akiba 71
'Alâ 51
'Alaisha 77
Alayyat 74
'Aliyat / Aliyyat 51, 52, 82
'Amaru 78
Amatâ / Amata 40-41, 42, 48, 49, 55, 56, 58, 69, 70, 134
Amataḥâ 27
Amatd'ateh 113
Amatnannaî 113
Amtallât / Amtallat 92, 159
'Anamu 69
Ananî 143
Ananidos 160
Annâ 107
Antonia 144, 192
Antoninus Pius 193, 194, 195
Aqamat 41, 50, 54-55
'Aqîbâ 205
Aqmê 41, 42, 50, 55, 60, 146, 172
Aqqamal 60, 146
'Argân / Argan 105, 164
Artaban / Artabanos 39, 46, 47-48, 61, 62, 63 144
Artaban Zabdûn 48, 62
Asoray 73
Aštôr 28
Atâ 113
'Ate'akab / 'Atê'aqab 70, 77, 78, 124, 204
'Ate'êm 142
'Atemâ / 'Atema 76, 147
'Atênûri 104
Atepanay 79
Attâ 59, 145, 159
Attaî 159
'Attarshuri 79
'Attay 71, 77, 78
Attéemm 159-160
Atthaias 78
Augustus 185, 189, 190, 191, 194
Aurelian 96, 171, 185, 197
Aušai 160
Azizu 82
Ba'adiyâ 45, 58, 59
Ba'alai / Ba'laî 71, 134
Ba'altagâ 47-48, 62
Babatâ 159
Ba'dâ 59, 146
Bagâš (Sagâš) 102
Bakray 79
Ba'lo / Balo 83, 206
Bana 83, 206
Barâ 50, 61, 144
Baraâ / Baraa 92, 159
Bar'ateh / Barate 45, 60, 70, 146, 148
Barates 68
Bar'ath 60
Barbarah 71, 134
Bare'a 73, 74
Barîkaî / Barikay 57, 72, 78, 142
Barîkaî Amrisha 142
Barnebû 148
Barqê 42, 58
Barûqâ 55, 56, 57
Bat-Abdai 45
Bat-Malê 41
Batmalku 70, 71
Batti 70
Be'eshegâ 145
Belaqab / Bel'aqab 25, 62, 91
Belhay 91

Bêlhazai / Belhazai / Belhazay 73, 92, 159
Belshûrî / Belshuri 41, 42, 48, 50, 54, 55, 57, 77, 89
Beltîḥan / Beltihan 34-35, 78, 79, 80
Berenike 40-41, 54
Berretâ 47, 50, 52, 61, 62, 144
Beththeis 160
Bithnanaia 84
Bogdan 101, 107
Bolaha 73, 78, 80
Bolaya 82
Bôlḥâ 44, 45, 48, 58, 59, 60, 61, 145, 146, 160
Bôlḥâ Nebôshûr 145
Bolhay 78
Bolhazay 71
Bolya 72, 73, 74
Bônnê / Bonnê 27, 137
Bonnur 78
Bonnuri 72-73
Boropa 69, 70, 72
Bôrrefâ 40, 113
Caracalla 185, 196, 197
Claudia 191, 193
Claudius 188, 190, 191
Commodus 194
Corbulo 59, 60, 61, 145
Dayyôn 71, 134
Dayyon, see Dayyôn
Diogenēs 84
Dionys 72, 78
Dionysios 172
'Divus Caesar' 191
Domitia 191, 192, 194, 203
Domitia Longina 188, 192
Domitian 188, 191, 192, 194
Drusilla 190, 191
Drusus 188, 191, 192
Edipus 73
Elabelos Barthe 160
Elagabalus 196, 197
ʾElâhbêl / ʾElâhbêl / Elahbêl / Elahbel 31, 32, 34, 89, 105, 110
Elahšâ 28
Elassas 28
Etnatan 92
Etpenîn 35
Faustina 190, 193, 194, 195
Firdushî (Paradasî) 126
Firmôn 158-159
Flavia Domitilla 192
Gaddâ 113
Gaddibol 76, 147
Gadîâ 124
Gaius Caligula 190, 191, 194
Gay 78
Germanicus 185, 188, 192, 194
Geta 196
Gnaeus Domitius Ahenobarbus 203
GRYMY 88
Habba 76
Habbata 73
Habbûla 103
Habîbîôn 48
Ḥabîbîôn Naṣraî 63
Hada 73
Haddûdan / Haddudan / Hadudan 27, 74, 89, 158, 159
Hadira 75
Hadîrat 34
Hadirat 79
Hadrian 185, 189, 192, 193, 194
Hagar 70
Ḥagegû 142
Haggâ 60, 146
Ḥaggagu 108
Haggat 78, 80
Haggay 74
Hagigu 75, 76
Haîdrâ 51-53
Ḥairân / Hairan 45, 58, 61, 71, 78, 126, 134, 173, 176
Hairan Hannate 71
Ḥalaphathâ 165
Ḥalaphtâ 57
Ḥalî 42, 49, 50, 54, 56
Halkash 73
Hanaina 73
Hanna 72
Harsha 73
Ḥashash 58
Ḥatrai 165
Haumal 70
Ḥennibel ʾAʿabî 126
Ḥennibelḥamṭûsh 139
Hermes 45, 48, 59
Herodian Hairan 171, 173, 174, 176
Ḥertâ 205
Hûrâ 59, 61, 146
Hurmuz 83, 206
Iabsumsos 208
Iamlichos, *see* Iamlikû

Iamlikû 24, 25, 35
Iarḥibôlê 109
Iedeibelos, *see* Yadi'bel
Imru 91
Jarhibôlâ 107
Julia 190
Julia Augusta, *see* Livia
Julia Aurelia Amata 71
Julia Domna 196, 197, 188
Julia Drusilla 191
Julia Maesa 196, 197, 188
Julia Mamaea 196, 197
Julia Soaemias 196, 197
Julia Titi 188, 192, 194
Julius Caesar 190
Kaisa 77
Kamnîn 47, 48, 63
Kephalon 74
Kîtôt / Kithôt 26, 27, 96
Konōn 84, 160
Lishamsh / Lišamš 26, 40, 91, 96, 126
Livia 188, 189, 190, 191, 192
Livilla 192
Lucilla 67, 68, 72, 195
Lysias 84
Ma'an 108
Ma'anay 79
Maflûn 42, 57
Mahuy 73
Maiša / Maisa / Maisha / Maîshâ 26, 78, 96
Makkai 164
Malaftâ 42, 49, 57, 58
Malakel 58
Malichos *see* Malkû
Malchusa 68
Malê / Male 42, 56, 57, 58, 71, 72, 76, 78, 82, 102, 143, 164
Malê Rabbâ 55
Malikû / Maliku 26, 31, 34, 72, 73, 75, 76, 78, 164
Malikû Attašuri 35
Malikû Obnît 25
Malkâ 140
Malkat 42, 56
Malkû / Malku 24, 40, 45, 48-49, 54, 55, 59, 60, 62, 63, 78, 79, 96, 126, 134, 139, 142, 143, 145, 146, 160, 172
Ma'nai Elahbel 31
Ma'nai 31, 34-35
Maqqaî / Maqqay 59, 82, 122, 145
Marciana 191, 192, 194
Marcus 74, 144
Marcus Aurelius 194, 195, 196,
Marcus Julius Maximus Aristeides 67-68, 69, 72
Mariôn 105
Mark Antony 185
Martâ 47, 62, 145
Martabû 144
Martî 147
Matidia 191, 192, 194
Mattâ 25
Maṭṭaî 40, 41, 42, 43, 54, 55
Mattanay 73, 78
Mazbê164
Meaiti 91
Mertabû 61
Mîkâ 25
Milonia Caesonia 191
Minucius Rufus 188
Modalla 70
Mokimos 28
Mokimos Akkaleisos, *see* Moqîmû Aqalîš
Mokimu / Moqîmû / Moqîmu / Moqimu 27, 28, 29, 42, 58, 70, 71, 75, 76, 78, 79, 82, 102, 113, 124, 142, 147, 163, 165
Moqîmû Aqalîš 24, 25
Moqîmû Gaddibôl 147
Moukianos 160
MTN' 88
MYT' 62, 89, 159
Nabay 71, 78
Nabî 41, 42, 54, 55, 56, 57, 134
Nabula 74
Nabushur 73
Nabuza 74
Nabuzabad 78
Naibanay 73
Nasor 173
Naṣrâ 47, 48, 62, 63
Naṣrâî 48, 62, 63
Nebô'dâ 59, 145
Nebôgaddaî 147
Nebôshûr 59, 60, 61, 145, 146
Nebôshûrî 45, 58, 59, 60, 61
Neboula 102
Nero 188, 191
Nesâ 103, 137
Neshâ 142, 143
Nîbnâ 45, 48, 58, 59
Nîdâ 62
Nikostratos 84

No'arai 165
Nurbel 73, 75, 78, 82
Odainath / Odaenathus 14-15, 168, 171, 173-179, 185
ʿOga / Ogâ / Oga 72, 76, 78, 164
Oga Borpa 82
ʿOgailu 72, 77, 78
ʿOgeilû / Ogeilû 27, 45, 59, 60, 61, 104, 145, 146
Ogelos Thaimaes, *see also* ʿOgailu 78
ʿOggâ Aqqamal 146
ʿOggâ 27, 42, 47, 50, 54, 56, 57, 58, 60, 61, 62, 63, 144
P. Aelius Theimes 89
Patroklos 84
Perdesh 159
Pertinax 67, 68
Piso 192
Plotina 191, 192, 194
Poppaea 191
Rabbâ 55
Rabbanâ 139
Rabbel 54
Rabbelos 28
Rabêl 109
Ragna 125
Ramay 71
Ramî 134
Refabôl 107
Regina 68, 72
[R]mallhâ 206
Sabina 189, 192, 193, 194
Saedei 28
Saʿiday 71, 78
Šalman 26
Šalmê 109
Samga 83
Sasan / Sassan 40, 41, 42, 43, 48, 54, 55, 56, 57, 58, 74
Septimia Batzabbay, *see* Zenobia
Septimius Odainath, *see* Odainath
Septimius Severus 197, 185, 188, 196,
Severus Alexander 196-197
Sewira 73
Shadilat 91
Shagal 69, 70, 72
Shahra 71, 159
Shalam 142
Shalamallat 48, 62
Shallum 73
Shalmaʿ 69
Shalman 96, 134
Shalmat 40, 47, 48, 50, 55, 62, 71, 74, 77, 79, 113
Shamâ 49, 56
Shamshigeram 47, 50, 62
Shebhaî 159
Shegel 159, 164
Shimʿôn / Shimeʿôn / Shimeon91, 126, 165
Shuʿadallat 69
Shuʿaday 78
Shullaî 134
Shulman 74
Shuraiku 72
Sîgâ 41, 42, 50, 55
Šimʿôn 105
Soados 160
Šokhaîaî 31
Šullâ 165
Taai 102
Tabnan 76
Tadmor 74, 75, 82
Taibbol / Taîbbôl 125, 147
Taîbbôl Qirdâ 147
Taima 159
Taimahe / Thaimaes 78
Taimai 202
Taîmʿamed 40, 48, 55
Taimarṣû / Taîmarṣû 26, 88, 96, 137
Taimassa 77
Taime / Taîmê 75, 77, 139
Taimi 92
Taimiša 26
Taîmshâ / Taimsha 55, 78
Tammê 45, 59, 146
Tema 71, 73
Thaimes 28
Thaimisas 78
Theophilos 137
Thomallachis 158-159, 160
Thrason 209
Tiberius 185, 188, 190, 191, 192
Timaios 74
Timon 78
Trajan 192, 194
Ubaidu 69
Ummabi 77
Valens 74, 144
Vespasian 192
Wahaballat / Wahballat / Wahballât / Wahballath 31, 35, 78, 79, 102, 113, 164, 171, 173, 174, 176, 179, 185, 189
Wahbaî 108
Wahballat Maʿnai 35

Warag 72
Yaddaî / Yaddai / Yadday / ʽYaddai 45, 47, 58, 62, 63, 71, 73, 91
Yaddîʽaî 147
Yadiʽbel 68, 77, 78
Yamlâ 56
Yarhai / Yarḥai / Yarḥaî / Yarhay 42, 50, 56, 59, 60, 61, 62, 68, 70, 71, 72, 73, 78, 83, 105, 107, 110, 144, 165
Yarḥaî Barâ 144
Yarhay Agrippa 68
Yarhibôl 103
Yarhibola / Yarḥibolâ / Yarḥibôlâ 42, 49, 56, 83, 206
Yarḥibôlê 158
Yaʽut 68, 107
Yerîʽbêl / Yedîʽbêl 105, 107
Zabda / Zabdâ 57, 72, 74, 75, 78, 79, 82
Zabdaʽate / Zabdaʽateh 73, 74, 77
Zabdelah 101
Zabdibel / Zabdibêl 92, 159
Zabdibol / Zabdibôl 42, 45, 57, 58, 59, 60, 61, 70, 71, 73, 74, 82, 122, 145
Zabdila / Zabdîlah 57, 73
Zaktaratay 77
ZBDʽTH 88
Zebaida 91
Zebeidas 28
Zebîdâ / Zebidâ 40, 55
Zenobia 7, 14-15, 69, 78, 79, 168- 171, 173-179, 185, 189, 197
Zerbâ 204
Zubaida / Zubayda 69, 70, 77

Index of divine and mythological names

Abgal 82
Aglibol 62, 85, 91, 158-160
Allat 88, 161-162
Arsu / Arsû 83, 85, 89, 206
'Ashar 82
Baʿalshamēn / Baalshamîn / Baalshamin 159, 163, 164
Baaltak 88
Bebellahamon, *see* Bel *and* Bel-Hammon
Bel 84, 85, 88, 90
Bel-Hammon 90
Benefal, *see* Fenebal
Blessed is his name forever / Blessed-Be-His-Name-Forev-
er / He whose name is blessed forever /
He whose name is blessed in eternity 78, 83, 84, 88, 90,
106, 163, 164, 165, 206
Ceres 189
Concordia 189, 190, 193, 194
Demeter 193
Diana 209
Dionysos 175
Eros 85
Fenebal 90
Fortuna 190
Gad of the gardens / God of the garden 83, 206
God of Nazala 91
Good gods 89, 90
Malakbel 62, 90, 91, 158-159, 160
Manawat 90
Medusa 175
Munʿim 83
Nereids 175
Pietas 189, 193
Rahim / Rahîm 83, 206
Securitas 190
Shamash 89
Temporum Felicitas 195
Vesta 189, 193
Victories 175
Yarhibôl 85, 163

Antique authors

Cassius Dio 192, 194, 196
Historia Augusta 168, 169, 171, 185, 192
Josephus 191
Lucian 84, 169
Pliny 174, 188, 192
Plutarch 169
Suetonius 188, 192
Syncellus 171
Tacitus 192
Zosimus 168, 171, 185